The Shariyat ·Ki· Sugmad

Books One & Two

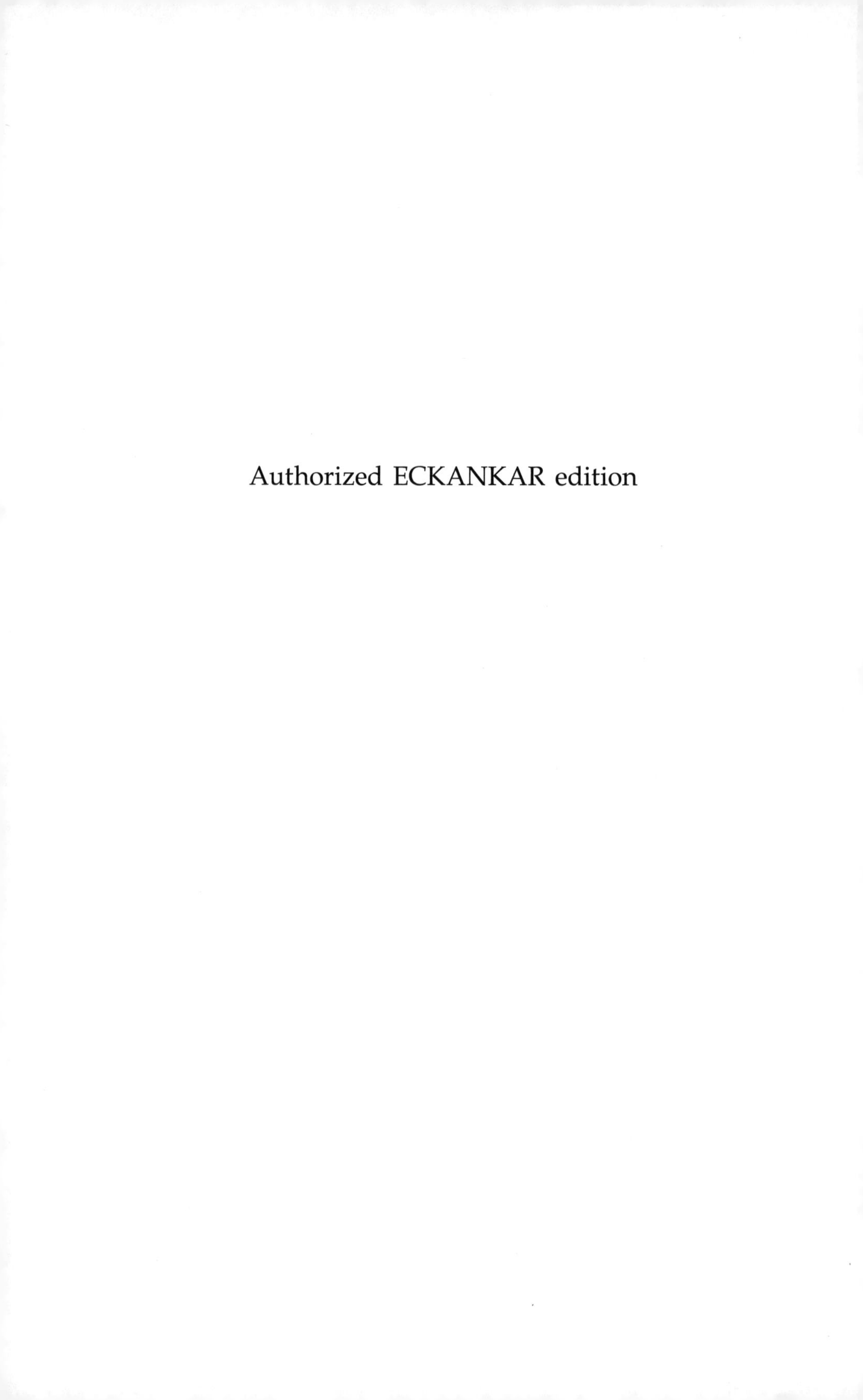

Authorized ECKANKAR edition

Books One & Two

Paul Twitchell

ECKANKAR
Minneapolis
www.Eckankar.org

The Shariyat-Ki-Sugmad, Books One & Two

 230953

Printed in USA

Library of Congress Control Number: 2023947315
ISBN: 978-1-57043-559-1
Third edition

∞ This paper meets the requirements of ANSI/NISO Z39.48-1992 (Permanence of Paper).

Dedicated to

The ECK Masters of
the Ancient Order of Vairagi,
who waited patiently for the right
time to give this message to the world.

Contents

Foreword

The teachings of ECK define the nature of Soul. You are Soul, a particle of God sent into the worlds (including earth) to gain spiritual experience.

The goal in ECK is spiritual freedom in this lifetime, after which you become a Coworker with God, both here and in the next world. Karma and reincarnation are primary beliefs.

Key to the ECK teachings is the MAHANTA, the Living ECK Master. He has the special ability to act as both the Inner and Outer Master for ECK students. The prophet of Eckankar, he is given respect but is not worshipped. He teaches the sacred name of God, HU. When sung just a few minutes each day, HU will lift you spiritually into the Light and Sound of God—the ECK (Holy Spirit). This easy spiritual exercise and others will purify you. You are then able to accept the full love of God in this lifetime.

Sri Harold Klemp is the MAHANTA, the Living ECK Master today. Author of many books, discourses, and articles, he teaches the ins and outs of the spiritual life.

Many of his talks are available to you on audio and video recordings. His teachings lift people and help them recognize and understand their own experiences in the Light and Sound of God.

* * *

The Shariyat-Ki-Sugmad contains the ancient scripture of Eckankar. These writings of golden wisdom which have always been hidden in the spiritual worlds have now been translated and published.

Book One is the first section of these works, which was dictated by Fubbi Quantz, the great ECK Master who serves at the Katsupari Monastery in northern Tibet.

Book Two is the second section of the works of *The Shariyat-Ki-Sugmad*, which was dictated by Yaubl Sacabi, the great ECK Master who serves at the Gare-Hira Temple of Golden Wisdom at Agam Des in the Hindu Kush Mountains.

The Shariyat-Ki-Sugmad contains the wisdom and ecstatic knowledge of the spiritual worlds beyond the regions of time and space. To read and study this highly inspired book will give you insight into the scriptures found in the Temples of Golden Wisdom from which these teachings emanate.

The essence of God-knowledge is laid down here. Those who follow ECK are involved in these writings of golden wisdom. *The Shariyat-Ki-Sugmad* is their bible, their everlasting gospel. All worldly doctrines on religions, philosophies, and sacred writings are offspring of this ancient scripture.

The Mission and the Writings of Paul Twitchell

When the ancient mysteries have strayed so far afield that only distorted fragments remain in the public mind, then the Order of Vairagi Adepts sends forth a chosen one from among its band to restore truth, such as it is, in the material domain.

In 1965 the time had come, and Paul Twitchell became the MAHANTA, the Living ECK Master. His was a short, rugged mission.

The high teachings of ECK had been scattered to the four corners of the world. Various writers had pieces of the true teachings but often attached strings—such as requiring students to become vegetarian or to spend many hours a day in meditation if they wanted to be true followers on the path to God. This was wrong for our day and age.

So in keeping with his mission, Paul Twitchell showed himself to be the master compiler.

He gathered up the golden teachings strewn around the world and released them from the cultural trappings and social aims which limited their spiritual radiance. He reoriented these fragments to show the direct path home to God.

By 1971 he had established Eckankar as a world teaching.

The fountainhead from which the ECK writings spring is the Ancient Gospel, the Shariyat-Ki-Sugmad, compiled by the Nine Silent Ones, whose main duty it is to gather up and sort out the unchanging laws that enfold every ripple in life.

On the inner planes are libraries connected to the Golden Wisdom Temples. The library alongside the main Temple on the Astral Plane is an enormous place of many roomy departments, much like the US Library of Congress, providing a comprehensive source of books and materials.

Good researchers—such as Julian Johnson, Paul Brunton, Carl Jung, and others—have come in and selected the paragraphs that suited their audience. Few knew the source of their inspiration.

But there was one who did. Paul's mission was to clarify, reveal, translate, and illuminate the sacred ECK teachings for all. And the great work continues on.

Every article or Wisdom Note by the MAHANTA, the Living ECK Master is taken from the Shariyat-Ki-Sugmad on the inner planes. Over 130 books later, the writings of Sri Harold Klemp continue to expand the body of spiritual wealth on earth.

* * *

Sacred writings inspire us. Yet by themselves they will always be imperfect translations written in an imperfect world.

The foundation of ECK is not in the physical writing. It's always within you as the Light and Sound of God. The MAHANTA can reveal all the truth you are ready to hear.

He awaits your invitation.

Introduction

The Shariyat-Ki-Sugmad, which means the "Way of the Eternal," is the ancient scripture of Eckankar, the science of Soul Travel and total consciousness.

It is possibly the oldest scripture known on earth. The Sanskrit writings, such as the Vedas, Upanishads, and Mahabharata, cannot be traced beyond four thousand years on this planet.

The Shariyat-Ki-Sugmad is said to have been known in antediluvian times, and before that on the so-called mythical continents known to us as Lemuria and Atlantis.

The Naacal records are reported to be among the first religious writings known to us, and they contain scattered references to Eckankar, or total consciousness.

Only two monasteries, one in the remote mountains of Tibet, and the other along the eastern slopes of the Hindu Kush Mountains, have any of these writings in their keeping on this physical planet. Other sections of the Shariyat are located on other planets and on other planes beyond this world.

These monasteries are so well hidden it is doubtful

anyone could find them, not even the Buddhist lamas who have the power to move about in the ethers at will. The keepers of these records are so careful in their guardianship that no one can enter these monasteries unless they are first screened by the monks, who can read the seeker's aura like we scan a daily newspaper.

Sections of the Shariyat-Ki-Sugmad, the guide for those who wish to reach the heavenly kingdom via the route of Eckankar, are kept in each Temple of Golden Wisdom, beginning on this Earth planet and continuing on each spiritual plane upward into the very heart of the Kingdom of God.

It is mainly kept—here on the Earth planet—in the spiritual city of Agam Des, which lies in the high wilderness of the Hindu Kush Mountains in Central Asia. Only those who are able to travel in the Atma Sarup, the Soul body, can reach this extraordinary community of Adepts and study these ancient scriptures of truth.

Eckankar is the basic foundation for all religions, philosophies, and scientific works in our world today. It is closer to being in its original form, as the science of Soul Travel, than any of the other paths to God. However, it is not just religion, philosophy, or metaphysics, for it is the ECK Marg, meaning the path of Eckankar.

It has been handed down by word of mouth from Rama, the first known world savior, who came out of the deep forests of northern Germany and traveled down to Persia, where he paused long enough to give these secret teachings to a few mystics whose descendents were to become the followers of Zoroaster, the Persian sage.

Rama then proceeded to India, where he settled and taught that man could have the experience of God in his own lifetime.

Eckankar was revealed to Rama by one of the ancient ECK Masters. It is likely that he was lifted out of the body and taken to the city of Agam Des, where the Shariyat-Ki-Sugmad was shown him and he was given the opportunity to study its contents.

No written instructions were available to the followers of Eckankar until about the thirteenth century, when Jalal ad-Din ar-Rumi, the mystic poet of Persia, hinted at it in his great poem "The Reed of God."

In about the sixteenth century, Kabir, the Hindu mystic poet, took it upon himself to unwrap the mysteries of the Ancient Science of Soul Travel.

He had quite a time with his adversaries, for everybody who believed in orthodox religion thought he was crazy and many tried to kill him. Those who were followers of the science of Soul Travel knew he was wrong to try to reveal such truth at that time. As a result, he was hounded until he could scarcely keep himself alive, spending most of his time in hiding.

There was a corruption of the original teachings by word of mouth, and several other paths came out of this. Some of these were Shabda Yoga, the Magi, the cult of Dionysus, and a few other mystery schools that are generally well known to us. Each school of divine knowledge branched off into its own particular way as a path to God. The six great religious systems of India are only branches of the God-Vidya (God-knowledge) that we call ECK. So are the religions of the West and every continent, including Africa and Asia. A study of *The Golden Bough,* by Frazer, will bear this out.

Basically, the main principle, or vital part, of Eckankar is out-of-the-consciousness projection, which is far beyond the astral or any other lower-plane movements.

It has been corrupted from the original source as man developed it in various parts of the world into a semblance of religion and worship. Man thus fell away from the main stream of truth and created his own gods and rituals. Thus we find there is some truth in the story about the Tower of Babel.

The Shariyat-Ki-Sugmad consists of twelve books, each book, on the inner planes, comprising twelve to fifteen chapters. These chapters average about thirty thousand words and are made up of cantos, or what we call verse in dialogue form, in which the SUGMAD (God) speaks to Its chief disciple, Sat Nam, sometimes called the Sat Purusha, lord of the spiritual plane of Soul, or the fifth region. He is believed by some to be the Supreme SUGMAD but is only the first manifestation of God.

Not all the writing is made up of cantos or free verse. Often it is straight narrative, or legends and stories. Sometimes it is in allegories or fables. But altogether it is the whole truth, concise in all its parts, and tells everyone what life really consists of and how to live it.

Statements of the highest spiritual nature are uttered by the SUGMAD to Sat Nam to show that the Supreme Deity wants all Souls to be lifted into the heavenly realm again: "I am eternal, therefore, I am free. All who come unto Me shall experience freedom of eternity.

"Freedom is a completeness within itself, for Soul must enter into the Divine Light or suffer the effects of the lower reality.

"The true reality in any universe of mine is Spirit, and he who looks upon It as giving him existence and experience is indeed a wise man."

The ancient books of the Shariyat-Ki-Sugmad are indeed the true Light and the Word of God: It takes up and discusses every phase of life in both the worlds of matter and the highest planes.

Those who are fortunate enough to be able to peruse its golden pages are indeed enlightened Souls. Usually, it is the Spiritual Travelers who make it their concern to study this golden book of wisdom and spread its light to those who will listen.

Indeed, as Rebazar Tarzs, the Torchbearer of Eckankar in the world today, points out, only the courageous and adventurous in spirit ever have the opportunity to see and study its wondrous pages.

Whatever truth each of us may receive is only in accord with our individual consciousness.

One will find within these pages an answer to every question man has ever devised to ask of any greater ones. All that which is truth is here now, within these pages.

Paul Twitchell

Book One

1
The ECK—The Divine Voice of SUGMAD

ECK is the totality of all awareness.

It is the omnipresence of the SUGMAD, the omniscience and the omnipotence, the allness of the divine SUGMAD in Its kingdom and the universes.

Life is concerned only with the primal Vadan, the Word of It. This is the essence of life. Nothing is greater than the Word of the worlds.

Hence the SUGMAD speaks to us only through the primal Sound. It has no other way of contact other than through the ECK, the creative energy. Out of this divine Voice all other sounds flow.

Those who are in It distinguish between the primal Word and the manifest worlds, between the original music and Its echo. They are able to point out the difference between the Dhunatmik Sound and the Varnatmik sounds.

The all-creative ECK is the Voice of the SUGMAD, out of which all other sounds arise. At the same time Its divine strains linger in all material planes as echoes of the original melody.

The Voice of the SUGMAD is the Dhunatmik, the Sound which cannot be spoken. It has no written symbol. Such is the music of the SUGMAD. The Varnatmik is the sound which can be spoken or written. Hence, the scriptures of the Shariyat-Ki-Sugmad can be spoken and written on the lower planes. But in the higher worlds it is only the heavenly white music.

The ECK is the Ocean of Love, a life-giving, creative sea, heard by the divine followers of the SUGMAD. Within the Ocean of Love is the total sum of all teachings emanating from the SUGMAD. It is the divine Word, for It includes everything that SUGMAD has said or done, and what It is.

The Voice of the SUGMAD includes all the qualities of the magnificent Being in the Ocean of Love and Mercy. It is a continuous process, flowing down from Its place in the Celestial Kingdom into all worlds below.

This Ocean of Love and Mercy projects Itself in the form of waves emerging out of a fountain. Since It contains the qualities of the SUGMAD, It can only appear on the lower planes—including the physical—as a form of consciousness.

Hence, as It reaches the Soul, or Atma, Plane, It manifests Itself as Sat Nam, in Sach Khand. Here this Divine Being becomes fully personified for the first time, manifesting all of the qualities of the SUGMAD.

Sat Nam becomes the personal creator, lord, god, and father to all who are religious followers. He is the source out of which the Voice, the Wave of the SUGMAD, flows to all worlds below.

Its Voice may be heard and seen by those who are able to participate in It throughout the worlds of the supreme Deity. It may be seen and heard only by those awakened selves, who have received the initiation from the ECK Adepts.

When the human consciousness in one has been awakened and he hears and sees the Wave of the SUGMAD, he is the enlightened. He hears the SUGMAD, sees It, and feels the omnipotency of It, for the ECK is the divine Deity expressing Itself in all that is visible and audible.

The Wave of the SUGMAD's Voice, issuing through Sat Nam, flows outwardly from the Ocean of Love and Mercy, reaching the vast boundaries of the spiritual worlds and of all creation. Then It flows back into the Ocean again, as do the waves created by a pebble dropped in a still pond.

Moving on It, all power and all life appear to flow outward to the uttermost bounds of creation, and again on It, all life appears to be returning to Sat Nam. Therefore, it is the returning wave of the Voice that Soul must look to for help.

The ECK Adept makes the connection, and the individual Soul is linked with this returning wave. It is then that Soul, or Atma, again starts Its journey toward the heavenly worlds, leaving all the worlds of mortality behind.

Thus the SUGMAD will speak to those who are obedient to Its Word, for It holds all life within Its hand. All shall have the Light and the Word if they listen to It and obey.

The SUGMAD has little involvement with embodiments. Its relationship is only with consciousness, striving toward a totality of awareness so every Atma will recognize Itself as being one with the ECK.

The SUGMAD is omnipresent, omnipotent, and omniscient in all life, and It desires to have every Atma share these qualities. He who listens and sees the living ECK will experience these godlike qualities and may use each for the welfare of all concerned.

Hence, the supreme doctrine is the Voice of the SUGMAD.

He who follows the golden arrow and crosses the mighty moat of heaven, where within the deep ravine sparkles and shimmers the strange translucent mist, enters into the secret kingdom of the holy SUGMAD.

The Voice that calls him is that which beckons all to take the first step upon the path to pass through the narrow gate and receive the graces of the Holy of Holies. Only he who is pure of heart will be able to partake of the arcane ecstasy and become aware of the divine ground of Being.

Within the Temple dwells the SUGMAD. Unapproachable in Its state except by the purest Atma, descriptions are unworthy of It. The Atma can only experience the SUGMAD in the state of freedom. Those who are faithful will be free and able to live in the radiance of It.

Fasting, eating certain foods, praying, beseeching, pleading, and the practice of austerities will never lead the Atma into the secret dwelling place.

The SUGMAD is engaged only with life and the Atma—never with forms, symbols, and objects. The Atma is immortal, cannot be injured, pierced, broken, wronged, drowned, or stolen.

The Voice speaks to all who listen. It speaks in the whisper of the wind, the roar of the sea, and the voices of birds and animals—in all things. It tells all who listen that It will never bring riches, fame, wealth, healing, or happiness to those who seek these mundane gratifications.

All who listen, obey, and surrender unto It shall have whatever is Its desire, be it riches, wealth, healing, happiness, enlightenment, or understanding of the divine wisdom.

The SUGMAD sends Its messengers into this world as warriors. None come as doves. They are the eagles who must seek food for the young. They are the shepherds who keep the wolves away from the flock.

The Adepts for the ECK are the swordsmen of the SUGMAD. Whenever they travel, the pace of karma is quickened. In their wake comes the storm that divides nation against nation and family against family. The elements of the wrath of the ECK bring down temples, demolish cities, and tear Souls asunder. It brings storms, floods, earthquakes, wars, and catastrophes.

Each Atma must fight Its battle against the storm of karma and the forces of the lower kingdom until victory is at hand. Then the realm of the SUGMAD is opened unto the victor.

The spiritually blind can never see the Light, nor the deaf hear the Voice of the SUGMAD. He who claims to be a master but is blind shall reap the harvest of wrath. The one who says he is a listener to the Voice but is deaf shall be torn asunder by his lying tongue.

The gods who are the messengers of the divine Voice know and see the blind and the deaf. They know the liar, the questioner, and the deceiver. They know that these shall not see the face of the SUGMAD.

He who has the eyes to see shall view the Light of the ECK upon the face of the MAHANTA. He who has the ears to hear shall gather unto himself the wisdom of the Voice of ECK within the worlds of the SUGMAD!

He who must know and see and hear shall be the perfect Soul. He has received purification and is ready to enter into the heavenly kingdom once again. He is an instrument and can talk with the Lord and be led by It.

Hence, wherever the Master goes, wreckage follows. For he is always the instrument of ECK. The purification of ECK, the Voice of the Supreme SUGMAD, causes the forces of the lower nature to cease. The cessation brings a warfare and, therefore, all know that life in the Pinda, or Physical, universe is a struggle between the spiritual and physical.

Man, the apex of the Pinda universe, is often the conveyer of the seeds of Kal Niranjan, the negative power. The Kal and its children do battle with the ECK and Its children. The war is always between these two powers, resulting in victory for the ECK for those who desire it so.

Whosoever wants the life of the ECK must remember the falseness of the Kal. Soul must exist upon the essence of the ECK. The Voice that speaks must be that which leads the chela into the true home of the SUGMAD, the Ocean of Love and Mercy.

Therefore, Soul must know that life and love are not in the voice of the Pinda consciousness. Nor are they in the voice of the Nuri, or Astral, existence; nor in the Karan, or Causal, world; nor in the Manas, or Mental, world. Life and love are only in the world of ECK. Unless one hears that which we know as the Bani or the Nada Bindu, the seed Sound from which all things grow, he has heard only the voices of these other worlds.

The wolves who come in sheep's clothing will sing the praises of the voice of the lower worlds. Heed them not. Listen only to the messengers of the Supreme SUGMAD. They who travel from the ECK to the regions of Jot Niranjan are like the prophets of old. They are the instruments the SUGMAD uses to give Its message to the universes.

The Voice is that Essence—the Holy Ghost, the Comforter, the Divine Spirit—that gives life to all. It has many names—Shabda, Logos, the Word, the Nada, Shabda Dhun, Akash Bani, Sultan-ul-Azkar, the King of the Ways, Ism-i-Azam, Kalma, Kalam-i-Illahi, Surat Shabda, Ananda Yoga, or Anahad Shabda. Others call It the Vadan, Dhun, the heavenly music, and other names.

Only those who follow the ECK Marg, the path of ECK,

know the truth that life consists of the Living ECK Master, the Bani, and Jivan Mukti, which is spiritual liberation in this lifetime. This is the way man leaves the Pinda and finds his way to heaven again. All must go this way. He might go another way, but the Marg is then slower. When his persevering efforts have brought him victory, he shall have the perfectly clear understanding that all he can do for himself is useless unless he accepts the way of ECK.

When one has definitely stripped off the Pinda values, then the ECKshar, the state of Self-Realization Consciousness, will burst forth, and the heavenly music will bring ecstasy. Upon this encounter he will find there is no path, for there is no place to go. All is eternity. He is at the unique and the fundamental center of All.

This is Jivan Mukti!

This is the deliverance, the disappearance of the illusion of servitude, because of man's unhappy conduct toward man. This freedom takes away his blindness and opens his eyes. It takes away his deafness and opens his ears. He proceeds, with the help of the Living ECK Master, the Vi-Guru, who is the Spiritual Traveler, to receive his initiation into the Holy ECK. Then all things are made whole again.

Thus he knows that the modus operandi is not the cause which precedes all form; It is only the instrument through which the First Cause operates.

He who looks upon the face of the mighty SUGMAD will never again be the same. He will thereafter be like the lion upon the trail of the deer. Hunger will drive him to the ECK Marg, and he will find the Holy Spirit in time, be it through the help of the Master, the Son of Heaven, or by his own way. But be aware, for he will find It.

Be on guard, lest he who seeks without the Vi-Guru, the Supreme Guru, find those who only appear as the Holy One, claiming to be angels or saints. Let none deceive the chela. If he who seeks is a chela of the Vi-Guru, he cannot be deceived by the Kal Niranjan. If he has not the armor of Spirit, he can be misled.

The Kal is treacherous, and the lower worlds are filled with those who desire to be recognized as great deities. A vision may be the creation of the manas. Man spends much of his time viewing creations of the mind, or manas. Such creations are not reliable communicants. Without the clear vision of the Vi-Guru—he who is the Master—and the tests given by him, one cannot be assured of what he sees or hears.

Every Spiritual Traveler, or Vi-Guru, will give the Word to the chela to call upon the Master. If the vision fails to reply, then it is false. He cannot see the holy Light, nor hear the holy Sound. He is the blind and the deaf whose eyes and ears are sealed until the Traveler arrives to unseal them.

Upon arrival in the worlds of true Spirit, there is no path on which to travel, no door to open, there is no gate, there is nowhere to go, because there is no need to go anywhere. This is the wonderful secret of the SUGMAD.

The SUGMAD is within every man, but due to ignorance, man is always seeking It on the outside; seeking Its Word in the noises of the Pinda kingdom.

It is true that the Word, the Voice of the SUGMAD, is difficult to hear, but it is easy to submit the Self to those who have It. It has always been the case that all have not received the Word, and yet they had the protection of the Travelers. Surrender to the Master, who is the instrument of the ECK, is the great pleasure of life. This path of surrender is only used by those who are mortals. He who is mortal must follow the way of submission.

Man must give himself to the Holy Spirit of the SUGMAD. He must let the Voice of Silence lead him into the heavenly worlds. If he who follows the Bani be brave, there shall be victory; but if he be fearful, only death of the mortal self shall result. Beyond this death of the Pinda Sarup, the physical body, there shall be nothing for him. He shall live in darkness and ignorance until the Vi-Guru sees him and has compassion on his suffering.

If the Vi-Guru looks upon mortal man with compassion in his eyes, that mortal shall be given the instant way into heaven. He shall find himself caught up in the twinkling of an eye into the Ocean of Love and Mercy. When the Vi-Guru turns his head aside and passes on, the mortal shall continue his life suffering until he learns to ask the Saint to show him the way out of the Pinda world.

Love comes to one in whom the Word has stirred. It is like the rushing of the mighty winds and the tongues of fire.

This message of love is translated from the Word of the SUGMAD to all the universes and to every living being. It is the message given to all entities living on every plane of the spiritual universes by the Living ECK Master of the highest Order. It is the difference between the recorded scriptures and the ECK.

It glorifies the living Master and gives to those who ask the Crown of Life—the holy initiation into ECK, approved by the Living ECK Master. No chela is ready for the initiation until he has undergone the trials of the cave of fire and the water test. These are all encountered on the path of ECK before reaching that spiritual level of initiation.

Thereafter, the chela enters into glorious life with the SUGMAD. But until then he will be blown before the wind like the chaff of wheat scattered over the fields. He will suffer the agonies of spirit until the burden seems too great and all is lost. He will drown himself in tears and pleas to the SUGMAD to give him amity and rest. But it will appear that the divine Deity has turned Its face away and the Living ECK Master has forsaken him.

He will yearn for peace and tenderness, but none will be forthcoming. All hope will die within him, and he will feel his life is unworthy of anything but the Kal Niranjan, the prince of darkness and materiality.

The Godman does not come into this world to make new laws, nor to destroy existing laws, but only to uphold the Universal Divine Law, unchangeable as it is. His message is one of hope, fulfillment, and redemption for those in search of the SUGMAD. He is a great cementing force, transcending all denominational creeds and faiths and presenting a way out of the worldly religious strongholds.

He travels high into the ethereal atmosphere of the spiritual worlds and, like the skylark, establishes an abiding link between the mundane life on earth and the pure spiritual heaven. All religions are subject to the Godman's love, and yet none shall bind him, for he gives to all humanity what is essentially sublime for every individual Soul.

The gulf that separates the pontifical heads on one hand and a truly God-intoxicated Soul on the other is vast. The God-intoxicated Soul who is the Living ECK Master combines in his person all that the scriptures contain and much more besides.

He is the living embodiment of all that is religious, the spirit of life lying dormant in others. He is the awakened Soul, transcending time and space and causation, holding the past, present, and future in the palms of his hands as an open book. He is the Master of the creative life impulse throbbing in all things visible and invisible, and is able to work simultaneously on all planes—Physical, Astral, Causal, or Mental, and even beyond into the supreme worlds of the Anami.

He is the Word made flesh, as spoken of by John the Apostle, and dwells among all races to gradually lead the aspiring Soul back to the eternal Godhead, from plane to plane with varying degrees of density. The ECK teachings, which he gives, promise a practical way out of the dense matter into the pure spiritual sunshine. The ECK, or Word, manifests in the Master and is revealed to those whom he may so choose to call his own.

His experience is a direct Soul manifestation, unlike those who work on the intellectual plane and quote scriptures in support of what they preach.

The only reason the Godman uses the scriptures is to correctly explain and interpret the spiritual experiences of Soul on Its journey homeward, in addition to the actual, practical inner events granted to individuals. Thus he leaves no room for doubt and skepticism.

All knowledge one has at this point is based upon sense perception or is derived from intellectual ratiocination. The knowledge the true, living Master gives is direct and immediate, coming from actual Soul experiences apart from the physical senses and human consciousness. His words are charged with the ECK Currents surging within him. They sink into the inner self of the listener, leaving little doubt about the existence of Soul experiences.

ECK is the golden thread, so fine as to be invisible, yet so strong as to be unbreakable, which binds together all beings in all planes, in all universes, throughout all time, and beyond time into eternity.

Since the first flicker of consciousness dawned on human intelligence, this thread was there, and it caused man to probe into the depths of himself to learn about the experiences of the inner life. Man is older than religions, but not older than ECK, for It predates all life on earth. It was in the beginning and the ending of all things, and is what sustains us in the present. Its very presence is the essence of the SUGMAD.

Thus man's being older than religions but younger than the ECK has caused him to wonder about this golden thread of life, and he has begun to look for the answers to the riddle of life. In the end he will learn all religions established so far throughout the world have their origin in the Godman, the Living ECK Master, who comes to this world, lives among humanity, and guides all footsteps to the Kingdom of God. Every religion in this world is a living testimony to this sacred truth.

The natural way back to God is known as Eckankar, the Ancient Science of Soul Travel, which is an exact science embracing the purest of the original teachings. It is the original of itself, and its simplicity, once grasped, is staggering to the intellect. It is the most ancient of all teachings, known to us in its earliest form through the Naacal writings, which are hidden in the Katsupari Monastery in northern Tibet under Fubbi Quantz. It is the original fountain from which all faiths spring.

It is the same basic truth which Yaubl Sacabi expressed so concisely during his time on earth many centuries ago in a few powerful words: "The SUGMAD is the essence of everything within us." Herein lies the key. There is nothing vague or complex in this statement, nothing which cannot be applied to all persons living in the physical world. Yet few people are able to step through the Tenth Door which leads Soul into the heavenly worlds. This is the basic principle of ECK. Heaven exists in all persons, and all persons have access to It.

All religions teach that God is within, but this is not true. It is not God, the SUGMAD, that is within every Soul, but the essence of God, or that known as the ECK.

The methods of Eckankar state explicitly how to find this state of consciousness which exists within Soul.

The road leading to this state, which is the kingdom of heaven, starts behind the eyes at a point between the eyebrows. This is the Tenth Door, which leads Soul to the original heavenly home from which It started eons ago. When all consciousness is withdrawn from the body to focus at this point, then the marvelous journey of Soul begins.

The human body does not have to die to make these journeys to God. Each visit will be only temporary until one leaves the body for the last time on earth. This is the art of death in life. The meaning of this was brought forth when Rami Nuri, the great ECK Master in charge of the Shariyat-Ki-Sugmad in the House of Moksha, in Retz, the capital of Venus, said, "He that wants life badly will never have it, but he that gives it up for the ECK shall have all life."

This is the true meaning of the death-in-life struggle, for once life is given up to serve only the ECK, he who does so becomes blessed. Truth is manifested when one seeking God wants to be shown the supreme Deity, for he has only to look upon the Living ECK Master to fulfill this desire. Gopal Das once stated that "whoever has looked upon the face of the Godman has seen the living image of God." This means the Living ECK Master has been sent to this world to serve and act for the highest reality. He has been sent by the Divine Power to administer to all who need him during his sojourn on earth.

"Those who follow the ECK take nothing for granted, for they must prove it for themselves. Only then will they know that God so loved them that He sent a Living ECK Master to bring Souls home to Him," Gopal Das said, repeating the words from the Shariyat-Ki-Sugmad.

The chela must prepare for the journey back to God. The way is a narrow footpath, and it is best to leave all baggage behind, for it is filled with desires and attachments. The chela must cast off the yoke that weighs him down. But the chela keeps asking himself, "Am I worthy of God?"

No one is worthy of God. It is only through the Grace of the SUGMAD that we become worthy. Only the Living ECK Master can bring this Grace to those who seek It, for he is the pure instrument of God on earth. So we must keep our faith with the Living ECK Master and live in his presence as much as possible.

In prehistoric times man took an enormous leap upward from the animalistic life with the development of consciousness. Now ECK is giving the human race the opportunity to take another equally great step upward into cosmic consciousness. The effect will enable man to make more spiritual progress by this second step than he made materially through the first.

The SUGMAD is what there is and all there is, so no name can really be given It except the poetic name of God. It is neither old nor new, great nor small, shaped nor shapeless. Having no opposite, It is what opposites have in common; It is the reason why there is no white without black and no form apart from emptiness. However, the SUGMAD, as we know It, has two parts—an inside and an outside. The inside is called Nirguna, which is to say It has no qualities and nothing can be said or thought about It. The outside is called Saguna, which is to say It may be considered as eternal reality, consciousness, and joy. This is the part man knows and remembers after experiencing the God-Realization state.

Because of Its joy in reaching this state, Soul is capable of enjoying Itself in play. This type of play is called lila and is like singing and dancing made up of sound and silence, motion and rest. In this kind of play, Soul will lose Itself and find Itself in a game of hide-and-seek without beginning or end. This is the joy the orthodox religions speak about, but in the losing of Itself, It is obliterated; It forgets It is the one and only reality and plays that It is the vast multitude of beings and things which make up this world. In finding Itself, It is remembered; It will discover again that It is forever the one behind the many, the trunk from which the branches of the tree grow—the tree itself. It knows again that Its seeming to be many is always maya, or illusion, art and magical powers.

The play of Soul is like a drama in which Soul is both the actor and audience. On entering the theater, the audience knows it is about to see a play, but the actor creates maya, an illusion of reality which gives the audience extreme emotions of joy or terror, laughter or tears. It is in the joy and sorrow of all beings that Soul, as audience, is carried away by Itself as the actor.

Among the many images of God is the Hamsa, the divine bird, which lays the world in the form of an egg. It is also the syllable *ham* that God breathes out, scattering all galaxies in the sky. With the syllable *sa* It breathes in, withdrawing all things to their original unity. The syllables *ham-sa* may also be heard as *sa-ham,* or *sa-aham,* which is to say, "I am THAT," or "THAT Soul"—what each and every being *is.* Breathing out, God is called in the lower worlds by the Sanskrit name of Brahma, the Creator. Holding the breath out, God is called Vishnu, the Preserver of all these lower worlds. Breathing in, God is called Shiva, the Destroyer of maya, or illusion.

This is the ancient truth without beginning or end. Soul is sent into the worlds of matter where It loses Itself and finds Itself. It always lives in various forms, in periods known as days and nights. Each day and each night lasts for a kalpa, which is four and a quarter million, (4,320,000) of our years. The day, which is known as a manvantara, is divided into four yugas, or epochs, which are named as in the throws of the game of dice—the first is Krita, or Satya; the second, Tretya; the third, Dwapara; the fourth, Kali.

Krita, or Satya, yuga is the Golden Age, the era of total delight in multiplicity and form and every beauty of the sensuous world. It endures for 1,728,000 years. Tretya Yuga is a shorter era which lasts for 1,296,000 years and is that period when everything starts to go amiss and every pleasure has some anxiety attached. Dwapara Yuga is shorter than these. It runs for 864,000 years, and in it the forces of light and darkness, good and evil, pleasure and pain are equally balanced. Last comes the Kali Yuga, lasting for 432,000 years, in which the universe is overwhelmed by darkness and decay, and Soul is lost in a delight which is hardly more than a disguise of horror. The form of Shiva takes place here, and the universe is turned to ashes and nothingness. This is when the Lord SUGMAD takes up all Souls to the Soul Plane, the fifth world, and destroys the lower regions in fire and ashes.

Souls who have been transplanted to this upper region find themselves in original unity and bliss. They remain in this kalpa of 4,320,000 years in a life of total peace, before the cycle starts again and they are returned to the new worlds of matter.

As God breathes out, the worlds are manifested. These worlds are not our own earth planet, nor those planets and stars in the sky, but the worlds we cannot see that are hidden in the body of the tiny ant or bee. The stars of our heavenly world can be contained in the eyes of a swallow. There are also worlds around man that do not respond to our five senses, worlds which are great and small, visible and invisible, and as numerous as the grains of sand on the seashore.

These worlds are levels of consciousness. They are

made manifest by the Lord SUGMAD, and it is the divine purpose that all beings pass through these worlds at some time or other. Each Soul will pass through the twelve paths, or divisions, of the Wheel of Becoming. This is the Wheel of the Eighty-Four, which goes the complete round of the zodiacal circle. It is here Soul spends eighty-four lacs in each zodiacal sign, and each lac is equivalent to one hundred thousand years. Eighty-four lacs amount to 8,400,000 years.

A wandering Soul, making Its way from birth to birth, may possibly be required to pass Its long and tiresome course through all these signs of the zodiac, provided Its karma calls for it. But there is an escape, and that is to meet with the Living ECK Master and accept him. The Master will link him to the ECK Stream of Life, and there do not have to be further births for him. He is now free of the Wheel of the Eighty-Four.

He will reach that place where he is no longer desirous of the fruits of action, as all within the lower worlds are seeking action motivated by desire for results, whether good or evil. This binds them to the Wheel of Becoming by their karma. Each will stay bound to it as long as their ignorance is prevalent and as long as none meet with the living Godman. Each must come to that position or level of spiritual understanding in which he knows that "I have come to be, and I shall cease to be," in the words of the ECK Master Peddar Zaskq.

One must set aside all ideas, opinions, theories, and beliefs and look earnestly and intently at the one great principle of ECK, the "I AM." Whosoever does this will find himself awakened by the knowledge of the divine Self, that there is no other center of the ECK than himself. Thus he is liberated while still in the human form, before the death of the body, and before the dissolution of all worlds at the end of the kalpa. He has reached the state of Jivan Mukti, liberation of Soul via the Sound Current.

On all sides, within and without, he sees all beings, all things, all events, as only the playing of the Lord SUGMAD in Its myriad forms. He has become the Coworker with the SUGMAD and cannot do other than the will of the Divine, for his will has become that of the highest. He no longer uses the terms "my Soul" or "your Soul," for now he knows he is Soul Itself and must at all times see from this specific viewpoint.

No one shall reach these joyous heights of Spirit unless he has been trained in the works of Eckankar. A specific attitude and viewpoint is necessary for the satisfactory utilization of the spiritual powers; he who uses them must be free from emotional bias and entirely detached and serene in his attitude. Otherwise, he will be a failure at traveling the path to God.

A knowledge of mechanics is not at all necessary for the spiritual works of Eckankar; it is the attitude that is all important and that determines the nature of the ultimate issues of God. This attitude can only be arrived at by self-discipline and purification of Soul.

Thus the greater ceremonial rituals of the initiation into ECK are unsuitable for the use of anyone save a trained initiate. But there are many minor rites that can be used by anyone who achieves a steady mind. Knowledge is secondary to all things in the spiritual works except for the issues at hand, to know whether it is right or wrong to take a specific course.

Every decision in life depends upon the factors that lie behind it. The Physical Plane, as the spiritually awakened man sees it, is the end result of a long chain of evolutionary processes that have gone on in the more subtle planes, the realms of the Soul, Mental, Causal, and Astral Planes. Consequently, every problem of human nature, every decision man makes on the Physical Plane, will have a magnetic field of its own, an aura composed of factors from each of these levels of consciousness. The initiate realizes this, because every action is composite. He must determine the relative proportion of these different factors and discern upon what level the action has its nucleus.

When man comes into the state of Soul consciousness, he realizes each plane of existence has its own laws and conditions, and these cannot be overridden by any power, however great, except by the will of the Godman. Each plane exists because of the one above it, to the extent that the powers and mechanisms can be adjusted and directed to its own conditions. Only the living Godman has power to bend any circumstances, conditions, and laws of any of the planes within the universes of God. He seldom does this; nevertheless he has the authority, for he is the manifestation of the Lord SUGMAD upon this plane and every plane within the worlds of worlds.

Man cannot change anything in life, but his own ego tells him it is possible. These are only the false whispers of Kal Niranjan, the king of the lower worlds, in order to hold Soul and trap It there. The sooner man learns his powers are puny, the sooner will he put his feet upon the path to God by the way of Eckankar. As soon as this is done, he will find himself being led by the Living ECK Master, who has taken over to assist him in reaching his true home again.

2
The ECK Sastras*

To understand the SUGMAD, the Lord of all universes, is to understand nothing. That known as the SUGMAD is the Allness of life, the fountainhead of Love and Mercy, to be named with any name you wish.

Spiritual essence is based upon the MAHANTA, the inner form of the Living ECK Master. This is the radiant form, often called the Nuri Sarup, which gleams like a thousand stars in the night. Until the chela is able to view and speak with the MAHANTA, and to travel with him in the worlds of spiritual life, he is without true realization.

To understand the SUGMAD, in the very beginning it is best to understand the MAHANTA, the living Godman. This is the affirmation and declaration of the SUGMAD, involving neither denial nor negation but a placing of full belief in the MAHANTA to know what God might be. ECK is the true path, and Its own spiritual practices laid down by the MAHANTA lead to true knowledge of the SUGMAD.

---

* Sastras: scriptures

Man should know that in Soul there is Being, Knowing, and Seeing. In the mind there is nothing more than thought, volition and analysis, while in the body there is only action.

All who become the channel for God will translate the ECK into the physical and spread peace to those concerned. Mind is the intermediate link between heaven and earth; therefore, it is good to use the mind as an instrument, allowing the spirituality of God to flow to all living creatures. Being an instrument of God, one asks not for solace, but only to give solace; one asks not for peace, but to give peace; and one asks not for happiness, but seeks only to give happiness.

The lives of the saints from the ancient Order of the Vairagi remind man that everyone can make his life sublime, while in the flesh. There is no mystery for him to seek, for all is as clear as the morning sun. Man must awaken and rise, tread the path of ECK carefully and with perseverance until he has reached the great goal, with no thought of rest.

If you aspire after truth, come, follow the MAHANTA; practice the Spiritual Exercises of ECK, experiment and realize the purport of the divine teachings. Do not praise nor condemn the works of ECK until Its truth is realized.

Man is a creature, but so is the god who rules the universes of matter. This god is the binding principle, whom those in ECK designate as the Kal, or Maha Kal. He is the supreme deity of all the known regions of the physical universe. Bound as he is, he binds all.

The idea of bondage comes from him and his Ahankar. He is the ruler of the spirito-material worlds, and as long as the unawakened Soul finds Itself inhabiting the realm of Kal, It cannot dream of release from the fetters of the Kal, that decrees all Souls should remain bound. It is the will and the struggle of Soul to become free.

Ordinarily Soul is confined to the planes of the lower worlds—the Physical, Astral, Causal, Mental, and Etheric, or the subconscious. It is also confined in the fetters of a three-conditioned consciousness called wakefulness, dream state, and dreamlessness. While encased in the bounds of the lower worlds, Soul has to be content with living in these conditions of Kal.

The awakened Soul, though, performs Its functions in the spiritual worlds while living in the physical state. This is the being that lives within the physical body. It is here he enjoys the foods of his senses, the body functions, and that which comprises life upon this plane of the material universes. This is the manner and life of the ECK chela, for he takes all within this life and enjoys it, knowing he is dead here and will not be fully alive until the body dies. Nevertheless, he does not reject the experiences of the physical senses and the body.

The Atma, living in the dream consciousness of the psychic states, enjoys the subtle things of life, as thought, emotional joy, intellect, and mind stuff. All this is essential for the bodies of the psychic worlds, the Astral, Causal, and Mental Planes. When Soul takes mastery over these states through dreaming, It becomes the supreme ruler of Its own universe.

The third state possesses neither wakefulness nor dreams. It is absorption in the state of being I AM! There is a consciousness of self-knowing, that the Atma has become an inhabitant of the world of Sat Nam. All the bodies the Atma has used on the planes of the worlds below are at rest, are in a dreamless, sound sleep. But the Atma is full in Itself, wise, and all-knowing about Itself. It enjoys the ecstasy of this high world and has the power to move wherever desired, to any plane of God below or above.

All existing life sprang out of the ECK, and exists only

by the presence of the ECK. In the beginning there was nothing but the ECK, the Word of the SUGMAD; unmanifested It was, and thence It arose into manifestation. The power within the ECK was polarized, and from It the vibrations of the ECK proceeded gradually, and innumerable worlds rushed forth into life and shape, as do bubbles rising from the bottom of a deep spring in globular forms.

Motion and action are always in the form of a curve, and from these curvilinear motions, or vibrations, were created spheres upon spheres in the psychic worlds below the Soul Plane.

The ECK is rooted and grounded in all life—he, she, it, I, thee, and thou. It is here, there, and everywhere; permeating all directions, east, west, south, and north; above and below; everywhere, in all seasons. All personalities and impersonal things have their existence in the ECK. The ECK is the symbol of individuality, the Sound and the Light. It is the music of the spheres, the light of lights. It is the theories and practices of all things. The creator, creation, and creatures are only the ECK.

Some scriptures describe the ECK as the Word, the Ego principle permeating the universes. It is all that and something more as well. All that is, that will be, and that was, is nothing but the ECK. All find expression in the ECK, the Word. All is manifested in the ECK and by the ECK. All are represented by the ECK. It is explicable. It is inexplicable. It is the personification of the SUGMAD. It is the essential whole and the essential part of the SUGMAD speaking and giving life to all life. It is divisible and indivisible, limited and unlimited, thought and no-thought, visioned and unvisioned; these are nothing but the ECK. It exists as the very essence in the motor and sensory currents of the physical, and in the mental and thought faculties as the very heart of each, and their existing life. It is the cause of all actions and deeds, and is the effect of all causes.

Thus, the ECK is the creative principle proceeding by agitation of motion in the polarized throne of the SUGMAD throughout the worlds and universes. It pervades everything, for nothing can exist without the ECK. As threads in cloth are woven and interwoven, as the particles of water fabricate the sea, all things in the spiritual worlds and all things in the material worlds are woven and fashioned of the ECK. All in existence, whether entire or in parts, is the ECK only.

ECK is the embodiment of all attributes of life, of spiritual enlightenment, of vitality and vibrancy. It is endowed with intelligence as opposed to *jad,* or materialism, and is the principle which finds expression in the word *chaitanya,* which in Sanskrit embraces all things noted here.

The ECK descends and ascends in vibratory currents, producing life in all forms; producing music inherent and inborn that gives joy to the heart of those who have the power to hear Its melody. The middle aspect of ECK is Light, and Its lower aspect is intelligence. It vibrates and reverberates through all worlds. Within the higher worlds It creates the Sound, the music of life; within the psychic worlds It creates Light, and in the worlds of matter It creates intelligence.

All in all, It creates, sustains, and gives freedom to that chela who is able to hear the Music of the SUGMAD, to see the Light of the worlds and to know with the intellect. With this comes freedom, the liberation that brings to Soul the very essence of happiness. This is the true freedom, the true happiness, and the true knowledge of God.

The liberation of Soul from Its gross body is the freedom which man has sought for centuries, in each reincarnation, millions and millions of times repeated. Ever hoping to find perfection in some path to God, but never succeeding until he reaches and accepts the MAHANTA. That perfection within him is recognized by the MAHANTA; he is taken under the MAHANTA's protection as the hen takes the baby chick under its wing to keep the world from crushing it.

By his nature, man can only grasp a particle of the totality of the SUGMAD by knowing and experiencing the God State, but can also realize It even more fully by directly linking up with Truth in such a way that the knower and the known are one. This is possible because human consciousness is dual. Man has two selves: the human ego, the self of which he is primarily conscious, considered erroneously as his real self; and the non-phenomenal self, the Real Self, the eternal Atma, the divinity within him. It is possible for man, if he so desires and is prepared to make the necessary effort and sacrifice, to realize and identify himself with the Atma Sarup. In doing this he is identified with, and comes into, the true knowledge of the totality of the SUGMAD.

Man must know that when he seeks God, he cannot find It. He must know that he cannot touch God. Nor can his mind exceed It. But when he no longer seeks God, then It becomes a recognized part of himself; It is always with him. He will come to know that God is a reality that has always been with him and has never left him; he cannot see It because It is hidden by the external senses that are used to see the world. These senses are not available in the inner world, for they have no use beyond matter. The inner senses are able to see all the outer world and the inner world. It is only by the use of the inner senses that the chela can find God, never by seeking It with the outer equipment.

When man comes to apprehend things as they really

are, and not as they seem to be to his limited perception, then he can know God. Not only will he then enter into the state of being, but he will enter into the immortality of the Atma and be transformed. He will become the Kitai, the enlightened one. This is the second stage of initiation on the path of ECK.

Reality is One, though religions call it by various names. This is what the sages have said to be One in asserting the interiority of divinity in Soul. This inner essence, the spark of divinity which is of the SUGMAD, is always hidden, for It exists at a higher level of human life as the potential of God in man. For It to become truth, there must occur the divine birth, the actual realization within Soul. It is then that man is raised to the Kingdom of God.

The language of man cannot truly begin to describe the sacred worlds of God, only the language of the senses can. His speech cannot be that of a spiritual Volapuk, a Silent One, capable of expression without limits, but is limited and contained in a space-time continuum. The man who can express his experiences in the realm of God does so by his deeds and shining countenance, not by words alone.

The ECK is not contained in space-time measures for It is out of space and time, and different in kind and degree from the worlds out of which the language of man is fashioned to describe the experiences of the senses. Thus the MAHANTA can only describe the glories of the SUGMAD in the environs of polarity with a language of opposites—nonpersonal and personal, supernatural and natural, subjective and objective, without and within. Each is truth within its various spheres, within the different levels of significance and awareness; but none, alone or combined, can express complete truth. The truth found in God is without opposites, while the conflicts of time and space are ever present in the worlds of physical phenomena.

The SUGMAD, like freedom, must be won and rewon many times, for freedom is an elusive element within the physical realms. This freedom is the ultimate reality of life, the ultimate result accumulated over the millions of incarnations of Soul on the physical plane. Upon meeting with the MAHANTA, the acolyte, the seeker of God, becomes the chela. The Living ECK Master is the SUGMAD manifested upon earth and designated to gather up all Souls that are ready and take them into the heavenly worlds again. He who is willing and voluntarily gives up his life for the sake of the ECK is taken up to the glories of God now. He gains freedom within a flash, yet as long as he is in the temple of flesh he will have to win his way back into heaven many times without ceasing, never giving up in the face of hardships and suffering which the Kal Niranjan lays upon him while he lives in this world. So he who will lay down his life for ECK will gain life everlasting, life eternal.

The only way the chela can attain peace of heart and rid himself of all burdens of karma is through the ECK. By his own efforts to leave this worldly state of consciousness and travel into the realms of the SUGMAD can a purified vessel, a channel for God, live in this world of matter while at the same time dwelling in the timeless spheres.

Understanding is without form and must be used. The chela must realize this, for he seeks, for the most part, in the outer worlds, the arena of matter, space, and time. The realization that understanding is a human means for gathering and storing impressions and experiences in the physical world brings Soul to the SUGMAD and the old knowledge of the spiritual realm. Only the single-minded actualizes his true potential and understands that understanding is for himself. It is not the same for all Souls, but differs with each.

There is no way to the SUGMAD except through the MAHANTA. This is the greatest understanding Soul may reach, but it must be direct knowledge, and not given him by another. So it is found that in Soul there is no ultimate knowledge but of Itself. This is what is sufficient for Soul and gives It immortality. Therefore, any speculation or philosophy about the SUGMAD is useless and meaningless for the human consciousness because It cannot be seen, heard, nor reasoned.

The only way the human state can express God, speak of It, or describe It, is in relation to the Kal. The lower element will not allow the essence of God to come through clearly to human minds. God can force Its own way, but only in dire cases of necessity will the SUGMAD express Itself in this world. This condition endures until the human element is conquered and Soul becomes One with One, when the two natures—the human and the divine—are united. This is when the Divine overcomes the worldly self and makes Itself known in the physical state. Few, if any, can find this state; fewer still ever solve the problem and attain this higher spiritual state of the supernatural life.

The state of God-Realization—attainment of the higher spiritual state of the supernatural life—is realized only in the personal aspect. This aspect is hinted at in all religions of the world. The idea of the SUGMAD as both impersonal and personal in Eckankar is expressed in the distinction noted between the ultimate Godhead, which is attributeless, and the MAHANTA, whose characteristics include the Trinity.

Those who have earned the titular distinction of MAHANTA serve their time in this world as the Living ECK Master, to gather up Souls and return them to their original home, the God-realm. For it was there they were created in Soul form and sent forth into the lower worlds along the grand circle route to take on the body form, life after life, until they eventually attained the spiritual awareness to recognize the MAHANTA. He brings them into this world, and has been with them ever since their first birth into the spheres of time, matter, and space. Few ever recognize the MAHANTA until they reach that certain position on their long journey through time and space when the scales fall from their eyes and he is seen in all his light and glory.

All earthly religious leaders fail with the majority, because they are not able to explain with precision the way of God. Few, if any, know the way of ECK. If they do, fewer still know it in a way to get it across to those who are hungering for the worlds beyond. Whosoever tries to explain the ECK without true experiences in the God-realm will not succeed. Whosoever shall have the opportunity to give and to teach ECK with experiences in God shall be successful.

He who has not been in tune with the ECK applies his knowledge to the pursuits of temporary gains and sensuous enjoyment, but the more spiritual realize that body and mind are but the outer and inner garments of Soul. The ignorant continually find themselves in touch with Kal at the lower level, while the spiritually enlightened find themselves in touch with the ECK at the higher level.

Soul is identified with the ECK, the essence of God, for Soul is that divine part of God which dwells in every man. The vibration of the solar sound unveils the true objective of Kal, but the Sounds of ECK reveal the divine reality of God within man.

It is only with the help of the MAHANTA that the chela can come to such a spiritual level of awareness that he can differentiate between the state of phenomena and the knowledge of the noumenon. Thus the ECK is a self-manifesting power independent of living forms. All living forms are composed of It, and all living forms are nothing without It.

ECK functions in the consciousness, the life states, and the embodiment of forms in cohesive unity because of the ties of love that unite them. This is not the same love as we find existing between human states of consciousness. The latter type involves love and death, for whosoever shall love another in the human state shall find death. Love should not be given in the human state from one to another unless it is done in a disinterested way. This distinct human love always destroys, while the superior spiritual love gives increasing life. The ECK forms the consciousness in man, and spiritual love lifts and unites Soul with God. This is at once an impersonal and universal action, and those who have reached this state are known as the Vairagi Masters.

The spiritually blind grope through life in unhappiness, fear, and uncertainty. Mentally paralyzed, they seek the false security of dogma, superstition, social approval, national and personal pride, and temporal honor. Living in the limited awareness of the intellect and in the sensuous state of the physical environment, their lives are darkened by a deplorable ignorance of the spiritual self and their inherent divinity.

It is the ECK that awakens man to full realization of his divine nature. Nothing else is capable of doing this. All those who seek this realization from the varied religions, cults, and isms will meet with failure. Only the ECK can transform the human state of consciousness into divine Self-Realization, and gradually lead Soul on to the God State.

To a man who has achieved Self-Realization and God-Realization, all religions, all philosophies, become just so many paths leading to the ECK. Through any of them, the seeker of God can reach the divine ECK, the immaculate path to the Ultimate Reality. To the man who has touched the robe of God there is no distinction of race or belief, no consciousness of nationality, and no religious difference. The ECK has cleared away all conflicts and oppositions from his mental processes.

Each created form of life, by its own nature, longs for the perfection of the SUGMAD. It yearns for its well-being in the spiritual worlds, not the material worlds. It aspires for the perfection of the Divine One, graciously brought about by Its Grace.

The most perfect object of love is the SUGMAD, for Its glory is shown only to those who are able to receive Its revelations. It is hidden from those who are entrapped in the snares of their own weaknesses and who, in the hands of Kal Niranjan, remain the docile captive.

The SUGMAD manifests Itself to the elect in this world in diverse ways, and these elect become the chosen people. Followers of the path of Eckankar are the chosen ones whom God has selected to return again to the heavenly realm and become Its Coworkers. They are the fortunate ones, the triumphant who have gained victory over the wiles of Kal Niranjan and who will reach the heavenly worlds again.

This beyond lies on the far side of cosmic consciousness, yet It is attainable to all who will make the effort to find It. It is the transcendent, so magnificent in Its scope and greatness—in comparison with the material universes—that the ego, the other worlds, and all therein are but pretty things against Its immeasurable, majestic background. It supports the universal activity of life. It embraces life with vastness, or rejects it from Its infinitude.

The ECK is the path, and to walk it is the enduring and unchanging way. All other ways are changeable and not reliable, for they can lead one only to the upper psychic planes. ECK is the nonpersonal and the personal path which takes the chela into the heart of God. Whatever is possible for the chela will be found on the way that is the highest, the Eckankar way, and no one may tread this path unless he is escorted by the MAHANTA.

The three aspects of the SUGMAD are different from the Trinity of Christianity and Hinduism, and also different from the Trikaya of Buddhism, since it covers all things in life. The triple aspects are the three bodies of the MAHANTA.

First there is the absolute primordial, the eternal MAHANTA, called the clear Voice of God, which dwells in the heart of the Ocean of Love and Mercy. There is no way to compare this with anything in Christianity, Hinduism, or Buddhism.

Second is the body of glory; the ECK, the Cosmic Spirit, the Sound Current which is in all life, giving existence to all things.

Third is the body of manifestation, the transformation, the historical MAHANTA. This is the Living ECK Master in every age, who is the Eternal One, the bodily manifestation of the SUGMAD.

The historical MAHANTA is the bodily manifestation of the eternal MAHANTA and is the aspect in which the Divine One becomes incarnate in human form. The historical MAHANTA possesses the same qualities as the Divine One in Its second aspect, and manifests them as far as they can be manifested within the limitations of human nature within a definite point of history.

Man must build upon the ECK, never on the Kal. When one is working with the Kal, he becomes paralyzed in his upward climb and is continually working on a destructive basis. Most Souls in the lower worlds are living in this sort of void. This is described by the Buddhists as Nirvana, the Void that is so highly praised. The main principle of karma is based on the Kal power, on destruction.

It is an axiom of ECK that whosoever tries to serve humanity will be a failure, but he who is willing and serves God is always a success in life. Few realize that the man who says his great desire is to serve mankind is speaking from the level of the Kal forces. It is one of Kal Niranjan's greatest traps to make one feel he is serving his fellow man. All those who heal the physical and mental aspects of man, who bring prosperity to man, who seek after peace for mankind, are deceived by the Kal forces into believing that this is God's design and will.

He who believes in social reforms for man is doomed to the lower levels of the Astral world, for this is but the work of the emotional body, which is the Astral body, working under the direction of the Kal forces. When the chela's spiritual eyes are opened he begins to see that the vast majority of works labeled as social forces, such as poetry, art, and music, have been created by the mind and are the Kal works of the Astral Plane, not of the true spiritual worlds.

The MAHANTA is the distributor of karma in this world, and what he says is the word of the SUGMAD. All the Lords of Karma are under his hand and must do as he directs. Hence, Eckankar is the spiritual refuge for all Souls. All are under the MAHANTA, although few recognize and accept him as the spiritual Avatar of the age. The spiritual body of the MAHANTA is always with all people at all times, and it cannot be replaced because some religions have a different name for him.

He has been the spiritual head of the world since its creation, manifesting physically to different races at different periods of human history as the vehicle for the

SUGMAD in the form to which they are most accustomed and by the name familiar to them. If the people were Hindu, he has appeared as Krishna, Buddha, or Vishnu, so they would know him. He was Zeus to the Greeks; Jupiter to the Romans; Osiris, Amun, Re, and Aton to the Egyptians; Jehovah to the old Judeans; Ishtar to the Babylonians; Varuna to the Aryans; Jesus to the Christians; and Allah to the Muslims. He has appeared to all in every age of this world. He is the secret force behind world historical events. None can escape the SUGMAD, and none be higher in this world and other worlds than the MAHANTA, the Divine One, who is the manifestation in body form of the eternal MAHANTA.

The MAHANTA will rebuild the temple and gather in the Souls who wander in darkness. He places before each Soul the two ways: the way of life, and the way of death. The moment comes when no man can resist the summons. Where can man escape death? There is no place he can go except to God, to escape death. He cannot escape death while he is in the physical state, for there is no charm against it.

The ECK of Itself is a whole sovereign state, a condition of spiritual thought bound together by the idealism and love of Its own peoples. The universes of the SUGMAD are complete with a hierarchy of highly evolved beings who govern all the worlds according to the laws of their own worlds, and in accord with the will of the SUGMAD. The only difference between the spiritual hierarchy and the structure of the governments of the physical world is that the SUGMAD is a monarch in Its government of the worlds. It rules singularly and by divine nature. There are no democratic principles found here, and we either live according to the Divine Laws or become rebels and resist. Then we suffer whatever results by dwelling in the world of matter and being a subject of the Kal Niranjan, king of the negative force.

When man is able to leave his physical state of consciousness and travel in the inner worlds, he comes to that state where he passes the beyond—and suddenly he finds there is no state of consciousness existing in such a place. He is beyond the Void of Buddhism, the Heaven of the Christians, and the world of No Thing of Jainism. He is in the state of pure Being, if there is a vocabulary capable of describing it. Language and sound fail him.

The whole fabric of mankind is in the prison of society and self. This is a tragic existence controlled by the Kal Niranjan in life after life. The Kal is the prison warden, and those who attempt to escape are usually independent. They believe in God, are stubborn and rambunctious; yet they, too, enslave themselves ever more securely in the prison of the Kal.

Man is both an exile and a prisoner, and his blindness is a darker imprisonment still. The inescapable confinement of Soul within this world is due mainly to the religion It follows. The church has become man's illusion and comfort. He parades before all people as righteous and spiritual, but he is like a rotten apple where the peel has a glossy shine but the inner part is filled with worms.

The physical infects the body, and the astral infects the body and mind. Both also infect the causal body. But then the physical will infect the body, the astral infect the physical, the causal infect the astral and body, and the mind will infect all.

In the relationships men have with one another, it is found that the astral and the mental have the greatest vitiative effect upon others. Those who stir up the astral waves and create disturbances among the human races suffer terribly without knowing what they did or how they did it. This is the danger of the psychic worker in this world. Be aware and do not have anything to do with them, for your ignorance will not be acknowledged nor be a reason for mercy when you face the Judge of the Dead. Your record here is what it is, and your next assignment, unless you are under the protection of the MAHANTA, will bring about more lives and further hardships, as one who violated the laws of the SUGMAD.

The mind infected by the Kal acts as a channel for the negative agent and infects other minds. The Kal elements which pour through the mind into the minds of the other persons become a poison which spreads from the youth to the elderly. No one living in the human consciousness is ever free from this unless he is under the protection of the MAHANTA. Age believes that it is triumphant because it has wisdom, but this is because the Kal wants the elderly to believe this; and the youth live in the rebellion of blindness because the Kal has set its course this way. None are free unless they follow the path of ECK. Orthodox religion will not save them, but will enslave all who follow it. Philosophy will furnish only a balm and salve for those who want to follow this never-successful path.

The MAHANTA is the messenger of the Absolute. There are none before him, and there will be none after him. All those who come to him in the present age have been with him since their advent into the world. He has developed them to this state of spiritual development so that by now they have reached the level wherein their recognition of him is apparent. He is able to accept each chela for what he is, and then put his feet on the path to reach the state of God-Realization within this lifetime.

Not all chelas under the MAHANTA will necessarily reach the state of either Self-Realization or God-Realization within this lifetime. Should the MAHANTA leave this life in his physical form before he has completed his duty with them, he will reappear again here on earth in another body to finish his task. He comes again and again in every age to take up the task of salvation with every Soul that reaches out or has reached out to him in some life. His duties with each Soul never cease; he is to take each back into heaven to become the Coworker with God. He has never left any Soul who has made contact with him, sometime, somewhere in the past, or in this life. Once Soul has made the slightest degree of contact with the MAHANTA, there is never any parting between them. He becomes as close to his loved ones as their own heartbeat, as their own breathing.

The body of the MAHANTA is the ECK. This is the essence of God which flows out from the Ocean of Love and Mercy, sustaining all life and tying together all life-forms. This is the consciousness of God, the very fluid that man lives upon. It is the highest form of God energy, and the greatest level of consciousness. The body form is merely the vehicle through which the ECK flows to uplift all life which comes in touch with the world. Without the body of the MAHANTA within the universes, things would wither away and die.

The MAHANTA liberates Soul from the grasp of the Kal forces. He is the good that dwells in the heart of every mortal creature. He is the beginning, the life span, and the end of all mortal creatures. He is the radiant sun, the wind, the stars of the night, and the moon. He is the king of heaven, of the sense organs, of the mind, of the consciousness of living. He is the spirit of fire, the spirit of the mountains, leader of all priests, the ocean's spirit, the greater seer; the sacred syllable ECK, the tree, the ant, the thunder in the heavens, and the god of fishes and sharks. He is time and the eagle, the lion and bear, the rivers of the world, the sustainer, the newborn babe, and the old man preparing to die. In all things is his face, and in all life is he the divine seed. In this world, nothing animate or inanimate exists without him. This is the Lord SUGMAD in action, and one atom of Its body sustains the worlds upon worlds. Not only is he the king of this world, but in all worlds, all planets, all planes.

Out of the shattering of man's image comes the death of his God, and with this comes the splendid vision of the worlds within worlds, bringing enlargement and release from this plane of flesh. No longer does the universe seem cold, impersonal and menacing, but aflame with the love of the SUGMAD. This vision is never superimposed upon another but rises out of the very texture of the cosmos. Man in his human state then begins to see it, only insofar as he has shattered the images of his past concepts of the SUGMAD.

The feeble denizen of this world feels as if he cannot trust himself to the ebb and flow of this immense spiritual universe. He needs to turn all his inner affairs over to the MAHANTA until he can, on his own, be responsible for himself. He must know that, despite appearances and the apparent evil flowing around him, he and everything else in it are safe. Freedom is impossible for one who does not recognize that the flow and ebb that pass through the MAHANTA to the world are guaranteeing him a safe journey through the lower worlds. The state of spiritual knowing, what we name faith, is impossible if faith seems to conflict with reason and possibility. One cannot believe without tolerance, and never can he believe in what he thinks impossible or unreasonable.

The experience of the MAHANTA, as one knows him in the human flesh, is that of man, but the chela is to look at what is known as the two sides of the MAHANTA. These are the human state and the spiritual body. There is the experience of the earthly man who walks and talks with his friends, who dies but rises again. There is the other experience of the spiritual ECK of the risen MAHANTA, an experience of a divine indwelling of the SUGMAD immanent in man.

It is unreasonable to isolate or overstress the historical element in ECK, since to do so can result in failure to grasp the timeless significance of the MAHANTA. Likewise, it is equally unreasonable to neglect or discard the ECK, for It is an essential part of the spiritual revolution taking place in every age, the constant conflict between the ECK and the Kal forces.

The idea of the MAHANTA as representative man appears sometimes to be quite startling to the traditionalists of religions. It need not be, though the eternal and essential Godman does involve seeming contradictions. The incarnation of the MAHANTA in every age is not only a showing forth of the divine drama being played out, but also a continuing portrayal of the human drama. This gives the only true promise of salvation, the liberation of Soul from the world of matter.

3

The Doctrine of the ECK Marg

In the beginning there was only the mighty SUGMAD, the Lord of Lords, the Absolute of all Absolutes, the All Holy of Holies, the All Merciful of Mercies, and the Omnipotence, Omnipresence, and Omniscience of all universes and worlds.

In the beginning, It slept; stirring not in the Ocean of Love and Mercy in that sphere where man has never trod nor any angel dwelled. It is not a land, nor place or abode, but a mighty ocean of splendor and love. It is the reality of all realities, the dwelling place of the SUGMAD, the Ancient One whom all creatures, beings, and men have worshipped through the ages.

In the beginning It was the Alpha that slept, but It ruled in Its slumbers over the mighty beings, elements, and creatures in the universes. Peace and happiness were everywhere, and little was there for the SUGMAD to concern Itself with over life and Its offspring. The sacred garden of esoteric wisdom in the Alaya Lok was delightful for those beings who amused themselves there, while the Almighty slumbered and dreamed new worlds.

In the eternity of the profound Ocean of Love and

Mercy, It stirred and aroused Itself from this deep slumber. Wild tremors came down through the universes, shaking the heavens and those beings in the sacred gardens. They paused, then looked up in astonishment at the parting of the firmament. They were amazed at the seeming wrath of the heavenly world that split with rolling thunder and crashing echoes.

The SUGMAD aroused Itself and looked out over the vastness of Its domain; saw only the creatures of Its making in play, amusing themselves without giving to one another. It whispered, and the Word went forth into the worlds of worlds.

The worlds shook, and all Souls flew to find safety, but none was to be found. They stood and trembled before the mighty SUGMAD, the God of all gods, and listened. "You have played when you needed to give succor and life to others; you must learn the Truth by dwelling in my mansions below. In the house of your Father! You shall return to my home when ready!"

None knew what the Voice of the Lord was saying. Yet all who heard Its Voice wondered. It was to build new worlds in which each Soul would spend Its youth, to germinate and spiritually unfold; to learn Its true nature and mission throughout the universes of God.

In the beginning all below the Atma world was only Spirit, that known as the ECK, which moved throughout the void. Everything was without life—calm, silent. Void and dark was the immensity of space and time. Only the supreme power, the ECK, the self-existing essence of the SUGMAD, moved within this dark gulf of nothing.

The desire came upon the SUGMAD to look upon this abyss outside the universes of Light and Sound. It desired to create new worlds, and It created these worlds below the Atma Plane. The desire came to It to create the zodiac and the twelve constellations therein, and to place living things upon each.

The desire came upon It to form the Sun, Moon, planets, and other worlds of the void; and It gave each thing life. In each was placed a different embodiment of flesh, but to the creation of Earth It gave the apex of life, called man. But first there were only rude forms of life.

It took the gases, which were without form, and scattered them throughout all space. Out of them were formed the planes, universes, worlds and planets, including the earth.

The gases solidified to form the worlds and all its heavens. Out of these came the water and the atmosphere; and darkness prevailed. There was no sound, for as yet the ECK had not entered into all the worlds of time and space.

After the atmosphere was created, the SUGMAD formed the outside gases and waters which covered the face of all worlds, and there were no land masses anywhere. So the SUGMAD looked and dreamed to see what It would do with these worlds It had created in the vast regions outside Its own domain.

It commanded the sun to give light and the atmosphere to open so that its rays could fall upon the worlds of darkness. Then light penetrated the darkness and made it bright and illuminated. The SUGMAD created the whirling masses in space, and the planets began to rotate around the suns within their universes, including the earth, and there was an alternating of light and darkness.

The light of the sun and the heat of the atmosphere met and gave warmth to the worlds. This brought life.

The ECK entered into the worlds of time and space and began to plant the cosmic eggs of life-forms.

Then the SUGMAD moved the gases within the bodies of the worlds and raised the lands above the waters. Life came forth in the waters when the sunlight penetrated the mud, stirring the cosmic eggs planted by the ECK, and life-forms appeared.

Again, the sunlight penetrated the dust of the lands, stirring the cosmic eggs planted by the ECK, and from these cosmic eggs life-forms came forth.

These life-forms were many, and they roamed over the lands and in the seas for yugas upon yugas. Then the SUGMAD looked again and saw that another embodiment was needed to complete the link of the life chain from mineral form to Spirit form. So It commanded that the apex of life come into embodiment, fashioned after the great Sat Nam, who is the first manifestation of the supreme Deity, and endowed him with power to rule the worlds below the heavens.

Then the spiritual workers created man and placed within him a living imperishable Spirit, called Soul; and man became like the living gods of the spirit worlds with intellectual powers, physical strength, and Soul. He roamed the worlds, living off the creatures of the fields, the fruits of the trees, and the products of the soil.

The mighty SUGMAD spoke to Its spirits and angels. "Lo, all those who have played in the fields of Heaven shall descend to earth and take the body form. Each will be given an adi karma by the Lords of Karma, to carry during his earthly lives. Each shall go through body upon body, reincarnation after reincarnation, until the day comes when he shall meet with me again in the body form in which I shall be known as the MAHANTA. Only when he is ready and has reached perfection, when all dross has burned away and he has gained spiritual maturity, will he return to the heavenly fields and become a worker in the spiritual realms. Until then he shall spend his time as Soul, in the lower worlds, learning his catechism and being educated to his true purpose in his heavenly home.

"Each Soul that is created shall go through the fires of the worlds below and be drowned in the seas of tears, agony, and unhappiness, until he cries out for me to reach down to him. Until he has been purified, until he has gone through all the mystic rituals, through the cave of fire and the seas of agony which give him perfection, shall my face be turned from him."

The imperishable spirits called Souls fell upon their knees and wailed their anguish to the heavens. The SUGMAD had spoken and commanded that they go down into the depths of fire, mud, and terror to receive their discipline, to become Coworkers with the Almighty. Life in eternity had been one of pleasure, play, and happiness, that no mortal being had ever known. To exchange that for a life of misery, unhappiness, and the burdens of karma was more than each Soul could bear.

The SUGMAD closed Its eyes and dreamed again. The wailing of the Souls did not reach It. The dreams that came were of creation that formed the worlds below. It created, and out of the creation came a manifestation of Itself, that mighty Deity whom all mankind knows as the Sat Nam. So mighty is He that few who approach can but believe that here is the Almighty, the Lord of Lords.

The floor of Heaven opened; and all Souls went tumbling downward through the worlds, through the planes and regions of light, darkness, the sounds of the wild winds, the universes and heavens. At last, each came to rest upon the worlds of matter—some in the newly formed planets of Venus, Saturn, Jupiter, and those named by man from his little world of Earth. Many came to the Earth planet and formed the consciousness of man in the flesh temple of the human body, to wear the cloth of misery and unhappiness, and take up the burdens of karma until at last, one day, each would be ready to return to the heavenly home.

Some accepted a human body, others came into consciousness as stone, rocks, minerals, birds, animals, and fish. But all manifestations of the SUGMAD received the consciousness of the lower worlds.

Then there were the rulers of the four planes which were established in the worlds of time and space. First, the SUGMAD manifested Itself in the last heavenly plane in Its own form, which became Sat Nam, the ruler over all worlds in the lower universe.

Under him was formed the spiritual hierarchy of Sohang, Omkar, Ramkar, Jot Niranjan, and Elam, each in order down to the last material plane of the lower universe. At the top of these material worlds the Prince of Darkness took his place to act as the tempter of Soul. He was given the name of Kal Niranjan.

Niranjan is the false power that symbolizes the negative. It is evil, the force that makes Soul believe happiness lies in material life. It is the Satan of the psychic worlds. All that are tempted by, and succumb to, its whispers of joy and riches shall remain in the fires of torture on the Wheel of Awagawan, or coming and going. This is the agelong cycle of births and deaths, transmigration, the reincarnation of Soul.

Niranjan is the power of mind. It is the psychic power, and those who live in ignorance listen to its sweet whispers of hope. It appeals to the vanity of human consciousness. But it can never succeed, for the Souls who have been pitched into the darkness of the universes shall someday give up and return to their heavenly home to be with the SUGMAD. There they will become workers in the spiritual field somewhere in the worlds of light and love.

Those Souls which follow the beckoning finger of Niranjan to organized religion shall take the wrong turn of the road. None but the Living ECK Master, who has descended to the worlds of matter to give all Souls an opportunity to return to Heaven, is capable of offering this opportunity. All others are false prophets and shall not be heeded.

Those who listen to Niranjan are listening to the false prophet. The sweet whispers of this negative genius are heard in the voices of those who make claims to be the prophets of the times and the preachers, clergy, and priests who represent the old orthodox religions.

Beware, lest they sway you to listen and change toward the Kal Niranjan, who rules the planets of the lower universes. Never talk of achievements in ECK, for this brings only disaster to the chela. Speak not of any achievement nor any loss, for it only brings about the retardation of spiritual attainment.

This is the way of the Kal. Its duty is to arrest the spiritual unfoldment of Soul, and the duty of Soul is to ward off these attempts of Kal.

The human consciousness is prey to autointoxication, for the Kal floods the consciousness of man with various poisons bred by various states of mind and emotion. The most poisonous of these states are fear, anger, worry, sentimental emotionalism, and envy. The destructive emanations set up by these mental emotional states clog the virility and sensitivity of the human race like a heavy pall. The emanations from terrified, slaughtered creatures add to the general aggravation of Kal's works with the human consciousness.

Truth can be understood only by one who is in a state of vigilance; therefore, none who are in a slack condition of mind will find it available. Truth is not in the heights but at the bottom of all things. It must be struggled for and sought after and come upon through earnest effort, through the stimulation brought about by suffering or striving, whereby the consciousness is prepared to recognize it. Truth always appears to be veiled, guarded, and hidden from the eyes of the profane.

At first Souls found little within the worlds of space. There are no boundaries where all is infinite, nor age where time is the only measure of change within the changeless, nor death where life is the indestructible pulse of energy in the heat and the cold. There is no morning, noon, nor evening, for what has always been and will always be, is just what it is.

As there was no beginning for every Soul who came into Its own recognition, there could be no end. But each found in living within the worlds of matter, energy, space, and time, that there is, and has been and always will be, continuous change in the appearance of things which, in the small chronology of finite perceptions, is the life of the human body known as birth and growth, evolution and progress, age and death.

Within the physical universe there occurred in countless eons a stupendous explosion that rearranged the destinies of the suns. One of these smaller suns, a white-hot incandescent splinter of the main sun, fell into the darkness, leaving behind vast streamers. Now shot too far out to return to its parent light, it formed a scattered field of light which came together in irregular orbits around the star it had left. Thus, the world of planets and its neighboring stars were born.

Smaller fires also, thrown far beyond the sun and close to the worlds, held in suspension by the pull of the two, moved over paths of their own. These millions of smaller fires were the scattered fragments of a new solar system, most of them useless. After cooling, after becoming small wandering nuggets of iron and stone, most of these fragments would in time go back to the sun or back to the world of solid matter, the earth.

The universe was not born in a moment nor a million years. It evolved through the ages from the white-hot sparks of the sun to the cold stone enveloping the furnace within its core. Then came the immutable laws to govern the worlds of the universe and bring harmony to the course of those planets that revolved around the hot sun.

Elements became precious within the soils of the earth and other planets. Out of the heart of the world poured the energies and rhythms and harmonies which were the only substances of God, and the only substance of all things that are.

Like its brother planets, the earth became a world of its own—a living world, but a simple one of elements where the energies and rhythms were greater than those which were to come in the form of bodies of animals and men. The world made numerous journeys around the sun, a hundred million times or more. Its gaseous body became a liquid, and the surface roughly divided into hemispheres and poles. There was no haste, for within the laws of the SUGMAD it was only preparing for the coming of a more complex shape of life.

Thus it became a new world where birth, youth, middle age, old age, and death denoted changes in the appearance of things. The energy of the living God shaped the forms which made the world a cradle of life, the home of civilization, and the graveyard of all embodiments. But never once did It keep the Souls of Its embodiments within this sphere of the universes.

The SUGMAD destroyed nothing and lost nothing in the process of change. It only used the world to refine each Soul that entered into it. It made the earth a place for greater destiny, through the energies of the ECK flowing down from the Ocean of Love and Mercy.

The long pilgrimage out of the darkness and into the light began in the mud and the slime, working upward into the apex of human consciousness. Something was gained from the cycles of sensate things through birth, age, and sleep, and into life again: They were born higher on the ladder of spiritual consciousness.

The sea was the cradle of life. The magic of the ECK energies formed the complex union of molecules and built a cell of life. The tenacious hold on life of the molecule for existence caused it to wed with others and make a complex entity with tendencies of reaction and response to its environment, the power to move in the water and seek food and protection.

The masses of molecules developed into protozoa and finally into the vegetation of the sea, and, after millions of years, into plants, sponges, and flowers of the watery depths. Minerals developed in the same form on the land surfaces, but the first form that started evolving toward human embodiment was the fish. The Law of ECK moved again in Its very mysterious way and saw the need of organs and faculties in these creatures. Some became aggressive, feeding upon those which had only the vegetation and plants of the sea for survival.

Intelligence came to the creatures of the sea. Simple as it was, it gave those without protection the only means of escape from the devouring jaws of the beasts that swallowed unwary fish. The size and speed of these scourges of the sea grew, developing appetites without parallel. They became sires of the shark, whale, and other mammoth monsters of the deep.

Some of these strange creatures came out of the sea to find easier prey. For a million years this saga went on, with the sea-born and the sea-living moving from the water to the land. Creatures with gills and fins developed lungs and legs in time. Many walked on hind feet, rearing in the air with crocodile heads and gleaming teeth. Into the dark, dank jungles they went, searching for food. They became stupendous bone-plated machines controlled only by a few lower reflexes, finding beetles as large as sparrows, and flying insects with a wing-spread of thirty inches, for their hunger. Anything that walked, crawled, and flew was food for their greed.

These were ancestors of the reptiles. They grew twenty feet in height and fifty feet around. The tail was massive and the skull as large as a grown ox, with broad powerful teeth six inches long. The claws on the feet were curved a little longer than the teeth.

The other species of brutes were just as fearful and frightening of aspect. They seldom attacked one another because of the thick armored skin. Some were vegetarian and others flesh eaters. They were moved by voracious hunger and fear. They were torpid mountains of bone and meat with the sluggish and cold-blooded nervous system of the reptile.

For millions of years these monsters ruled the earth. A few of them became the dragon species that lived on the ground. But smaller dragons took to the air, flying on wings. These were more dreadful than those that walked on the ground.

The ECK's experiment in dreadful creatures came to a sudden and dramatic ending. The dragons that had ruled for millions of years perished within a few centuries, unable to adapt to climatic changes. Too sluggish to migrate and having too little intelligence to understand the coming danger, they froze to death when the great ice age took place.

The ECK was now ready for another kind of creature for experiment and for the first time turned to those to whom It had given sympathy and care. These were the creatures of fear who had lived in dread from the day of birth to the day of death. The destruction of the killer beasts came about in a harsh world, so now the ECK prepared the earth for a more noble experiment for the SUGMAD, the coming of Souls into this world.

The ECK softened and beautified the great, formidable earth, covering the mountains with forests and scatterings of wildflowers over the hills. The valley teemed with butterflies and singing birds. Lights and shadows were given to the morning and evening of the day. Now the mammals entered into the world and became the forerunners of this genus, including man, today.

These were the milk-givers that housed the unborn in their bodies, not by eggs as their fierce predecessors had done. They gave their young care after birth, for now love had entered into the world. The age prior to this was one of tremendous savagery, for often the dragons and other beasts ate their young hatched from eggs, or one another.

However, this was not a gentle age by any means, for still there were the savage beasts, such as the cat family, the saber-toothed tiger and all its kin, the bear, dog, and wolf. There were giant hogs and mammoths, flesh eaters all of them.

There were two great clans: the killers, who ate only flesh and who spent all their waking hours stalking and killing their prey, and the timid beasts that fed off the earth. Out of these clans came men, who originally were leaf eaters and lived in terror of the killer beasts that stalked and trapped them.

Souls that came into this lower environment had to take on the embodiment of flesh in order to exist in the vibrations of this material world. But man had no place to live, for he was prey to the brutality of the flesh eaters. He was not a creature with fangs, claws, and muscular strength. What strength he had was not enough.

He could not venture into the waters, for there the beasts awaited ready to tear him apart. In the jungles were the huge serpents and deadly insects; on the prairies were the wolves. There was no spot on earth for him to safely lay his head. He had only one place to live, and that was in the trees.

So it was in the high treetops of the forest that he built his home to be safe from the prowling animals that killed him for food. Not the primate, but the Soul and form of man himself. He developed an amazing agility to swing through the higher branches. For ages he was a treetop tenant, rarely venturing to the ground. He drank water from the leaves and ate the foliage, and made his bed in a tree crotch. He scorned the endless spectacle of slaughter which went on beneath him. But the day came when he was to descend to the soil of earth and leave his distant cousins still in the treetops.

At first he walked on four feet, then learned to stand upright, and what was a creature now became a man because he could think, and by thinking he could protect himself. Thereupon, he found a persistent pattern of behavior that set him free. Never again could his supremacy be threatened nor his foe be more than his slave, for they were the beasts of the forest, the birds of the air, and the creatures of the sea.

Then human consciousness came into being, and man became the supreme creature upon the earth.

He developed thought and the ability to use it to protect himself against the flesh killers and the environment. He found shelter in the caves and fashioned weapons out of sticks and stones. He found that the female reproduced his species, and he lived in family groups. At first the female was taken by force, for man was a strange and violent creature belonging to the bloodstained and bestial past of the human race. A headman or chief was selected to supervise the family and the tribe which gathered around him.

Civilization formed in a primitive manner, and there

appeared in the world the first ECK Master, who was without name. He was important to the human race because his task was to minister to their needs and give to all succor and wisdom.

Primitive man believed that stones and trees were homes of the spirits who served under supernatural beings who ruled everything. Soul was not yet developed enough in man for It to understand and know what It was seeking. But It lived in a universe where the laws of the world are different.

Sundered from all things by gulfs and far dimensions, the ancient world of Polara, the Garden of Eden, loomed upon the horizon. Stretching from the greater sea in the east to that in the west, this civilization was known for its great forested lands to the north, the steppes-dwelling creatures, and the fierce desert of the rich eastern lands.

This was the beginning of the races of man upon earth. Within the world of the past and before the dawn of recorded history, at the western extremity of the continent of Europe, Asia, and Africa, the Polarian, or the Adamic, race of pale copper-skinned people dwelled. Out of the forests came man, walking upright. His first act of worship was for the luminous power that scattered darkness and evil. It was a great golden eye, like a wheel, or a halo of glory, rising majestically out of the underworld with the heat of its body spreading over the whole hungry earth.

The first Polarian man was Adom the Rabi, and he stood on the summit of a hill. His female companion, Ede, stood back with bowed head as he addressed his Sun-god. He prayed for food, protection from pain and enemies, and well-being for his woman.

He was granted everything but freedom from pain and emotion. He knew when the danger came, for out of the forests came another creature walking upright like himself, who wanted the female. The battle was bitter, but Adom won and drove off his foe. He produced a man-child and another; and human history began.

Gradually the creatures gathered and formed a clan. Slowly they hacked out the forests, fought the flesh eaters and won, until a civilization was born on the edge of the rivers that flow through the continent called Asia.

Malati, the first ECK Master of record, was sent by the SUGMAD into this world to give man his first spiritual knowledge of God.

For men drifted apart, fought one another for domination over tilled lands, trade, women and slaves, and what little wealth they had in precious stones. Slowly the ECK was building Its species. Then came the race of men called the Hyperboreans, and this became the age of the same name, the second root race of mankind.

The Hyperboreans were the clans that drifted onto land where there was perpetual sunshine. The rains fell heavily upon the forests and created the jungle growth. The north wind never touched the heart of this world, and the face of man became darkened by the sun and jungle regions.

Where the Polarian man was a tiller of the soil, a shepherd and a hunter, his successor was a higher being who built cities and founded a civilization in the heart of the equatorial jungle. He developed weapons for fighting, and pots for holding his food. He elected a king to rule over the mighty empire of Melnibora.

The empire lived on for a hundred centuries, ruled over by the fierce Varkas kings. They swept across the jungles and over the heat of the sands to the north, conquering the wild tribes of men with white skins.

They made slaves of the conquered, forcing them to work in their fields, in their weapons shops, and in the homes of their nobility. The kings ruled by the formless terror called sorcery, with powers greater than anything witnessed prior to their times and for centuries to come.

The Varkas used their awful powers to conquer their subjects and their foes. They cast spells upon the masses and dealt in terrible mysteries with the dead. Some of the kings conquered time and lived for centuries. They ruled through the priests who were known as the Zuajirs. And these priests were more terrible than their masters.

They were ruthless, giving quarter to no man when captured on the field of battle. The victim was killed or saved for a fate more fearful than anything man could believe. If he was saved for the stables of the nobleman or to work in some household, the captured was indeed fortunate.

Living in secret and teaching to those who would give ear was the great Kai-Kuas, the Living ECK Master of these times. He was discovered by the Varkas and slain.

This was an age when man literally ate man, for he was hardly out of the jungle and felt that all life was his deadly enemy. He believed that in order to survive, he must serve his god, the sun, and when night fell, it was the destruction of their god. When it rose again in the morning, its worshippers knew the sun had won over the powers of darkness and evil.

Along with this, it was their simple belief that the people of the north with their pale skins were evil and, therefore, must be subjected. They conquered and ruled the world as the first of the races to go out trying to subject its fellow men by the sword.

Soon they began to lose their hold on the known world, for the ECK experimented with Its own species and founded a third root race known as the Lemurians. This new race, living in the land of Lemuria, was brown-skinned with a highly developed sense toward being civilized.

The Lemurians had the greatest civilization known to the world. It developed on the great continent of Mu in the midst of the western ocean, and spread around the world with many subempires. It was a tropical country of vast plains. The valleys and plains were covered with rich grazing grass and tilled fields. There were only low rolling hills and no mountains, for the peaks and ranges of great heights had not yet been forced up from the deep centers of the earth.

The air was soft, the vegetation constantly bloomed, and life for the millions of the continent's people was gay and happy. Ten tribes made up the bulk of the citizens, each distinct but living under an emperor named Ra Mu. The empire was named the "Empire of the Sun."

Ra Mu was the representative of the Supreme Deity, although he was not worshipped. The deity was worshipped through symbols, and all believed in the immortality of Soul, which eventually returned to the Source from whence It came.

The reverence of the Lemurians for their deity was so great they never spoke Its name and even in prayer and supplication addressed It always through a symbol. However, Ra, the sun, was used as the collective for all the deity possessed as a supreme entity.

The people of Mu were highly civilized and enlightened. They were gentle, peaceful, and lived together without savagery. As citizens of the great empire which stretched from rising sun to rising sun—an empire upon which the sun never set—they were under the protection of Mu, the motherland of the earth.

The ruling race of Mu was exceedingly handsome, with brown or olive skin, large, soft, dark eyes and straight black hair. They had other races—the yellow, brown, and black people—but these did not dominate. They sailed the seas and discovered new lands, inhabited and established colonies around the globe, built great temples, stone palaces, and carved gigantic monuments.

Within the continent of Mu were seven major cities, where the religion, science, and education centers existed. There also were many other large cities for trading and industry, for, as the center of the world as it came to be known, Mu was the land where all came for learning, trading, and commerce. The rest of the world formed her colonies.

Into this world came Geutan, the third great ECK Master, who served the people of Mu and warned them of the coming destruction of the world.

When this continent was at its zenith, the center of world civilization, it received a terrible shock.

The rumblings from the bowels of the earth, followed by earthquakes and volcanic outbursts, shook her southern parts. Gigantic, cataclysmic waves from the ocean rolled over the land, and the cities went down to destruction. The volcanoes belched out their fire, smoke, and lava. The flat continent reared up, and lava beds formed cones which became rocks.

After this, the people of Mu gradually overcame their fright; cities were rebuilt, and trade and commerce were resumed. Generations passed after this visitation, and when the phenomenon had become history, Mu again became the victim of earthquakes. The whole continent heaved and rolled like ocean waves. The land trembled and shook like leaves on a tree in a storm. Temples and palaces came crashing to the ground, and monuments and statues were overturned. The cities became heaps of ruins.

The land quivered and shook, rose and fell. The fires of the earth underneath flamed forth and pierced the clouds. Thick black palls of smoke hung over the land,

and huge cataclysmic waves rolled through the cities and plains. The terrified people sought refuge in their temples and citadels, only to be driven out by the fire and smoke.

During the night the land was torn apart, and down it went into the dark waters of the ocean, claiming the lives of millions of people. The waves rolled over and met in the center of the land, seethed and boiled, destroying the earth's first great civilization.

A few islands were left where mountain peaks had been raised in the catastrophe. Those people who survived this terrible event became the race of the South Sea Islands.

From across the world there came next into existence the Atlantean race, the fourth root race, or the red race, who lived upon the continent of Atlantis in the great ocean between the eastern and western hemispheres. It grew steadily with large cities and fair lands, with tilled fields and deep valleys. The people worshipped the supreme deity they called Tat, who represented the four corners of the world; East, West, North, and South.

Atlantis replaced Mu as the center of the world and became the greatest civilization of its time with learning, trade, and commerce. It had over a hundred million people living on its lands. But this world was rife with magic, and its king-priests, called the Tat Tsoks, were wizards of cruelty who ruled over all with an iron hand.

Castrog, the Living ECK Master, came into this world to teach these people that the Supreme Deity was not happy with their ways and dealings in black magic. He suffered the death of the sword for his troubles, but not before warning the king that his lands and people would soon die under the waters of the sea.

One generation later the catastrophe which had sunk the land of Mu brought death to all the fourth root race, leaving only a dark, unsmiling ocean to greet the sailors who dared to cross its surface.

The fifth root race, the Aryans, developed the magnificent empire of Uighur in central Asia in the Gobi Desert. It was a mighty land stretching from the Pacific Ocean across central Asia and eastern Europe. The history of this empire is the history of the Aryan race. Its capital city was in the Gobi Desert, then a fertile land and large in the sense that it was the center of the world in its day, with a highly developed civilization.

The Living ECK Master, Rama, first known to the civilized world of the Aryans, came out of the high valleys of Tibet to the capital city of Khara Khota and began preaching Eckankar. But he was hounded out of the empire and went back into Tibet, where he founded the monastery of Katsupari in the northern mountains.

From there he went into India to teach the great science of Eckankar to its teeming masses.

The sixth root race is the yellow race, coming on the heels of the gradually fading Aryan race. It is the Mongoloid race of the East, which has its life center in the world of the North, where many do not penetrate. The ECK Master who will come into this world of semidarkness and light will be Regnard. This race is yet to fulfill its destiny on the earth planet. It will meet destruction by fire, earthquakes, and tidal waves.

The seventh root race will be the golden race, and they will be called the Zohar people. They will come from a far distant planet to colonize the world after its destruction by another great catastrophe in the twenty-first and twenty-second centuries. The attempt to put colonies on this planet will fail, and eventually, after several centuries, these peoples will withdraw.

The ECK Master who will be responsible for the spiritual welfare of this race will be Sepher.

The SUGMAD will then withdraw all Souls from all planets and constellations into the heavenly worlds where they will sleep until It has repaired the damage to the lower-world planets. Those who have to return will then be sent back again to finish their spiritual development in this world.

4

The Kingdom of the SUGMAD

The great doctrine of liberation taught by the MAHANTA is set forth here for all who have earned the right to know. If he has the ears to hear and the eyes to see, all knowledge and glory will be given unto him.

Every Soul is liberated from the material worlds upon initiation by the MAHANTA, who has been granted this power by the SUGMAD. As the representative of the Supreme Deity in all planes below the Anami Lok, he in turn releases and transfers the consciousness of spiritual freedom to all who desire to have freedom through the ECK.

Release comes at the time of initiation, not at the translation of Soul from the physical body at death in the material plane. Those who become the initiates of the Inner Circle of ECK live out their lives in the physical plane and are transported at the time of death into the higher worlds without standing in the court of Yama, the King of the Dead, where all uninitiated Souls must go to receive judgment for their earthly actions.

The uninitiated are those who have not received liberation through initiation from the MAHANTA. Baptism will not fulfill the necessity of liberation. Neither will the joining of any cult, religion, or faith. Only the Living ECK Master has the power to initiate Souls and take them to the regions of light.

The initiated Soul is transported from the temple of flesh at the time of death by the MAHANTA, to confront the clear light of the Atma Lok. It has left behind the body and will never return to embodiment on this earthly planet. It is now free and will take up Its assignments in the Kingdom of the SUGMAD for eternity.

Faith is the first step on the secret pathway to heaven. Unless the chela believes in the MAHANTA, has faith in the ECK, and trusts the SUGMAD—completely—he has spent his time worthlessly.

The faith that one has in the MAHANTA must be that of complete understanding and surrender. Whatever the MAHANTA sees, knows, and understands about the ECK chela is his own secret. He never tells but expects the chela to give a degree of obedience and observance to his desires, all of which are for the benefit of the chela. He never expects anything less than self-surrender of the chela to the divine will that is working through him as the Inner Master.

Those who cease to believe in the MAHANTA must pay the price. The payment is in accord with their degree of capability. Since the Inner Master is only the vehicle for the SUGMAD, all persons who are following the path of ECK must look to him as the representative of the ECK power on earth.

He is not the Master of anyone who is not following the path of Eckankar. He is the Avatar, the Master, the guide and vehicle of the Divine Being for anyone who is immersed in the spiritual works of ECK.

The MAHANTA takes over the spiritual life of whomever approaches him to become a chela. He guides him through his worldly life and helps him to resolve all his karma here before being translated into the other worlds. Upon entering these worlds permanently, the chela finds the Master still guiding him spiritually. At no time does the MAHANTA ever leave one who has become his charge, regardless of whether or not the chela tries to break his ties. The tie is never broken inwardly—perhaps outwardly, but never on the inner planes.

The ECK Master establishes miraculous power in the chela when they meet for the chela's last incarnation in this earth world. Thus when the chela is ready, when he has reached that stage of spiritual development, a meeting with the Living ECK Master is inevitable.

When any man or woman has earned the right to stand before the MAHANTA, there is no power in the universe that can keep him away from the Sat Guru. The two must meet, for the spiritual law commands it. But in every case it is good karma that brings the individual to the MAHANTA. The proof is in itself, for when the chela is ready the MAHANTA will find him.

The MAHANTA is prepared to take the chela into the heavenly worlds of the SUGMAD. These worlds are the Atma Lok, Alakh Lok, Alaya Lok, Hukikat Lok, Agam Lok, and the Anami Lok. It is above the Anami Lok where dwells the Lord of Lords. This is also the true home of the Atma, that particle of God which has been sent down into the lower worlds to receive purification.

These are the pure worlds of the SUGMAD. It is the universe of the ECK, where there is neither time, space, matter, nor motion. It is where all karma and reincarnation have ended, and the Atma is a part of the whole, but individual in Itself. It is here the Atma receives, by choice, Its mission in the lower worlds to become a Coworker with God.

The bodies of man within the lower worlds assume the

embodiment of sex, either male or female. Thereby, reproduction in the lower worlds, especially in the material universes, is accomplished through sex. But within the heavenly world of the Anami Lok, Souls are reproduced by the Lord of Lords reacting upon Itself. Therefore, every Soul is a particle of the divine source which is known as the Supreme Being. Each is a spark of the Divine Self.

The Atma—Soul—is a neuter atom of the divine source of life. It is neither male nor female, masculine nor feminine, man nor woman. It is both within the worlds of God. It does not assume a body until reaching the worlds below the Atma Plane, the fifth plane.

Thereupon It takes a body of either sex in the beginning, usually that of the male during Its first incarnation. Following this, It will take the body of the female; thereafter, during Its millions of incarnations in the physical worlds, Soul will alternate between male and female bodies, each time learning some lessons while gathering karma and working off karma.

The good karma will be kept, while the negative karma will be given up as the burden of learning the lessons of life. The final goal of good karma is to bring the chela to the Living ECK Master and to learn the true path to the SUGMAD. This is the very highest reward of good karma, assuring the chela of his liberation from the Wheel of the Eighty-Four.

The true works of Eckankar take the chela into the heavenly world to become a Coworker with God. There is nothing higher than this. When the chela asks what his mission is in life, he should be told that becoming a Coworker with God is the only purpose of Soul's existence.

He begins his true spiritual life in the Atma Plane which is known to all as the Soul world. The classical name for this plane is the Sat Nam, who also is the ruler of this world. This is the first realm of the SUGMAD, the pure Being, where Soul finds Self-Realization. It is the dividing plane between the worlds of pure Spirit and those of the material worlds. The Sound here is the single note of a flute. The chant one gives is the name of the Divine Being, the SUGMAD!

The next plane is the Alakh Lok, known as the Invisible Plane. Its classical name is the same, and the chanting here is *Shanti.* In the Hindu language it means *peace.* This is the second world of the SUGMAD. It is ruled by the great being the Alakh Purusha, who at times seems harsh and without consideration, although the chanting in this world does not seem to fit the nature of its ruler. The sound of the ECK here is the wind, sometimes roaring and sometimes very gently sighing, like a breeze in the treetops.

The Alaya Lok is the third pure spiritual plane above the Atma region. It is the true shining world, sometimes called the Sach Khand. The chanting here is a sort of hum, like that done with the lips closed tightly and humming a worldly tune. The description here is of endless worlds, for it is so vast, so far beyond any conception of man's intelligence. The ruler of this plane is the Alaya Purusha, a mighty being whose very presence fills every Soul with awe as he passes through this world.

The Hukikat Lok is the fourth world which Soul must travel through on Its way to the SUGMAD, the center of all universes. This is the highest state Soul usually reaches. It is the plane of God-Realization where Soul learns the God-knowledge. The Sound is like the music of a thousand violins. The chanting is the word *Aluk.* The great being here is the Hukikat Purusha, the Lord of the fourth world of pure Spirit.

The Agam Lok is the fifth world, the Inaccessible Plane.

Few Souls go past the Hukikat Lok into this world. It is a world of immense space, so much greater than any which the mind could ever conceive. The Sound here is delicate music, something that cannot be described. It is like the music of woodwinds—faint, sweet, and beautiful. A melody that gives Soul great ecstasy. The word here is *Huk,* and it is pronounced *HOOK.* The lord of this world is the Agam Purusha, and he is the guardian of the Anami Lok, the nameless plane.

The Anami Lok is the world of the Supreme Being, the SUGMAD. This is the Lord of Lords, the highest of all Beings, and Its home is the Ocean of Love and Mercy. It does not live in a palace nor dwell on a throne, as many believe. Its home is the mighty center of the universes, the very heart and core of all life and existence. It dwells in the center of this mammoth ocean where all is like a whirlpool, sending out Its Word to the worlds upon worlds.

The Word, the Voice of the SUGMAD, goes forth like a wave from the center of a pond and sings Its way through all the planes in many different songs and melodies. Each is the living Word, creating and giving life to everything in each world. By Its very life—this ECK, the essence of the SUGMAD, the Spirit of all things—life exists.

When It reaches the end of the worlds It returns like the wave, gathering up all Souls ready to do God's work. They are returned to the true home and become Coworkers with God, having completed their mission in life.

The true gospel of ECK is to give every chela Truth. This Truth is to lift him into the worlds of Light and Sound: the Kingdom of the SUGMAD. Thereby the spiritual law of God acts upon the fact that it is possible for every Soul to unfold spiritually, in a greater or lesser degree, in one direction or another. He may seek to order his life and his relations with the SUGMAD on the basis of the knowledge that he must become a Coworker with the Divine Being.

The chela must practice *pratyahara,* the complete withdrawal of consciousness from the environment around himself. This is true on every plane of the universe below the Atma world. The chela cannot fail to do otherwise, or he will delay his ascendance into the heavenly Kingdom of God. He shall delay his true mission, which is to serve out his spiritual responsibilities in a world of heavenly good.

Heaven is the ultimate state. It is where Soul goes to meet Its Maker and decide upon Its final mission in eternity. Soul alone must make the choice of what It shall do for Its missionary assignment. This is the freedom of choice which the SUGMAD gives to all Souls. No other form of life has this privilege.

Soul sometimes enters this universe as a thing of lower embodiment. Generally, It enters into the minerals of the earth, where It will dwell for an age. In succession It becomes the flower, the fish, a denizen of the seas and waters of the lands, a serpent, a creature of the air, the treetop things, a four-legged animal, and after many such incarnations It enters into the body of man.

Man lives only with himself. He is the ablest of all the creatures of God, for the use of the divine power of ECK is at his fingertips. He learns to use this and to liberate himself from the Kal power which rules the lower universes. But it is only with the spiritual assistance of the MAHANTA that he is able to do this. The mind, of itself, is of little use to him except to live within the physical plane.

The mind is only an instrument for the Atma to use within this world of matter. It uses the mind and the physical and mental faculties like one uses a machine. Man is only an animal without the Atma. He is the physical body known to all in the spiritual works of ECK as the *Isthul Sharir.* Unless the chela denies the existence of matter, this cannot be disputed. It gets hurt, sick, and dies, to return to the soil from which it originally came.

Within the Physical body is that starry and subtle body, the *Sukhsham Sharir* or Nuri Sarup, the light body of the Astral world. It sparkles with millions of particles like stars shining in the worldly heavens. It is through this body that the mind and Soul can communicate with the Physical body and its world. But it will take shape according to the character of the individual. Therefore, the chela knows what his Astral body is according to his natal ECK-Vidya-scope. When the Physical body dies this Nuri Sarup stays as the instrument of expression on the Astral Plane.

Within the Astral body is another body, more subtle and much lighter, which is called the *Karan Sharir.* This is the Causal body, which is quite distinct from the Astral. It is named this because it is the real cause, containing the seeds of all that is ever to take place in the individual's life. This is the body that the Living ECK Master reads for the past, present, and future of the individual.

The other body enclosed within the Causal body is the Manas, or Mental Sharir. It is much more refined than the other two bodies. It would appear to the eye as a blue globe of light and has a humming sound when in the presence of another. Its function is to act as a transformer for thought between the mind and the Astral body. It is creative to an extent, but only because it receives impressions from the *Buddhi Sharir,* which is known as the Etheric, or subconscious, mind.

The Buddhi Sharir lies between the Mental body and Soul. It is regarded as the part of the mind body which acts as a sheath between mind and Soul: It is very sensitive to impressions from Soul, and its function is to receive and transmit impressions between mind and Soul on the one side, and between Soul and mind on the other. A perfect record of every experience the individual has ever had in any incarnation within the countless ages of Its existence throughout any plane is stored here. These can be read by the Living ECK Master by use of the ECK-Vidya.

The Atma Sarup is the Soul body. It is the Atma Sharir which dwells on the Fifth Plane, the dividing line between the material worlds and the true spiritual regions. It is a broad, universal world that takes in the whole of all things, including the lower and the higher universes. It is an extremely sensitive body and is, in Its natural state, a perfect vessel of the Divine Being. Only by Its compulsive lives in the bodies of the lower worlds does It appear to become imperfect. It becomes covered with a sheath, making It seem imperfect, but this is only the illusion of the Kal forces.

Spiritual liberation comes when one finds himself established in the Atma Sarup. The recognition of enlightenment within the state of Soul consciousness brings Light and Sound at this particular plane, which is a blazing illumination similar to the light of ten thousand suns. The roaring is more thunderous than ten thousand waterfalls.

It is here Soul enters into Self-Realization. It finds Itself in the state of self-awareness. The universal mission of being a Coworker with the SUGMAD is rapidly realized in Soul's state of self-knowledge. It knows and now is ready to advance into the heavenly worlds of true Spirit. It has no other purpose in life, and all attachments to the life in the lower worlds are lost. The values of materialistic things leave the senses of the mind and body, for now Soul is in control of all life around Itself.

All Souls must, in the beginning of their creation, descend into the bowels of Turiya Pad. This is where the SUGMAD declared they must dwell until each becomes once more fitted to serve It and not the pleasures of desire.

The highest form of belief is faith-belief in the SUGMAD. The higher always encompasses the perfection of the lower. To act as if we are. This is the secret of believing, of having faith in the SUGMAD. "Believing is not believing," so says the Lord of Lords to all Souls who descend into the ash can of the universes.

"I say unto you, believe in my Word. For the day shall come when you shall doubt all things. The earth shall be rocked in its last convulsion, and when ye have spent life after life seeking and finding nothing, then ye shall offer up everything to me, begging for the life which is already yours for the faith in me!"

And the Lord of Lords spoke again: "To him who will love me and will observe my commandments will I manifest myself, and he shall be one with me and I with him."

Those who love the SUGMAD shall be taken unto Its heart and given the kingdom of heaven. But those who do not love the SUGMAD and wish to go their way shall not have the kingdom of heaven nor any of its parts.

This must be written on the heart of every Soul, for all things and all life are concerned with the Lord of Lords. If the Tuza, or Soul, chooses to forget and gives Its devotion to Kal Niranjan, that Tuza shall become a slave and have only the transitory objects of the lower kingdom, ruled over by the Kal alone.

Soul journeys through the worlds of the Kal. Whenever It finds it is time to leave the physical vehicle in which It has abided for Its time in this lower world, then a preparation is made to enter into the Astral body, the first of the inner bodies.

This Astral body becomes truly awakened with the advent of Soul, for the physical and all states of consciousness are left in the outer body. It dwells in this first inner vehicle for a relative period of time, then either proceeds into the Causal body, or returns to another physical embodiment. This is known as reincarnation.

Soul must leave the physical body at the death of this temple of clay and journey into the next world. This passing is called the *Kangra Sambha.* It is known as the supraspiritual experience of Soul. Thus, it leads to a knowledge of the greater worlds beyond the physical senses. This journey, the Kangra Sambha, takes place between the Physical worlds and the Astral. This is the Bardo of Tibetan Buddhism, the purgatory of the Christians. It is the duty of the MAHANTA to assist the Atma when It passes from the physical body and enters into the Kangra Sambha period of Its journey.

After this death of a physical vehicle, the Atma is taken by the Living ECK Master to whatever subtle region of the inner worlds It has earned. No Soul that is an initiate of ECK will have to account for Its deeds and actions within the lower realm of the Kal world. It is through with all earthly karma and must now begin to work out the karma of Its actions on the Astral Plane.

The Physical world is a world of turmoil and strife. Never shall there be any peace in it. This is the way of the SUGMAD. It is so designed that the Pinda worlds shall have nothing but strife, for the good of each Soul that must dwell therein. For these worlds are the testing ground of Soul; the place It must spend Its long periods of existence, creating perfection and spiritual maturity.

Should the Soul not be an initiate of the Living ECK Master, It must stand before Dharam Raya, the Judge of the Kangra Sambha, and receive Its just award. There are no complaints nor favors, and justice is rendered to all.

Each Soul knows It is being judged and must consent to the judgment. It is then taken to the region or condition where It has earned Its residence, be it good or bad. It remains there for a fixed time according to the judgment rendered. After Its time has expired, It is then returned to this world, or some other world, to once more begin a new life in the physical body. It takes up where It left off, somewhere in one of Its past lives, and starts once again, depending upon Its karma.

The Kingdom of the SUGMAD is imperishable. Thus, when Soul enters into this region of Light, It either remains or is given a mission somewhere in the lower kingdom. But It knows immortality and the joy of serving with the SUGMAD to keep the vast universes running smoothly.

Soul derives benefit from all the SUGMAD gives It through the grace of the Lord of Lords. It is so far removed from Its true home that without the spiritual benefits of the perfect Sat Guru, the MAHANTA, It cannot find Its way back.

All chelas on the path of ECK, though belonging to different historical periods and various times of study under a Living ECK Master during their past lives, have now come to the level in this life to be completely released from all karma, or else to make progress toward resolving that karma so each may be liberated within the near future.

Many, started by the force of their spiritual exercises, have already reached certain levels in their unfoldment. But all of them have not yet reached the final stage. This is why they are still struggling to find the way. Some of them have stopped at the First Plane level and others at the Second. Only the ECK Masters have reached the fifth stage of spiritual development, where they enter into the Atma Plane at will. They have gone far beyond this stage and entered into the Anami level with the true Godhead.

This is the place of the original departure of Soul toward the lower regions. During Its downward journey, Soul goes through such intermediate states as the Agam Lok, Hukikat Lok, Alaya Lok, Alakh Lok, Sat Lok, and the Saguna Lok (the subconscious, or Etheric Plane); Brahm Lok (the Mental Plane); Brahmanda Lok (the Causal Plane); Sat Kanwal-Anda Lok (the Astral Plane); and the Pinda (the Physical Plane).

Once in the Physical worlds the curtain of memory is drawn down over the mind. Here Soul struggles for centuries, through life after life, wondering if the journey through time is worthy of Its efforts. A few will rise into the Astral world and feel this is the true Kingdom of the SUGMAD. They feel Soul originated here and has returned home again. This is the illusion of the Kal, whose responsibility is the play of the universe, the sport of the gods; to amuse itself at the expense of Soul struggling toward the true Godhead.

The follower of Eckankar is never alone, for the MAHANTA, the Living ECK Master is always with him in the Atma Sarup, or Atma body. The chela may never realize it but, nevertheless, it is true. Once Soul has joined with the ECK Master upon the true path of God, there is never a separation. The chela may wander about for many lives trying to find himself, trying to return to the path, but the Living ECK Master has never left him. He never recognizes this because of the veil of materiality that has covered his eyes.

Each ECKist should practice the Kundun. The Kundun means the presence of the Living ECK Master. Whether or not he can see the form of the Master, he must try to hold a conversation through mental whisperings. He should listen for the answers which come via the intuitive or the mental arena. He should never be in doubt that the

Master has spoken to him from the inner world.

If the chela practices looking into the Tisra Til—the Spiritual Eye—where the Inner Master, the MAHANTA, dwells in every Soul, he will find him there.

The chela first meets the MAHANTA in the first region of the Astral worlds. This is the next station above the Tisra Til. It is known as the Ashta-dal-Kanwal, the lotus center of eight petals, located just below the true center of all the Astral worlds, the Sahasra-dal-Kanwal. This is the great city capital of the first plane beyond the Physical world.

Between the Ashta-dal-Kanwal and the Sahasra-dal-Kanwal lie the Sun Worlds and the Moon Worlds, sometimes called the Lightning Worlds. Here is where the chela who practices the Spiritual Exercises of ECK meets with the MAHANTA to travel into the far worlds for Self-Realization; to eventually enter into God-Realization, where he will have the whole of divine wisdom.

The MAHANTA is able to be seen by all his chelas simultaneously, for he is of the ECK Itself. Being the Spirit of all things he is, therefore, capable of giving the secret teachings to all initiates of Eckankar, or to protect and give them all the necessities of life. He knows what goes on in the minds of every chela and all people. If he so chooses he knows the thoughts of animals and of every embodiment of life.

He is the true Master. If the chela practices the Spiritual Exercises of ECK, then at a point between the Sun Worlds and the Moon Worlds he will enter the zone known as the Ashta-dal-Kanwal. It is here the great change is made which alters his life and his method of procedure. This change is the meeting with the MAHANTA, who appears just as he does in the physical body, except his radiant body is more beautiful and brilliantly illuminated. The MAHANTA appears and greets the chela with great joy. From that moment on the two are never separated throughout their lives, whether it is in the physical world or on the spiritual planes. The form of the MAHANTA is always with the chela from the moment he enters into the path of ECK, although the chela does not see him as a general rule.

The ECKist must always practice the Kundun, the presence, whether or not he can see this inner body of the Master. It can, however, be noted many times by the outer manifestations of things such as the protection gained, the great feeling of love which surrounds the chela, the improvement of his welfare, and the attainment of spiritual knowledge. All is given freely to the ECKist after he has passed into the higher worlds via Soul Travel.

It has been mentioned that above the Atma Lok (the fifth world) are the high worlds. This is the region of the ECK Masters, and there are numerous planes still further above which have not yet been revealed by these Adepts. Out of love for all the struggling masses of humanity, they are now able to bring forth the description of the worlds above and below the Atma Lok.

There are two worlds of the mind, the Brahmandi and the Pindi. But the chela is not concerned with these, for they are within the lower worlds and must be used to carry on the business of the world with the help of Soul. Soul becomes so attached to the mind that It is caught in a downward pull toward the lower physical regions. The mind and sense organs receive their power of action from Soul. Once Soul, the Atma, turns toward Its true home in the heavenly worlds of the SUGMAD, all Its attachment to the physical worlds begins to decrease.

When Soul reaches Its home in the Atma Plane beyond the regions of the Brahm, the mind, It is freed from all bonds whether they have been causal, astral, physical, sensual, or mental. Attachment to the world is then only in name and can be terminated at Its own volition.

The rope of the conscious tie with the spiritual self can only be cut when the Atma reaches this abode. This is accomplished by Soul freeing Itself from the chains of the mind and senses. The unconscious part of one's life, which is controlled by the Etheric, or subconscious, mind, consists of the mind, senses, vital organs, and the worldly patterns of karma which have been established from past lives and must be cut by the Living ECK Master.

The highest of all the spiritual regions, the Kingdom of the SUGMAD, cannot be described in mortal language. It is the Anami, the nameless region. Sometimes it is called the "untold region." This is the beginning and the ending of all worlds. It is the love and power of this world that vibrates throughout the worlds by the force of the SUGMAD, the first principle.

Five worlds below the Anami, the Kingdom of the SUGMAD, is found the Atma Lok, which is highly effulgent and pure. It is the world of pure Spirit and consciousness. It is the beginning and ending of all creation of the lower worlds. The currents emanate from this plane and spread into all regions below. Sat Nam, the great ruler of this plane, is the true manifestation of the SUGMAD and is the creator of all the worlds below. The ECK flows down from this world, manifesting embodiments and the entities who inhabit all the worlds below.

This is the home of the ECK Masters. They are the embodiments or incarnations of the Lord of this region. Love, mercy, and bliss reign here eternally. All those aspects known as death, karma, sin, evil, and pain are not found in this region. This is the first stage of the journey to God in the true spiritual worlds. Until Soul has reached this plane It is still in the clutches of the Kal Niranjan in the planes of the Universal Mind Power.

The SUGMAD incarnates Itself as the MAHANTA, the Living ECK Master to give the truth of the path of salvation in simple language. During the present Kali Yuga, the dark age, all humanity has become tormented by the thousand ills of poverty, disease, plagues, and wars instigated by jealousy, which remove man from the path of Truth.

The agents of the Kal, who call themselves men of God, have concealed and done away with all truly religious scriptures. They have replaced them with the pseudoscriptures, and claim they are the books of God.

The ECK Masters have for centuries explained to the people the mystery of the ECK, the Word, in their own written and spoken language. They have given the words of the golden scripts—the Shariyat-Ki-Sugmad—and initiated disciples into the true teachings of Eckankar. Therefore the teachings of the SUGMAD are upon every plane of the universes of universes. Each plane has a portion of this holy manuscript, in accord with the understanding of the chelas who reach this plane.

Those who watch over and guard the golden scripts of the SUGMAD are the nine unknown Gods of Eternity. They are different from the ECK Masters who act as the teachers, instructors and watch-guards for the portions of the Shariyat-Ki-Sugmad kept upon each plane. The nine unknown Gods are the keepers of the Divine Flame of Wisdom. They let only a few into their temples to learn the deeper knowledge of what the secret truths might hold for them.

Man loves miracles. But a religion based only on miracles or a show of the supernatural powers cannot endure permanently. As long as a doctrine or principle is not fully comprehended by the reasoning faculty in its spiritual aspects, it is not likely to stay with the mind for any length of time.

Many profess faith in ECK outwardly but have not given up their longing for materiality in their hearts. This lack of faith is due to their ignorance of the spiritual works of ECK. Often they do not take the pains to read or study properly, nor do they listen to the MAHANTA. They criticize and harp upon their pains and troubles, often blaming the Living ECK Master, and in their ignorance they do not understand that this is a dangerous practice. Everything they say against the MAHANTA and the ECK will return and take from them. Their losses are due to their own thoughts and actions.

The chela who has the society of the MAHANTA, the perfect Vi-Guru, will partake of the Grace of God and love. He has started upon the true path to the Kingdom of the SUGMAD. There is a difficulty here, too, for often the Vi-Guru is apt to be regarded as an ordinary man serving his own interests, and the chela may refuse to submit himself wholly to the discipline which the MAHANTA asks of him.

The MAHANTA does not desire that worldly people in large numbers flock after him. He prefers only those who are eager for the realization of God to them. He does not perform miracles for people to see, but moves in the mysterious ways of the Lord. The true disciple does not believe in the miracles which the MAHANTA may perform at varied times but instead believes in the teachings he imparts to give each a lift into the heavenly worlds.

Slander and criticism should strengthen the faith of the chelas for the MAHANTA, the Living ECK Master. Only a true devotee can resist the evil effects of malicious opposition. To put up with insult and slander is a mark of true love. None but the true lovers and devotees are able to rise above the fear of censure and the world's disapproval.

The Lord saith, "Slander or mockery of the followers of ECK is a guard for the market of love and a cleaner of its dirt.

"Only those who love the ECK, and listen only to the music of the heavenly worlds, will enter into the true Kingdom. They will repel the scorn and slander of the world like water falling from the rubber-tree leaf when the rain falls from the sky.

"He who believes in me shall be saved. He who scorns my loved ones shall suffer in the fires of the tormented and shall not enter into the heavenly kingdom until he repents of his words and deeds."

5
The Spiritual Hierarchy

Those who follow Eckankar are never alone. The presence of the Living ECK Master is always with the ECKist, regardless of wherever he is in the invisible worlds or whatever he is doing in his life.

Fortunate is he who believes in the Living ECK Master, the MAHANTA. If he has faith in the MAHANTA, in the lords of the other worlds, and the ECK Masters, then he will have good fortune in wealth and health. He will be known to his neighbors as the most fortunate of all men.

If he believes in the Kal Niranjan, the king of the Kal (negative) worlds, he will be unfortunate, for he will be a slave, a man who suffers and has great hardships. He will have neither money nor health. His faith in the king of the Kal worlds will only bring him misfortune and unhappiness in any world where he may dwell. The face of the Living ECK Master is turned away from him, and the spiritual lords of all the worlds know him not.

Only the God-governed shall inherit the worlds. The false belief that there is something besides the SUGMAD and the perfect spiritual creation is thriving in the lower worlds and is responsible for the discord in the human race. This false belief that there is life, substance, and intelligence without the SUGMAD is an illusion which the Kal Niranjan wishes for each Soul in the human embodiment to possess.

This false belief is the counterfeit of spiritual reality. It is the illusion of the material senses that sees only the material universe inhabited by physical beings, each with a limited mind of his own embedded in matter.

This erroneous concept gives rise to the idea of faith in something other than the ECK. Belief in anything except the ECK is false and does not alter reality any more than a passing cloud would permanently hide the sunlight. Most chelas, including those who follow the ECK, are too hidden in the matter world, the illusions of the Kal.

All in the lower regions, except the ECK, is controlled by the Kal. When in humility one is able to look away from his wrangling, self-assertive human consciousness—his own and others'—recognizing his true spiritual identity, then he recognizes himself.

The foundation of all is uncreated, uncompounded, independent, and beyond the conception of the human senses and verbal definition. Nothing can describe what this is. Neither the term *God*, nor the term *Anami Lok*, can be applied to It. To realize It is to attain the MAHANTA state. Not to realize It is to wander in the Kal worlds.

Not knowing the source of all, beings err. They are overwhelmed by the darkness of the unconscious Kal power from which springs ignorance and error. So immersed in error and so obscured by ignorance, the seeker becomes fearful and bewildered. From this state springs the concept of the individual "I," the ego, and the "others."

It is only when these have gained strength and matured in all beings that there is an unbroken current in the evolution of the lower embodiments in the worlds of the Kal. It is here that the five passions of the mind reign. Lust, anger, greed, attachment, and vanity flourish, and they produce an interminable chain of the Kal karma.

Thus, the root source of error among lower beings is unconscious ignorance. It is only through the power of the SUGMAD that each of them is able to realize the radiant innate Self in all living things.

There is a remedy for this ignorance, for the Lord says, "He who asks in my name shall receive all blessings, provided he is worthy.

"But if he is one who gives my message to the world and acts at all times in my name, he shall be among those who are indeed worthy and greatly blessed."

This is the promise of the SUGMAD. If the chela gives in the name of the Living ECK Master, all is blessed and he shall receive. If he gives all in the name of the SUGMAD, the chela is also blessed. Little does the nature of the deed change, and he is blessed, for he is indeed worthy.

All blessings are given in the name of whomever the chela calls upon. Such blessings are often passed directly from the MAHANTA, the Living ECK Master to the chela. Often the blessings may be passed down by the spiritual hierarchy, and the nature of the hierarchy is complex, yet simple.

In the beginning, the SUGMAD rested quietly in Its abode in the Ocean of Love and Mercy. Outside Itself there were no other planes, universes, nor worlds. Not a Soul, being, nor creature existed. Only the SUGMAD lay dreaming in Its eternal realm. And while It dreamed, there began the formation of the worlds inside Itself.

First, It formed the Anami Lok, where dwell only the endless realms of a nameless Void. Because the SUGMAD was not pleased with this creation, It dreamed again.

Second, It formed the Agam Lok, where dwell only the inaccessible realms of a world where there existed no life nor creatures. Because the SUGMAD was not pleased with this creation, It dreamed again.

Third, It formed the Hukikat Lok, where dwells the first accessible realm for beings, Souls, and entities. But because the SUGMAD was not pleased with this creation, It dreamed again.

Fourth, It formed the Alaya Lok, where dwell the endless worlds of no-thing. These came to be called the Sach Khand planes. Because the SUGMAD was not pleased with this creation, It dreamed again.

Fifth, It formed the Alakh Lok, where dwell the invisible worlds where no creature, no being, and no thing is ever seen. Therefore, it was called the Invisible Plane. Because the SUGMAD was not pleased with this creation, It dreamed again.

Sixth, It formed the Atma Plane, where now dwells the Soul of everything in repose. It is here the SUGMAD became wise in Its judgment about the worlds to come.

The SUGMAD slept in Its abode in the Ocean of Love and Mercy, but It was not pleased with what It had created. So It dreamed more to understand what It had formed in these planes.

Again It awoke and looked out over the vast firmaments, wondering what belonged in them. It dreamed again and sent Its Voice rolling through these vast worlds upon worlds. Its Voice became the heavenly music and spoke the Word which rolled through all the magnificent planes. The Word of the SUGMAD became the ECK, the Spirit of all existence. Out of this came the lords, rulers, Souls, and all beings which the SUGMAD had dreamed.

And out of this also came Its son, the MAHANTA, the consciousness of all heavenly bliss. There were then the SUGMAD, the ECK, and the MAHANTA, all of which were the one great Reality.

The Lord spoke unto the MAHANTA and said, "I have created the worlds of bliss and happiness. Yet there is spiritual immaturity in all my creatures. Therefore, I must create the lower order of worlds, the planes of matter, space, energy, and time. The worlds where there is shadow, light, and embodiments."

The SUGMAD stretched Its hands over all the firmaments and created the worlds of the Triloki, which consists of the regions between the negative pole of creation and the Atma Lok.

Within these regions It placed the elements of matter, energy, space, and time. Here the SUGMAD created the law that nothing could exist except in relation to its opposite, called the Law of Polarity. Without time there could be no space, without mountains there could be no valleys. Without shadows there could be no light, and without evil there could be no good. Nor could there be ignorance without wisdom, or age without youth.

But the SUGMAD was not yet pleased with what It had created, so closing Its eyes It dreamed again. This time It formed the spiritual hierarchy of all the universes.

The hierarchy began with the SUGMAD, followed by the ECK, and the MAHANTA. After this came the Living ECK Master, the Adepts of the Order of the Vairagi, the lords of each plane within the higher worlds, the guardians of the Shariyat-Ki-Sugmad; and then the lower worlds were formed for those entities named the Atma, or Soul.

Over these worlds, which are three in number, It placed the Kal Niranjan, lord of all the negative worlds. With this, It formed the Kal force, which originated and flows out of the Niranjan as its source. Subordinate to the ECK, the Kal, however, takes precedence over all life in the lower worlds. But it is still subject to the will of the SUGMAD.

The SUGMAD was not pleased with what had been done

in Its lower worlds, so It slept again and dreamed. Out of this dream came the lords of the lower worlds. Next the Lords of Karma were formed, the devas (angels), the planetary spirits, bhuts, elementals, man, and all the creatures subordinate to him—the fish, the animals, reptiles, plants, and stones.

All these were formed on the many planes of the lower worlds; the stars, planets, and the material worlds of matter, energy, space, and time. Then the SUGMAD slept again and dreamed that all Its manifestations needed life, so the ECK was sent into all the universes and worlds to create activity.

With this the SUGMAD gave all the worlds Its highest creation, the Atma. The Atma, or Soul, had to be perfected, so It was sent into the worlds below, only to return to Its true home when perfect.

Upon each plane the SUGMAD placed a governor, or ruler, who was to act as Its channel for the powerful energies flowing out from the Ocean of Love and Mercy.

In the beginning, when the Supreme Deity wished to bring the universe into being, Its first step was to create the first focus of action. This can be said to be the first step downward to the nether world.

The first focus of action was the ruler of the Anami plane, named the Anami Purusha. This is the lord of the first world, a being so mighty its very presence is beyond the imagination of man. It was brought into existence as the first individual manifestation of the Supreme One. All subsequent creations of life embodiments were now to be carried on through this first individual manifestation.

The supreme creative ECK energy, working through the Anami Purusha, brought into existence the mighty being of the Agam Lok plane, the Agam Purusha. Through him came the Hukikat Lok and its lord, the Hukikat

Purusha. Again through this great being, the SUGMAD formed the Alaya Purusha, who became the lord of the Alaya Lok. The Alakh Purusha was the next individual manifestation of the SUGMAD, and working through him, the sixth lord, the Sat Purusha or Sat Nam of the Atma Lok, was individualized.

The Sat Nam was appointed to carry on all creative activity below that division of worlds, in the lower planes, consisting of the Etheric (Saguna Brahm), Mental (Par Brahm), Causal (Brahmanda), Astral (Anda, or Turiya Pad), and the Physical (Pinda).

The region of the Atma Lok is the Sach Khand. Sat Nam, the lord of this world, carries on all creative activity below. It created each region. At the same time each region was created, the lords of each were created and assumed charge of their respective planes.

Over all these lower worlds the Kal Niranjan was given the responsibility of exercising the power of the negative force. This Kal force was formed to have the strength to give life and body forms for each Atma which came to live in these negative worlds.

First Sat Nam formed the Saguna Lok, the upper division of the mind world. Over this It placed the ruler Saguna Brahm. He has jurisdiction over all entities and beings living on this plane.

Second It formed the Maha Kal Lok, the mind world. Over this It placed the Par Brahm, whose duties were to make all seekers of God believe this was the top of the worlds, the final resting-place. It performs this duty well, for many believe, upon reaching the Maha Kal Lok, that they at last have come to the true home, the abode of the Almighty.

Third, It formed the Brahmanda Lok, the world of the Causal Plane. Here It placed all the karma and recalls of Souls which reincarnated from life to life on the physical plane. Over this world It placed the Brahm, whose mighty features make one wonder if this is God. Brahm is the deity that the lower-world religions all think is the SUGMAD, the Lord of Lords. Their mistake is in the illusion established by the Kal Niranjan.

Fourth, It established the Turiya Pad Lok, the Astral world. Over this region It placed the Niranjan as king of all entities and beings. This is the world where Soul gets Its training in perfection so It may return to the heavenly states again. The Niranjan here is not the true Kal Niranjan but only an offspring.

The Order of the Vairagi, which is the secret legion of ECK Adepts, was now able to establish its work on the many different planes of the universes of universes.

At the head of the Order is the MAHANTA, the living embodiment of God. As the MAHANTA, the Living ECK Master serves in the world of matter, energy, space, and time, called the physical universe. He is responsible only to the SUGMAD.

All the Adepts of the Order of the Vairagi are under him, until he relinquishes the Rod of ECK Power and passes on to another plane of existence. He is the manifestation of all the spiritual essence of God, that which selects a physical embodiment and uses that body while serving in this world of matter. The worlds over which he rules are every plane from the Ocean of Love and Mercy to the lowest of the physical universe. He functions equally upon every plane in the Atma Sarup and uses the physical body as the instrument to serve in the physical worlds.

He places these magnificent Adepts in charge of the Shariyat-Ki-Sugmad, the Holy Book of the ECK Order. They are the guardians of these works, and upon each plane an Adept of the Order of the Vairagi is in charge of a section of this Book of Golden Wisdom. A section of the book is within the Temple of Golden Wisdom on each plane as designated by the SUGMAD.

The planes and guardians are as follows:

1. The Ocean of Love and Mercy—the SUGMAD.

2. The Anami Lok—the Padma Samba is the guardian of this section of the Shariyat-Ki-Sugmad. It is kept in the Temple of Golden Wisdom known as the Sata Visic Palace.

3. The Agam Lok—the Adept here is the Mahaya Guru, guardian of the Holy Book at the Kazi Dawtz Temple of Golden Wisdom.

4. The Hukikat Lok—the Adept here is the Asanga Kaya, the guardian of the Holy Book at the Jartz Chong Temple of Golden Wisdom.

5. The Alaya Lok—the Adept here is the great Tsong Sikhsa, guardian of the Holy Book at the Anakamudi Temple of Golden Wisdom.

6. The Alakh Lok—the Adept here is the Sokagampo, guardian of the Holy Book at the Tamanata Kop Temple of Golden Wisdom.

7. The Atma Lok—the Adept here is the Jagat Giri, guardian of the Holy Book at the Param Akshar Temple of Golden Wisdom. This is the House of Imperishable Knowledge. It is the highest Soul can go, as long as It is attached to a physical body, to study at any of the Temples of Golden Wisdom.

8. In the worlds below the Atma Plane (where the Shariyat-Ki-Sugmad is kept for those who are able to study its golden pages) is the Saguna Lok (Etheric world). The Adept here is Lai Tsi, guardian of the Holy Book at the Dayaka Temple of Golden Wisdom in the city of Arhirit.

9. The Par Brahm Lok (Mental world—the Adept here is the Koji Chanda, guardian of the Holy Book at the Namayatan Temple of Golden Wisdom in the city of Mer Kailash.

10. The Brahmanda Lok (Causal world)—the Adept here is Shamus-i-Tabriz, guardian of the Holy Book at the Sakapori Temple of Golden Wisdom in the city of Honu.

11. The Anda Lok (Astral world)—the Adept here is Gopal Das, guardian of the Holy Book of the Askleposis Temple of Golden Wisdom in the city of Sahasra-dal-Kanwal.

12. The Pinda Lok (Physical world)—the Adept here is Rami Nuri, guardian of the Holy Book at the Moksha Temple of Golden Wisdom in the city of Retz, Venus.

13. The Prithvi Lok (Earth world)—the Adept here is Yaubl Sacabi, guardian of the Holy Book at the Gare-Hira Temple of Golden Wisdom at Agam Des, the home of the Eshwar-Khanewale (the God-Eaters) in the Hindu Kush Mountains.

14. The Surati Lok (Mountain world)—the Adept here is Fubbi Quantz, guardian of the Holy Book at the Katsupari Monastery Temple of Golden Wisdom in northern Tibet.

15. The Asurati Lok (Desert world)—the Adept here is Banjani, guardian of the Holy Book at the Faqiti Monastery Temple of Golden Wisdom in the Gobi Desert. The section here is only an introduction to the Shariyat-Ki-Sugmad. Chelas are usually taken here to begin their study of the holy works in the dream state.

The MAHANTA is the Godman, the Ancient One who reincarnates again and again in the world of matter. He comes in every age, every lifetime, to gather up those who have failed to accept him in the past. All who have surrendered to him in any particular life and accept him as the Living ECK Master work out all karma before their translation from the body.

The MAHANTA is the father of all who have studied with him in the past. During each incarnation he takes on another body and personality. Those who have followed him in the past and have reincarnated again will always find the MAHANTA. They will come to learn that all who follow the path of ECK are the chosen people of God.

The MAHANTA is the Avatar of his time. He is concerned only with the spiritual development of all Souls. He takes care of karma and helps to resolve it for those who come under his guidance on the path of ECK. He also takes care of the karmic pattern of the human race, all life within this universe upon whatever planet it may be, and also the life that exists on the other planes within the God Worlds. He does all this individually and collectively. He uplifts all Souls, no matter what plane they may be upon.

He is in all places at the same time because he is Spirit, the ECK. By this very reason he is able to be with all who follow the path of the holy science of ECK. He has nothing to do with psychic phenomena, nor will he perform miracles merely because someone requests he do so. He appears to those in danger to warn them and will take care of all the chelas of ECK.

There is only one to whom the MAHANTA bows in humble submission. This is the Supreme Lord, the SUGMAD. Its sovereign will is the only law the MAHANTA recognizes, and the universal law of all laws—love. While living on earth in the human form, though, he will break no law of man, but supports all good governments. His life and works are universal. He does not belong to any race or time, but to all nations and all times. Correctly, he is a citizen of the macrocosmic worlds, a being which has entered this world to bring the Light to all peoples.

The MAHANTA is generally a family man—he is never an ascetic, nor does he ever encourage austerities. He will advocate keeping the body healthy, as it is his duty to serve the world.

The MAHANTA, the Living ECK Master lives in the world,

although he is not of it. He has come to help all those who desire it, and enters the stream of humanity to give this help. Yet he himself stands aloof from the waves of human passions. He has attained all virtues. He believes in the highest degree of strength; spiritual strength which cannot be separated from the moral qualities of mankind. This strength is the strength of love. He is stronger than any man in intellect or spirit, for he has unlimited power, and yet this strength is combined with the noble virtues of the humble and gentle. All people find in him inspiration for the development of noble character.

In the realm of religion the MAHANTA is a paradox. He has no theology. He teaches none, yet he is the greatest religious leader on earth. The system of ECK, which he teaches, is not an orthodox religion, although it leads to the most complete and enlightening religious experience. He is universal in all the teachings of ECK. Not having a creedlike religion, he never deliberately antagonizes any creed, sect, or religious institution.

He never finds fault with anyone or anything, but draws the line sharply between God and Kal. To correct errors in the chelas, the MAHANTA often points out the opposite virtues, frequently in examples.

The MAHANTA is omnipresent, all-pervading, except in his physical limitations. Spiritually he has no limitation, but the body is not the MAHANTA. It is only a covering of one of his instruments. He can leave the body and work on any of the spiritual planes at his own volition. He has no limitations, being one with the SUGMAD.

All the Living ECK Masters have taught, "I and the SUGMAD are one." In the process of the development of the MAHANTA, all Living ECK Masters, in their days on earth, wore the mantle of the MAHANTA and expanded their godlike qualities in common with all men. The Living ECK Master is, therefore, the divine man; a real son of

God. Yet every man has in him the latent possibilities for the same expansion to mastership. He only requires the Living ECK Master to help develop it.

When the Master gains MAHANTAship he attains conscious oneness with the SUGMAD. This is the distinguishing quality of the Living ECK Master. He knows his relationship with the SUGMAD and is able to consciously exercise his powers as a son of God. He is literally part of the all-embracing ECK, partaking of Its qualities, and is the chief instrument which the Supreme Being uses in Its universes. It gives Its boundless love to all mankind through the MAHANTA.

A vital difference exists between the MAHANTA and a departed Master. The chela cannot follow a Master who has left this plane and gone into the other worlds. The departed one cannot initiate anyone on the spiritual path. He has nothing now to do with the earth world. Neither can anyone follow two or more Masters at the same time. Here one is following only principles in the light of the universal cause, but not the Living ECK Master.

No child can get nourishment from a deceased mother, nor a sick man from a departed doctor. The Masters of the past ages have left this field of action, and so their work here is finished. Neither does one follow a book because it is said to be truth. No man can get truth out of a book. It must come out of himself. Therefore, all who wish the truth of ECK must follow the MAHANTA, the Living ECK Master. The SUGMAD cannot instruct, or give man the needed help on the upward path, without the MAHANTA in human form to act as Its instrument and spokesman. The greatest stumbling block for man is that he cannot see all God's manifestations.

Those who cling to a Master who has translated from this earth world are in error. He is not dead, but he has left the field of action in this region of matter. He is no longer in touch with humanity; his work is elsewhere. The discipleship of the chela must change to the successor.

Men must recognize that feelings provide no proof in religious matters. The MAHANTA will try to teach the chela to discount feelings as proofs of religious dogma. Only the Living ECK Master can offer the chela a definite method by which he can prove all things for himself.

There is one way to know the Living ECK Master is authentic. That is to see him on some higher plane where assumption is impossible. If the MAHANTA is seen in his radiant form, the chela knows this is the true Master of Eckankar. It is only when the chela is ready that he will see the MAHANTA in the radiant form.

Whenever the chela finds the Living ECK Master, he should follow him with unwavering faith and determination and accept him wholeheartedly. If the chela runs up against karma and burdens, he must hold a steady hand on himself and wait while these are being worked out by the ECK Master.

Hold all and wait. The questions that are in one's mind will be worked out eventually without a word from the Master. The light becomes stronger, and the darkness vanishes in the reorganization of the inner man and his thinking processes and habits. Do not make the mistake of trying to fit the teachings of ECK into the old ways of thinking. Drop all, and start over again.

It is not possible to enter into the kingdom of heaven except through the teachings of Eckankar. The path lies with the MAHANTA, and all who come to him will have salvation and liberation from worldly affairs. Unless Soul does this and follows the path of ECK with loving obedience, it is impossible for It to enter into the Ocean of Love and Mercy and become a Coworker with God.

Each Soul that becomes a chela of the living MAHANTA starts working out Its karma for permanent entry into the kingdom of heaven. If It is initiated, this is assured, for all karma will be resolved, and the Lords of Karma will never again bother him at the end of his earthly existence. When he enters into the next world, should it be on one of the lower planes by the will of the MAHANTA, he must work off his karma on that plane. Should it be on the Astral Plane, he must stay for a period until his astral karma is worked off. This is true of every plane below the Atma region. However, the ECK Initiate of the Second Circle will rise above any of these lower worlds upon the decease of the physical vehicle. He will enter into the Atma world at once, escorted by the living MAHANTA.

However, if any chela or initiate leaves the path of ECK for another way to the heavenly worlds during any particular embodiment on earth, he must expect his karma to be extended. His karmic burden increases as he gathers more, going through incarnation after incarnation searching blindly for what he has given up. Not knowing, not seeing that the Kal Niranjan has blinded his eyes to the glory of the heavenly worlds.

He cannot leave the path of ECK expecting to find salvation and liberation in the Prithvi Lok (Earth world). No one but the living MAHANTA can take him out of this plane of matter. He will again someday meet with the Living ECK Master, when ready, and enter permanently into the kingdom of heaven.

Woe be to him who tries to travel another path of religious doctrine or spiritual works while at the same time a chela of the Living ECK Master. He will suffer the penalties of his folly and not know what has created his adversities. If he becomes an initiate in Eckankar, there shall be no wavering from the path unless he wishes an adverse life and falling into disgrace. If he accepts titles, rewards, and so-called benefits from others who are not on the path of ECK, there will also be the same adversities of life.

He must have that burning faith in the ECK in order to find the liberation of Soul. He must never allow anything to disturb this and take him away from the path. If he should try to enhance and advance a teaching of the lower order, or another order at the same time he is following the path of ECK, there will be little spiritual unfoldment for him.

The ECKist recognizes no other religion, although such exists in this physical world. Nor does he recognize any metaphysical teaching, occultism, or any world theological faiths, creeds, or cults, all of which claim to be the way to God. The ECKist, however, does not condemn any of these, because they are, in a sense, all under ECK, as each has its origin in the ECK. These are only the chelas of the Living ECK Master who have strayed from the path and established a faith of their own. It is like the shadow of truth. Whoever wants the shadow instead of the Light is foolish.

Man will take to religion, even if he has to invent one. The weak need the support, and although it is an illusionary product in the spirit-matter worlds, it shall not be taken from man. Every man must seek the path of ECK for himself, and walk upon it for himself.

A spiritual darkness will brood over the world, and all men who walk upon the surface of the earth will be sick from it. Except for the Satya Yuga, the Golden Age, there is a physical and moral deterioration of man in all other yugas. Moral corruption eats into the vitals of the human race, and none but those who follow the path of ECK are immune to it. Practically every man, except the ECKist, is lost in the dense forests of morality because each is blind. He suffers from spiritual amnesia, for there is no memory nor recollection of his true home.

In addition to this mental and spiritual plight, many suffer from physical illness, heartbreak, and are otherwise worn and weary. They fumble and stumble, not knowing where to find the Living ECK Master. They pray to their God, but there is little answer. Each is looking for miracles that can happen, provided they recognize the Master is waiting for each and all.

The entire human race is but an aggregation of driven slaves from childhood to old age, while cares and anxieties multiply. They wait only for death, and this death is the doorway into the kingdom of heaven. The human race is told by the priests and religious fanatics that death is the mystery. But for the ECKist there is no mystery in the phenomena of death, for he practices dying daily and visiting the heavenly worlds. When the time comes for this phenomena to take place in the Pinda world, it is found he can leave the body under his own volition.

The ECK Initiate is dead in the Physical body but always alive in the Atma Sarup. Thus each man needs to know himself as Soul, living in the body of the ECK (Spirit). He must realize he is not the physical vehicle, that it is only an outer garment used for protection against the coarse vibrations of the lower worlds.

The chela is never converted in ECK. Conversion is not a part of the works of Eckankar. He is transformed and transmuted instead to the body of ECK. He repents of karma, that is, gives up the Kal and accepts the MAHANTA as his spiritual guide. This is the ECK side, and there is always the factor of total surrender of the human consciousness to the MAHANTA. This is not an emotional (astral) experience.

Any man who makes claims he is a master, adept, or savior of the human race and still speaks of being an incarnation of a past life is false in his claims. Only the Living ECK Master can truly say that he is the Ancient

One, the incarnation of the ECK (Spirit) and the MAHANTA Consciousness. No others can make this claim.

The chela must learn that cleanliness of the mind and body is a necessity in the works of ECK. He must take care of his body, keep it clean at all times, see that it is free of odors, and that his hair is properly trimmed. He must keep his mind free from the pollution of worldly affairs, such as lust, anger, greed, attachment to worldly desires, and vanity. These are the five passions of the mind. But he cannot allow them to infest his mind, for they will in turn infest the body.

The laws and rules for the ECK chela are simple. These are to give harmony, purity, and perfection of Soul. This constitutes heaven while in the physical vehicle. One can discern this heavenly state in the proportion that he relinquishes the false concepts of the limited, mortal consciousness of man. He must yield himself, the inner self, to the one divine ECK. Peace and well-being then enters into his human experience of life.

He who enters into the works of Eckankar becomes an Acolyte. He is put under the spiritual discipline of ECK, prior to his true induction into the invisible order. He is a probationer who must prove his worth before entering into the true works of Eckankar.

He must practice the disciplines of ECK. The first is to have cleanliness of mind, that no words which would pollute the air enter into his mind. He shall look upon all men as creatures of God and this only; for they, like himself, are temples who shall eventually become Coworkers with God.

He must, in mind, fast continuously from all Kal thoughts which could infect his mental state and consciousness. Through this he learns the powerful awareness of the presence of the Living ECK Master, who is with him constantly. He learns not to be deceived or dismayed by the conflicting world around him. He knows that all universes, regardless of whether or not they are under the rulership of the Kal Niranjan, are really worlds of perfection, harmony, and good.

He learns that patience is the greatest discipline of all the spiritual works of ECK. By patience he can endure life, hardships, karmic burdens, the slanders of men, and the pricks of pain and disease. He keeps his mind steadfastly upon the Light of God, never swerving, never letting up on his attention to the goal of God-Realization.

He comes to know humility and chastity in his life on earth and that all his responsibility belongs to God, not to anyone nor anything within this physical realm. His loved ones, family, and relatives are the images of God, mirrored in this worldly life and embodiment to serve the SUGMAD, the Supreme Deity.

He soon learns that humility is opposite to kani, the ego. He will not let this false concept of his worth to the Master and to the SUGMAD stand in his way to reach the heavenly states. He knows that vanity is only a trap of the Kal Niranjan and that he will become a fool if he lets himself be enslaved by the Kal.

He will come to discriminate between all things, recognizing that there is no good nor evil, no beauty nor ugliness, and there is no sin. That all these are concepts of the mind, the dual forces in the matter worlds. Once he recognizes and understands this, he will then be free of all the Kal traps.

He will be ready to enter into the Kingdom of God, the Ocean of Love and Mercy.

He will be the ECK, of Itself.

6
The Living ECK Master

The Living ECK Master is always higher on the spiritual scale of God than any saints of the worldly religions. An unbroken line of ECK Masters have been the Living ECK Master during their respective sojourns in this world, which means each, in his time, was the direct manifestation of God, the divine channel which God uses as Its voice to speak to the worlds within Itself.

Hence, the Living ECK Master is omniscient, omnipotent, and omnipresent. Each who has served his respective time in the worlds of God, including the physical plane, is known as the MAHANTA, the Vi-Guru, the highest of all spiritual Masters throughout the universes of the SUGMAD. None are higher than the MAHANTA, for he alone possesses the shining consciousness of the SUGMAD.

The saints of the various religions have never been placed in the same category. Therefore, they should never be considered in the same distinctive class as the Living ECK Master. Those whose training has been in the traditional religious manner would possibly resist this statement of golden truth. Truth has never been told in the physical worlds. It has been hidden from the eyes and ears of the profane by those who wish to make slaves of the masses. It has only been a control factor in the managing of men to keep their attention riveted upon one particular religious object; this is the foundation of the religions of the world that claim to have Truth. There is no basis for this consideration, and that is what it is, a consideration of the worst sort.

Truth is no being's prerogative nor any religion's singular strength. Since everything in this physical universe is controlled by the Kal Niranjan (the negative power), we have nothing that can say it represents the ultimate in the perfect sense, except Eckankar.

Since the ECK is the original, primitive source of all life, It is closer to Truth than any orthodox religion, philosophy, or church. Those who point fingers at ECK, claiming that here are false teachings taught by false prophets, are not aware that they are themselves misled by the Kal. None of these detractors are enlightened with Truth. They can quote only from the sacred books of their representative religions, strictly stating their own interpretations. None have any further advancement than the Astral worlds and usually the lower subplanes of this first region beyond the physical senses.

Neither do they have any experience in the ECK Life-Sound Current. Few, if any, can do anything more than preach the message of the Kal. They are the agents of the Kal, establishing the delusion that their purpose is to give out truth, but this truth is that of the negative power. Theirs is the message of the Universal Mind Power.

Kal agents promise more abundant life in the name of their saviors. They give the impression that nothing is greater than their own words. This illusion is furthered by the fact that life somehow always manages to upset any faith they have in their gods.

This brings about disappointment, frustrations, and unhappiness. It never gives any glimpse of the true reality. Nor does it bring enlightenment, or knowledge of survival of Soul. Like the donkey with a carrot dangling before its nose to keep it moving, forever out of reach, the man who follows these Kal teachings goes through life with false hopes. For hope is all he has, and never faith.

The Living ECK Master points out again and again that each man can have the joy of immortality if he follows the words of the ECK. No other religions or masters can give the complete Truth except the Living ECK Master, who is the MAHANTA, the resurrected Spirit of God, the ECK, serving all Souls in every universe of God.

While he serves out his mission as the MAHANTA, he has to do duty not only upon the earth and every planet, star, and constellation in the material world, but in every plane within the universe of God's universe. Hence, he is the Living ECK Master and the MAHANTA to every Soul, regardless of where that entity may be living. Whether It be in hell or the Ocean of Love and Mercy, the MAHANTA is with It, as well as with all other Souls. The Soul only has to recognize this to understand and know this miracle of life.

All others who claim they are the messengers, preachers, or the voice of God do so for some materialistic motive. But the MAHANTA has none; he serves God; he is the servant of God; he is the servant of the servants of the Lord because he has been selected and given the command. His life is so directed that even in the physical world he does not accept anything from life but always gives to those who seek him out.

Yet, woe to those who take advantage of his generosity and his efforts to give. These are the false followers, the seekers of the material things of life, the parasites who attempt to feed upon the ECK which flows out of the MAHANTA, the perfect instrument of God.

Man is apt to be this way and will oft seek out the MAHANTA to pour out his woes and personal issues. He asks for everything, and in return for resolving his problems and for success or materialistic gains, he promises his faith, everlasting devotion, dedication, gratitude, and payment in monetary means. These are only insincere promises, for the MAHANTA knows that when a solicitor has received his gift from God, via the Living ECK Master, he generally forgets, in his joy, to offer his gift. He honestly intends to fulfill his promise of payment, but the Kal activities stir within him, and again his desire for physical well-being becomes greater than his longing for God.

This longing is forgotten in his workaday life in the material world. He seeks love and comfort by every possible means, and those metaphysicians and doctors of the mind and Soul who promise him a kingdom on earth are only false prophets.

If they promise him rewards in heaven after life here on earth, this, too, is a series of false promises. The kingdom of the ECK is so far beyond this world that few, if any, recognize the life which they can have if only they would follow the path of the ECK Truths.

If the MAHANTA bestows gifts upon the solicitor, then he is the most fortunate of the fortunates, for it means that he basks in the favor of the Living ECK Master and seeks nothing further in life. He has met and found the true Vi-Guru and must now start his spiritual journey to God.

All Souls struggling to find their way to the true path of God—the way of Eckankar—will eventually seek out the Living ECK Master. Each will come to know that life itself is the elemental part of ECK, and it is only because of the will of the SUGMAD that all Souls have existence.

All religions have had a beginning and an ending. Whenever the history of the human race is examined, it is found that many religions have existed on the physical planes, but few have lasted beyond a thousand years. All world religions, therefore, are materialistic in nature and worship the wrong power, the wrong God. Unless a religion has for its basic teaching the Living ECK Master, the Sound Current, and the Light, it will not have longevity. Few, if any, religions have such elements in their teachings.

It is the will of God that Souls have existence. This is the doctrine of the ECK, the way of Truth. No man comes to the SUGMAD except through the MAHANTA. Life has no existence but for the love and mercy of God. Only Soul can have life because It (God) has willed it to be.

The man who solicits the gifts of God for health, monetary means, and worldly love only keeps the ECK from entering into him and healing all aspects of his life. To ask is never to receive, to question is to defeat one's own purpose with God, and to make promises which knowingly are false is to annul one's advancement on the spiritual path.

To ridicule, to scorn, to speak mockingly of the words of the MAHANTA, and not to have faith in him and the cause of ECK, is to bring woes on the advocator of doubt. It brings his karmic progress to a halt, increases his incarnations in this world, and causes him to suffer untold hardships.

The ignorant and the naive will never understand, nor shall they learn except by experiencing the slow death brought about by their own overt acts against the MAHANTA and the ECK. This is actually creating overt acts against the SUGMAD.

Self-assertion, self-righteousness, self-will, and self-seeking at the expense of the ECK, likewise, brings untold hardships of life for one who indulges in these things during his life in the spirito-materialistic worlds. Not only does this occur for him in the physical world, but upon every plane of existence. He who takes up such Kalistic virtues is never at peace with himself. But he shall become like a fine crystal globe—to ping just right would cause it to break into a thousand pieces. No man should wish this upon himself but should seek God for Itself, and never for any personal motivation.

Religion speaks of peace after death for man. But this is only a lower-world teaching. It is not true, but only a promise to keep man happy, a promise he is going to be free of the trials and tribulations of this earthly life. But not until Soul has gained the realization of the SUGMAD shall It become peaceful and have harmony with all life. This is possible not only after death, but while It is still living in the physical embodiment.

The chela keeps wondering when he will reach that moment of meeting with God. But it will never come, for, if he would realize it, he is already at that moment. Rather, he is at this focal point in eternity, for the SUGMAD is always with him, in the form of the Living ECK Master. The chela is always in the present, for the present is always eternity. God is with him all the time as the Living ECK Master, every moment of his life.

Therefore, the chela should recognize that if God is with him, then the Living ECK Master is always the presence he experiences constantly. He should understand this and have it written upon his heart, for the MAHANTA is the vehicle God uses to reach every Soul Who will listen. This should be kept in mind constantly.

Privacy is a necessity in the life of every ECK Master. He must have it, or he cannot give the inner service to mankind as he should. But with the way men try to use him for their own means and motivation, he generally has little privacy and much less rest.

The chela must be dedicated to the ECK. Dedication is his greatest asset. He must give this dedication to the MAHANTA, the Living ECK Master because he is the only manifestation of God that can be recognized by those in the human state of consciousness. If the chela is not possessed of this quality of dedication and loyalty to the path of ECK, his incarnations are lengthened in this world, and he shall not be able to enter into the next worlds at the end of his present life.

The Living ECK Master is not a therapist, as understood in the physical world, nor at any time does he pose as one. If the chela or the nonchela considers him as such, they are defeating their own purpose. He is a healer, one who can read the auras of chelas and others, one who knows the past, present, and future of the human race. But he is not a therapist, nor a fortune-teller, nor a finder of lost articles. He is none of these things, but a manifestation of God upon earth. He is a miracle worker but never attempts to prove himself when called upon to do so. He does not perform wonders simply because someone challenges him to do so. He will not perform magic nor give himself over to tricks as many believe he should do. But he proves himself in mysterious ways to everyone. He gives of himself and is forgiving of all others. He never considers anything, nor anyone, as an enemy. He knows it is the Kal Niranjan who is trying to defeat him, but this is the way of God.

He points this out to all who question him and say he should bring his mighty powers into action to be rid of the Kal Niranjan. He does not battle, nor destroy anything that is a creature of God, for the Kal is also part of God's own divine power put here to act as the purifying agent for all Souls.

The MAHANTA, therefore, allows all things to have their freedom. He gives each power through God because this is the way of life and must be done in accordance with God's will.

The trouble with religion is that one individual appears in what might be a perfect manifestation of God, and so begins a worship of that manifestation. Most of these manifestations are only social, Astral, or Mental phenomena, and they deceive the worshipper.

Such an individual is but a man-made object, established by the Kal power to give man something to keep his mind from Truth. This is the way of all orthodox religions.

Orthodox religious leaders appear to follow out this trend because of the difference on thought and worship of their respective desires.

This is all because few, if any, realize what they are trying to establish in the field of worship. It is simply a crude manifestation which is little more than a symbol with considerations pouring into it and impressing the mind so it will stay with men until the end of their earthly time.

Most religions have been rewritten again and again and reinterpreted until there is little vitality of the primitive teachings left anywhere in any worldly path. When a religion begins to lose its force in this world, it gradually dies away as all have in the present and past.

Thus, the ECK is the true faith. Its teachings are from the ancient original source, pure and unadulterated in Its message. It is direct from God in Its Ocean of Love and Mercy, and is given through the pure vehicle, the true instrument, the MAHANTA, and is the highest message of the SUGMAD.

The Master always presents the straight path to God,

but it is the chela's relationship with the human element in others that manages to upset and divert the Master's way to heaven. Or it is man's relationship with himself which brings about the ingredients of human problems on the physical level of life.

The Living ECK Master strives constantly to take the chela out of the earthly games level, but he never makes rules nor rituals, never lays down laws and proclaims his way to God as the better way, although all know it is. He knows that all worldly religions are pseudo and in the minority, but he seldom states this in any of his works. He never asks that anyone follow his path and abide by his own conduct and words. He knows that many men cannot do this, as they have established their own consciousness in orthodox religion and will be offended should he demand they follow him.

All worldly religions are for the benefit of the leader. The Living ECK Master teaches all who listen to his word that it is Truth, and the chela must learn to separate Truth from false teachings. Until the chela has learned to do this, he is apt to wander about in this world of mind and body through centuries of reincarnations.

The Living ECK Master is above civilization and culture. He knows that all there is in this world is life and embodiments. These are forms with which he seldom, if at any time, has any relationship. He works only through each Soul, which is the divine spark of life within each embodiment.

The MAHANTA is always born near or on a large body of water. His birth is always mysterious, and men of ordinary birth do not know his origin. Nor does any man know who his sires might be, their true names, or their true origin.

The ECK enters into the womb of a virgin, the queen of heaven, who has submitted to the true Spirit of the universe. The consciousness of the MAHANTA state is planted as the seed and carefully nurtured in the womb. When the embodiment of flesh is brought into this world, a man-child is born. It starts its unfoldment over a period of years until the state of perfection is reached, in adulthood. Then the chosen one learns he is the Living ECK Master of his times.

There is never a time when the world is without a MAHANTA, the Living ECK Master, for God manifests Itself again and again in the embodiment of the chosen one. It is constant and always in the worlds. For in the Living ECK Master does It find perfection, as he is the true instrument for the SUGMAD, the Vi-Guru, the Love and Spirit of the SUGMAD.

All life springs from its origin in God, but manifests in the perfect body of the SUGMAD via the MAHANTA. This is the living Quintan (five), or the fivefold bodies of the MAHANTA. This is the greater part of the SUGMAD which is the Word made flesh in the lower worlds. The MAHANTA thereby has a body which functions as an instrument of God upon each plane throughout the worlds of Spirit, including the true spiritual planes.

Therefore, the Living ECK Master has existence on every plane in the lower worlds in a body: the Physical, Astral, Causal, Mental, and Soul. At the same time, he also exists in the nonbody form which is the ECK. Above the Atma world (the Soul Plane), he is entirely without form and is completely omnipresent. While living in the five lower planes he is omnipresent, while at the same time existing in the MAHANTA state in each world and administering to those entities and physically embodied Souls as deemed necessary, as well as to his own chelas and initiates of Eckankar.

All religions born upon this earth speak of their saviors having three bodies, or three states, which are known as the Trinity. These are the lower states of consciousness which millions have accepted and put their desires and ambitions into to have saving grace. ECK never speaks of any orthodox religion as being beneath the true spiritual works of God, but merely makes it known that these religions are the offshoots of Eckankar, the original source of all life.

All men and all entities existing in every universe of God will, in time, come to know each exists because God has given all life through the perfected state of Its manifestation on earth and upon every plane in the universe. The MAHANTA is Its only manifestation, the Light of the worlds, the Voice of God, which is heard in every corner and closet of every plane. When he speaks, the Voice of God is heard. Every word that he utters is Truth to all men, entities, and creatures.

He gives life and allows the actions of every man and creature upon earth and throughout the heavens of God to do all deeds in freedom of respective consciousness. For each and all he is the vehicle of God, and he is able to give all things and be all things to all through the power of the ECK.

The MAHANTA is a law unto himself. So oft does he speak of life itself as being his servant, but he commands heaven and earth, yet never does he allow himself to be worshipped perfectly as man. Only as the MAHANTA, the perfect consciousness.

When Lai Tsi, the perfect ECK Master of China in the ancient days, stood upon the hill and preached the sermon that gained him the title of perfection as the MAHANTA of his day, he was approached by a disciple who asked, "Master, who are you?"

"Whom do you say that I am?" Lai Tsi asked.

"You are the MAHANTA, the perfect Master," said the disciple.

"If this is what you believe, you have gained the true enlightenment of God. From this day you have entered into heaven and will be at my side."

Man earns himself a place in heaven when he recognizes the MAHANTA and knows him for what he is. The world that follows the dictum of the Living ECK Master and fulfills his slightest desire does so only so it can gain for itself. The MAHANTA gives, regardless of the motivation, if he knows that the gift will be a gain for the solicitor.

To knock and receive is not always the motive for the Master to fulfill a request. He who asks must gain it by earning the gift. The gift to anyone is that which God gives via the MAHANTA. But it is the decision of the MAHANTA as to who may receive and who is worthy of the gift.

All may be worthy yet cannot receive the gifts of God because the heart is not ready. If one wishes to have a gift from the SUGMAD, his heart must become pure and gentle. He cannot receive when filled with doubts, lust, unhappiness, and dread. Only those who are dedicated, happy, and love God are able to receive the gift of God that the MAHANTA passes to each who has earned his rightful place in the heavenly kingdom.

When shorn of the time-sense, when knowledge of space has left the human consciousness, then shall the chela be relieved of the anxiety of experiencing life as a succession of problems—past, present, and future. The barriers of time and space can be broken by accepting the MAHANTA as the true one and by entering into the spiritual view of life, as the unfolding of all life is eternity. Eternity is an expression of life without a sense of time and space, already established by the SUGMAD. Once the chela surrenders to It and accepts as valid that the ECK is the source of all life, his concepts of eternity change his human consciousness into a state of God-knowing—the divine consciousness.

Man's essential nature is primarily a spiritual desire for God. He must pray that the eternal ECK will visit Itself upon him and that the living Master will appear to remove any doubt and act as his divine guide. Then all the lower aspects of human nature will be filled with the holy Light and Sound. When this divine visitation is given unto him, then does he become worthy of any gift of God and able to serve in this world as a Coworker with the MAHANTA.

Each Soul can be liberated so It may stand upon the high summit of the spiritual mountain and view the world. This is a symbol of the understanding each chela in Eckankar will reach. This is eternity—the view from the hilltop of spiritual vision. The eternal view that is seen is the wholeness of life, free from time and space of the lower worlds.

Perfection may seem far from the human state of consciousness, but one can be thankful that perfection is divinely true in the present, now, and not in some distant future. If one looks, he will find divine power in the human situation as well as in the spiritual situation. Man can always bring out in the human self the divine Truth. He only has to be himself.

As man deepens his understanding of the divine ECK, his outlook changes. The ECK, which is the essence of God, is divine love, and being love It naturally provides only the good karma of life.

The ECK is uninterrupted, continuing, eternal. It is the reality of all life manifested here in this world in the embodiment of the Living ECK Master. When one sees beyond the views of this world, he is living in Spirit. He can avoid all the anxieties and dangers of this worldly life by lifting himself again to the top of the spiritual mountain. He looks neither to the past nor to the future, but to the present, the now, knowing that the SUGMAD lives only in the present. He knows that with each step he takes he is on hallowed ground, for the MAHANTA is always with him.

The Word of God within this world has already been done. It is the state of man's consciousness which has not unfolded but will continue to unfold. The chela is ever developing and can reach the state of spiritual perfection only if he will accept and believe what is taking place in the activity of Soul.

The Living ECK Master embraces all humanity because he is the only channel that can do so. He is able to live in an enlarged state of present consciousness and few, if any, can ever do this. Certainly none of the ancients could do this, although many were able to experience the good of life. If the chela is seeking eternity, then he must first look for it within his own orbit. Since the Living ECK Master is in this circle of being that is the personal and universal self of the chela, then the latter must seek it with the Living ECK Master.

Once he has established the recognition of life as it is, then the knowledge that he is immortal comes to him. He experiences the ending of all karma which has been the Kal cause and establishes only the God-given karma within the world of worlds.

Eternity is experienced by the chela in Eckankar when the MAHANTA takes him to the top of the spiritual mountain and lets him view the scrambling activities of the little selves among the masses of humanity. From this position the view is not limited to the senses of the human consciousness, and there is no time-space sense. All below him are desperately trying to scramble up the mountainside to the summit where the view is eternal and the spiritual atmosphere is clear. To live in the world of humanity, as the chela must do until the end of his days in the physical embodiment, he must constantly dwell on the spiritual summits of God.

Soul is the all-inclusive consciousness of the individual established in God, and outside the concepts of the aspects of the lower worlds. It has been named static, but It is not this, for Soul is dynamic within the worlds of God Itself. It is a state of awareness which experiences life through the spiritual senses. The spiritual senses are able to have perception, conception, and realization.

Man consists only of Soul. There is nothing else which can give the physical self life. He has body, mind, and Soul. He is Soul but has not yet recognized this. His spiritual senses have not yet been activated, so he does not know Soul is the only thing he is in eternity.

Soul is a spark of the divine ECK. It has three attributes with the SUGMAD: It has a perception of eternity through inner sight, hearing, and knowing, but mainly knowingness; It has conception of all that It gathers in through the inner senses—that is, an understanding of what has been seen, heard, and known; It recognizes or realizes Its relationship with God through God-Realization, Self-Realization, and Mind-Realization. Soul realizes that It is part of the whole of ECK, not with God. As a divine spark of the ECK, It can have a realization that It is the ECK Itself. No man or Soul has ever, in the true state, felt he, or It, was whole with God.

It is through these attributes that Soul controls the body which It occupies during any given time in the world of matter. The control of the body and environment depends on the strength and realization It has gained through these three attributes. This again depends on the degree of Its awakened consciousness. This is an explanation of why each man is different from another. This is also in accordance with the Law of Spiritual Evolution which establishes inequality in all things and beings and their continued effort for spiritual unfoldment.

The MAHANTA is not only the Living ECK Master, but a living example of the philosophy of Eckankar, the high priest, and a fountain of knowledge for ECK. He is one who knows divine law, government of the heavenly worlds, and the workings of the human mind and Soul, as well as the art of spiritual healing, magic, prophecy, and miracles.

The love of the Living ECK Master for all chelas is on the highest plane and should not be considered in any other manner. When the gift of love is passed to the chela, he should be contented, for it has been his privilege to gain the inner heights through the MAHANTA. If the chela is happy in this, then the reality of God shall be his own realization.

It is best not to make contact with the Living ECK Master in the physical but through the inner level, for all comes as the secret teachings from the heart of the MAHANTA to each chela under his protection and guidance. This is the inner way, and all who come unto the MAHANTA shall be lifted up into heaven.

ECK is always at war with the Kal Niranjan and all the orthodox religions, mass societies, and civilizations created by the Kal. Therefore, orthodox religions and the masses have always tried to hinder the progress of the ECK in the lower worlds.

Those who follow the Kal are mainly interested in the effects of materialistic power. The subtle play of the Kal is an intricate working of power forces among the various minor forces in these worlds of its own.

Yet on the opposing side all the power of God must reach these worlds through the perfect instrument of the MAHANTA, the Living ECK Master. There is no other way, for he is the distributor of the power. All may see the example of this in the material life here on earth in the same manner, and they recognize that each within himself is a distributor of this power which gives life and creation to their environment.

The Living ECK Master is appointed to his high position and is expected to defend the God power and to defend the works of ECK and the chelas who have put their interest in ECK. The Living ECK Master is not allowed to retire from his field of action in this life until another is ready and trained to replace him.

When the Living ECK Master's position is attacked by revolt or by dissatisfaction among the followers of ECK, he will defend himself. Not in the way many would expect, but in ways that few can recognize. The defense will come from the inner planes and by means of the ECK. Those who revolt or become dissatisfied cannot bring about any attack upon the Living ECK Master or his position in life. If they try, there is always the swiftest of retribution, which is not always recognized by the receiver nor those who might have observed the occasion.

Those who are the children of ECK are the sons and daughters of the divine Sound Current. They are the heroic people of their age, and they could suffer at the hands of the orthodox who wish to keep the doctrine of the ECK from spreading.

Man cannot receive any more than he can give. This is truth for every state of consciousness. It only means that if he petitions the MAHANTA for a gift, he must have the state of consciousness for receiving it. If he does not, his petition is wasted. He cannot receive healing if he is not ready for it in his own consciousness. If he is desperate and grasping at straws, there is little opportunity for the fulfillment of his petition. If he seeks the Light before he is ready for It, expecting miracles, it is not likely he will have the miracle. But if he seeks the Light and Sound and is in the state of preparation for It, then he shall receive the heavenly gift from the MAHANTA.

The wretched, the poor, the unhappy, and those who are in need are drawn unto the MAHANTA, for those who are poor in heart are the greatest recipients of his love. His weapons are love, the spiritual works of ECK, exhortations, and giving of himself.

He goes among the poor, the young, the wretched, the wicked, and the unhappy to spread the Word of ECK. He gives only love, faith, and joy to all he meets, whether it be an embrace, a kiss, a coin, or a coat. But to each he meets he gives all he has in spirit in the realm of the material world.

The Living ECK Master rejects all violence, all acts of force, and accepts his obligation to the society and order in which he lives. At the same time he refuses to obey any man-made law which interferes with his spiritual freedom and that of his chelas, which are the limitations put upon the body, heart, and Soul. The Living ECK Master recognizes the law of God.

The ECK is life, and the MAHANTA lives and creates life, for all things are made of ECK in accordance with the will of the SUGMAD. God took the ingredients of the ECK which are parts of the divine body of the SUGMAD, the shining dewdrops of the Ocean of Love and Mercy, and created Souls and life in which all nonbeings and beings live.

The true qualities of the Living ECK Master are indestructible. His chief quality of love can never be destroyed no matter what the enemies of ECK may do to him. Nor can any destroy his immortality. He may be put to suffering by men, caused pain and grief, but never can any bring about the true destruction of the reality of the MAHANTA. He is permanent because he is perfected Soul, above the physical forms and physical substance. Never was he part of the perishable and impermanent. He is free from all that the ordinary man suffers, grieves over, and mourns in his losses and happiness in material gain.

The Living ECK Master is above time and space. He is God's essential expression and is never separated from the source of true wisdom and reality. He is able to see the past, know the future, and give healings, happiness, and create miracles for those whom he loves and those who believe and can accept his gifts. For all those who have reached the state of consciousness of the knowing level shall realize who they are and shall be ready to receive the gifts as dispensed by the Living ECK Master.

The work of the Living ECK Master has already been finished with every chela who comes to him to be lifted up. He knows what the chela is ready to receive before the petition is made. He gives all to the chela in advance, but if the chela is not ready, there is no recognition that he has already received his gift. When the chela is ready, the gift shall be recognized and received with the joy and blessings of the Living ECK Master.

Those who are taken to the summit of the spiritual mountain by the Living ECK Master are the fortunate ones. Here, independent of time and space, above all the lower worlds, they see all the joy and blessings of life.

All reality stands out in its shining splendor, and the Music of the heavenly ECK is acclaimed for all who have reached the summit. Below, the work of the divine ECK has already been done. It unfolds Souls who are in the lower worlds as long as each is within the tentacles of the Kal, and until each comes to realize It is living in the world of illusion.

Until then, each Soul exists in unreality. When the recognition of Itself comes in Self-Realization, It then will accompany the Living ECK Master into the heavenly worlds to find Its spiritual responsibilities in the worlds of God.

7
The Transcendence of Love

The major mistake any chela can make with the Living ECK Master is to keep everything with himself in the personal realm.

This includes his own problems, and this is especially true of those who do not follow the path of ECK yet will call upon the MAHANTA to fulfill their petitions.

The question of love enters into the subject at hand. If the chela or the nonchela really loves the Living ECK Master, neither would make any petition for the fulfillment of personal desires through him. It is natural, when one is desperate and has no other way out, to make some contact through the physical channels available to ask the Living ECK Master for spiritual assistance.

It is not necessary, though. He should not have any demands made upon him through physical and material mediums but only via the inner channels. Therefore, if the pseudolove of any chela or nonchela tries to obligate the Living ECK Master by making extraordinary demands of him, there will be repercussions.

The Master should have the freedom to work in the universal cause of ECK. Instead, he has many people constantly demanding him to take care of any problem they may lay at his feet. These are the people who cannot accept love. If the MAHANTA speaks a word of love to the chela, it must be taken in love by the one who accepts it.

The greater the following of the MAHANTA, the greater will be the demands made upon him by those in ignorance. Few know they are to take their own responsibility in life, for whatever they have is due to their own karmic patterns of life.

Those who profess love for the Living ECK Master must be sincere. If they are not, it is a useless gesture and useless words. Love does not come to those who seek it, but to those who give love. It is a binding force between Souls who have nothing to give but themselves to one another. It is not a physical force of any nature, but one of deep, tender compassion ready to give all should another demand it.

This love must be great for the Living ECK Master. If he should ask any chela to give up everything in life for the ECK, this should be done. Nothing should stand between him and the Master. Any opinions, any thoughts, any materialistic things, and any feelings should be given up to follow the MAHANTA. Unless the chela is willing to do this, then he is not ready to enter into the spiritual worlds.

There are adversaries of ECK who will try to suppress the true spiritual works. Their behavior is abominable, for they are not sensible but panic and viciously attack ECK. Their attempt to repress ECK is damaging to themselves. Many pseudomasters will attempt to attack ECK and Its followers in order to stop the true message of Its reality. They cannot abide anyone who is not in agreement with their ideas and level of consciousness and who does not attempt to worship them as personalities.

This is proof they have no love within themselves.

Those who follow these pseudomasters and abide by their words, mimic them in manner, and parrot their words against the ECK shall suffer. There is no proof of any spiritual development within these persons, for they are only the agents of Kal.

It is wrong for anyone who makes claim to seership to publicly broadcast doom and disaster about an individual without that person's permission, or without first giving warning to that individual. This is a lack of love on the part of the so-called seer. This is proof he is neither a seer nor a master.

Too many claiming seership have made their reputations, in all times of human history, by using others as their targets and victims. It has made for some a reputation in prophecy in a vicious but Kalistic way.

The so-called prophets do not understand the laws of love, nor do they have any understanding of the laws of Kal that underlie all their statements. What they are doing is setting in motion, by public acclaim, some target for disaster, a series of vibrations which will eventually bring about troubles for their victims.

Such practices are always carried on in the psychic planes and have been during all recorded history. These peculiar persons create an aura of fear and awe, so they take advantage of it and strike down the foe and enemy with psychological effects made by fierce utterances and dreadful forewarnings.

If these pseudoprophets had any insight, it would be to their greater credit to serve their fellow man by quietly warning him and breaking up the vibrations which are going to bring harm to him. Not doing so shows a lack of universal love on the part of these pseudoprophets.

Since these people are only looking for applause and acclaim, they manifest a great deal of their public utterances for public eyes and ears. This is only an ego builder, and they do more harm than good. They do not seem to understand that love for their fellow man is greater than their own petty egos.

The religionists of the world claim that when the whole human race comes to the path of love, all evil will disappear from the world. This is not a rational solution, for few ever find the source of true love while living in the physical consciousness.

The fundamental requirements for meeting the MAHANTA, the Living ECK Master are humility, love, and freedom from the bonds of any worldly religious creeds. Therefore, not many Souls will have the privilege of meeting the ECK Master. Moral goodness has nothing to do with meeting the MAHANTA, nor do great intellectuals have any primary qualifications. It takes a Soul that has earned the right during Its past lives. All those who do come to the Living ECK Master have been with him in the past, not as the personality he now presents, but as Soul formed by the whole body of the ECK, the Word made flesh.

As one follows the path of ECK he will soon be assured he is on the right road to God-Realization. He will become stimulated to greater love and charity for all. He will eventually be guided into the heavenly worlds where consciousness is blended into the divine Current, where Soul shall only see Light and hear only the Music of ECK.

The very heart of the doctrine of ECK is love. This love is that divine essence which unites all reality and brings together all Souls. The higher Soul goes into the other worlds, the greater this becomes. Love is the bond which holds the worlds together. It is the living ECK, the Spirit of the SUGMAD.

When man turns his attention to universal love, all suffering ceases. This does not mean that all mankind, at any given time in this world, will collectively give universal love. This is not in the consciousness of the human self.

If one begins to look for love, he will find it. If he puts any conditions on love, there will be obstacles. If he questions and argues with those who are the Arahatas, the teachers of ECK, over points in the spiritual works, he has not advanced on the path. None like to be told this, but, nevertheless, it is true. Those who bring up points to be debated are still in the mental realm, and as long as they are there, they will constantly have qualms and will debate love, freedom, and the meaning behind the words in the ECK books and those of the Living ECK Master.

He who is in this stage will search out the hidden meanings behind the MAHANTA's words. He will seek significances where there are none. He will look for some reason for the Living ECK Master's acts. He will seek answers in everything, but there will be none. He either accepts what is written in the holy works of ECK, or not at all. This is hard for those who have always been able to question and seek logical answers to all their questions.

The questioner, or seeker, must learn to control his curiosity. He must learn discipline, control of his thoughts, and to know whether his decisions and judgments are correct. He must settle down to some answers for himself which must be raised and answered within himself—not by the MAHANTA, nor the Arahatas, but by himself. Then he knows without knowing. He understands without understanding and sees without seeing. He knows that whatever is said by the MAHANTA is not of the physical temple worn by him, but of the ECK which flows through the embodiment. Whatever is written and whatever is said is not a symbol of any divine reason, purpose, or logic. But it is that which is from the original fountain of God and is not of any earthly origin. Therefore, there is no significance to what is said or done, but It is what It is! Nothing more, nothing less.

The vital importance of love is to love all life without qualms, without wisdom or religion being uppermost in the mind of the lover. When one is of a pure heart and has the noble purpose of ECK as his goal, he can, impelled by love, set about doing the work of the SUGMAD on earth under the direction of the MAHANTA.

Love is the keystone of the works of ECK. Without it no chela can enter into the heavenly kingdom. There is one direct command, and that is to love one's fellow man and to love God more. Whosoever can measure up to this standard shall be ready for the Kingdom of God. But whosoever gains such love for the world can expect to gain nothing from the world itself. The Kal shall see that whosoever desires God while living in this world shall suffer for it.

Those who listen to the MAHANTA and obey with love in their hearts shall find love everywhere. They shall receive the love of God and shall abide in the love of the Living ECK Master.

Those who love the Living ECK Master shall be loved by the SUGMAD. In love of this nature one finds freedom, but until one learns to love the Living ECK Master he is in the bonds of the Kal.

No Living ECK Master ever works through a medium. He teaches that all wisdom is gained by changes in consciousness through contact with the ECK. Soul Travel is an individual experience, a realization of survival. It is an inner experience through which comes beauty and love of all life. It cannot be experienced in rituals and ceremonies, nor bottled in creeds.

The confusion in understanding ECK comes because every man's experience is different from every other man's. But the idea that man can get something from God because of his petty human love is erroneous. This is not the kind of love which one should believe is true. Strength without love produces the brute. Love without strength produces the weakling.

The SUGMAD is love, wisdom, and power. It is omnipresent, all-pervading. The Living ECK Master is the same, except he has physical limitations. But spiritually he has complete freedom and is a replica of the SUGMAD. The body is not the ECK Master; it is only a covering, one of his ready instruments, just as the Astral, Causal, and Mental bodies are only vehicles for him to use when on these different planes.

The MAHANTA may instantly rise to those worlds above the planes of human and psychic activity where consciousness expands to limitless love, wisdom, and power. On returning to this plane he has total recall of just as much of it as can be retained in the compass of the mental area. The Living ECK Master is infinite himself. If he has a hundred followers or a hundred thousand, it makes no difference. Each one will see the Living ECK Master in the inner chambers of his own individual self, wherever he may go. This, of course, must again depend upon the development of the chela's spiritual faculties.

The Living ECK Master always brings Light and Love into the world so all men shall profit by them. Not just his own followers, but the world of itself. Each of those who follow him should be caught up in the fire of his love. This love begins in each like a tiny flame, then begins to consume them until they love all because it is life, and life is God.

This is known as the holy fire. When the chela catches the spirit of the ECK, he immediately becomes fired to serve It. He is burning with the fever of the holy fire within himself, the ECK driving him on mercilessly toward fulfilling his destiny in this world. He becomes relentless in his striving to get out the message to others and may be considered a missionary of the ECK.

This holy fire is a burning love for all things, all people, and all life. It is the love of God seen in the smallest blade of grass, or in the eyes of a newborn babe. It is the love of God stirring in Soul to find Itself, to give away everything which is holding It back materially in this physical world. It is ready to give up all the mental qualms, emotions, and attachments to anything in the material plane. It cannot help Itself; It is a babe in the power of the Lord. Everything but God is the anti-ECK, and It considers all as Its enemy unless it is part of what Soul knows as the ECK.

The holy fire of ECK is principally the love of God which has taken over the person who has surrendered himself to the Living ECK Master and found that this is the only path to complete liberation. The word *surrender* may be insufficient. It is not to be confused with its worldly connotation. It is that the chela fully trusts the Master in every department of his life. He puts his spiritual interests in the hands of the Living ECK Master.

The chela never surrenders anything to the MAHANTA which he must keep. It is merely that he puts his trust in the knowledge that the Master will take care of his spiritual guidance. He accepts the aid and guidance of the Living ECK Master over a path which is unknown to himself. The Master is the guide, for the chela starts out in a wilderness and must be carried out into the calm of the spiritual worlds.

But the MAHANTA will never impose his own will upon any of his chelas. It is a cardinal principle that the Living ECK Master never interferes with the freedom of his followers. He is very careful of this, for he seldom gives a command, merely advises, and never attempts to dominate the intelligence of others.

Complete surrender means that out of perfect confidence and a great love, the chela will gladly follow where the Living ECK Master leads him. By giving himself up to the Living ECK Master, in this sense, the chela gains everything, which ends in perfect liberty in the spiritual worlds. Yaubl Sacabi stated, "Give the ECK Master all you have, and he will give you all he possesses!"

Love, as it is known to the human consciousness, is only involvement with astral influences. It is emotional freedom one seeks; to be rid of this involvement of the astral influences. Until he can be rid of these, he is never able to understand and know true liberation.

Human love, which is involved with sentimentality and physical love, is that part of the human consciousness influenced by the five Kal passions. These are *kama,* or lust; *krodha,* or anger; *lobha,* or greed; *moha,* or attachment; and *ahankara,* or vanity. Of these, man is influenced mainly by moha, or attachment. Here is the heart of man's karma, the very reason why he keeps moving constantly on the Wheel of the Eighty-Four, the continued round of births and deaths in this physical world.

This is the type of attachment which means delusive attachment, or infatuation. It is perhaps the most insidious of the five destructive passions. It is the one which makes the human consciousness believe that it can love all life, that it can love anyone outside itself. The truth of the matter is as Rebazar Tarzs once said: "He who believes he has a great love for another, be it a fellow being or God Itself, usually loves himself more."

Once the human consciousness becomes absorbed in ECK, it has little time for anything else. The individual must decide whether he wants to be absorbed in himself or absorbed in God and the works of ECK as distributed via the MAHANTA. Liberation of Soul is the one reason why man is in this world. Nothing else counts, but it is the sole purpose of the Kal Niranjan to keep Soul in this world, by using moha, the attachment to material things in life.

The Kal Niranjan keeps men blinded to their own higher interest through the five passions. This particular passion, moha, or attachment, is the king of procrastination. It keeps the chela from attending to his spiritual interests, the Spiritual Exercises of ECK.

Should physical death come before man finds liberation, he will go through a period in the Astral world. He may be as asleep, or he may be aware of what has gone on around himself. But then he is given rebirth again into the Physical world, not remembering his sojourn on the Astral Plane, nor that he has lived past lives. He has not rested spiritually, and the Kal power takes him, in hand again and leads him through the deep forests of worries and hardships of life.

He does this over and over again until one day he meets again with the Living ECK Master. This time he recognizes the MAHANTA as the one he has been searching for all these many lives. It comes upon him like a burst of the sun from behind a cloud following a storm. Then he realizes what has happened to him, and love for the Living ECK Master begins pouring out of him.

He realizes now that it is karma that binds the worlds of the lower planes together. The universality of the Law of Karma is one of the chief factors which binds life together, and not only human life but animal, plant, and mineral life as well. All these compose one big family, with a complicated and inseparable history and an inseparable karma. This is what man mistakes for love. It is not love but actually karma that binds him to all life here and on the psychic planes. He thinks of it as love because there is nothing within his mental capacity nor vocabulary that is capable of thoughts of love.

Then man begins to look at karma and wonders about it. When he comes under the great living Master he starts to realize he has substituted love for attachment. This attachment is actually the karmic conditions of life that are holding him here. Once he gives up this attachment for life, he will begin to think in terms of a love which is a greater force than any other in this world or on the inner planes.

If man could possibly grasp the principles of karma, which he believes to be love, then there would be a complete change in the social structure of society in the physical worlds. He would then know that instead of having to pay off everything as a debt to the Lords of Karma, he would be able to take the way of Light and Sound through the ECK. He would know that in order to gain true love, all he would have to do is break his karma. This can be done by giving up his attachment to the things of the material worlds.

Man believes that peace comes through this lesser form of love. This is the great illusion of life, the works of the Kal power. Every man should know without prejudging that all life in this world pays for all it receives. There is no exception. If he does not give the highest love, without attachment, he is apt to pay for it somewhere in this world.

Every man must first seek to give love if he expects to receive it. He must give it under every circumstance—even though he is abused, mistreated, and given unnecessary hardships in this world. A demanding love is like a shadow, for it has no substance. If anyone demands love in return for what he has not given, all is lost.

The cure for evil is the unobstructed Light and Sound. Evil is but a shadow, a lesser light and sound. It is nothing but the darkness which can become light through love. No one can ever come to the MAHANTA except through the way of love.

When their good karma brings Souls into the presence of the Living ECK Master, it is because they have earned it. Their appearance may not indicate this good karma but, nevertheless, they have reached a place on the spiritual path which earns them the right. Their good karma was not utilized to bring them worldly position and wealth, but applied to secure for them something vastly more important. That is the Darshan, the meeting with the Living ECK Master. Few come with good bodies or prosperity, but with something far more important, and that is a capacity to love. This love is an inheritance that brings them to the MAHANTA. They have but one idea and know nothing else, that the Living ECK Master will take them out of the misery and depths of this world. This is all that is needed. It does not require worldly goods of any nature, nor the need to have great knowledge. It is the good fortune of anyone who finds the Living ECK Master.

The MAHANTA loves every Soul more than Soul loves Its defilements. This is truly the characteristic love of the ECK Master. If the MAHANTA did not love his chelas more than they love themselves and their defilements, there would be little hope for any of them to ever reach heaven. This is the love of the Living ECK Master which surpasses all human understanding.

This is why the individual Soul must always go through tests while on the path of ECK. All the living Masters have gone through the same tests, have resisted temptation, have shown splendid loyalty to the SUGMAD and the highest characteristics of a Master. The chela who enters into this path must always maintain such an attitude in the presence of temptation and hardships. He must never weaken nor waver in his love or his loyalty to the SUGMAD and the Living ECK Master.

He who is fortunate to gain the attitude of true love

shall have independence. Man must remain in this world as long as he has a single duty to perform, but he is not to love the world. He must not become so bound up with duties or family or worldly interests that he forgets his most important interests. He must never forget that one day he will leave friends and all possessions, and he never knows what day he shall be called upon to leave them.

Not only does he leave his own body. He can take nothing with him except his inner possessions. All material things and people belong to the passing show on earth, for they have only a temporary interest. These material possessions are not his own. They have never been, nor ever will be. They are the property of the Kal Niranjan, the king of the negative worlds, and man's attachment to them is only temporary. He must never regard them as his own, but as a loan to him from the Kal Niranjan for the day, the moment that he may both serve them and use them. When he comes to this attitude, he has reached the *vairag*.

The wise never give thought for the dead, nor for the living, in sentimental emotions. That which belongs to matter, heat and cold, pain and pleasure, and the values of beauty and ugliness, is impermanent. They come and they go, and nothing shall halt them, for these are the elements of the Kal, the negative power. The man who believes they are the core of his life shall suffer rebirth and death century after century until the day comes when he is able to cast the scales from his eyes and recognize the Living ECK Master. Then shall he see and know that the dweller of this world is vulnerable to the traps of the Kal. Only Soul is free and cannot be forever held to the world of physical matter.

When one acts while dwelling in union with the Living ECK Master and renounces attachments while remaining balanced evenly in spiritual and worldly successes and failures, then he has been liberated. This equilibrium is called Eckankar. Yet there is always compassion for one who works only for the fruits of his labor, who wishes to be rewarded for his deeds and actions in the physical life.

No man can reach God practicing any path except devotion to the SUGMAD through the MAHANTA. One must be detached from all love of material things and events, from all concern about them. The chela attains this attitude—because his love is centered above the perishable things of this world—and reaches the heavenly planes.

From the love of objects of the senses, man has desires; from his desires rises anger. From anger proceeds delusion, and from delusion come confused memories and senses. This destroys his love of God, and from all this he perishes. But when he is disciplined and places his love in the MAHANTA, then does he move among the objects of his senses free from pleasures and free from pain, but mostly free from self-indulgence.

Worldly peace can bring only the pain and unhappiness of life, for all peace is a momentary stilling of the senses which builds up a greater desire and bewilderment for the chela. He who detaches himself from the worldly peace of life shall achieve inner peace and shall be worthy of entering into the kingdom of heaven.

He shall have love for the things beyond the senses and shall hear the voice of the Lord speaking. Then shall he be devoted to life with the Word and form of the MAHANTA in his heart, and shall attain supreme peace and an eternal home in heaven.

Only when one abandons his love of life, his love of material things and his anxieties, does he then begin to know God. Until then, he shall wander about the face of the earth life after life, incarnation after incarnation, until that day when he shall meet with the Living ECK Master and see Truth as the many splendored love.

The three attributes derived from Soul's relationship with God are love, wisdom, and power. Of these three, the greatest is love. Man understands this more than he does the other attributes. Reality has but one attribute, and that is love. All love is given to Soul when It is linked with the ECK, the Audible Life Stream.

One becomes the *bhakti,* the devotee, who loves all life more than he loves himself. He discards all rites and ceremonies and seeks to follow the Living ECK Master through the force of love only. When one reaches this stage of spiritual development, he finds the Living ECK Master always in his inner vision, waiting to meet him at a point beyond the Sun Worlds and the Moon Worlds. This is the pure astral zone, where the lover of God enters a zone called the Ashta-dal-Kanwal. At this point the whole course of his life is changed.

It is the meeting with the Living ECK Master in his radiant body. This is the MAHANTA's Nuri Sarup, or Light form. It is the Living ECK Master appearing just as he does in his physical life, except now his body is more beautiful and filled with a brilliantly illuminated light. The radiant ECK Master greets the chela with much love, and from there on the two are never separated throughout the journey to still higher regions and eventually to God. This inner form of the MAHANTA is always with the chela from the moment of his initiation, but often the chela cannot see him. Yet from this moment on, the chela can see and communicate with the Living ECK Master on the inner planes as well as the outer ones.

There is no one else on earth but the MAHANTA who can and will utter the Word which liberates the chela and puts an end to his uncertainty. He is the only one who can release Soul from Its prison, in this world. Otherwise there is no escape, for Soul is overwhelmed by the separateness of Itself from the universe of God.

This new stage in the life of the chela brings about a remarkable change in him. Up to this time his success has been partial. He has had the opportunity to test the exercises of ECK and repeat his individual mantra. From this moment on he may discontinue his chanting of the mantra, for he will not need it. He is now in the presence of the MAHANTA, the living Master, whom he may view constantly. This is the Dhyana, which inspires love for the Living ECK Master and the Master's love for him.

It is well in the beginning for the chela to understand that his greatest exercise is to look steadily at the Living ECK Master's form, particularly the eyes, be it in his inner vision or simply a picture of the Master. If one does this during his contemplation period, looking steadily into the eyes, he will find himself going into the other worlds more quickly than any other method. By softly chanting the Master's name and gazing steadily into his eyes, he has the twofold essentials of the spiritual exercises, the zikar and the Dhyana.

It is at this point that a great occurrence takes place. He will contact the ECK, and Its perfect sounds will bring about changes within him. He will find himself listening to that Music of the ECK within himself with increasing attraction and love. He will never want to leave It or to miss one note of Its delightful strain. The chela who has reached this point will find that half of the preparation for his journey is done. While before he had to exert his willpower to focus the attention on the sounds of ECK, now it is difficult to withdraw the attention from It. The Living ECK Master and the ECK are attracting him, lifting him higher with each effort he makes. He does not understand this, but it is his devotion and love pulling him ever higher with each step on the spiritual ladder.

He will have the most ardent wish to go on forever looking at the eyes of the MAHANTA and listening to the sounds of the ECK. One takes for granted, before he starts on the path of ECK, that he is to become well grounded in the fundamentals of righteousness. He must practice the dharma, the Law of Life itself, in all aspects of his life. This means doing what one ought to do while an ECK chela. Without doing this, he cannot make a start in life.

There is no pranayama in the practice of seeing the MAHANTA during this Spiritual Exercise of ECK. The chela must sit in the proper position, with his mind detached from the world and fixed at the spot between the eyebrows, bringing all his attention to focus upon the singular eye. This has to be done if one is to go inside and behold the MAHANTA. He softly chants the sacred name of God, beholding the MAHANTA with a loving gaze in the radiant form. The zikar comes first, and then comes the Dhyana, the vision of the radiant form of the MAHANTA. Following this comes bhajan, the spiritual exercise of listening to the Music of the ECK. No path to God has this form of exercise, mainly because none know the ECK Dhun, the Sound. They miss the most vital part of the realization of the SUGMAD in their lives.

This leads the seeker of God to the first experiences of Samadhi, to the actual going inside and stepping out onto the Astral Planes where he meets with the MAHANTA in the Nuri Sarup. Higher than Samadhi is the Nirvikalpa, in which the seeker of God cannot distinguish himself from the ECK Itself.

This is gained when the chela enters the Fifth Plane (the Soul region) with the MAHANTA. It is here he beholds himself as pure Soul after leaving behind his material sheaths. Few, if any, can attain this state without traveling the path of ECK in the company of the MAHANTA. No one can get his release from the net of karma without the Living ECK Master.

It is love that brings the chela to this spiritual stage in the heavenly worlds. It is love that makes civilization on this Earth Plane, and that love is the essence of pure Spirit. But the SUGMAD can never reveal Itself to anyone with a contaminated mind. The consciousness must be somewhat pure and ready for the ECK force to enter into it. Love makes this possible, and unless this quality is ingrained in man, he must struggle until his consciousness becomes ready to accept it.

Adjustments to the discipline that the MAHANTA suggests is the better way for the chela. It must be taken seriously and rigidly followed. This is what is known as the narrow way. One does not fit himself into this narrow way, but he adjusts himself accordingly. He does the best he can without upsetting or disturbing his own way of life. Until he does this, time is wasted in trying to find himself and what the MAHANTA is willing to do for him to assist him spiritually in this world.

Yet it is love, and this quality alone, which will gain him greater favor with God and the Living ECK Master. Love and desire to serve make for greater spiritual unfoldment on the path to the SUGMAD.

8

The Supreme Attainment of the Chela

The human body of the chela is Kal, the negative force. The body of the Living ECK Master is also Kal. Yet there is a difference between the two. The body of the MAHANTA is that of the ECK, the conscious creation. The body of the chela is that of his subconscious drives and desires from his past incarnations.

Both are made out of the elements of the Kal, which is maya. Each is then maya, but the Living ECK Master is conscious of it, and the chela is not. The MAHANTA is the master of Kal-maya, and the chela is its slave. The difference is the knowledge which is sacred and divine and hidden from the sight of man.

Until the chela becomes an initiate in the works of ECK, he is unable to know and understand he is the slave of the Kal Niranjan. It is then he begins to enter into the ECK, which is all-embracing and omnipresent, whether he is conscious of it or not. But when the chela raises the ECK from his subconscious potential state into full consciousness by opening the Spiritual Eye to Its Light, then only can Its nature become an active force in him and free him from the deathly isolation of the Kal.

This is synonymous with the transformation of the mind and body into the state of Nirvikalpa, the highest state of enlightenment, known as God-Realization.

Only in the state of Nirvikalpa can we realize the ECK as the body of the SUGMAD, that which we know as the ECK Itself. It is in this state that the chela can see the MAHANTA as the personification of Truth. This is the state of suchness, the ultimate and unconditioned nature of all things of life.

One realizes this state by converting it into the ever-present consciousness of the human state. Thus, he who is in this state finds himself in an all-consuming focus of experience in which the elements of the little self are purified and integrated in the universal Self.

The law which all seek to know is the great principle of life. Its simplicity is amazing, for it is summed up in this statement: Soul exists because God loves It. In other words, all life exists because God so wills it. This is the very foundation of life, the whole of the philosophy of Eckankar. There is nothing more and nothing less. All life is built upon this basic principle of God. If Soul did not exist, there would be no life anywhere on earth or on any of the planets, nor on the many planes throughout the universe of God.

If the chela could only grasp this very simple principle of life, he would have the entire philosophy of Eckankar in his hand. But so few can, because they cannot grasp the simplicity of it. They want to make it complex. This is why many fail in their search for the realization of the Almighty. Only when the transfiguration of body and mind has taken place does one enter into the understanding of the suchness of God and the very heart of Its being.

One must protect himself not only from without but

from within, and often from the most natural impulses. He must watch out, for the Kal Niranjan will attack him from the Astral, Causal, and Mental Planes as well as the Physical Plane. The attack that comes from these inner planes will be more subtle than he can imagine.

When he is first in harmony with the illuminated force, It will increase like a violinist going up the E-string. He will believe that the Sound cannot go any higher and the Light will have to stop at what is considered the last point of its brilliancy. But the Sound will rise higher and higher, and God will bring the fortunate one from note to note like a deaf child being taught to hear or a blind child being taught to see.

Burning off of karma is the state of rechemicalization. It is something man must go through while living on this earth. Man should be able to do this under the Living ECK Master. If he is under any other guide here on earth, this is not likely to happen. He will be receiving more bad karma than good and will be overbalanced on the negative side. He needs to be balanced only in the middle way, not on either side. Only when he can walk the middle path of ECK can he leave the Wheel of the Eighty-Four and find the gates of heaven.

The MAHANTA is always engaged in a dialogue with people, but his decisions and influence are constantly in a struggle with the opinions of man, which were formed by traditions and orthodox religious thoughts. Many men develop ideas on the rights and wrongs, the supposed motivations, the possibilities and impossibilities of each religious situation. Some of their ideas are well-based, some uninformed, some absurd.

The ECK which can be perceived by those who are not chelas is only a shadow of It. It takes on a different aspect according to the different viewpoints of the many planes of existence. Their crude perception of It does not include any concepts of Its possibilities for happiness and enjoyment. They see only glimpses of It in the works of the ECK around them.

Feeding the Kal force into the thought stream of this earth world builds an invisible body, a thought form, which is acceptable to all those who are susceptible. But those who allow the ECK to be fed into themselves shall do just the opposite, building an invisible force of love which shall protect, give life, and lift all they meet, see, or know into higher awareness.

God never reveals Itself to one who has an impure mind. Only when the stress of life has brought man to the verge of exhaustion—when the bruised body, the humiliated mind, or the weary self cries out for the Master—will there come into his life the true Light. It is away from the applause of the crowd, the stage of life, and the wild cries of adoration that man finds himself confronted with the possibility of God. It is only in silence that he practices the Spiritual Exercises of ECK and finds the heavenly world. This is the underlying and absolute law, the essential message of the teachings of Eckankar. No one can find it in any other way.

It comes through the Living ECK Master, and not until man comes to that stage of life when he must give up everything will he find all things necessary to his spiritual being.

Man is impressed by the remarks of worldly religionists that all truth is one and reality is the same for every man. This is not truth. Truth is a variation of experiences, and there cannot be any standard measure made of it. Those eternal truths which man speaks about so vainly and with such pompous pride are hardly more than mouthing words. He cannot prove what he says, nor can he debate them except from an intellectual viewpoint. Such statements are not truth. Anyone who experiences

Truth knows it for what it is and has little to say about it. There are no words nor feelings which can express experience in the esoteric worlds.

The chela must seek love and wisdom before he attempts to have any experiences in the life beyond. He knows that if he surrenders himself to the greater cause of life, he will gain these attributes of God. But he also knows that if anything can save him from physical death—the transition of life from the matter world into the spiritual world—it is the Living ECK Master.

The Living ECK Master is always seeking the spiritually starved people of this world. He brings them more than bread. He feeds that spirit within them which is always urging them toward God. He is the ECK, the father, mother, and all things to all people. Where one may find him a friend, another will find him the Living ECK Master. Where one finds love in him, another will find wisdom, and others may find hardly anything else but severe discipline. Each views the MAHANTA from his own limited consciousness. He is all things to all people. Some will love him intensely, while others may dislike him with equal intensity. But no one will ignore him. He will be the target for attacks from all directions with every possible means that the Kal can invent, using the human consciousness.

Only the way beyond thought remains, the way of extended consciousness through Soul Travel. This way, or path, reaches far beyond the frontiers of primal thought into the realms of esoteric experience through the inner vision and spiritual sound of the ECK.

The language of words is replaced by the language of feeling, and the language of feeling is replaced by that of visual symbols. Then the language of visual symbols is replaced by that of sound symbols, in which the vibrations of Light and Sound are combined on a scale of experience values until they become mentally exchangeable.

Should Soul cease to spiritually unfold, It will, after the death of the body, go into the seven worlds of Avernus, the dark realm of the Astral Plane where many evil Souls must spend time. There is no purely evil man, nor is there a purely good man. However, many who border on the edge of evil, or who are tainted with some evil, must spend time in this dark world. Instead of extending himself into the higher worlds, he who has gained too much of the negative karma and overbalanced himself in this way must spend time in this vast world and later reincarnate into life again for the opportunity of regaining what has been lost in his spiritual unfoldment.

Once he has established himself and started working toward the good of existence, he will no longer spend time in these lower Astral Planes. After he has met the Living ECK Master and established himself upon the path of Eckankar, he will never have to reincarnate on this plane nor in any of the underworld planes. He will find himself ready for the heavenly worlds and will not return to the physical region again. He is assured of this by initiation into Eckankar.

Before one studies Eckankar the mountains are mountains, and the oceans are oceans to him. However, if he should have an insight into ECK through the guidance of the Living ECK Master, then the mountains are no longer mountains, and the oceans are no longer oceans. Later, when he has reached that state of God-Realization, he will find the mountains are again mountains, and the oceans are oceans. This, however, is a different state of consciousness, for now he recognizes them for what they are, nothing more. He puts no significance upon either the mountains nor the oceans, for they are now a part of the reality of the matter worlds.

Where there is an understanding of spiritual love, there is neither concern with what life might be nor care for the worldly life. Where there is an understanding of ECK, there is no concern for searching for divine knowledge. Men believe the body can be preserved with material foods alone. There are cases where the body is preserved but life does not exist, and yet man believes that he is alive. He is not alive until he is filled with the ECK. He is not living, nor does he have survival after the translation from the physical body, until he has been fed the food of the ECK by the MAHANTA.

The wise man is one who stores up the ECK within himself and at the same time distributes the spiritual love which is within himself. He is not one who gives his compassion to a few but to all, whether or not many understand this. He is able to live among the wretched, the thieves, the unhappy, robbers and fools, for he accepts life for whatever it is and gives love to all. He is the wise one who is able to give all he has to his fellow man. He finds love for those who greedily accept what he gives, and they shall be blessed a thousand times for his love.

Whosoever is beaten, whipped, scorned, mistreated, and derided while performing any of the works of ECK shall be blessed a thousand times over by the SUGMAD. He shall be freed of his karma and taken into the heavenly worlds where peace and joy shall be his eternally.

Whosoever shall suffer at the hands of the unbelievers while performing any works of the ECK, or in the giving of himself with love in the name of the Living ECK Master, shall be freed from the Wheel of Life and shall have no more worldly karma. He shall enter into the worlds of ECK (true spiritual worlds) and there live in peace, joy, and service as a Coworker with the SUGMAD.

Blessed is he who shall give love in the name of the

MAHANTA to any man or entity who does an injustice to him, regardless of whatever plane he may be dwelling upon at the time of the injustice. Whatever love the ECKist gives to another in the name of the MAHANTA, he shall in turn receive love a thousandfold over.

Whosoever passes from his own physical body shall have heavenly awards if he whispers at the time of his passing the name of the MAHANTA. He shall instantly be gathered up into the arms of the MAHANTA and taken into the worlds of spiritual splendor. He shall never have to return to this universe of physical matter again. It matters little whether his length of time on the path of ECK has been two minutes or two hundred years; if he remembers the name of the MAHANTA at the translation from his earthly life into the other worlds, he shall be liberated and immediately initiated into the ECK.

Should he not be conscious at the time of his death, whoever is with him can perform the rites by whispering the name of the MAHANTA, which impresses it upon the inner self and reaches the true being of the departing one. The same may be done for those who, upon the last conscious moment of their earthly lives, accept the MAHANTA as their spiritual guide just before translation into the other worlds.

Many are called to the path of ECK, but few are ever chosen to become the true initiates of the nine worlds, and fewer still ever become eleventh-world initiates. The highway into the kingdom of heaven is narrow, and the way is strewn with the spiritual corpses of those who have failed. Only those who give up all for the love of the MAHANTA can ever reach the gates of paradise. This is not the heaven of the orthodox religionists, but the true world of the initiates who have earned their place in it.

He who listens to the Living ECK Master and obeys him will have his love and will be freed of his worldly karma. He will enter into the spiritual worlds a free Soul. If the living Master performs a miracle of healing, of bringing justice, or giving one something of a material nature, be not surprised, for it is his nature to do such things when necessary. He will not perform miracles with fanfare, trumpets, or great pronouncements, but in silence and secrecy. He is the only one who can do such things. All others are false masters, false prophets, and false when they try to give and they have no means to give. No one but the Living ECK Master is the divine channel for these gifts of God.

Seek no favors from the MAHANTA, for he gives when he sees that gifts should be bestowed upon those who are in need. The seeker who is searching for some gift seldom has earned or needs it.

He who seeks to keep his life shall never have it. But whosoever loses his life in the love of the MAHANTA shall have it in eternity. And whosoever shall give of his material life to the ECK shall have it thricefold returned unto him in spiritual blessings. No man with riches shall enter into the Kingdom of God, for he shall leave them on earth with his temple of flesh, and both shall rot away into oblivion.

The chela must learn that in order to travel at will in the other worlds, he must first learn to break his covenant with the material worlds that are so solidly real to him. It is not a mark of power for one to travel in the inner worlds, but it is concerned with consciousness. This alone makes it possible for the chela to move at will on all higher planes of life.

There are an infinite number of planes within the universe of God. They blend and shift from one state to another. The vibrations are frequencies of which the ordinary man is not aware at any time. He believes he is a body to which breath gives life with such an impact that it creates the impression he is a physical body only. This is an illusion established by the Kal force which makes him human and limited.

The chela lives in a world of many mansions, but he can learn to live on any plane. As he learns to break his agreement with this world, freedom will begin to come into his life. In time, he learns to accept the liberation which the Living ECK Master brings to him. He comes to control himself and not be controlled by matter or illusions. Anyone who is afraid of the Kal Niranjan will never be able to control himself. He does not try to control or manipulate matter, for this is useless. It scatters and disperses his energies to do anything outside of trying to control himself.

Those who speak of their Soul, or finding their Soul, are only working in the direction of the emotional (astral) nature. They do not mean Soul Itself but the emotional self, which is so often mistaken for Soul.

Hence, the Living ECK Master is the only one who truly knows what Soul is. He has taught since the beginning of time that one should never speak of Soul as "my Soul" or "his Soul." This is the negative connotation put upon It. He is the only one who can release Soul from these lower Astral Planes, the only one who can take Soul across the borders of death and bypass the Angel of Death.

Those who have borne their karma and do not look upon their own affliction with floods of unhappiness will be blessed by the MAHANTA. Nothing is given, and nothing is taken away. The MAHANTA does not adjust the karma needed by the chela to develop spiritual responsibility. As the chela unfolds along the path of ECK, he reaches the higher spiritual worlds where the MAHANTA is ready to give of the divine gifts and take away what is not of any further use to the seeker of God. Thus one finds the illumination of the consciousness only through Soul Travel.

The matter world is but an extension of consciousness with a crust of solidity that must be broken. All the illusions of the Kal are but a part of material creation. This is fluid and bends to the creativeness of Soul. Those who retreat from life and do nothing are as bound in matter as are those who believe in the concept of a solid universe. Body and spirit are not separated from life but are a part of it as much as Soul. The nature of this world is change and impermanence.

It has been stated that the Living ECK Master can release Souls from the lower Astral Planes. This is also true of those who have reached the Ninth Plane of God under the Living ECK Master. These initiates of the Ninth Circle are privileged to name the Souls they want released, making it possible to unchain a dependent relative or anyone with whom they have close love ties.

Those who seek God shall never have the Light nor the Word. But he who does not seek God shall have Its Voice which will guide him into the heavenly kingdom. The seeker does not like nor does he dislike, for there is only a hairbreadth of difference between the spiritual kingdoms and those of the psychic regions.

A chela who wants Truth can never be for or against anything, for the grappling between acceptance and rejection is the failing of the ECK within one's consciousness and the delight of the Kal. One does not take and reject, nor does he drive away pain by pretending it is not there. Pain will vanish, as all other problems will, by seeking serenity in the heavenly state. Whoever stops all movement in order to find rest only finds himself restless, and if he lingers over any extreme, then he is both restless and lost.

In order to understand the Living ECK Master, stop talking, stop thinking, stop analyzing him and his worldly actions, and then you will understand all things. If the chela will look for the Light and Sound within the Living ECK Master, all things will be revealed to him.

The MAHANTA is different from the outer form which the chela can see and talk with at all times. As the inner self, or the Inner Master, he is able to be in all places at the same time. He is the universal Spirit which is in all life and which manifests to every chela in the specific form that appears as the physical body of the Living ECK Master.

The chela has security when he is accepted by the Living ECK Master. He has gained liberation, salvation, and entered into the kingdom of heaven whether he is aware of it or not in his outer senses. He is now able to survive death. This victory over death is the greatest triumph of Soul. It is his privilege to have this knowledge and the grace of God bestowed upon him while living in this physical universe.

Those who seek God shall never have the Light or the Word, for It can be gained only through the Living ECK Master. Those who look not for God shall have Its Voice, which shall guide them to the Living ECK Master, who will lift them into the heavenly kingdom.

Every chela who wants to enter into the true realization of ECK truths shall and must become the extreme devotee of the SUGMAD. He must have the dominating faith that to serve the cause of ECK is the only purpose of his life. Only then will he succeed in becoming the ECKshar.

There is little need to seek truth; just stop having views. Do not adopt or reject, nor examine truth or pursue it. When the chela accepts the Living ECK Master for whatever he is, it is found there is no separation; no acceptance; no giving up of anything, yet the surrendering of all he has within himself. Soul makes no distinction in any part of life. Therefore, there is no preference or attachment, thought nor disagreement, and, of course, no separation between the MAHANTA and the chela.

Only the SUGMAD supports the universes. Those within the lower worlds are made up of the perishable, and those of the upper worlds are made up of the imperishable, the manifest and the unmanifest. Soul, forgetful of the Lord and of the fact that Its very existence depends upon the Divine Being, attaches Itself to pleasure and thereby is bound to the lower worlds. When It comes to the SUGMAD via the Living ECK Master, It is freed from Its fetters.

When the chela asks, From whence do we come? Why do we live? Where shall we find peace, happiness, and rest in the end? What has command over my life to give me happiness or misery? then the law of God states that Soul has existence because God wills it. Thus, God loves all life so dearly that It allows Soul to exist. If It did not love life, there would be no life-forms in this universe, and all would be barren. Time, space, law, chance, matter, primitive energy, and intelligence are only the effects of God's love for life and only exist to serve Soul in Its journey to find liberation and freedom.

The Soul is not the cause for the law which brings happiness or misery. Not being free, neither does It act as the prime cause that brings about the opposite. As the free Self It has the opportunity to establish Itself as the prime mover for bringing about happiness and letting life be what it should be. It does not establish life but exists because life itself supports Soul as the prime consideration of God's love for every individual Soul within the universe.

The vast universe of the lower worlds is but a wheel. All beings and creatures existing within this universe are subject to birth, death, and rebirth. The one God, the

SUGMAD, exists only. All else is a part of Its beingness. It alone presides over all. It dwells as the self-conscious power in all beings and creatures. Its universe of the lower planes revolves like a gigantic wheel, and round and round go all beings and creatures until each meets with the MAHANTA and finds the straight and narrow path of ECK.

As long as Soul believes It is separated from the ECK, It revolves upon the wheel in bondage to the laws of the Kal Niranjan, which are birth, death, and rebirth. But when, through the grace of the MAHANTA, It again realizes Its identity with him, It revolves no longer upon the wheel. It has found immortality.

Whosoever realizes himself as pure Soul knows that only by transcending the worlds of cause and effect through the Spiritual Exercises of ECK is one liberated. He learns that Soul is imperishable, that all within the lower planes is but the shadow of the true substance of the SUGMAD. Only the SUGMAD is the one Reality behind ALL. Only Its body, the ECK, is what communicates to all Its creatures. Only the MAHANTA is the instrument of this communication, this Reality which flows out of the SUGMAD to all Its beings, creatures, and worlds.

Thus, it is known that the MAHANTA is the ECK in his spiritual body. He is the paradox of the worlds of God, for while serving in the Physical body in the lower worlds upon the material planes, he is also serving in the spiritual worlds in the Spirit body. As the ECK, the Spirit of the SUGMAD, he is able to be the whole and thus with all who recognize him as the Master. This is true, therefore, mainly of his own chelas. He manifests to his own as they can accept him.

As the ECK, the MAHANTA becomes the all-pervading and omnipresent, transcending time and space, protecting those who are his beloved chelas and giving life to all that exists. He is the ECK, superior to all. Alone he stands; changeless, self-luminous, and living within the world, yet not living in it. He is the Master, the ruler of the whole world, animate and inanimate.

Man's consciousness of Truth is the substance of his demonstration. To change his level of consciousness is the ECK chela's purpose under the MAHANTA's guidance. Unless this is done, there is little need for the chela to stay on the path of Light and Sound. It is not the gaining of knowledge, but the understanding of Truth. Those who seek knowledge will learn that this is not the ultimate goal of the ECK chela.

Consciousness is the ECK, but not God Itself. The moment the chela has a consciousness of himself as the ECK, he has established himself in the Word, the Voice of God. This is the realization of Soul that occurs on the Fifth Plane. This leads into God-Realization, the ultimate goal of all chelas who follow the path of ECK.

Every Soul is the spiritual spark of God invested in a physical body. The body does not have to die for Soul to reach the spiritual universe during the time that It resides upon earth. Man does not have to become anything other than what he is in order to have divine guidance, divine protection, divine wisdom, and divine understanding through the Living ECK Master. He must recognize only that God is and that he himself, as Soul, also is.

Soul is never anything else but this. It is always in eternity. It is always in the present NOW. It is always in the heavenly state of God. These are the three principles of Eckankar which It must come to understand and know well. Out of these principles springs the doctrine and philosophy of ECK. There is nothing more to say, and there is nothing less to say.

By the realization of these three principles, the chela becomes a transparency for the divine impulse. He comes into a greater awareness of the divine plan in this world and his part in it. He now rests in the arms of the MAHANTA, the Inner ECK Master, and relies upon him to give him this divine guidance.

As he rises higher in this spiritual realization, the great discovery of life is found. The majestic law of God upon which the three principles of ECK rest is "Soul exists because the SUGMAD wills it."

God loves all life so dearly that It grants all Souls existence. It gives life to all beings, entities, and forms. Without God's love there would be nothing—a void and a blank space in all worlds. Therefore, when the chela begins to understand this and know Truth, he has entered into the true worlds of God above the Atma Lok, the Soul Plane.

The SUGMAD gives of Itself, but It also seeks that every Soul take up the path of ECK and find Its way back into the heavenly realm. But Soul must follow the narrow way as the SUGMAD wills, and not as It desires.

9
Visions of the SUGMAD

Within the visions of the SUGMAD are the followers of Eckankar who, in some way or other, betray the Living ECK Master.

Many, in their finite consciousness, fail to recognize the Master's true nature and thus cannot understand nor control themselves in allowing their tongues and deeds to react to the MAHANTA and his words. Being in the flesh, they look upon him as man; but in Spirit, as the Living ECK Master, he knows all that goes on within each of the ECK chelas, although he never says anything. He knows how each will end his life upon this earth; whether he will stray from the path or be critical, upset, and unhappy with the Master; and whether he will betray the Master during his sojourn as an ECK chela.

The Living ECK Master knows everything about the chela, as well as his reactions to the tests and trials given him. The Master is never surprised when a chela leaves, giving up in a quandary and unhappy because the MAHANTA has not given him the desires of his heart. He knows the suffering each chela may have during these periods when separated from the Living ECK Master.

The MAHANTA is not concerned with what either the chela or the public thinks about him. He expects misunderstandings to arise or the masses to attack him, and he knows that some chelas, regardless of how much love is poured upon them, will betray him because of their lack of self-honesty. Those who quarrel with the principles of ECK, or the knowledge of who and what the Living Master is to this world, had best examine themselves.

When one tries to correct the Master's works by suggestion or argument, he should take interest in what he is doing rather than accept these extremes. Often the Living ECK Master establishes certain forms of speech or written phrases which baffle the chela completely. But if the chela is open to what is being said, there is nothing which is perplexing. These are the tests of the ECK Master to see what the chela will take. If the chela accepts it for what it is, then the test is passed. It does not matter how the word is given, as long as it is given out to the chelas.

The intellectual purist will never be able to advance on the path of Eckankar. He is so busy trying to find mistakes and errors in the sacred writings of ECK, as well as others, that he overlooks what is necessary for his spiritual growth and defeats himself.

There are many ECK chelas who will complain and work up unhappy attitudes to compensate their egos. What they do not understand is that this is a destructive attitude and they are defeating themselves. The MAHANTA will never speak out to them to correct this attitude but will quietly and without notice pull away from them. There is no way in which they can pull the MAHANTA down to their level of consciousness. This is the very thing they wish to do.

It is self-defeating to deride the works of Eckankar,

to try to defy the spiritual influence of the ECK or look upon the SUGMAD and the Living ECK Master negatively, or with the eyes of Kal. The ECK Master has always been a figure of controversy in the materialistic world and will always be, for he is a spiritual giant in the flesh. He could bring peace and happiness to this world, but it is not his purpose. The races and people of the earth are willing agents of the Kal power. They perform his duties to keep any spiritual influence out of this materialistic world, including that of the Living ECK Master if at all possible.

The mission of every Living ECK Master is to find those who have a deep desire to prepare for returning to their true spiritual home, the Ocean of Love and Mercy, where each will become a Coworker with God; to prepare as many as possible during their earthly lifetime to become channels, or instruments, for the divine power. This will give them the opportunity to be able to assist the Living ECK Master in his work and to lift others in spirit, to help him prepare them for their ascent into the Ocean of Love and Mercy.

Since it is the mind which creates the human body and controls it, it follows that the more it reflects and is filled with the body of the ECK, the more it will be able to influence and transform the physical body. This transformation brings about perfection in greater abundance in daily living. Not the abundance of materialistic life, but in the fulfillment of Spirit. It gives perfection in Spirit and in love for the chela who is able to reflect this to all with whom he comes in contact.

When the chela reaches this vastly important state of transformation, he is able to see the illusory body (often called the phantom body, a concept of the physical body which is as misleading as the maya-illusion belief). Many define this world as maya, but the ECK chela should not think that the world is deprived of all reality—only that it is not what it appears to us. Its reality is only relative. It represents a reality of a lesser degree which, when compared with the highest reality, the Ocean of Love and Mercy, has no more existence than the objects of a dream or a cloud formation. Only the ECK Masters, the perfectly enlightened ones, have access to these higher worlds to make such comparisons.

Bodies are the expressions of an inherent law whose reality is undeniable, even though they are products of the Universal Mind Power, known as the Kal force. Though the body and mind are products of these worlds, and the individual personality is both mind-made and illusory, it does not mean they are unreal. The mind that creates them has made them real in this world, for they are necessary for Soul to use as an instrument while here.

The body and personality do not disappear the moment we become aware of either as products of the mind, nor when we become tired of either. As soon as these products of the mind take material shape, they must obey the laws of matter, energy, space, and time. No Master, regardless of his degree of spiritual unfoldment, can arbitrarily change or annihilate the material properties and functions of the body. He can only transform them step-by-step, by controlling them in their initial individual states until he has reached a certain level of spiritual perfection.

The Living ECK Master reaches this state in time to take over his position as the spiritual emissary of his times. He is not restrained to any particular place. The ECK Masters who have received the Rod of ECK Power only relate to those in this world who will listen to the true path and to those who come seeking true knowledge.

The ECK Masters are not linked with any orthodox religious cause or dress. They are free personalities, for they are neither a party to one nor a foe to the other. They only impart knowledge of the way to reach God. Those who apply themselves to the path of Eckankar will succeed, and those who keep themselves aloof and far away from ECK will not succeed to the higher levels of the spiritual worlds.

The mission of true spirituality can only be carried on successfully by the Living ECK Master. It cannot be entrusted to those who have not reached the worlds above the Atma Lok. Whosoever attempts to reach God can only go through the MAHANTA, and not through those who are seeking the possession of the world. Be not deceived by such people. Do the Spiritual Exercises of ECK, and meet the MAHANTA in the other worlds.

To be with the MAHANTA inwardly and enjoy his talk, his blessings—to see the ECK power working amid the mortal coil—is an ultimate experience. The Living ECK Master's connection with his chelas is eternal, unshakable, and loving. He desires to see all chelas rise to spiritual heights and continually pours his love, protection, and grace upon them, making them more receptive to the ECK.

The understanding of survival in the higher spiritual states of existence is linked with certain esoteric experiences, which are so basic in nature they can neither be explained nor described. They are so subtle there is nothing to which they can be compared, nothing to which thought or imagination can cling. Yet such experiences are more real than anything in this physical world. More real than anything that the senses of the human consciousness can experience, touch, taste, hear, or smell. This is because they are concerned with that which precedes and includes all other sensations, and mainly because reason, logic, and intellect cannot be identified with any of them.

The ECK follower knows that it is only by the means

of symbols that such experiences may be somewhat expressed to the world. These symbols can only be hinted at and are not invented. They are spontaneous expressions which break through the deepest regions of the inner self and are brought forth outwardly.

The forms of divine life in the universe break forth from the seer as vision, from the mystic as Light, and in the ECK Initiates up to the Fourth Circle as Sound. But the Mahdis, the Initiates of the Fifth Circle, have vision, Light, and Sound. The higher each goes on the planes of the worlds of true Spirit, the greater the vision, Light, and Sound become.

Therefore, the chela now understands that sounds coming from the mouth of the Living ECK Master are not ordinary words but the true Word, the mantra, the ability to create an image in its pure essence. All he says becomes knowledge, the truth of being which is beyond right and wrong; it is real being beyond thinking and reflecting. It is the ECK force speaking through the Living ECK Master. It is beyond true contemplation, as every Mahdis, the Initiate of the Fifth Circle, will come to know. It is the simultaneous awareness of the knower and the known.

A personal mantra, the secret word which fits each initiate, is an instrument for linking up with the ECK. With its sound, it brings forth its content into a state of immediate reality. The Word is the ECK power, not merely speech. The mind can neither evade nor contradict it and will often wrestle to keep from accepting it. But whatever the Word expresses, by its very sound it exists—and will come to pass in each of those who use it. The Word is action, a deed immediately calling forth reality. It is not merely a sound, but an action of the ECK in motion upon whatever plane the initiate is performing.

The secret of the hidden power of the ECK—sound or

vibration—forms the key to the riddle of the universe and creativeness. It reveals the nature of God and the phenomena of life understood by the ECK Masters throughout the ages. The very sounds of the vibrating form a universal harmony in each element throughout the whole world.

The knowledge of the creative Word lives deeply within the heart of every ECK Initiate. Each learns this early in his study of the spiritual works of Eckankar, for It is the very heart of all life. He who has the true knowledge knows that in the lower worlds there exist both creative sounds and destructive sounds, and that he who can produce both can, at will, create or destroy. But only the Living ECK Master has this power, for it is given to him who will sustain life for all.

The Holy ECK, or the Word, must be practiced in silence. Only those who have received the Word in initiation can be given the blessings of the SUGMAD through the MAHANTA. The practice of the personal secret word of each initiate shall be done vocally when alone or silently while in public. He shall practice not only the kamit, the Law of Silence, with his secret word but shall practice the silence in his own affairs with ECK and whatever is given him in the secret teachings.

Whatever the MAHANTA, the Inner Master, gives him in secret through the channels of the inward self, he shall keep secret and not speak of to anyone else. He shall practice this law of silence with others who are not to be told any of the deep secrets of ECK. He will not speak about the MAHANTA and their inner relationships, nor of his affairs in the works of Eckankar. Those who do are violating the very heart of the works and shall have to pay in some manner or other.

One may discuss the outer works of ECK with those who are interested and seeking spiritual security. He may discuss the outer works for those who want to learn more in order to take up ECK as a chela and follow the pure path into the heavenly world. However, one shall never give openly the esoteric or the secret works of ECK, especially those who have become initiates in Eckankar.

Every chela will, at some time or other, be confronted with the riddle of faith. Each will be attacked by the Kal in some manner or other because of his relationship with the ECK. This faith will be tested by the pseudomasters and the false prophets. Many will speak to the chelas in the name of another religion, as a master, or what they call the true faith. Some will speak in the name of the MAHANTA and ECK Master. But they speak with false tongues, for none but the Living ECK Master has the authority to speak in the name of the SUGMAD.

Anyone, from a king to a barber, who wishes to listen to the teachings of ECK from the MAHANTA, follow him in his missionary wanderings, or join the ECK Satsang (the formal fellowship of ECK disciples) is free to do so. But in all, the original transgression in ECK is ignorance. This is not merely an absence of knowledge, but the wrongness of attitude. The approach of the ECKist to God is through the MAHANTA, with the attitude of separation of Soul free from the lower selves.

Soul must be freed of all skandhas. These are ideas, wishes, dreams, and consciousness of the lower self which creates attachments to the physical realm. When Soul approaches God with only love to give, then It is accepted into the heavenly realm. All the riches and wealth of the earth and its companion planets cannot get a single Soul into the heavenly worlds. The way is love, nothing else. This is the only path an ECKist travels.

Love comes through the practice of the kamit which is the Law of Silence. No one can enter into the state of love until he knows loyalty, devotion, and love for the

ECK. Until he surrenders to the MAHANTA, giving up everything to gain love, his life shall be narrow and selfish. His loyalty, faith, and devotion are his survival factors, both in the world of human consciousness and the worlds of the psychic senses. No physical survival factors are concerned when the body is destroyed through accident, bullets, or disease. But much can be accomplished in saving the body and repairing it if disease or war brings injury to it, and it can safely pass from the cradle to death without any harm or injury. Yet many men are taken away due to such factors as stupidity, mental instability, and lack of faith, devotion, and loyalty to the ECK.

The initiates, mainly of the Fifth Circle, do not suffer from insanity, instability, neurosis, or worry. They can stand up under the sufferings which the Kal force tries to inflict upon them. Resistance to disease, accidents, and other poor physical survival factors are common to these spiritual ECK Initiates. The higher one goes in the initiations, the greater become his survival factors, both in the psychic and the spiritual worlds.

It is quite wrong to think there is no personal self, that is, a human consciousness. When one rises above the human consciousness and its states of mind passions, then It dwells in the spiritual states. But Soul is never without having to live within the human consciousness as long as It has a physical body and must dwell in this world. This means that survival is in the Soul state and not in the human consciousness.

The chela does not annihilate the human self but takes it as part of the whole being until it is eliminated by physical death. He must never leave the physical body while the body is still alive and try to stay in the other worlds permanently. He must learn to live in the two worlds at the same time, knowing that the death wish is only in the human consciousness and never in the spiritual self.

The death wish is instilled in the human consciousness. It is there when one feels that nothing gives happiness and, therefore, it is impossible to ever meet with any spiritual success. Those living in the human consciousness will seek happiness through orthodox means which the old religions and philosophies of the world teach. Neither are of any value to the chela who wants to get into the heavenly kingdom.

Orthodox religions represent the human and astral states of consciousness, while worldly philosophies are concerned only with the intellectual or the Mental Plane. All these are only of the psychic world and give only the teachings of these planes which are under the Kal Niranjan. It is his desire that all who live in the human body have the wish of self-destruction implanted within them. This keeps Soul trapped in the lower worlds under his rule. It is his duty to see that all Souls are kept here. Therefore he must resist the ECK from taking them out of his domain.

It is also his duty to see that man is filled with woes and miseries. It is part of his plan to see to it that as many as possible in the human state of consciousness hinder the work of the Living ECK Master and all those who follow him in the lower worlds. This is the way the Kal works, although he has little success when he attempts to interfere with the Living ECK Master and his mission.

The Kal encourages suicides, self-destruction, unhappiness, apathy, discontent, disruption of communities, and complaints. He encourages lust, anger, greed, attachment to material things, vanity, abnormal sex activity, craving for drugs, alcohol, tobacco, gluttony, gossip, obscene literature, useless card games, laziness, thinking ill of others, taking offense easily, criticizing the actions of others, lecturing on mistakes of others, chronic fault-finding, scolding, nagging or blaming others for things that go wrong, vile abuse, cursing others, fighting, quarreling, or trying to inflict injury on others.

He also encourages miserliness, hypocrisy, perjury, misrepresentation, robbery, bribery, trickery, bigotry, self-assertion, a show of wealth and power, gaudiness in dress, and the exhibition of a domineering attitude. He dearly loves titles, honors, degrees, procrastination, worry and anxieties, divorce, controlling others, mob actions, deception, ridicule, resentment, murder, tyranny, boasting, and exaggeration. The Kal assumes great intellectual knowledge, long and unnecessary periods of meditation, shabby beards and hair, and untidy dress.

These are among the many things which the Kal power will try to encourage in any chela. It will even try to bring about a break between the chela and the MAHANTA. It will create all sorts of doubt in the chela's mind as to what the MAHANTA is doing and why it is being done. It will bring about an estrangement between the ECK Master and the chela. But at no time will the Living ECK Master ever be disturbed at such foolishness, for he can see through the illusions which the Kal establishes for anyone who falls into such traps.

The chela who allows himself to be persuaded by the Kal power is only adding to his karma. He should not let himself fall into slovenliness of appearance or mind. This adds to the karma of whoever does it. He should know that any of these patterns of physical, psychic, and other lower-plane habits are only karmic in nature and often considered overt acts against others.

Those who fail to give dignity and respect to their neighbors, elders, and loved ones will have to suffer the consequences. Those who fail to love and try to understand the MAHANTA are placed in a long series of incarnations until they come to this state in some future life.

All the works of ECK, therefore, are based upon three tenets. First, the works of ECK form a nucleus for the universality of life through the spiritual hierarchy of the ECK Masters. Second, they promote an opportunity for all those who desire to earn their way past all karmic burdens and enter into heaven for eternity on passing from this lifetime through death. Third, they will prove to all persons that survival throughout eternity is possible through experiences under the guidance of the Living ECK Master, here and now.

Therefore, one has to think about life as being just It. There are no disclosures given in what are called the right views or understanding: right purpose or aspiration, right speech, right conduct, right vocation, right effort, such as the Buddhists give. What the chela is seeking is simply one thing. This is the Truth, and once this happens he will find that nothing else matters. The eight steps of Buddhism are concerned with the mental regions, which have always been under the control of the Kal forces. Therefore, the ECK chela cannot afford to put his mind on the lower elements but must at all times receive the guidance of the Living ECK Master, who eventually will separate knowledge from Truth for him and show him the gap between them.

Knowledge lies in the lower worlds. It is the bane of the seeker after God, and no chela has much interest in this quality of the psychic world. Of course, it is of immense value in the lower-world kingdom, but at the same time it has little value in the true spiritual worlds. Most chelas will go through this phase of unfoldment and think of titles and knowledge as the ultimate. But this is wrong, as neither have anything to do with the true value of life. A chela who is completely ignorant of any academic knowledge and psychic erudition or wisdom can be great in divine wisdom because of his ability to contact the world of God.

He knows without having gone into the art of study. This knowing holds a strange quality that no wisdom of life in the lower worlds can furnish. It is something that reaches out and tries to touch each individual, if such Souls have readied themselves for it. It will make no effort to enter the consciousness of the individual unless that Soul is ready and willing to accept the higher understanding of life. Thus it is said that the ECK only accepts those who are willing and ready for Its divine gifts.

The insistence in ECK on the proper use of will and mind in the lower worlds is part of the need for living in both the physical and spiritual realms at the same time. The psychic world was purposely left out because it is the mental area and included in what is termed the physical and spiritual realms. Actually, the chela lives in three worlds: the human consciousness, psychic consciousness, and the spiritual consciousness simultaneously and singularly.

This is the explanation of Soul Travel, but too many think of it in terms of phenomena. It is not psychic phenomena, but that one can inwardly see the Living ECK Master and hear him talk; can see him walking on the street through the inner eyes and can hear him talking with the inner ears. One can visit the worlds beyond the physical body with the MAHANTA, the Living ECK Master through this inner vision. It is inner travel, the moving of one's consciousness from one state to another.

When the chela's spiritual eyes are open, he sees the Living ECK Master, talks with him in the nonverbal tongue, and listens to the secret teachings with nonphysical ears. Many are not able to do this because they do not believe; others cannot do this because they allow their little selves to get in the way; another group cannot do it because they are depending on psychic phenomena, and if they have no abilities in this field, they will fail completely.

When one contacts the Living ECK Master in the other worlds, he is doing it personally. It is not something psychic, but something deeply spiritual. It is beyond conception or understanding. It is Soul movement from one plane to another, not the movement of the various bodies of man, which is dangerous.

No entity can take possession of anyone's body when he is Soul Traveling. He has no need of the silver cord, for it is dropped when he enters the Atma Plane (Soul region) and picked up again when he descends to the body. He gathers up the profound teachings of ECK as he moves about the realms of the upper worlds, the true universes of God.

Those who need the Living ECK Master will always stay with him, but those who feel they are beyond this are wrong in their thinking. They have not examined the truth and will go afoul of the illusions established by the Kal. They will find that nothing can revive them except the fresh spirit of ECK, the winds from heaven. They cannot hear the true melody of the ECK, nor hear the Living ECK Master's words inwardly or outwardly. They can neither understand nor grasp the true nature of the works of ECK. Neither can they find the MAHANTA within them at all times. They will see him occasionally and have a revival of faith, but then it will leave because this is impermanent.

To have permanency, the chela must have faith and live in the presence of the Living ECK Master, whether or not he can see him with the inner eyes or hear him with the spiritual ears. It is always true that the Living ECK Master never leaves anyone with whom he has established his love. He gives of himself and does not neglect the chela and his affairs.

The secret word which the initiate receives during the initiations of the different circles (planes) is not merely sounds to be repeated to oneself, but powerful expressions of the ECK power. Such words do not act of themselves but through the inner self which experiences them. They do not have any power of their own; they are only the means of concentrating already existing forces. They are like a magnifying glass; it contains no heat of its own but concentrates the rays of the sun. It transforms these rays from a mild warmth into a burning heat. The same applies to the secret word of the initiate. His word transforms him from the confused, doubtful seeker into the incandescent lover of God.

Those who confuse the hidden knowledge of their personal word are like the primitives who believe in sorcery. Scholars who try to discover the nature of these words with their philological knowledge often come to the conclusion that such words are meaningless. Yet it is known that those who have received a personal secret word in their ECK initiation have gained in their unfoldment. This is a tradition among the followers of ECK over the past centuries that has proven to be an expression of the deepest knowledge and experience in the realm of spiritual life.

Those who have received a personal secret word from the MAHANTA, whether it is through one of the Mahdis (initiates of the Fifth Circle or above) who can give the initiations or from the MAHANTA in person (outwardly or inwardly), shall never reveal their word to another without permission. It brings the spiritual unfoldment of the chela to a halt. He will not have any more advancement until given another secret mantra to replace the other.

The philosophy of the secret teachings is built around this phase of Eckankar. In ancient times the ECK Masters, as members of the Order of the Vairagi, taught orally and inwardly. The teachings were rarely, if ever, put in writing. The teachings were therefore given mainly in the inner sanctum, meaning that all were given individually to the chelas through the inner channels.

This meant then that the chelas were chosen by the MAHANTA, as they are today. Every Living ECK Master chooses his chelas, and few are let go. If they do wish to go, it means they leave voluntarily and it is mutually agreed upon. If a chela decides to leave the Living ECK Master on his own without first discussing it, then he has problems to face which are more severe than ever. He has left the ECK Master and gone into the wilderness alone to face the wild beasts which will devour him. It is typical of the vain chela to announce he is leaving without asking permission.

No chela who has asked permission to leave the Master's care has been refused, for the MAHANTA gives him freedom to do as he wishes. He does not warn against the dangers the chela will face after leaving the protection of the Master. Neither will the Living ECK Master refuse to take him back, should the chela wish to return to the fold of Eckankar.

If a chela decides to leave the Living ECK Master, the Master will not punish, nor will he give any indication of what might happen to the chela. This is for the chela to learn on his own, for the experiences he meets are his own. It is when the chela leaves the protection and guidance of the Living ECK Master that the Kal Niranjan will pounce upon him and start his negative works.

The specific qualifications for the initiate are a basic knowledge of the main tenets of the sacred scriptures of Eckankar, a readiness to devote a certain number of years to the study of the spiritual works of ECK, and practice of the inner teachings under the guidance of the Living

ECK Master. Thus the initiate will find that the esoteric knowledge is open to all who are willing to exert themselves sincerely and who have the capacity to learn with an open mind.

Just as those who are admitted for higher education in academic institutions in this world must have the necessary gifts and qualifications, so have the Living ECK Masters of all times also demanded certain qualifications from their followers before they initiated them into the inner teachings of ECK. Nothing is more dangerous than half-knowledge, or knowledge which has only theoretical value. This is why the SUGMAD has placed within the worlds a living representative of Itself.

The experiences of Soul in realization of Itself and Its mission can only be acquired under the guidance of the Living ECK Master and by constant practice. After such preparation, the individual secret word is used, and all the accumulated forces of Its incarnations are aroused in the initiate. This produces the conditions and power for which the word is intended. The uninitiated may utter any specific word or mantra as often as he likes, but it will not produce anything for him.

The secret of the special individual word for each initiate is something not intentionally hidden. But it has been acquired by self-discipline, concentration, inner experience, and insight. Like everything of value and every form of spiritual knowledge, it cannot be gained without effort. In this sense it is like profound wisdom that does not reveal itself at first glance because it is not a matter of surface knowledge, but a deep realization of the inner self.

This is also true of divine love. One does not see and grasp it at first glance, but it grows within him like the acorn of the oak in the earth. Gradually it opens the consciousness of the receiver and flows through to the world, changing all about it.

10
The Purpose of the Kal Power

The SUGMAD's purpose in establishing the Kal worlds is to train each Soul to reach the perfection of being a Mahdis, an initiate of the Fifth Circle, which is being a Coworker with the MAHANTA, the Living ECK Master.

It is the purpose of the Kal power to temper each Soul in the art of life so It can come to the MAHANTA as a chela. Hence, he initiates every chela who can become qualified after two years of study on the path of Eckankar. He wants every chela who is eligible to become an Initiate of the Fifth Circle.

Therefore, the Kal Niranjan was created and is subject to the laws of the SUGMAD. His duty is to create hardships, illusions, and make the path of life more difficult for each Soul who must travel through the lower worlds trying to reach God. These illusions are to make Soul believe that nothing exists beyond this world. But all in all, the SUGMAD intends these lower worlds of the Kal to be the school of life which all Souls must attend before moving on to the heavenly path of ECK.

Until the lesson is learned that these worlds are only regions of illusion, none will meet the Living ECK

Master. One will struggle forever upon the path until the day it dawns on him that all the glories and wealth of these worlds are merely the toys and playthings of the Kal Niranjan. Then will he find the MAHANTA awaiting him.

The MAHANTA is the key to all things for the chela in ECK. He is the great Soul, free from the illusions of the Universal Mind worlds under the rule of the Kal Niranjan. He is the only link between man and God and, therefore, it behooves all to enter into the path of ECK to find their way to the SUGMAD with the assistance of the MAHANTA. He is the linkup with the divine Deity and is able to give the initiation that puts the chela in true contact with God.

The MAHANTA is not a citizen of any country, although he will physically live in one and obey its laws. But he is a citizen of the whole universe of God and is known as a man of God. He is the universal man who is here to give the chela the right way to God and nothing else. When anyone appeals to him for material help, it depends on whether or not the MAHANTA believes it is best to give it. If he believes that it is needed, then it will be done. But if it is a hindrance to their karma and their spiritual unfoldment, it shall not be done.

He who hates the MAHANTA will hate God, and he who loves the MAHANTA will love God. This is what is known as the cell of self-cognition, for man of himself can do nothing. It depends mainly upon God working through the great instrument of Itself, the MAHANTA, whose several bodies act as channels for the ECK power on every plane throughout the universes of God.

However, the key to the survival of Eckankar in this world is the MAHANTA working with the Mahdis, the Initiates of the Fifth Circle and above, who are his chief channels for the ECK power. It also means that the ECK Satsang is equally important to the survival of ECK in this world and upon every plane of the spiritual universe.

The MAHANTA not only works in this world as a true channel for God, but upon every plane of the spiritual worlds. The Mahdis are able to work only in this world and in the first five planes as distributors of the ECK power. But they are only qualified to do this by the love of the MAHANTA, who allows each to be a channel for himself and the power that flows through him. There is no other way to be linked up to God except through this method.

Therefore, ECK and Its message are distributed through the MAHANTA to each of the Mahdis for every plane in the lower worlds—the Physical, Astral, Causal, Mental, and Etheric. Each Mahdis depends upon the MAHANTA for this, and acts as a channel only because he allows it. Also, there must be ECK Satsangs, not only in this world but upon each of the lower planes, for each acts as a collective channel for the distribution of ECK power.

So long as the ECK controls the ECK Satsangs, It is in the position to give life to the individual and the Satsang, respectively. This is the reason for Its longevity in this world, for It cannot be destroyed. Defeat or the dropping out of an ECK Satsang does not dissolve It or even make an impression.

The heartbeat of ECK is faith in the SUGMAD and the MAHANTA, whether the chela belongs to an ECK Satsang or performs upon his own, while the believers in orthodox religions put their faith unwittingly in the Kal Niranjan. This type of faith is only an opinion, fixed in the minds of men. When all the relatives and absolutes of any Kal-directed group are brushed aside, the individual finds himself alone. This is not true of those chelas who follow the ECK, for the ECKist knows that the presence of the Living ECK Master is always with him. He is never alone.

Moralistic power is the only force by which the Kal

Niranjan can operate. The Kal has no other force in this world than what we call the forces of nature. But moralistic power works best in man because of the consciousness of human nature. Man lives by this moralistic power which builds churches, civilizations, and societies; he makes laws and enforces laws through it.

The ECK power is above the dichotomy of good and evil, for It is only the power of the true nature of the SUGMAD. It cannot be otherwise. It leads Soul back to heaven; It has no other purpose. The true purpose of the Kal, however, is to hold Soul within the lower worlds, torment It, bring It hardships, and build Its life in the depths of negativism through centuries of incarnations.

Within this true physical realm, the Kal Niranjan works through the human consciousness. The Kal force performs best in the political and religious arenas, for here it is working through the absolute rule of a single body of consciousness, or that of a single individual.

No matter how the system of representation, or delegation, of the orthodox religious system is arranged, there is necessarily an alienation of the liberty and freedom of individual Souls. All religions use bodies, minds, and Souls, for without exception the ways they seek for power are varieties of absolutism.

This is true especially of the worldly religions. These systems fail to recognize that though man is a social being and seeks equality, he also loves independence and freedom.

The desire for personal property, in fact, springs from man's desire to free himself from the slavery of tribal or state-owned beingness, the primitive form of society. But property, in its turn, can go to the other extreme. It can violate equality and support the acquisition of power by the privileged minority who are generally behind the religious systems of the earth and other worlds.

Each chela in Eckankar must listen to the voice of the Living ECK Master, for he is the speaker of the Word of the SUGMAD. Each ECKist will eventually become an Initiate of the Fifth Circle (plane). He is then a citizen of the Fifth World and must perform all his living acts within this new universe. Thus the fifth dimension is where he begins to live truly in the spiritual Light and Word.

It is no mishap that he reaches this state of spiritual unfoldment. He then becomes the agent of the MAHANTA, and he has the ability to work in silence, but at the same time openly, as Coworker with the MAHANTA. But he himself always has to confront the Kal power, for it will assault him again and again, each time trying to create doubt, trying to break through to create schisms and bring about unhappiness with the spiritual works of ECK.

The works of Eckankar are revolutionary and eternal. The ECK changes all things once It is allowed to enter into the consciousness of the individual who is earning his daily living. No matter what the situation may be or what that individual does, and regardless of his position on the social and economic scale of society, he has become a channel for the ECK to change the environment within his own world.

The Living ECK Master uses him as a subchannel to pass the power of the ECK into the world and revitalize it, to make important spiritual changes which will reflect in the social, political, and economic stature of man.

Therefore, the chelas of ECK must not be restless or desirous of changes, but must serve the Living ECK Master wherever he is and wherever it is possible, here and now! The chela must act as a channel for the ECK where it can best be done—at his job, in his home, and in his social environment. He is always working in silence, always open to let the ECK change all his life around him. By being watchful and aware of this, he can see what changes are made.

When the chela eventually becomes a Mahdis, an initiate of the Fifth Circle, he may be chosen to initiate chelas in the name of the ECK Master. The Mahdis must train each ECK chela who is in his ECK Satsang or within his designated area. He must go out among the uninitiated and see that they are, in some manner or other, led to the Living ECK Master.

It is the duty of the Mahdis to bring those Souls who are ready into ECK to be lifted into the upper regions of pure spirit before the holocaust strikes the worlds of the Kal. The end of this era, the Kali Yuga—the Iron Age, when all is in darkness and ignorance—will come in a few thousand years.

The MAHANTA appears again in this world to gather up Souls to return to the true heavenly home. Wherever he goes and whatever he does, the great ECK power clears the way like the whirling winds of a storm. It breaks up the old orders and reestablishes the new within this world. Everywhere the ECK destroys systems established by the Kal forces and injects the spirituality of Soul into the social order and spiritual life of man.

So it is proclaimed that the path of ECK must be taken. A man's lust for possessions and his mad, desperate scramble for material things have become such that the spiritual work of ECK granted by the SUGMAD is the only way; otherwise, this world would be on its way to becoming a veritable desert. Thus the attack on the Kal power continues in the quiet quest for salvation.

It appears that man has been cursed by the SUGMAD because of the standards of living in this world. While man uses up the resources of nature at an alarming rate, it is only the natural result of the speeding up of race karma in the last yuga before the destruction of this universe.

It is the last of the yugas, when mankind and his fellow

creatures will be destroyed in their respective embodiments and each Soul lifted into heaven to sleep until the reforming of the lower worlds. Those Souls who have taken up the path of ECK under the MAHANTA shall be liberated from this destruction and sleep, and become Coworkers with him.

In the lower worlds, men rule by politics and thereby with orthodox religions. Hence, religions become a system of socioeconomics to control man's mind and body. Most world religions have a foundation in the economic systems of their times. Every social order since the start of man in this world has had a religion for its own followers. It has promised the glories of heaven when one dies: suffer on earth, and get the reward after death. This is the creed for keeping an exploited society quiet. It has also formed consumer societies throughout history which have created wars and left man in poverty. It has destroyed the natural resources of man and formed a spiritual desert on earth.

As long as this condition exists, man cannot find himself and therefore suffers in spirit. He is ignorant and does not know what has happened to him. He is without a spiritual guide: desperate, seeking and desiring to meet the savior who can halt the wars, bring back the natural resources, and give him comfort in body, mind, and spirit. He has not yet learned that the Living ECK Master awaits his decision to turn to the spiritual path of ECK and find freedom for himself.

All this brings man to the point where he considers himself able to make judgments and form decisions. He is not really able to do this until he has reached the state of the Mahdis. Therefore, he rebels even at calling other men *sir*. This comes from a variation of the title *sire*, which is taken from the word *Sri*. It reflects the early relationship between the spiritual ones who have attained the

Kingdom of God and those who are still seeking. The efforts of the MAHANTA are directed against this sort of relationship and against all authority of one man over another. For it is said in Eckankar that whosoever puts his hand over another to govern him is a usurper and a tyrant. The ECK declares him an enemy. The Living ECK Master wants no barriers between himself and the chelas of Eckankar.

The ECK is always the new-old religion, fitted for the times in which it exists. The human race always needs ECK, for ECK is life itself. This means ECK is the religion of the people because It is positive in Its effect. There is always the need for ECK because man becomes negative; hence the ECK flows to fit any and all generations.

The proof that the religions of the past are no longer valid can be seen in the performance of the codes of the churches and their priests. Man pays lip service to his churches, synagogues, temples, and mosques, while the life he leads is without ethics.

The ECK chela does not seek utopia, which is the perfect society, for all things perfect have ceased to grow. The world changes with each generation, and man always changes. Hence the concept of utopia, or perfection, is imperfect. This is the mistake made by those who are ruled by the Kal Niranjan. They think that once their promised land has been achieved, all progress will stop, that their millennium will have been reached. The SUGMAD knows no halting. The path of ECK is forever.

The powers that the SUGMAD may delegate to Its channel, the MAHANTA, are wondrous. Because of the goodness and mercy of the SUGMAD, the Living ECK Master has powers which cannot be comprehended by any average man. He may build, and he may destroy, but he always maintains an equal balance within the universes where he lives in his many bodies.

Man desires to be entertained instead of seeking out the message of ECK. He is conditioned by the Kal power to seek amusement instead of God. If the wrath of the MAHANTA should be incurred, he could speak the word that would bring about the destruction of man's source of amusements, or even man himself. Although it is rare that this would occur, man in his ignorance often attempts to play with the fire of the MAHANTA's wrath. This is seeking self-destruction through ignorance.

Man will normally seek God when his struggle for survival on earth is great. When man's economy is lowest, his struggle is greatest, for he believes that his survival is linked with his materialistic life. It is then that his prayers for help are greatest, but they are in vain. He is not asking for the true survival of Soul, but only the survival of his materialistic universe.

But when a civilization has an economy of abundance, man's mind turns away from spiritual survival to publicly provided entertainment. The average man is not capable of programming himself. He cannot think up tasks to occupy himself spiritually, for he has never had to. He has evolved under conditions where the time and energy available to him were programmed for him. There was very seldom time for spiritual things, and purely traditional aspects were provided by the church. Festivals were a great relief and source of entertainment. Man never got a chance to become bored with them. He played the games laid down by his church or religion, and this occupied most of his time since the beginning of the history of the human race.

If man is to survive in the physical universe, then he must find time for creative activity in spiritual things. Until this comes about, within a group with time to do something besides subsist in the materialistic worlds, there is little opportunity for the spiritual sensitivity of man to develop. But time spent in contemplation does not automatically produce spiritual results.

In all the civilizations in this world, especially those of the noncreative, average man, mankind has formed for himself predetermined, ritualized activities. This is what can happen to an affluent society, as well as a welfare state, if the leaders do not establish a spiritual or religious time for the common man.

What destroys every social order is the growth of an immense leisure class. It no longer becomes a subsistence culture; other nations must support it. When the populace is offered free food and shelter, the spiritual growth of the nation goes down. Because of this leisure, it gives no incentive for self-programming activities. It usually goes into eclipse as a nation with self-destructive tendencies.

Man always wants something to do, to have some trinket he can play with to take up his leisure time. If he has not the creative abilities to learn Soul Travel, he must come to rely on a government that will see that his leisure time is channeled in the direction to which he is a slave and dependent.

Man does not like to read. It requires that he engage in a great deal of mental activity. He has to visualize the actions from the words, imagine the voice tones and the facial expressions. The average man is not up to such creative labor.

The ECK, therefore, is what he needs. It is all. Each thing he comes to learn is the ECK. The bird singing in the tree is ECK. It is transcending and descending all in the same motion. As It descends, It also transcends and vice versa. Truth is for those who know, those who come to know and never question it. They realize that questions are never satisfying and never answered.

"He who loves me will love me for what I am. He who hates me shall hate me for what I am not. Those who question all the works of ECK shall never know Truth and shall always be bothered with questions. None shall ever know Truth. It is not possible to have Truth and at the same time ask questions about it," says the SUGMAD.

Thus it is that the ECK Satsang is really the key to the spiritual works of Eckankar. So long as the Satsangs have sufficient chelas who are open as channels for the ECK to reach the non-ECKists within their communities, nations, and on all levels of consciousness, then will the ECK survive.

Therefore, the Satsangs become absolutely important to the collective body of the chelas, as each forms an enormous channel which can control the spiritual affairs of this world and the worlds beyond. As a collective body, the Satsang brings harmony, peace, and happiness to the individual, and to all entities within the universes of God.

This is the real secret of the works of ECK, and as long as the ECK Satsangs hold their related positions, none can be resolved by the Kal power but only by the MAHANTA. Defeat of the power of the ECK Satsangs will never take place, for any attempt to do so does not make the slightest impression on the Satsang and the chela concerned.

The Light and Sound of ECK therefore uses the MAHANTA as the major channel for Its work within the worlds of God. It is through the MAHANTA that the chela may be established in the ECK Satsang or act alone as the channel through which the MAHANTA works in this world.

Man has been taught to want certain things in this materialistic world. Now he must reverse himself, for since he has solved the problem of the production of abundance, he must now take stock and work out his path to his destiny, which is Eckankar. The overwhelming majority of mankind is working either on methods of destruction or on the creation of new products which people do not actually need or want. Instead, mankind should be working on spiritual unfoldment: the curing of man's ills, delving into the secrets of life, plumbing the ocean's depths, and reaching out to the world of God through Soul Travel.

The words of the MAHANTA alone can change the world, completely and irrevocably. He is the only being who has developed his spiritual perception beyond any point known in the history of the human race. Generally, he contacts those who are ECK chelas, but there are many times when he communicates with whole groups of people or individuals outside his own followers. So often he uses an ECK chela as a channel to pass on a thought to a large body of persons within a certain area. He is always in contact with every ECK Satsang or collective body of Souls, as well as with every ECK chela on a personal and individual basis.

If he so desires, the Living ECK Master can make spiritual contact with the whole of mankind or all beings in any country at any time, regardless of language barriers. He can make contact with any entity on any plane, regardless of which plane. He keeps the inhabitants on every plane throughout the universe intact and working on mutually common causes, whether or not the causes have the appearance of ECK to the outer senses. Yet the ECK is the underlying factor, the essence of life, which only the Mahdis can recognize in all languages, religions, and philosophies everywhere. All life therefore flows out of the ECK; and all religions, philosophies, and sacred writings are based upon the ECK and Its original source, called the Shariyat-Ki-Sugmad.

Races and persons at different levels of consciousness will divide the ECK into various parts because of their lower states of thought and spiritual development. Few have the level of consciousness to accept the ECK. This is the reason why many fail to understand and grasp Its meaning.

Few can understand and know what the ECK may do. It is so vast, so magnificent in Its scope. The select few who come to It are actually the most fortunate of all the followers of the spiritual paths. These Souls are fortunate because they have come to the apex of their training in the lower worlds and have passed the tests established by the SUGMAD and administered by the Kal Niranjan. They are indeed fortunate, for now, after long centuries of spiritual training and incarnations, they have reached their last life on earth and have come under the guidance of the MAHANTA.

He takes them under his wing in loving care and is thereafter with them wherever they may be, whether it is on this plane or any of those in the heavenly worlds. He always stays with those whom he has given the initiation into ECK, whether that person has left this physical body or not. It is also generally known that the MAHANTA may stay with his own chelas, those he has initiated on earth or the spiritual worlds, whether he himself has passed on from this life or not.

Man will go nearly insane if he cannot label everything. He simply must have an explanation for all things. Three-quarters of the human race spends its time wandering about aimlessly. The Living ECK Master comes forth from out of the secrecy of his existence whenever man needs to be pulled out of the dark ages.

Human character is determined by environment rather than heredity. Human faults are imparted by bad training and karma. The vices of the young spring not from the Kal; they are derived from the defects of spiritual training in this life and past lives.

Mystery is not a satisfactory term to describe the experience of God. It is only an intimation of something more profoundly significant, often recognized in a flash. But an understanding of its significance does not always follow such an experience in one's life. The curtain, unnoticed, is sometimes moved aside, and other curtains also, so Soul can see Its own self and thus reveal the mystery of what It truly is. Then the curtain drops in place again, and a measure of oblivion descends.

God has had thousands of names, but none of them is apt. This Reality has sometimes been called the good, beautiful, and true, to name a few. Philosophers term It the Absolute, or Ultimate, Reality. Western mystics say It is the Godhead and in general know it as God. It is Brahma and Paramatma to the Hindus; the Beloved of the Sufis; the Tao, or Way, of the Chinese mystics. The Buddhists say It is Nirvana. But none of these is the true reality of the SUGMAD. This is the ultimate of all realities. It is the Ultimate and is so far above all things that few ever achieve It.

There is no name for this True Reality, for names set boundaries. Therefore, all the above that are known by name are within the world of the Kal. Those which are listed here, with the exception of the SUGMAD, are only Fourth Plane phenomena. If something can be labeled, it is still within the world of the mind, the Fourth Plane, which is the final region still under the influence of the Kal Niranjan.

This is why the SUGMAD takes as Its name the Ocean of Love and Mercy: the world of the unknown, the unknown Itself.

Mystics and poets are generally introverts and do not have good relationships with the outer worlds. They are supremely fortunate in that visions of reality sometimes come to them unsought. But they are even more fortunate if they are able to induce these visions.

The extroverts are not so fortunate, for generally, when they glimpse this reality of God, they are so shocked into fearing for their sanity that they will back away without any further contact. They are also uncomfortable in the presence of anyone who has had such experiences and can handle them. They will label such an experience a mental aberration or go to see their physician.

When one is concerned with the pure element of the divine reality, he finds no words to speak of It, for It cannot be set apart from Itself. To say It is material in nature is to label It, to play with words.

Man's consciousness cannot be easily divested of symbols. The mystics use all sorts of terms such as divine bliss, infinite love, and others. But the labels are merely those of the mind trying to grasp what is unknown to it. This has been done for centuries and is not limited to any faith, religion, person, creed, or cult. The ECK has been found in many parts of the world, from the beginning of time to the present, having made Itself known to some but not to others.

The ECK never plays favorites but always reveals some portion of Itself to those who are persistent and obey the instructions laid down by the Living ECK Master. So many times Its concern is with the economics and politics of nations in which Its mystics are inhabitants, but this usually turns out to be a phenomenon of the Mental Plane.

The ECKist who reaches the stages beyond the level of phenomena becomes intoxicated with visions of the True Reality, and he no longer cares for conventional forms. He grows beyond propriety, religion, philosophy, economics, and other materialistic forms which become suffocating to him.

If the cynic believes the esoteric experiences of divine

reality are illusions, he must suffer for his ignorance. No ECKist who has had intense or prolonged experiences doubts the validity of them. But what is brought forth from the initiated is difficult to communicate to those who are the uninitiated. Life, as it is in the materialistic worlds, sadly rejects the experiences of the ECKist and the validity of the Living ECK Master.

Therefore, we find that all ECKists, regardless of their spiritual status and nationality, are still disciples of Eckankar. Whether the chela is living on the Physical Plane or the Atma Lok (the Soul Plane), he never feels he is in a separate world or state. He is still under the general authority of the ECK, and the individual laws of the separate planes are to be obeyed, and homage paid to their various rulers and spiritual governors. He does not feel like either a citizen or an alien, but rather like a modern traveler who goes through each country as a tourist or for business.

The entities of each plane look upon their existence there as sort of a contract of service. This is the way it should be, for whether they consciously realize it or not, all are actually the children of the ECK kingdom. In this way it makes no difference what religion or path Soul may adopt for Itself, It is a full citizen of the kingdom of ECK. All Souls belong to this kingdom, whether they desire it to be so or not. The longer they resist this, the longer anyone withstands the ECK, the longer they continue their existence on the Awagawan, the Wheel of the Eighty-Four. Since the beginning of time, all Souls—regardless of their faith, creed, religion, philosophy, cult, or sect—have had the consolation that they are full citizens of the kingdom of ECK.

Servitude on earth in the human form, or in any of the psychic planes, is a small price to pay if it purchases a ticket to the true Kingdom of God, which is by the way of Eckankar.

The ECKist finds there is only one MAHANTA at a time within all the universes. All other ECK Masters in the Order of the Vairagi, the Brotherhood of ECK Masters, are known as the Maharaj.

Every Maharaj is subordinate to the MAHANTA, the Living ECK Master, no matter who he might be, for the MAHANTA holds the ECK Rod of Power. It is given to him on the twenty-second day of October. The MAHANTA holds this Rod of Power until he translates or passes the Rod of ECK Power to his successor and takes an esoteric position within the Order of the Vairagi somewhere in the universes as a spiritual worker of great importance. Then he, too, becomes subordinate to the next MAHANTA, or Living ECK Master. He becomes a member of the spiritual hierarchy, where before he was the head of it and responsible directly to the SUGMAD.

Besides the Maharajs, there are the Mahavakyis, who are known as the Silent Ones, for they have charge of all the universes and the affairs on each plane. All Souls within all universes are within their orbit of affairs. Their duties are to see that every Soul, regardless of Its spiritual status, has the opportunity to enter into the Kingdom of God here and now. It makes little difference which plane the Soul is on. It depends on the individual Soul to do what It will with the opportunity presented to It. All the Soul has to do is recognize the opportunity, thereby forgetting any religion, creed, or faith It has followed, knowing that each was only a step on the way to ECK, the true pathway to God. One then learns that every Soul living somewhere in the universes of God is actually a follower of ECK.

Unless the individual has planted his feet directly on the path under the guidance of the MAHANTA, then he has wasted time and effort. The lower paths of philosophies and religions are necessary, but none will last forever.

Soon he will find that upon reaching certain spiritual levels, he will be able to meet with the Living ECK Master and resolve all his problems both spiritually and physically. He will find that all religions, faiths, and philosophies are merely necessary steps to reach the ECK. It is all part of the overall omnipresence of the ECK. Nothing can exist but for the ECK, and unless one has himself rightly placed within the ECK, knowing It for what It is, then he is still on the treadmill of the Kal.

He will find that philosophy is merely a psychic means of studying religions through the intellect. He will know that religion is the means which the Kal has established to take control of the masses. Kal puts emphasis upon the mind and body consciousness so that Soul cannot express Itself freely. It is only when one goes beyond the intellect into the spiritual arenas that the ECK is truly known.

The ECK is the true reality, that shining essence of the SUGMAD which cannot be found by worldly eyes, senses, and perceptions. It is only found in the true self, that which is known as Soul. With the ECK comes the Sound of the flute of the SUGMAD. This is what Soul is, and none can deprive Soul of It once It has been experienced. It is something beyond words and sounds, symbols and signs.

Until Soul returns again to this state of consciousness, It will always struggle in the meshes of the Kal. It is the purpose of the Kal power to keep Soul trapped until It learns Truth and starts on the path to perfection, the path of Eckankar. These are the responsibilities and the mission which God assigned the Kal Niranjan.

11

The Way of ECK Perfection

The very reason why most occult, metaphysical, and spiritual writings (including the sacred works of the orthodox religions) in this world fail is that too many who write them never realize that knowledge alone is not wisdom. A catalog of facts and opinions, by itself, does not constitute either literature or perfected works of any nature.

Most Oriental religious literature and most Western sacred works lie mainly in the field of knowledge and historical facts. Some parts, of course, contain wisdom, but generally they are only legends and myths expressed in poetic form; they are merely stating what the writer wants the orthodox followers and readers to believe.

The sacred mystery of the ECK lies in the initiation of the Ninth Circle, for when one comes to this level of spiritual growth he does not wish to live in this life anymore. He becomes dead, only to awaken when the body dies. He sees nothing in the sacred writings of orthodox religions and does not wish to read them or refer to them again. He seeks no glory, no titles in this life, and will reject all those given him. He becomes honest to the point of pain for himself and cannot find happiness in anything in this world. He has no interest in social reform nor any wish to bring about adjustments in this life for the masses; he only wants to see that each Soul has the opportunity to gain salvation through ECK.

ECK does not pose as a remedy for the illnesses of this world, but is only a path to spiritual freedom. The MAHANTA can change the world and its history, but there is little likelihood that he would ever do this. Every Living ECK Master has come to this world to impart spirituality to a materialistic age. He gives an extra spiritual push to every era of mankind. But there is always a fixed time for such divine workings, and when the time is ripe, the Living ECK Master who has made his appearance in this world during each respective age of mankind reveals his true nature to the world. Not one has differed in this essential doctrine.

The chief commandments of ECK, running like a golden thread through the teachings of every Living ECK Master, have all been based upon the teachings of the SUGMAD. These divine ones come out into the public when their help is most needed, when spirituality is at its lowest ebb in some country of the world or planet, and materialism is apparently victorious.

Each Living ECK Master, in his respective time, has laid down the spiritual law again and again to help those who follow the path of ECK. These laws, which are truth, have always existed to lead man to God. But the priestcraft has taken the laws of ECK and made them into tenets for organized religions. Therefore the idealistic spirit and the motivating force that prevailed during the time of each Living ECK Master all but disappeared under the weight of orthodox dogma.

Therefore, the Living ECK Masters have always had the responsibility to not establish new religions, cults, or mystery schools. Instead they rejuvenate the religious thoughts of all people, instilling a higher understanding of life into them.

The founders of dogmatic religions usually passed away, leaving little. Later somebody would invent dogma from the words the founder preached, and a religion was established. All religions, regardless of what they are and who founded them, are from the same source, the ECK.

ECK is life itself, the Audible Life Stream. The time is coming that will bring ECK to the world as a universal spiritual belief. Mankind will accept It. ECK will serve all races of people and all countries. The way is being prepared to enable the MAHANTA to deliver the worldwide message.

This will come when there is total chaos and confusion everywhere; when the world is rocking in upheavals, earthquakes, floods, and volcanic eruptions; when both east and west are aflame with war. Then is he needed most by all mankind. The whole world must suffer, for the whole world must be redeemed.

When such conditions are at their worst, the Living ECK Master will make himself publicly known and will declare his mission to the entire world. He shall, by his spiritual powers, speedily bring all conflicts to an abrupt end, bringing peace once more to all nations. Then mankind will rest from all conflicts on all planets within the world system.

No one should require the Living ECK Master to fit into that person's image of what a spiritual giant might be. Few ECK Masters will ever fit the popular image of what the masses think is a Godman. ECK Masters act too independently of the general social concept, doing as they wish and usually living a life of their own and never bothering anyone.

The problem existing among the orthodox religions is

a lack of understanding on their part that destroys communications. It is not that disciples of any orthodox religion lack an opportunity to communicate, but most are intolerant of ECK. Most orthodox followers believe only in their traditional faith. This gives each, they think, all the answers to life and its problems. Therefore they refuse to accept any ECK chela's point of view. This is a trap of the Kal force and is dangerous in the lower worlds.

Thus the ECK chela must proceed with caution when he wishes to pass the message of ECK to others. Few want to listen, because they have been steeped in their religious traditions and believe that everything else is wrong. Their founder's name has become a part of the woof and warp of their lives, and if anyone speaks of anything being greater than him, there is danger. This is why it is courageous to be an ECKist. But the ECKist must sacrifice and go forth to spread the message of Eckankar.

He knows there are dangers, because the Kal force will use any of those who are wrapped in orthodox religions to get rid of him. They will do it in some manner or other, if at all possible. But the ECKist must know that life alone cannot teach him all he wants to know about ECK. He knows, though, that if the ECK uses him as a channel, all will be well. Consequently, he cares little for what happens to his human body, for nothing can stop him. He cares little if all things in his material world are taken away. If he loses everything but himself, nothing matters but spreading the message of ECK.

The strange influence of the MAHANTA on all who see him in person, or as a spiritual being when they can open their Spiritual Eye and see him in the Atma body, is indeed fascinating. Those who can feel reverence for the spiritual quality in him without belief in ECK are indeed rare. But ignorance of his spiritual greatness does not bar materialistic persons from tasting the radiant influence of spirituality emanating from him.

Those who come to the Living ECK Master and say they are inclined to follow his teachings are told to associate with those who have had spiritual experiences. Contact with such persons will assist in bringing out the latent spirituality in anyone. Those who have had such experiences are usually the Mahdis, the initiates of the Fifth Plane. Therefore, the society of such people is very important as the first step, and often it is the last, as the MAHANTA often will say to seekers of the SUGMAD.

The Mahdis are above the Mental Plane; therefore they are not to practice magic. This includes both black and white magic, for the practitioner will come to regret it if he does. He will learn that the use of magic for anything, regardless of what it might be, will bring effects that are not good. If he uses it to heal others or to injure anyone, then it is wrong. In healing anyone with a bodily affliction, it is the ECK that does so, not the magic which is part of the Universal Mind Power, or that known as the Kal force.

When the Mahdis reaches this level of spiritual unfoldment, he must then begin to let the ECK use him completely as a channel. Then he starts to become all things to all people. To those under the law, he becomes as one under the law, though not being himself under the law. To those outside the law, he becomes as one outside the law. To the weak, he becomes weak, and to the strong, he becomes strong. Therefore, he becomes all things to all men in order to help and possibly lead some to the MAHANTA, the Living ECK Master.

Life for the Mahdis becomes a cinema play, unrolling its episodes from the cradle to the grave. Instead of seeking truth through any of the psychic means, he looks for the real, the enduring, the eternal principles of ECK. He does not look for ECK in the illusionary, for It is never there.

The power of ECK can conquer any aberration of life. Millions labor under the illusion that their emptiness, their guilt, and their lack of purpose are due to their material and environmental associations. If any lack a spiritual purpose in ECK, then life will become dull for them. It is contemplation and belief in the MAHANTA that can bring about a new life.

It is only the MAHANTA who can cleanse Soul and forgive all that has been created in this world of materialistic values. The MAHANTA gives each Soul a new challenge and purpose. He brings about the imperishable things which man has created for himself. When the chela has taken away all his false concepts of life and sees only the divine sense, then he no longer runs after another man's opinion. He understands and knows truth.

Whosoever looks deeply into himself and perceives only discontent, frailty, darkness, and fear need not be afraid nor curl his lips in scorn. But let him seek the MAHANTA, who can be found within his heart. It is then that he will become aware of the ECK and Its purposes for him. He will learn that his own divine nature will reveal Itself in him, and that he will no longer walk indifferently. He will learn that no one is excluded from the divine nature of the ECK consciousness, that it is only man that excludes himself from It.

It is the man who thinks he may live as freely as his unconsidered desires prompt him who does not see the reckoning of such an attitude. He is binding his life to a hollow dream if he persists in this thought. If he has had the experience of knowing his true self, there will never be any hatred for another.

Anyone with ego-consciousness often confuses this with self-knowledge or Self-Realization. He takes it for granted that if he has ego-consciousness, then he knows himself. But the ego knows only its own contents, not the true self and Its contents. It knows only human and psychic knowledge, and only too often those in this ego-conscious state measure their knowledge by what the average person in their social environment understands. Psychic and social facts are, for the most part, what make up the human psyche. One is always coming up against the prejudice that such a thing as Self-Realization could not happen with him or in his environment. And on the other hand, he meets with equally illusory assumptions that merely serve to cover up the true facts of such cases.

The concept of unity, which is supposed to embrace the universe and all its action, is titanic in scope and potential. He who dares to examine this concept soon discovers that it leads into something too great for understanding, for it leads to the ECK. An alternative becomes imperative, for if he is an extremist, he abandons normal life to become a hermit. If he finds this too impossible, he rejects his ideal completely and lives the unexamined life with all its unhappy consequences. The only good solution, both personally and socially, then, is compromise. Man must particularize and reduce his god to a form that he can handle, thereby distorting and sometimes obliterating the original image.

When man is allowed to proceed naturally with the reduction of the image of his god, the image will conform to the social and political expectations of the civilization of his times. Every major religion in the world has evolved a hundred species to fit man's image of the various types of gods that he seeks. All this attests to the needs of man for what is known as the examined life. These compromises are vitiated by the panaceas that lead to dogma. But if anyone should recognize the fallacies in the dogma of the orthodox religions, he usually comes into an understanding of the ECK.

Man insists upon talk and exposition, but the ECK cannot be put into words. Sometimes, however, a profusion of images and metaphors are used by the ECK Masters. The problem here, however, is that a spoken language is the expression of the Kal, and it presents a hardship of how to get a positive image in the demonstration of ECK to this world.

Philosophy and worldly religion describe the SUGMAD in negative language. Neither deny It, but both are too often emphatic that the existence of Reality is not true. Actually, there is no vocabulary that can express the truth of the existence of Reality. Reality is Truth, though the ECK chela finds so many interpretations of truth that he cannot help being confused. He tries to get into the heart of truth, but it always eludes him in some manner because he cannot get a mental grasp of it. This is the problem of language: it exists only in the mental realm to express itself vocally to the external world. Since Truth is beyond the mental realm, it cannot be grasped except through the internal vision.

This is why Eckankar can be described as the Everlasting Gospel. It is not available to the senses of the Buddhi, the function of the mind that discriminates and decides. Chitta, the function which takes note of form and beauty, sees these things in truth but is unable to pass them along to the Buddhi. Manas, the other function of the mind, called the mind stuff, the Universal Mind Power, only has the power to receive feeling and taste. But the Buddhi, being thought, must discriminate and decide what is best to give to the outer world as a good representation of itself.

Thus, if not governed by Soul, the mind does not allow for anything but itself. It causes man in the masses to find dynamic living too difficult and fatiguing. The average man requests codification of life; he looks for laws to live by and for somebody to provide them. To reach out for anything beyond this is too much for his senses and his understanding. This is what makes the ECKist a special person, for he is in the ECK and lives in dynamic dimensions. He knows that peace does not come when an oligarchy, a government, or some ruler decrees peace, nor does order come through ossified rituals of legislation.

Every ECKist knows that this sort of external peace and order will sooner or later flounder, creating difficulties and eventual destruction for itself. It has nothing to do with the SUGMAD and Its works. It is something which the Kal uses to exploit the masses for its own interest, for behind all this is the Kal, trying to trap the mind of every individual Soul.

Belief in a creed is not always due to religious feeling, but is more often a social matter. As such, it does nothing to give the individual values to live by. For support he must depend exclusively on his relation with the ECK, an authority which is not of this world. No lofty principles nor creeds of orthodox religions can lay a spiritual foundation for the ECK chela. It is simply empirical awareness, the incontrovertible experience of an intensely personal, reciprocal relationship between the chela and the MAHANTA. This has nothing to do with either the physical world, reason, or logic, as human consciousness knows them. But it does have everything to do with the ECK consciousness.

A clear distinction must be made between what is essential in Eckankar and what is haphazard. The ECK doctrine has naturally been preserved in a form suited to those Souls It could reach since the beginning of the universes. This is especially true in the lower worlds.

Many have been called, but few are able to comprehend

and understand the ECK. Those Souls who do are then consciousnesses that are open to the ECK for gaining awareness. They serve in the lower worlds or wherever Soul is needed.

Every ECK chela must grasp the tools of the spiritual works of Eckankar in the field of mystical experiences. He must know there are two types of spiritual experience, both of which are found in the works of ECK. First is the extrovertive spiritual experience, and second is the introvertive type. Both are attempts at the apprehension of the full experience of the divine reality. But they are reached in different ways.

The extrovertive way looks outward, through the physical senses into the external world, finding there the greater experience of the divine reality. The introvertive way turns inward, with an introspective manner of seeing through the inner senses and eyes to find the greater experience of the divine reality beyond the human consciousness. Naturally, this type of experience should outweigh the extrovertive way in importance. In the course of human history the introvertive way becomes a major resource to depend upon for decisions and changes of events and nations.

The extroverted seeker, with his physical manner, including the five external senses, will perceive the same world of trees, hills, concrete roads, and household furniture as most people generally do. But he sees something which the average person does not see. He observes that these objects are transformed into something through which the ECK shines to illuminate his senses. So many of those who have been called mystics and seekers of God have found the spiritual experience of life in blades of grass, wood, and stone. These types of extrovertive mystics have always pointed out that God is in everything.

The extrovertive seeker has the ability to know and

separate the ECK from the material things of life, yet he can see that the ECK is the very substance of all life in such things. This puts him above the average man, who has a lesser understanding which does not qualify him to see the ECK as the whole or everyday life as the divine reality.

This understanding of the extrovertive mystic passes beyond the sensory-intellectual consciousness into the conceptual intellect. However, the distinction between the ECK and these things has not wholly disappeared. The extrovertive mystic is generally one who finds all things identical—such as grass being the same as stone—although each is different. Mostly these extroverts are the poets, metaphysicians, and religious writers.

What they are saying is a complete paradox, in fact contradictory. But paradox is one of the common characteristics of mysticism. Paradoxes arise because the chela is dealing with the elements of psychic power, better known as the Kal force. The Kal always deals in mystery and paradox, for everything in its universe consists of dichotomies. The Kal is always presenting the two sides of the coin in order to bring about confusion and complexity. This is what causes any mystic to question the affairs of the SUGMAD. Dichotomies always bring questions, because few within the human consciousness understand the two-sided view of life.

The mystic is not an ECKist, and neither is an ECKist ever a mystic. The mystic is one who has never gone beyond the Mental worlds. He deals in the mystification of the spirito-psychic worlds. The true worlds of the SUGMAD, which lie above the Atma Lok, have no complication nor mystery. They are what they are; the whole element of these worlds is simply Truth. When one has moved into these worlds and placed himself upon one of these planes, he is therefore part of them and never questions. All things are as they are because it is proper and fitting for them to be this way.

He never questions, never indulges in the mystification of life, but leaves all things as they are. He knows that the extrovertive mystic is simply a psychic who has gained a little more insight than most seekers, and that he is halfway on the path to reaching the Fifth Plane. This is the experience of the sensory-intellectual. He sees only what has been granted him: a perception of the world as being transfigured and unified in a single reality. Some identify this single reality as God, and others do not, but it all ties in with the same thing, the ECK. In most societies, however, this type of experience leads to pantheism. Nevertheless, the experience of the extrovert is important in making headway on the path of ECK. Yet it is not the end of the road, as so many believe.

The success of the introvertive experience depends on shutting out all physical sensations from one's consciousness. Average men believe this to be easy. One can shut one's eyes, cover one's ears, and hold the nose. He can avoid taste sensations by keeping the mouth closed and empty. But no one can simply shut off the tactile sensations, for it is difficult to be rid of organic sensations. But this is what the chela must learn to do to enjoy the subjective, that is, the introvertive experience. He must learn to thrust tactile and organic sensations out of his conscious awareness, into the unconscious. Neither does he go to the trouble of holding his nose, plugging his ears, and emptying his mouth. The only thing he does is shut his eyes and close out all organic sensations.

After this is done, the chela then drops all sensual images from his mind. This is the most difficult part of the contemplative exercises, but it is possible. After this, one stops the thinking and reasoning processes within himself. Having gotten rid of the whole empirical content of sensations, images, thoughts, and presumably all emotions, he will find that his desires and volitions will disappear, since they normally exist only as attachments to cognitive awareness.

All consciousness of his human self will then have disappeared. Often the chela will go to sleep when this happens, or become unconscious. The total suppression of the whole content of human consciousness is what the introvertive mystic claims to be able to achieve. He claims that the sensory-intellectual consciousness disappears and is replaced by an entirely new kind of consciousness, which he calls the mystical consciousness. Although the yogis and many of the Eastern mystics use this modus operandi, it turns out to be the wrong way to reach the spiritual consciousness. There is a difference between spiritual consciousness and mystical consciousness. The former is the highest, when one reaches and enters into the state above the Atma Lok, the Fifth Plane. The latter is only reached when one enters into the Mental realm.

Samadhi, a mystical state of consciousness, belongs in this area of the psychic worlds. But Nirvikalpa, a spiritual state of consciousness, belongs in the area of the true ECK worlds. This leads to detachment, which eventually takes the chela through the varied initiations into the Ninth, when he becomes a member of the Order of Vairagi, the ECK Masters.

When one reaches the Samadhi state of consciousness he becomes one with the Kal, but it appears to him that he is one with the divine source of life, the SUGMAD. This is why many have said that the Godhead is pure nothingness, a desert and a wilderness. Here again the mystic is talking in metaphors that are useless to the chela.

The chela needs no such explanation of the SUGMAD and the ECK, for within the worlds of the true spiritual universe, It is Light and Sound. This is all there is. One does not need to find explanations for the Light and Sound, for there are none. Soul knows and understands instantly what goes on in the worlds of the SUGMAD, and never questions. Soul just knows and does not call this knowing either religion or philosophy.

In the study of inner-world experiences, most men believe that the mystical experience and the religious experience are the same; and actually, neither of these are the same as the ECK experience. There is an important connection between mysticism and religion, but it is not nearly so direct and immediate as most people seem to think.

The mystical experience has been described here. The experience of the religionist is of some undifferentiated unity which is often interpreted as union with God. But this is only the interpretation and is not the experience itself. The great problem here is that most Souls do not have a sufficiently analytical faculty to distinguish between the experience and the interpretation. The ECKist usually has the proper training, so that when he comes into an experience of this nature, he is able to distinguish between the real, the pseudoreal, and the unreal.

The introvertive experience often gives the experiencer the feeling of melting away into infinity. The religionist will experience a blazing light which seems to be the center of all things. But each is only reaching the same point in the high Mental Plane, and is being deceived by the Kal Niranjan into believing this is God. The ECKist enters into the Atma Lok, the Fifth Plane, with the assistance of the Living ECK Master. He is not at all misled by the Kal into believing that the Brahm world, the Mental Plane, is the ultimate of all planes. Neither does he believe that the Saguna Brahm Plane, which is the unconscious world, is the last of the path. He knows that the path of

ECK ends in the SUGMAD. He will strive onward until reaching this world, this Ocean of Love and Mercy. Nothing will or can hold him back, for it is the guidance of the Living ECK Master which takes him into the highest worlds of all, where he receives his spiritual mission and becomes a Coworker with the SUGMAD.

Whether the seeker understands it or not, it is true that the mystical experience will bring him into intimate association with the religion, culture, and civilization of his times. It does not have any tendency to make him a member of any particular creed or sect; it will not basically change his traits. If he is a Hindu, he will remain a Hindu. If a Buddhist, he will remain a Buddhist.

He will believe in whatever is the scripture of his particular society and civilization. His background and religious tendencies will be part of the culture to which he belongs, and his faith in the religious scriptures of his country will be the guidepost and the strength for his spiritual drive. The framework of which creed he will fit his experience into will depend mostly on the culture in which he lives.

However, it will be found, on close scrutiny, that most seekers are using mysticism merely as an escape from life and from its duties and responsibilities. The mystic can retreat into a private ecstasy of bliss, turning his back on the world and forgetting not only his sorrow but the needs and sorrows of his fellow men. His life becomes narrow and selfish.

The preoccupation of man in his waking state is for comforts and for survival as long as possible; he looks for any state that gives him joy, regardless of whether it is a mystical state or a state of material comfort. He lives through periods of skepticism and drops his skepticism when he feels that the comfort states are leaving him.

When such states of comfort are regained, he once

more establishes himself in the persistent ideal of ease and happiness with his materiality. He knows, lives, and is aware of life as the part of his physical and human senses. Other than this there is little else in life for him. He accumulates material possessions and gives back to life the least he can, but always in hopes that it will return him greater rewards.

The evolution of his consciousness is always slow. It takes many lives to reach anyone of this nature. He goes through the evolution of life in matter and the evolution of life in mind power. But to him the ECK is only a word which merely states the spiritual phenomena of life without explaining them. Neither is it any good for him, because he has to extend himself and gains little, according to the material world. Life then becomes a form of veiled consciousness. He objects to stepping any further into a more evolved state.

Thus, the ECK is not a doctrine, It is a perspective. It is not a philosophy, but a mood. It is not the ECKist who makes ECK, but the ECK which makes the ECKist; and this ECK is all of life.

The materialist is one who always sees the variety and not the reality of life, who wanders on from birth to rebirth trying to find what might be the answers to his permanent desire for creature comforts. The ECKist finds that whosoever wants life shall live, and whosoever wants love shall have love. But whosoever wants hatred shall suffer through the hardships and pangs of discomfort from death to death, through life after life.

The ECKist need not ask what to do with his life and his efforts in life, for the ECK engulfs him constantly and gives him task after task. He becomes a conduit through which flows an electric current of power. This current becomes him, until he can no longer feel the difference between It and himself. He cannot recognize where It begins in him and leaves off in him; It compels him to accept Itself for whatever It might be. It is the ECK power, using him as a channel.

After he has accepted It as part of himself and allows It to use him, his life cannot be otherwise. He wants It to continue to use him as a channel, and keeps himself open to the ECK at all times.

The lower self must learn that it cannot exist in eternity, as it belongs to the Kal Niranjan. Since Soul does not belong in the lower worlds, except to live in them temporarily, then all Its communication should be with the ECK.

No problem is given man which is greater than himself. Each being is tested according to his capacity; none are tested beyond it. Each problem which man encounters has a spiritual solution, and each person has his troubles at the point where he is most negative and vulnerable.

Whosoever knows one thing therefore knows fully all things, for Truth in one spiritual thing is inseparable from the Truth of all things. If one knows himself, then he has Self-Realization; but if he knows a single factor about Truth, he certainly knows all Truth. The mind of man and the mind in man are One. This is the law of the lower worlds, and that which so often betrays the seeker of the divine.

Man should never seek to become one with God, for he is then falling victim to the Kal Niranjan. He is catering to the impermanent, and not to that which is eternal. Only the SUGMAD is eternal and can give life in eternity. What men call God is impermanent and cannot give life to any except in the psychic worlds.

Trying to bring together the lower self and the higher self to make them one, in order to enter into the worlds of ECK, is to bring about defeat. They do not mix, for none are as far apart in poles as these two qualities. The lower represents the Kal, which is the negative power, and Soul represents the ECK, which is the higher power. The twain shall never meet, for the lower, being of the Universal Mind Power, must step aside and be left behind so that Soul can enter into the heavenly worlds.

Spirituality and the sciences of man are also separated by the same factor. Spirituality represents the highest in man and the universe, while science is only representative of the negative or materialistic. Mind does not seek truth, but only the material and what is needed to survive in the world of the Kal Niranjan.

All that is life is the ECK. Thus the eternal paradox and eternal truth of ECK is within all. It is only the chela who has the insight to look into life and find the ECK behind all things, working slowly and quietly to bring about the spiritual change which is the true purpose of the SUGMAD.

12
The Sacred Works of Eckankar

Every chela of ECK is a special person. He is special because all his protection is from the Living ECK Master. Though he has been under the protection of the MAHANTA for many centuries, yet has ignored his presence, it does not keep him from receiving the MAHANTA's blessings.

The ECK chela is always cherished, beloved, and protected by the ECK Master in every act of the chela's life. He is taken care of in every possible way, furnished with life, love, and the generosity and kindness of the Living ECK Master. The chela does not have to call upon the Living ECK Master to fulfill any needs in his life, for everything is taken care of without request.

Desires are the least of the chela's worry, for he is never without the protection of the Living ECK Master. There are times when he may feel that he is in disfavor, but this is never true. The Living ECK Master may stand aside and let the chela go through a certain test because he needs the experience. The MAHANTA is always testing the chela in one way or other, for he knows that this is the way to keep the chela aware and always watchful of what life may bring him. Sometimes it is pain, for pain is often the creator of awareness, and sometimes it is hardship, but if the chela will recognize this, he will know that he is most fortunate, for the MAHANTA is merely putting him through some karma in order to reach a higher level.

Most fortunate is the chela who receives the blessings of the MAHANTA in some manner or other. If the MAHANTA touches the chela with the tip of his finger, shakes hands with him, or kisses him, the gift of the Lord is passed from ECK Master to chela. The Master is only the medium, or channel, by which the blessing is passed from the SUGMAD to the chela.

The chela must be spiritually developed to such a high degree that he inspires a subtle peace of mind and serenity of heart in those who are the noninitiated. He must give joy to those around himself. Dignity and sweet humility are the twin traits of the ECK chela, and he cannot be otherwise. He is ready to go forth to preach the gospel of ECK to the world, revealing Its secrets to those who are ready to listen. He will show that the MAHANTA is the divine one who has taken upon himself the human frame for the emancipation of Souls.

The Living ECK Master alone connects one with the ECK, the Sound Current. He is the incarnation eternally present on earth for this purpose, and he knows who is ready here and now. The chela, in his work to assist the spiritual ECK Master, finds that men are hopelessly immersed and imprisoned in mind and maya. Seeing the true MAHANTA within the form of the outer body brings salvation and permanently puts an end to all unworthy desires.

As moths are drawn to the flames and hummingbirds to the honeysuckle, so the nonbeliever is drawn to the chela, who in turn is drawn to the MAHANTA. Without being drawn to the MAHANTA in this way, the inner fires of faith are never kindled and devotion never aroused. Without these, no grace may ever be bestowed by the MAHANTA, and the goal of Ultimate Reality never gained.

The body is the temple in which Soul dwells while on earth. It is transient and perishable; subject to birth, growth, decay, and death. The senses of the body often lead the individual astray so that he follows the false teachers, prophets, and pseudomasters. These are only the Kal working through the lower forces.

The ECK must be first in the thought and deeds of every ECK chela. Until he has reached this stage of life, all things seem useless to him. However, all else must be forgotten. Only ECK should be first in his life. Life becomes worthless, damaging, and without any meaning whatsoever if he has not accepted ECK as the supreme reality in himself.

The chela's stream of consciousness, which is a worldly concept of thought as a continuous procession of experiences and memories through time, must be imbued with the ECK. It must be filled with everything that is the ECK, instead of those forces which are known as the Kal power, or the lower-world psychic things. One has to bring himself into agreement with the ECK and not the Kal forces. When he has reached a certain agreement with the ECK, this stream of consciousness pouring through his mind will be changed to make him a channel of the divine reality.

The jumble of thoughts pouring through the individual's mind are from habit. They have tremendous influence on the individual, and certainly are not truth at all, but only the reflection of the nature of Kal. Often, by picking out a thought here and there to verbalize, one sees that thoughts are often a stagnant stream of dead matter which are constantly raised by Kal Niranjan in order to bring about influences to keep Soul caged within the body.

The attempt to render into words the totality of one's thoughts at any given moment presents difficulties. There are not enough words available to make it possible. Thought, at its simplest being a rather wide band of perceptions, often confuses the chela who does not know what should be selected for his best interest. This is why one's concentration must be upon the ECK rather than anything else. Once the consciousness of the individual is put upon the ECK and filled with It, there is no problem, for every word, thought, and deed is of the highest order, and he follows Its dictates naturally.

The confusion here is that man believes human beings think in words, but this is not true. Man thinks in images within a stream of consciousness. Most of the time the stream of consciousness is really what predominates in the neurotic and psychotic mind. It never has good recall, and only occasionally can it be shut off in order to get the individual fixed in some sort of stillness within the inner self, to get him outside his psychic state of consciousness.

Those who allow this stream of consciousness to control their lives are in very poor states. Whenever a thought foists itself upon the thinker and persists in spite of his wishes, the thinker is in trouble. He must be able to call up practically any thought or memory within his whole realm of knowledge without going through his stream of consciousness.

Most religious and metaphysical systems within the earth world lean too heavily on this stream of thought association. Out of it come the twin negative emotions, hatred and fear. This leads to the doctrine of wars and destruction and the pursuit of power, which keeps the world in an undesirable state of turmoil.

It means, then, that the mission of the MAHANTA on this earth is to stir the millions of noninitiated into revolt against all orthodox religions. It also means that anyone who opposes the MAHANTA in any of the worlds is foolish, for the ECK will swiftly work in retribution. There is no wasting away of the MAHANTA's strength, for it is of the power of the ECK. He does not have to prove anything, for all is there as clear as life itself. While the priest can prove any religious proposition by quoting texts from some sacred scripture, the MAHANTA proves it by his very existence.

The mainspring of every civilization is its church. When that decays, the civilization decays with it. But with the ECK, one finds no decay, for Its strength lies in the SUGMAD, and hence It is all-powerful. Because the Living ECK Master is always with every civilization in history, those who follow the ECK find that it needs no human state of consciousness to guide it, as orthodox religions do.

No one should exploit the good and gentleness in man. But those trying to gain power in this world do so, be it in religious or other matters. To anyone who is not spiritual, spirituality always looks like hypocrisy.

Man is able to tell what comfortable lies he likes to others, but he must beware of telling them to himself—not because it is immoral, but because, unfortunately, he will not be able to deceive himself. One cannot live happily with a person he knows is a liar. Those in the human state of consciousness will always be ready to deceive others, while living in frustration from such states themselves. The Living ECK Master knows what is going on within each of them, but he says nothing. Every individual who lives in this attitude must himself be subjected to what he practices.

All ECK Masters who have come here to live upon this earth plane and to give spiritual assistance to those ECK chelas who desire to follow must be, above all things, sincere, honest, and above reproach. But whatever they do in their human lives will have nothing to do with their spiritual lives; the two are often in opposition with one another.

By his inner powers, the Living ECK Master looks at the inner state of the chela, not the outer self. If any are worthy, they will qualify to be given the higher initiations and will receive the true spiritual instruction about the royal road of ECK. At times the MAHANTA will openly discourage some, because they are not inwardly receptive. He never pays heed to one's caste, color, or nationality. He is ever steady in his outlook upon all, and he sees the ECK in all, though few see It in themselves.

It is by these same inner powers that he gives chelas secret instructions at long distances, without speaking or using the written word. He will often send one of his own Mahdis in the Nuri Sarup to those who are in need of instruction and initiation. The MAHANTA knows the inner states of all chelas and anticipates their actions and questions. At times his behavior may offend the general public and even some chelas, but the true seekers of the SUGMAD recognize what this means to themselves and the public.

When the initiated one is ready to cross the Bhava Sagar, the tumultuous ocean of birth, death, and rebirth, he knows the MAHANTA is ready to assist him. He will not have to face the Angel of Death nor the Judge of Karma, for the MAHANTA will not let him be touched by either. He is taken by the Living ECK Master to that place in the high spiritual planes which he has earned during his life on earth. Neither will he be compelled to return to this earth world in another incarnation.

The chela should never expect nor ask that the Living ECK Master fit the image which he has formed through reading and listening to others about any pseudomasters.

All are pseudomasters except for the Living ECK Master; he is the only authentic Master within this world. Many seekers of God make their own image of what they expect a Master to be, and, learning that the MAHANTA does not fit this image, they become disappointed. They look too much for gentleness and kindness and all the virtues which they believe should be the main qualities of a Master. They look for love, when perhaps what they believe is love does not exist. Their disappointment is too deep for retreat. Sadly they turn away, only to learn that what they are seeking does not exist within this world.

The MAHANTA is kind, gentle, and loving to whomever he believes needs these qualities for spiritual growth; to others he might appear to be understanding, but firm and sharp in his discipline. He treats everybody according to their spiritual growth and helps each unfold individually on the path of the SUGMAD.

The ECK is the unity in the midst of diversity and multiplicity, which means that all the functions of life preexist in the SUGMAD. But It expresses Itself through the ECK in the worlds of Its own making. So it's found that the ECK is the cause of all life, for It is the medium which the SUGMAD uses to reach all existence. The universes, then, are the effect of the ECK. Nothing can appear in the effect which was not already in the cause. The cause is ever present in the effect because it is as much in the whole as the ECK is in the SUGMAD, and the MAHANTA is in the ECK.

Separation from the MAHANTA is pain, and unity with him is peace. All is within the MAHANTA, for all within him is in the ECK, as well as in the SUGMAD. When this understanding rises in the Atma, there is a great burst of knowledge and unfoldment which gives It peace and happiness. All conditions of space, time, and causation are within the ECK. All the universes are within It, and so is the reconciliation of all opposites. Yet It is attributeless and possesses the works of the SUGMAD, in the being and nonbeing states.

Therefore, whoever lives in the whole, and in whom the whole lives fully, is alone in his holiness. Few can share it with him, for they do not know what it is and cannot understand anyone in whom it dwells.

In finding himself, man turns his consciousness to the MAHANTA and allows the Living ECK Master to fill it. By doing so he passes through the limitations of the little self into the nonlimitations of the SUGMAD Consciousness.

It is in the little self that man craves to burst the bondage and become freed from all ills, find personal immortality and salvation. He fails, for he believes that the ECK can be brought into manifestation by either written or spoken words. The truth of this is that the true Word or name of the SUGMAD is Dhunatmik. It resounds within the chela, and never without as many believe. There are the two forms of the Name. First is the Dhunatmik, which is the soundless word, and second is the Varnatmik, which is the sound of the word in many forms. The Dhunatmik exists in those regions where language is not needed. It is the smile of the lover who finds that his love exists in the heart and not on his lips nor in his deeds. One can never express in words or deeds, gestures or symbols, what the spiritual ears hear.

The Varnatmik is the great Sound of the Physical, Astral, Causal, and Mental worlds. It is heard by the inner and outer ears, in many forms, but always as the echo of the original Sound, the Dhunatmik of the upper worlds. The chela must always take care to distinguish between the echo and original. The Dhunatmik can never be heard by the outer ears; therefore, the inner ears must be attuned to the higher vibrations of the true SUGMAD worlds.

The creative primal music of the ECK is always vibrating throughout all the universes of the SUGMAD. It is the voice of the divine reality, the SUGMAD, vibrating into all regions like a great wave. When this primal force leaves the heart of the Ocean of Love and Mercy, It becomes the ECK, which is the Dhunatmik—the soundless, wordless Music. The Varnatmik is the Sound which breaks into many sounds, and is manifested in the lower worlds.

Those who seek God always look for the one who is able to converse with the Dhunatmik, the Inner Word: One who knows the way of the ECK. Every Soul is released through the ECK, brought out of the darkness of matter, and set free through the MAHANTA, in the form of the Sound Current. As soon as the pure consciousness is established within him, he actually hears the ECK Current, the Dhunatmik, which is not heard by the outer ears.

At first he does not know from where the inner Sound comes, but he instinctively does know It comes from the direction which he must take. Without consciousness of the Sound, he would be in darkness. It reaches down from the Ocean of Love and Mercy, pulling Souls out of the darkness of the lower worlds into the heart of the SUGMAD.

Through the ECK, the Dhunatmik, comes the creation of all the universes and all the creatures and beings, and man himself. In heaven and on earth, no other name is to be given It but that of the ECK; by ECK alone can man escape the bondage of worldly ills and the Wheel of the Eighty-Four.

The divine and direct method of the ECK is natural and innate in man; there are no substitutes for It. It is found within Itself. Without devotion, Soul is not purified; and without the purification of Soul there is little that man can do for himself. He must remain faithful to the Spiritual Exercises of ECK. He must set aside the gross and seek only the pure within himself, for without this there can never be any success in hearing the Sounds of the ECK or dwelling in the heart of the SUGMAD.

The human form and mind are gross embodiments which can never have direct contact with the Dhunatmik. This ECK Dhunatmik is the cause of the consciousness in man. The essence of the ECK must be joined with man's consciousness to remove all earthly vestures that separate the two. It is through the ECK that Soul descends into the darkness of matter and mind and becomes bound. It is also through the ECK and the MAHANTA, the living embodiment of the ECK, that Soul is lifted out of this darkness of matter and mind.

Unless the seeker finds the MAHANTA, who is conversant with the ECK, he shall be unable to return to the true Ocean of Love and Mercy. The way of the ECK is the only escape from the caged condition of maya, the veil of illusion which keeps one in the world of matter and mind.

When the chela is no longer encumbered with the mind, he is free, happier, and finds life in the SUGMAD. Nothing can limit his activities or bar his perceptions. But he learns that knowledge of universal nature is possible only by means of a human body. All the kingdoms of the universe have their corresponding sheaths in the human system: the Physical, Astral, Causal, Mental, and Etheric. Into each sheath are woven the ECK principles, ranging from abstract factors of conscious life to relations and laws governing natural facts. Also, each plane has both the universal and individual aspects. The bodies of each individual are a microcosm in which the macrocosm dwells.

The ECK of Itself has no body. But this ECK—and not God or the SUGMAD—is in everybody, everything, and is no-thing. Therefore, the body and the embodied are not separated; they are not the same, but similar. Each Soul is given a body to wear for a divine purpose. This is the field of karma, and the human world is the place of karma.

There are those who serve the MAHANTA for desires and selfish purposes, and those who tirelessly strive for Truth. There are those who, for fear of pain, birth, death, and other common calamities, seek sanctuary with the MAHANTA to escape them. Finally there are those who, having known Reality, have established themselves in It; they alone love the Truth for truth's sake; these are the children of the ECK.

At the time of initiation the chela is imparted vital secrets, which facilitate his growth and speed up his karma. The highest, perfect directions for the Spiritual Exercises of ECK are given. These help him unfold his inner hearing and inner sight, and with them he begins his ever-growing inward and upward pilgrimage to the SUGMAD.

At initiation the MAHANTA personally, or through his Mahdis, connects the chela with the ECK Sound Current and accompanies him all the way through the regions of Light until he reaches his home within the Ocean of Love and Mercy. All men caught in the meshes of matter cannot be released until the MAHANTA connects them with the inner ECK Current. No man can tune himself in to the Sound Current, for it is only the MAHANTA's own initiatory power that can do this for him.

Soul is connected with the Sound Current at initiation only by the MAHANTA, whether he is there in person or not. He may have one of the Mahdis, an initiate of the Fifth Plane, do this, but the Initiator is only an instrument through which the initiation and connection are given.

When the connection is made, the chela develops the ability to travel by himself, in the company of the MAHANTA. He is more than able to overcome the downward pull of mind and matter, and keeps ascending toward the regions of true Light. When there has been enough progress made on the path of Eckankar, he cannot gather any more negative karma. The earthward pull has ended, and the upward pull becomes more powerful and acts upon Soul.

It is always the individual Soul, the conscious man, that is initiated and animated. Therefore, the age of the physical body will have nothing to do with the initiation, and the effectiveness and efficiency of the initiation depends on the competence and compliance of the one who receives it. The inner states of consciousness differ in different individuals. The MAHANTA animates and quickens the ECK mantra, making it a mass of radiant energy; he injects his own consciousness and its subjective Light into the chela receiving the initiation, and the chela then feels the shock of spiritual consciousness. It is an unspeakable feeling of blessedness which comes upon him.

Blended in consciousness with the MAHANTA, it is then that the chela rises to planes within planes. This inner elevation of consciousness results also in the expansion of consciousness. It is then that the initiated one finds an added knowledge of himself and those glories of the ECK which await him. He reaches these heights by the grace of the Living ECK Master; he would have been unable to reach them if he had not entered onto the path of Eckankar.

The initiate, who with great devotion is purged of his dross at the time of initiation, enters through the single eye—the straight and narrow gate—into a tremendous expansion of consciousness, which transports him with joy into a state of beingness he has never before known.

Thus begins the chela's journey to the SUGMAD; he walks on the straight and narrow path, which is as sharp as the razor's edge, and listens all the while to the ECK Sound Current. All this is accomplished while the chela is in full possession of his faculties. He finally arrives at the court of Sat Nam, ruler of the Fifth Plane, and sees this great being in Its radiant and inexpressible form. Then he realizes that the SUGMAD, the ECK, and all the rulers of the vast universes throughout the spiritual kingdom of the SUGMAD, are all one in one, and that, in reality, each is the MAHANTA, the Living ECK Master. This is the greatest of all discoveries, for the MAHANTA is formless in spite of having form. He is of spiritual form and material form, being many things and many forms.

The chela will come to the point where he cares nothing for cultural creeds, philosophies, civilizations, and societies. He knows they are only pale offshoots of the true Reality. The holy current of the ECK is all that counts for him while living in the physical form, but he knows that he now is of two worlds. The coming and the going of the bodies of man are of little interest to him, for he knows that this is the way of the world. But when initiated into Eckankar, all are free from the births and deaths of the body. All are then at rest with the SUGMAD in the Ocean of Love and Mercy.

The journey to the SUGMAD begins at the Tisra Til, the Third Eye, and from this point Soul ascends upward. Soul is cut free from all material toils and from the Kal, who has restricted It from the beginning of Its journey in this world. Proper training under the direction of the MAHANTA after initiation will work wonders, and the seemingly impossible becomes possible. The finer senses become active and aware by right use, as directed by the MAHANTA. At first the ECK Sound Current is weak, often imperceptible, but variable. However, by continual training, a transformation takes place, and the Music of the Spheres is heard quite distinctly. Its divine and delectable Sound is of a sweetness and serenity unsurpassed by any.

This Music draws Soul upward by Its strong power, like

a powerful magnet. It purifies all which Soul picked up as dross during Its sojourn on earth. As the awakened consciousness makes Soul partake of the joys of heaven, It becomes a greater channel for the MAHANTA to use for spreading the message of Eckankar. Thus Soul, severed from maya and its illusions, its seeds of desires, its hopes and fears, is liberated and established in the great Reality of ECK.

By contemplating upon the Living ECK Master, the chela discovers the fickle and faltering nature of his mind. The MAHANTA removes mortality and the lower nature from Soul and gives It strength and firmness. There is only a singular sense of purpose within the God Worlds, and this brings Soul into Its own reality. It separates illusions from truth and brings to Soul the recognition of Itself as a channel for the MAHANTA. Soul establishes Itself in the true light of the SUGMAD by this recognition, and few, if any, will reach these heights unless they bring themselves to that point of getting rid of the ego and accepting the MAHANTA as their spiritual guide in life.

The ECK Satsang is important to the chela, for it is a part of his being in the works of Eckankar. Without the ECK Satsang, the true potential of the chela never becomes an actuality. Unless the grace of the SUGMAD is upon the chela, there is never born a deep aspiration for heavenly things. He cannot receive these blessings unless the ECK helps his heart to understand and hunger for truth. People cannot be made to become spiritual. This is the greatest mistake made among those who desire truth but who make no effort at finding it. They believe the Living ECK Master can give them spirituality.

This is not true, for spirituality is born in the heart of man by the grace of the Supreme Deity. When one attends an ECK Satsang, he becomes refined in the presence of others and moves in grace toward becoming an instrument of the SUGMAD. He becomes closer to the MAHANTA in spirit, and they can communicate secretly. The relationship between the two is of a love greater than words can express; it is the highest of any love.

The Living ECK Master has a relationship with the chela which is an ever-present inspiration. In his presence the chela finds that the dormant vitality within himself becomes a dynamic actuality which strengthens his spiritual unfoldment. The devotion of the chela for the MAHANTA is divine and, therefore, their close relationship is sacred, strong, and permanent. As the chela makes his way upward, the true love between him and the MAHANTA grows, and there is never any chance of its diminution.

To utter the Word, or the ECK mantra, in a special arrangement, is to build one's own future in the other worlds. This is especially true of building in the Akasha, the primal matter force. The ECK enters into the composition of all beings and things of life. It is the primary Sound of every world within the universes of the SUGMAD. The sounds of the oceans, the whistling of the winds, the rustle of trees in the forests, the beating of drums, the noises of great cities, the cries of animals, and the words and emotional sounds of people are the natural elemental sounds of the ECK.

All words are but forms of the ECK, for each is a modification of the inner Sound. This consists of the primal Sound of life and matter. The substance of the atom, its vibration, and the equality of the Sound which are inseparable in reality and in consciousness. Within the psychic worlds is the cycle of sounds. It is important that each vibration has a start, a continuation, and a finish.

Vibration is the manifestation of action by the ECK, but initiation is by the SUGMAD and carried via the Sound throughout all the universes. The chela learns this secret from the MAHANTA after his Seventh Initiation.

He begins to understand that the number of vibrations

is the principal secret of the production of all sounds. Vibration arises in one of the Kal worlds because of the presence of substance, the reality in it. Sometimes, if the chela is on the higher spiritual planes of the SUGMAD, he will find that vibrations rise only under his origination, and not by fixed law. However, all such vibrations take place in a moment.

The ECK Sound is produced by such a vibration in the higher worlds. Because there is so much Sound, there arises the inarticulate Sound. On the lower planes the opposite is working: for each of the sounds without articulation, there must be equal sounds with articulation. In these worlds the sounds, or vibrations, must work opposite one another, the inarticulate against the articulate. This makes perfect vibrations within the matter worlds, and until these are matched, there can be no music, nor words, nor sounds from man. Therefore, man must have silence and sound in equal portions, for if one overbalances the other, then he will have pressures from the inner powers which will pull him one way or the other. It could even bring death to his physical body.

For example, if man spends too much time in silence, as those pseudoholy men do, sitting in caves in the vastness of mighty mountains, they are not fit to serve their fellow men. They do nothing for themselves nor anything for the race of men. They become selfish in their desire for silence and receiving the powers of the ECK. When living in this state, the individual is apt to lose all he has tried to gain.

When man spends all his time with the other extreme, which is noise, he is soon driven crazy. He cannot live in this state for long without losing all that he has desired of the SUGMAD. Therefore, unless he balances the periods of time for receiving and giving out vibrations, there will be an imbalance in him which will bring a loss of spiritual growth.

The right act is the act which best serves the progress of all. It shall bring the greatest good to the greatest number of people. It shall put all beings of all worlds in accord with the will of the SUGMAD.

The chela never consciously makes such efforts to do the right thing for all, for if he did, much of his time would be spent in trying to decide what would be the most universally just thing to do. He gives himself up to the MAHANTA and allows the Living ECK Master to work through him. Whatever he does is always in the name of the MAHANTA, and therefore, most of his actions will be right. But opposition to right action will always be strong, so he must consider that there will be good and evil times, and proper and improper seasons for doing right actions. He should not have to put his mind to making such decisions, but rather let the ECK use him for right deeds, as It knows best.

True judgment takes into consideration the necessity of the circumstances, the requirements of the particular spiritual evolution, and the time period and world system in which the particular Soul in question dwells. But there is a main aspect to this, and that is love for all life. Right speech, right duty, and right hearing are of the same pattern. By depending upon the guidance of the MAHANTA, by becoming a divine channel, one falls into the patterns of right acts, right speech, right duty, and right hearing. By all this, he finds true spiritual growth and eventually works out all his karma in one lifetime. He enters into the heavenly worlds at last, never having to return to this plane in any incarnation.

During this life on earth, one finds conflicts with his domestic duties to his household, state, and country. He is often called to duty for defense of the homeland, or to take part in some political act, for some act of good for humanity, or for a religious or moral purpose. Sometimes the call of Soul will cause the individual to cast aside everything to follow it. The call of the MAHANTA is the highest of all, for it is the spiritual beckoning of the SUGMAD to come home again. This call is imperative and cannot be weighed against any other condition.

If he is willing to give up everything in his life to follow the call of the MAHANTA, then let him do so. It means that he will have peace of heart but will suffer in body and spirit from the taunts and insults of life around him. He must be forever dedicated to the MAHANTA, for being so, then will the grace of all life be given to him, whether he is in rags or wears rich garments upon his back.

He shall receive little praise for what he gives in life to the divine reality, nor shall anyone appreciate his sacrifices. He will be reduced in social and human stature, but his spiritual self will be like a shining giant among pygmies. He will be in love with all people, all creatures, and all life. But he will be reviled, spat upon, and hated for the spiritual light he carries with him.

He will find the MAHANTA's name torn to shreds, his life always in danger, and his reputation continually shattered. The masses will not like truth being thrust upon them, and they will be used by the Kal to destroy whatever body, or vessel, the MAHANTA wears at the time he is in the world as the Living ECK Master.

It is only then that the chela realizes that life here on earth as the spiritual channel for the MAHANTA is not without its dangers and problems. He truly learns then who the MAHANTA really is; he learns what spiritual greatness has been thrust upon the MAHANTA. He learns that he himself is to become a coworker in the field of the divine reality.

He will also learn that, although the MAHANTA is with him every moment, day and night, he is truly in a lonely position. No one knows or understands the spiritual cloak he wears, except a handful of those who follow the ECK. But he will know that always he is in the protecting love and light of the MAHANTA, the Living ECK Master, and no harm can ever touch him.

Thus ends the first book of the Shariyat-Ki-Sugmad.

Book Two

1
The Eternal Dreamer of ECK

In the beginning it is said that the influence of the ECK on world history is and has been enormous; but few other than the ECK Masters and a few chelas have realized this. However, once the chela becomes a Mahdis, an initiate of the Fifth Circle, he begins to realize the universal importance of Eckankar. Not only in this world but in all the worlds of the SUGMAD.

The noninitiates in this world are many, but those who have reached the Fifth Circle of initiation soon find that to establish oneself with the SUGMAD is a rare thing indeed.

The Divine Dreamer sends out Its dreams to man via the MAHANTA, the Living ECK Master in all Its worlds, to arouse individual Souls in their sleep state to seek once again the heavenly kingdom. The Kal Niranjan sends forth its illusions via the negative channels to offset the divine dreams. It is hardly ever successful.

Therefore, dreams are part of the emotional states of man. He lives either in the ECK or the Kal emotions, but hardly ever in the neuter, the nonattached, states. But the dream state is real to the true dream of the Mahdis, for the Living ECK Master sees that it must be of truth.

Few know and few believe that dreams are mainly of the emotional fabric of life. This emotional state is originated on the Astral Plane; hence, the initiation of the Second Circle of ECK is that of the Astral Plane. Emotions are experiences rather than behavior, as the material and mental scientists of the physical world have led man to believe. The mistake made in the world of physical science is that emotion is originated on the Mental Plane and is therefore subject to the realm of thought.

This is not at all true, for emotion is not a mental phenomenon. The ECKist must work in the plane of feeling instead of thought where the emotional state is concerned. Naturally this is the force of the Astral Plane and nothing more.

The ECK Initiate knows that the emotional state is that by which the dream state finds its true nature in this world. Soul lives in the constant state of dreaming, for emotions are awareness on a certain level. This is the awakened state of the astral sense; and while within this state, one knows and realizes all perceptions in the Astral world.

The basic awareness, then, of the astral senses is emotion, and this is linked with instinct. The twin instincts of the emotional state are love and aggression. Both are consciously experienced in man, for every charge of either is generated on the Astral Plane through feeling.

Pain is the basic feeling. It is an astral emotion which arises when the ECK force comes in contact with the Kal at a singular point in the body. This means that emotions are aroused on the Astral Plane and then sent through the physical body, making one aware of whatever has happened at any given point in the body.

Thus the emotions build up vibrations which are wavelengths of feelings. These vibrating rates are either speeded up or slowed down according to the energy charges of the instincts, which can be set in motion or relaxed in nature.

The relaxed instincts, for peace of mind and heart, may be to the disadvantage of the chela, for those instincts may cause him to reject the knowledge that Soul must follow the destiny of ECK and this alone.

The whole history of the physical universe is based upon the emotional state of man in the astral sense. This means that the civilization of those nations which have accepted the orthodox religious idea, that of the principle of man born in sin and who could not be saved until the savior made it possible, was able to create some stability among the races.

No pagan religion or culture could withstand the force of the idea that man was born in sin and would never have any release from it until he accepted the messiah of his own people, according to the religions of the earth planet. But this idea was and has been established by the Kal forces; and man, finding this is a false premise, has learned he is in a quagmire of troubles arising from a multitude of new ideas. One of these comes from the new values which man puts down as arising from the intellectual senses.

The idea of man born in sin is one of the oldest pitfalls which the Kal Niranjan could plan for keeping Soul in ignorance of Its true glory; the pitfall that It must spend a certain amount of time and incarnations in this world in order to become purified to enter into the heavenly kingdom and become a Coworker with the SUGMAD.

The truth must be found in the heart of the ECK, for all that is needed for true liberation is the Master, the initiation, and the Sound Current. This alone is the truth of the whole purpose of the SUGMAD for Soul's existence in the lower worlds. All the doctrines of man being born in sin, to be purified by the appearance of a messiah who dies for man's sins, are of a Kalistic belief.

Man is not saved, but Soul is redeemed by the MAHANTA, the Living ECK Master. No other being is capable of giving Soul true freedom after Its multitude of incarnations spent on earth in search of redemption. There is no other way of redeeming Soul's spiritual sanctity for entering into the heavenly states of the SUGMAD.

ECK is life, and life is ECK, and the MAHANTA, the Living ECK Master is The Way, regardless of what is told in any religious scriptures. He is the transformer, the divine channel for the ECK.

No religious faith can continue successfully unless it has a living Master at the head of it. This Master must be one who is adept at the spiritual truths, both in the physical form and that which is the inner self. He is both the Outer Master and the Inner Master.

Unless one has come to the Living ECK Master and accepted him in complete faith during one's lifetime, he must serve many lives, meeting with the MAHANTA during each life, searching, and waiting for another golden opportunity to take up the path of ECK and leave this world forever.

The opportunity comes again and again for every individual Soul who has spent time in this world. The MAHANTA has been with each Soul time and again, but few accept him. They can neither see nor understand the divine glory which flows through him, which can take each into the heavenly worlds to live forever as Soul.

The rejection of the MAHANTA is sad indeed, for it means that the seeker must go on looking, reaching, and trying to find the heavenly path of ECK and the Living ECK Master who will take him into the Kingdom of the SUGMAD. But he seeks in vain, for there will never be anyone but the MAHANTA to give him life, to give him the way to the eternal source of all things.

The ECK life makes no sense without foundations in the ECK doctrine and practices. Indeed, the whole thesis of the ECK chela's life is that he does in his own peculiar way what all ECKists are called upon to do; that their vows are a specific way of carrying out the initiation promises, and that their community life is a particular manifestation of the life of the ECK, the body of the MAHANTA of which they were made a member at the initiation of the First Circle.

Because the ECKist believes that Eckankar is not an isolated sideline but the working out in specific terms of the principles of human life, this means that the ECK chela's life is a particularly clear specification of spiritual existence, which of course is why it can be so completely satisfying at the natural human level, as well as the spiritual and supernatural levels.

If the seeker is going to depend on some private revelation before making a decision to become a follower of Eckankar, he may risk waiting a long time. It does not work in this manner, for revelation in ECK usually comes at a time when he has entered into and become a part of ECK Itself.

Every chela in the works of Eckankar can or could have everything that he wants and needs in the material universe, except what he really wants and needs. The alternative of any desire in this world is meager and not at all heartening.

Symbolism is not a part of Eckankar, but that which is, is the importance in the true spiritual works. A physical action seldom symbolizes anything, for it is actually a simple action and nothing further. Personal feelings are hardly important in ECK; whenever anything has to be done, the chela is the means to the end for the ECK and the MAHANTA, the Living ECK Master to use as the subchannel in this world.

The asanas, postures, and motions of the yogi; the rituals of the religions; and the genuflection and prayers of the metaphysicians are therefore useless. None touches the heart of the SUGMAD, for It does not require worship and love, but faith, devotion, and responsibility to Its cause and principle. Love and action are always secondary.

There is an ancient principle in the world of religion: If one reputable man dies for the people, then all the sins of society can therefore be made as white as snow. What a man's character has to do with the whole of the human race is hardly worth the trouble of dying for, in all matters concerning himself and others. The old feeling that one must do something for others is a negative idea which must be a part of the nature of the Kal force which works in him. It is only an aspect of the material world, and nothing can be settled unless the chela has the true enlightenment of the ECK.

Until this is settled, nobody can expect anything from their religious inspiration and training. Being free from sin will not take anyone a step further on the path to God. It takes the Master, the Sound Current, and initiation to enter into the kingdom of heaven. Because of this, spirituality always looks like hypocrisy to the nonspiritual.

Those who have had realization of Soul know that the SUGMAD *is*. The fool is convinced that nothing greater than himself exists. But he who knows, when he hears of It, he understands It. And whatever is understood exists in the understanding. Assuredly then, that which exists as It is beyond all understanding; but whoever knows this realizes that the realization of It is not in understanding alone. If It exists in understanding alone, then It could be conceived; therefore, It is understood only when the chela allows It to swallow him and digest him. When the chela lets himself surrender to It, It accepts him as a divine channel to be used in all the worlds of the universe.

Nothing is more symptomatic than the gulf between faith and knowledge. The contrast is so enormous that the chela is often so amazed that he will completely drop out of the spiritual works of ECK. He is concerned with the materialistic world in which he lives and also in the spiritual world of the Second Grand Division. He finds that historically all the ECK Masters have existed throughout time within this world, some suffering and dying at the hands of their fellow men, some working miracles and dying quietly, and others becoming well-known figures of their day who had the confidence of the leaders of their time.

The rupture between faith and knowledge is a symptom of the split consciousness which is characteristic of the mental disorders of the individual during any lifetime. It is as if two different persons were making statements about the same thing, each from his own point of view, or as if one person in two different frames of mind were sketching a scene of his experience. This is what is known as mental dissociation, a neurotic disturbance which has bothered practically every society known in the history of mankind and the leaders within each social and racial group.

When the collective dissociation exists within a race or social structure, then the spiritual works of ECK cannot penetrate the group in which it is a part. The work of the MAHANTA, the Living ECK Master becomes more difficult. The collective group is pulling apart, because the individuals within the social order have established this dissociation within themselves. They go in all sorts of directions, and it is hard for the MAHANTA to get the message of ECK across because of this rupture between faith and knowledge. But once the MAHANTA can establish a bridge between himself and the people who are living in this state, it's found that the supremacy of the Word, the ECK, which is central to the ECK faith, takes hold and begins to heal this rupture.

The ECK chela enjoys a great advantage when it comes to answering the crucial questions which have hung over every civilization since the beginning of time. All his experience flows from the SUGMAD; therefore he has a certain amount of spiritual experience in matters which lie beyond the range of human knowledge. But like most of those Souls who venture into the heavenly worlds, he first has a transcendental problem with the God-knowledge.

Man confuses self-knowledge with the knowledge of his conscious ego-personality. One who has any ego-consciousness at all takes it for granted that he knows himself. But the ego knows only its own contents, not the psychic self and its contents. Man measures his self-knowledge by what the average person in his social environment knows of himself, not the real spiritual facts, which are, for the most part, hidden from him.

In a relative way, the psychic self of man behaves like the body with its physiological and anatomical structure, which the average person knows very little about. What is commonly called self-knowledge is therefore dependent on social factors, on what goes on in the human mind. Hence, one is always coming up against the prejudice that negative things should not happen to him; and, on the other hand, one meets with equally illusory assumptions about the alleged presence of qualities, or masters, whom he believes are protecting him, but these are merely rationalizations to cover up weaknesses and unhappiness in himself.

This includes a broad belt of unconsciousness in man, which is defenseless against all sorts of influences and psychic afflictions. One can guard against psychic afflictions only when he knows what is attacking him. Self-knowledge is not of much use in this particular case because it is a matter of getting to know individual facts, and theories do not do much good in this respect. Most of man's ideas, knowledge, and fears are based upon theory; for he knows very little about himself despite all the scientific work done by the world's scientists. When man accepts an idea and wraps around it emotions such as the astral feelings, he is likely to establish a do-or-die feeling.

This is the cause of martyrdom in man. He becomes infatuated with an ideal that is religious or political and dies for it, if the occasion calls for such sacrifice. This is merely a state of loyalty which belongs to the Astral Plane. It is the strength of man's feeling in his cause which brings about this sort of physical and useless death. The ECK Masters look upon this as suicide, or self-destruction, and shun it, for nothing seems more useless than to bring about their own physical death by some feelings of stubbornness which amount only to astral emotions.

There have been some deaths of ECK Masters which could be termed martyrdom, but these are unusual cases. Generally the ECK Master stays away from the issues of the day, which mix politics and religion; he teaches only the purity of the heavenly doctrine of Eckankar. He knows that many will be against him because of the stirring up of the Kal forces, but nothing seems to worry him in this respect. He artfully keeps away from the issues which bring on a confrontation with certain so-called authorities in the materialistic worlds.

The teachings of ECK are the pure doctrine in this world. There are no others which can reach the same level as ECK. Therefore, the ECK Masters know that it is useless to argue and try to convince those who are not ready. Almost all orthodox religions and occultisms are only on the astral level; so the MAHANTA, the Living ECK Master will not allow himself to be drawn into any controversy over the orthodox religions and ECK. He knows that such arguments are foolish and nothing would be gained by anyone who is involved in them.

The release of the chela from the wheel of life when he enters Eckankar is that point when he begins to accept, and stops all his questions. The riddle of the question is forever plaguing the neophyte, for he never understands that no question can be put without an answer. Yet all questions are on the mental level; but the answers are always available before the question. In other words, there are always the answers to the problems of life, without the questions existing. It is the doubting in the mind of man which leads to questions. This doubt arises when there is a lack of confidence.

When asked how to deal with people who are skeptics and doubters, the Living ECK Master says, "I trap them. I get them where they cannot ask any more questions."

When man cannot understand his problem or something which is unfamiliar to him, he is doubtful and asks questions. He must live by established traditions and forms. He must follow out a unified pattern of behavior and live with others who do likewise. Otherwise, his whole pattern of life is upset. If he is not living close to the source of the divine ECK, he might think in terms of not being able to do anything. This is because he is still living in the patterns and binds of society and not yet able to break through the boundaries of liberation.

All life, therefore, becomes an awareness of small things—such as being occupied with the things of the senses. He is aware of speaking, breathing, hearing, seeing, walking, tasting, opening and closing the eyes. He should be beyond these things, for his attention must be put upon the greater reality of life. That of Seeing, Knowing, and Being.

As long as the ignorance about the MAHANTA, the Living ECK Master prevails, the individual Soul is constantly reborn into the world, rising or falling in fortune and station according to Its deeds and their consequences, which is karma. These are various levels above and below the physical world through which the individual Soul may pass in the course of Its reincarnations. These are the psychic, the animal, mineral, plant, and the realm of ghosts. Until It awakens to full self-knowledge, Soul may undergo reincarnations for amazingly long periods of time, touching the highest possibilities of pleasure and the lowest depths of pain, going round and round upon the wheel of samsara for thousands and perhaps millions of years.

All the ways of liberation offered by the various orthodox religions generally must take Soul through the endless cycle of reincarnation until It becomes awakened to Its true self. But ECK gives the chela a concise way which is not known in any other path to God. Once the chela steps onto the path of Eckankar, his karma begins to resolve, and his reincarnations become fewer. When he is initiated, it means that never again will he have to return to this physical and material world. From the moment he steps upon the path of ECK, his spiritual life is under the protection and guidance of the MAHANTA, the Living ECK Master.

The problem with the religions of the world is that one who has gained insight into the nature of the ECK soon learns that they are but social institutions. Their liberation involves, among other things, the realization that it is a myth and not a fact. It is a liberation from certain social injustices, but not a liberation from karma and the gaining of spiritual unfoldment which leads to God-Realization.

Many who are ignorant of the psychic dangers on the path to God will clamor to become initiates of anyone who is supposedly a guru or master. They seemingly want this most important ritual as quickly as possible, without preparation, whether it's the first day they meet or not.

In their eyes the initiation is practically the same as joining a church through baptism, or receiving a lodge degree. One thing seems to be held out to them, should they receive the initiation: that no matter what their development is, they will have certain mystical experiences and will be in a position to command material success for the rest of their lives.

The promise of any successful materiality is nil, although there are some pseudoteachers who say that by joining their group, through initiation, there will be great material success in store for each and all. Others promise spiritual rewards immediately. None of these promises are worth the words that are spoken; they are like shouting into the winds which rage over the stormy ocean. The MAHANTA, the Living ECK Master will not make such promises, but he will state what the initiate can expect after going through the initiation. Neither will he allow anyone to enter into the outer initiation until he has had two years of study in Eckankar.

This is done to build up the stamina of the chela to withstand any spiritual hardships which might arise from working off his karma. If he should initiate the chela at the start of his introduction into ECK, there might be reverberations against the way the chela is accepting ECK. It could prove to be too much for him, and he could become discouraged and quit ECK. So many chelas do this in those religious programs when they are accepted as initiates from the day they enter into their respective paths. This often creates a guilt pattern in the chela, and he becomes resistant to any teachings of wisdom in the future.

Any initiate who violates the tenets of Eckankar will automatically be dropped out of ECK. This means that he will be put back in his spiritual unfoldment and will not have any opportunity for growth until the MAHANTA, the Living ECK Master has reinstated him.

The ways of the initiation offer release from the endless cycle of reincarnation through the awakening of the true self. Accordingly, the divine play of ECK goes on through endless cycles of time, through periods of manifestation and withdrawal of worlds, measured in units of kalpas. A kalpa is a span of 4,320,000 years. From the human point of view, such a concept presents a terrifying monotony, since it goes on aimlessly forever and ever. But from the divine viewpoint, it has all the fascination of the repetitious games of children, which go on and on because time has been forgotten. Yet it has reduced itself to a single wondrous instant of time.

This is not an expression of a formal philosophy, but the experience of a state of consciousness. This means, then, that the only way to cut through these kalpas, or yugas as they are sometimes called, and make a more direct path to God is through the ECK initiation. No one can get off this terrible Wheel of Awagawan, the Wheel of the Eighty-Four as it is known to most God seekers; until one steps upon the path of ECK, he is always on the wheel, which creates millions of problems and karmic conditions.

Release from the Wheel of Awagawan is that which is called Moksha, or liberation. On the whole, it would be best to say that the ECK philosophy is somewhat built around the liberation from this wheel through the MAHANTA, the Living ECK Master. Unless the chela takes the initiation via the Living ECK Master and does it seriously, then he cannot expect to be released from the Wheel of Awagawan, which will carry him through the kalpas of life for millions of years.

The ECK language is always confused with factual language, so there is little or no clear distinction between the Divine Deity as described in terms of conventional thought, and God as It is in reality. This is true in all aspects of the works of ECK for those who are ECKists. To the conventional mind, the puzzle of the ECK philosophy is that it has so much to say in the matter of language and the liberation of Soul that one cannot grasp it unless he is trained in the way of Eckankar.

What is being said here is that according to the liberation experience, there is so much said of what it is not, and little or nothing said of what it is. This is naturally bewildering, because of its lack of relation to things which are considered important in the life of the individual. If it's without content as an experience, why seek it? Why does it hold such immense importance in the ECKist's scheme of life?

It can be said that the vessel, the body and Soul of man, is empty and must be filled. This is the negation of the experience, but it must be considered, for without negation the experience is not of importance to the individual. In the value of emptiness must come the movement it permits, but the emptiness must come first. The filling up is needed in order to understand the fulfillment. This is why the ECK teachings concentrate quite frequently on the negativeness of self, on liberation of It from the so-called concepts of truth.

It proposes no idea, no description of what is to fill the void of the inner self, because the idea would exclude the greater truth which the inner self is seeking. Therefore, the practice of discipline must now enter into the scheme of liberation of Soul. This is the unfoldment and disentanglement of Soul from every identification It has had on every lower plane in the material or psychic worlds.

Soul is total consciousness. It has the complete knowledge, love, and power that all men seek, yet few realize that these qualities are within themselves. They look to the outer instead of the inner self. The liberation of Soul is, of course, freedom from the surrounding materiality which has all but made a prison for It in the lower worlds. When Soul leaves the physical body to journey into the far worlds, It usually does so through the Tisra Til, the Third Eye. It meets the MAHANTA, the Living ECK Master after passing through the gate of the tenth opening, who escorts It into heavenly worlds where It experiences the joys and bliss of life.

However, the first thing which is noticed here is that all time and space dimensions are different from where It resided in the physical world. The laws are different, and the beings and entities all abide by rules unknown upon earth and its respective planes. Soul must again become used to these new laws, and as It passes through each plane, similar to the time zones and nations of the physical world, It finds different ideas along with new laws and ways of life. Each time It enters into another spiritual world, It finds that the laws are vastly different from those of the area which It has just passed through. It takes adjusting to keep up with the travel from one plane to another.

The measurement of reality, therefore, comes when Soul realizes during Its flight into the higher worlds that understanding is a perception of the spiritual senses and not a fact or event in Its travels. It is also found that to isolate any part of the spiritual universe as a single fact, all by itself, is impossible. This is the greatest mistake that most men make. They cannot grasp any of the spiritual life as a whole, much less their physical existence, and as a result find themselves chasing illusions instead of reality.

In ECK there is the unmistakable tone of sincerity which makes the action which is not studied and contrived. Whosoever thinks and acts with a split mind rings like a cracked bell, one part standing aside to interfere with the other, to control, to condemn, or to admire. The true self, or Soul, cannot be split, for It's like the sword that cuts but cannot cut itself.

The illusion of the split comes from the mind's attempt to be both itself and its idea of itself from a confusion of fact with symbol. To end the illusion, one must stop the mind from trying to act upon itself, upon its stream of experiences, from the standpoint of the idea of itself which is known as the ego.

Therefore, the action taken for correcting this phenomenon is sitting quietly and doing nothing. This is the basic Spiritual Exercise of ECK. If there is any action brought forth from sitting and doing nothing, it is spontaneous. Such an action is particularly subtle and extremely hard to put into words. If one wants to weep, then he does so because it is spontaneous; and if he desires to laugh, he does so. The display of emotions is not to be considered in this action because all things are done with a spontaneous effort.

This natural sincerity makes all ECKists different from others. For all those in ECK know that they cannot find the SUGMAD by taking thought, nor can they even seek It by not taking thought. In all, it's known that one begins the road to God by accepting the divine first in thought, and later dropping thought to make the contact.

The ideal is not to discover the original self, but to allow Soul Its own recognition. This self-recognition is the same as the child who one day suddenly discovers he is a person who must have responsibilities and establish his own life here in this world society. Soul's recognition of Itself is, in a sense, made in the same manner.

This recognition comes through the daily routine of the ECK spiritual exercises. Mainly through the nonaction that is sitting still and doing nothing. This is a deceptive action, but then the chela soon learns that ECK is subtle and that he must be constantly aware to catch what is going on within himself. If he sits still and expects life to grow around him quietly like the grass does, then he may be disappointed.

This is the paradox of Eckankar. One sits still and does nothing, but on the other hand he must be ever watchful to grasp the subtle opportunity to go with him wherever the ECK Master desires to take him.

The fear of the unknown, the doubt, and the lack of insight in the chela can cancel out all aspects of Soul Travel. This alone can take the chela completely off the path of ECK, for if he cannot accept what is taking place within himself, if he has problems understanding and believing the subtleness of the experiences which take place within himself, he can leave the path of ECK claiming that it is of little value to him, that he is wasting his time and energies trying to be a success at Soul Travel.

What these people do not understand is that the Eternal Dreamer makes contact with them at varied times while they are in the state of sitting quietly and doing nothing. Sometimes this can be compared with the experiences that take place in dreams. When the chela comes out of his exercises, he may wonder if this was a dream or reality. He might dismiss it as something which happened during a dream state and never give it full consideration as an experience which comes with the inner movement of the ECK within himself.

The identification of the mind with its own image is paralyzing to the chela who seeks Self-Realization and

God-Realization. This image is fixed from out of past lives, and finished as far as the ECKist is concerned. He wants nothing to do with this image, but it tries to react on him while he is doing the Spiritual Exercises of ECK. The mind cannot act without giving up the impossible attempt to control itself beyond a certain point. It must let go of itself in the sense of trusting its own memory and reflection, and in the sense of acting spontaneously on its own in the unknown.

However, it will not dare take chances, for stepping into the unknown is a fearful act to the mind. This is why the ECKist often seems to take the side of action, as against contemplation, and the spiritual exercises are sometimes described as no mental action or no thought. This is also why the MAHANTA, the Living ECK Master sometimes demonstrates ECK by giving instantaneous and unpremeditated answers to questions. When anyone might ask the MAHANTA for the ultimate secret of ECK, he might answer, "Nothing."

No thought is action on any level whatsoever, physical, psychic, or spiritual, without trying at the same time to observe and check actions from outside. The attempt to act and think about action simultaneously is self-defeating, for it starts the mind whirling in a circle—like the wheels within wheels. From the viewpoint of mind, this brings about feeling and action which is wrong, for feeling blocks itself as a form of action when it gets caught in the act of observing.

Too many who are seeking God-Realization expect the experience to be dramatic, something that is earthshaking and will strike them like a club on the head. However, this is not always true because such experiences often are without drama, in the sense of being something startling. Every ECKist knows that the experience or revelation comes like a thief in the night; it comes with strange subtleness.

Often it is hard to grasp, for one doesn't recognize the realization for what it is and will often cast it aside and complain that after taking the path of ECK nothing has happened. This is only the lack of awareness and definitely a lack of understanding of what has happened to him. He sees something; he has a revelation, and yet nothing happens for him because it is too personal. He asks dozens of persons what this means and gets dozens of answers, none of which fit his own case. Many of the answers are negative and discouraging, which tends to destroy whatever revelations he might have been having over a period of time.

The main point here is that the chela must decide whether the revelation is reality or not. All such revelations are usually inward and very subtle. If the MAHANTA, the Living ECK Master appears to him inwardly, then he should make a decision whether this is reality or not. The revelation is so personal that he cannot allow any outside interference. He cannot discuss it with anyone except perhaps the MAHANTA, the Living ECK Master, and if by letter, it should be put down in writing carefully. If discussed vocally, then it should also be done carefully.

Every ECKist who has a revelation of the MAHANTA or the SUGMAD must make his own decision whether it is true or false. The decision does not depend upon anything else. It is a most personal experience with him and must be treated as such. It is a part of him like eating, sleeping, and emotions. No one else should know anything about it but the MAHANTA, the Living ECK Master, who will see, know, and share the experience with the chela.

The MAHANTA, the Living ECK Master knows at all times what goes on, and the ECKist should realize by now that he is never alone in his life regardless of whatever he is doing or wherever he might be. He should know by the living experience that the presence of the

MAHANTA is known through seeing and feeling. That this is reality and no one can take this from him.

All life becomes a realization that the MAHANTA is always present, and that the ECK makes life a joy to live. If the chela errs at any time, there should be little need for discouragement, but one of joy, for he can now compare the errors with the joys of his life.

2

ECK, the Everlasting Gospel

The message of Eckankar, given by the MAHANTA, the Living ECK Master, is the Voice crying out in the wilderness. It is the true doctrine, and he who hears it with ears that can catch the spiritual significance will come to know it as the Everlasting Gospel.

To see the perfect truth of ECK, as It is, demands and compels the subjugation of Soul. This is the Everlasting Gospel, which, in Its majesty and uniqueness of pure truth, necessitates a suspension of the personal activity of thought. One ceases to assert his thought against It. He is passive before It; but in that passivity, which requires the utmost opening of his receptiveness, is the supreme form of activity.

What is man when, having been possessed by the ECK, the ECK has ceased to possess him, and he is possessed by himself again? He is not what he was in the beginning of life upon this earth; he is changed by the knowledge that he has been the actual and is the potential vehicle of God. He is changed by the knowledge of the beauty and wonder of worldly things. It is through the vision of the Kal, in the momentary perfection where he personally enters into the state of awareness in the human sense and looks at what he believes is the true perfection.

He looks at the price of this experience which can be bought for a song, or wisdom for a dance in the street. But hardly does he realize that the truth must be taken with sacrifice and tears in the desolate places where none exist but himself. He must look to himself only for the experience of Soul, for the secret of ECK is that it is neither natural nor revealed. It is given without fanfare. Reason and logic, as man knows them, always change under the influence of the Sound and Light. Divine knowledge is always creative, but it is always difficult to understand. When the eternal individuality of things is recognized, Soul is in abeyance. The infinite in all life is at one with the infinite in man. In this sense the SUGMAD becomes as man is, that man may be as It is. If man can see eternity in life, then at every moment of given knowledge, he knows not merely the particular thing but the mode in which it is real; the mode in which all things are reality which are in the spiritual realm and in which alone they are real. The mode is, of course, eternity!

The true ECK knowledge is above abstraction. Confusion between the psychic and the truly spiritual lies within the lower worlds. Therefore, all religions are one according to the principle which rules the lower worlds, the rule as laid down by the Kal Niranjan. This deity who rules the lower worlds tries to make it appear that all reality is the same, that all religions are one. This is not true, for ECK, of Itself, is not a religion; therefore It cannot be one with any religion, philosophy, or doctrine.

ECK is the Audible Life Stream, the essence of the SUGMAD, the Holy Spirit, and the science of God-Realization. It grows out of the experience of Soul Travel into the state of religious awareness, which the subject gains at his own volition via the Spiritual Exercises of Eckankar. The latter is correlated only with the movement of the inner consciousness, Soul, in those spiritual regions above time and space. ECK is involved in these regions in which all is omniscient, omnipresent, and omnipotent; hence God Awareness. All religions, philosophies, and sacred doctrines are the offspring of Eckankar.

Eckankar is different. It is the Ancient Science of Soul Travel. This is the projection of the inner consciousness which travels through the lower states into the ecstatic states in which the subject feels that he possesses the awareness of the religious experience of being. This is done through a series of spiritual exercises known only to the followers of this science.

The state of perfection is a condition of free unfoldment of identity, through the continual annihilation of the lower self in all its forms by Soul, as It travels through all the planes to reach the heavenly worlds. To explore the vision of individuality, which strives to be free from the chains of the lower world and Kal, is that which inevitably allows passage from the human consciousness state to the individuality of Soul.

To hear one's own Self shriek with terror as It approaches the borders of time and space to sail off into the boundless worlds where only the Void exists is like hearing the cries of the infant. Man is terrified of freedom, for if he reaches the boundless ocean of no-thing, he finds himself freed; and instead of accepting his freedom, he considers it a burden and only seeks to lay it at the feet of another.

The answer is simple, for he who enters into eternity knows that freedom and knowledge are eternal. He knows that the freedom of divine wisdom is to be free of all things and have only responsibility to himself. He becomes the universal man who knows all things in life, and has control over his own destiny.

Every man who enters into the delights of the heavenly world is lonely in the human consciousness, for there are none with whom he can share his delights. Yet within the heavenly worlds he is never lonely, for the very vision of heaven keeps him company forever.

Man's personal experience of liberation is the liberation of his neighbor, the community in which he dwells, his state and nation, and eventually the world. His liberation eventually reaches out and touches all things in life, for he is linked with the very essence of things within the universes of God. He cannot expect to have any experience in life, be it negative or positive, and not have it affect the next person.

The gulf between eternity and time is absolute, and when Soul is in eternity, It is not in time. In the living physical body, Soul is at the point where time and eternity meet, where It and the human self strive together, where the impersonal and eternal are with the personal and temporal. This creates the conflict and strife in the human state of consciousness. But conflict is possible only between things of the same order—and time and eternity are not of the same order.

Nevertheless, they meet in the human self, and the fine point of their contact is that of forgiveness. The eternal forgiveness of all things in life becomes the temporal forgiveness of love. Man cannot love his enemies and kill them at the same time. But forgiveness is possible even while men slay; yet it is not possible, for once man learns to love, there is nothing within this world that man wishes to slay.

Eternity is a condition into which the ECKist enters after physical death, and Eckankar may not merely condone war, as it does, but often it might employ war if necessary to protect itself. After all, the ECK is at constant war against the Kal force within the lower worlds.

Man must not think that if he asks the MAHANTA's help while facing a serious problem, the SUGMAD will remove it to suit man's desires. It works in a different way; the problem itself may remain, but man's approach to it, his understanding of it, will change as a result of his petition. Whereas it may seem a very difficult, even insurmountable battle to face, man will be given the help needed in resolving it. It does not matter in what field the problem may lie, for this is immaterial; all man needs to do is ask the help of the MAHANTA, the Living ECK Master, who can intercede for him, but only in accordance with man's spiritual unfoldment and his karmic needs.

Man's rebellion against Kal is natural. He is involved with those many things which enslave him, like government, taxes, business, the law, religion, education, media, law enforcement, and body chemistry which is known as medicine. He battles to untangle himself from these forces of the Kal Niranjan, but few have any success until they come into the presence of the MAHANTA, the Living ECK Master, who will raise them above all these things. It is then that they can become detached from these aspects and traps of the Kal and make themselves free. It is only then that they can participate in this world and its negative nature and receive whatever benefits are needed for the human body and its senses.

It must be remembered that all complaints and all arguments against the ECK, which are directed at the MAHANTA, are the works of the Kal. Such assaults on the MAHANTA are those which originate from the Kal using the minds and consciousness of those persons within its power to destroy the MAHANTA and the ECK, if at all possible. These are the works of Kal, who uses religions, ministers, and lay persons to bring about the downfall of the ECK because It is truth. There will be those who call themselves ECK Masters and disguise themselves under the robes of the ECK, but they are prophets with false faces who are lying to take in the ECKists; but few, if any, who are truly followers of the ECK are ever deceived by these agents of the Kal.

In order to break the hold that a problem may have upon the mind of a chela, the MAHANTA frequently persuades him to try to solve a false problem unknowingly, by acting consistently upon its premises. This often releases the chela, who suddenly sees through many problems of his own and finds liberation. However, religions feel that the state of liberation they may enter into is the cosmic consciousness or mystical experience. But this is not true, for the ECKist, once released, goes into a much higher state than this.

The ordinary egocentric consciousness is a limited and impoverished consciousness without foundation in reality. Whether its basis is physical or social, biological or cultural, remains to be seen, but there is no doubt that release from this particular limitation is the aim of Eckankar. Nothing else matters but this liberation from the limitations of the egocentric consciousness. Few can understand this, and many go wandering off the path in search of the material things of life: money, health, and physical happiness.

The role of man within this world is to play a game, in a comedy or drama. The ECK chela understands this and has the right to refuse to play the game. He is taught to look at the incessant working of his mind and the physical activity displayed by his body. He should succeed in understanding, in noting that nothing of all that is from him, is him. He, physically and mentally, is a multitude of others.

This multitude of others includes the material elements, the ground from which he came, and that which makes up his body. On the Mental Plane it may include many beings who are his contemporaries, the people he mingles with or with whom he chats, what he reads, and the actions of those he watches. Thus he becomes a part of all that surrounds him.

Anyone asking about ECK does not know ECK. Although one may hear about ECK, he does not really know about ECK. There is no such thing as asking about ECK. There is no such thing as answering such questions. To ask a question which cannot be answered is vain, and to answer a question which cannot be answered is unreal. And anyone who meets the vain with the unreal is one who has no physical perception of the universe, no mental or spiritual perception of the origin of existence.

This is not because the ECK is inherently mysterious, but because the problems of human social needs are artificial. The ECKist acts without calculation, and he never looks for results. He lays no plan, for there isn't anything within this universe in which he is interested for achievement. Therefore, if he fails, he has no cause for regret, and if he succeeds, he has no cause for congratulations. He does not know what it is to love life and hate death. He does not rejoice in birth, nor strive to put off death. Whatever comes into his life is no cause to lead his heart away from the ECK, nor let the human seek to supplement the divine.

During his lifetime man must be faced with the great social lie, that falseness with which he is confronted by the Kal power. This is the illusion, the maya of his life. The great social lie is that he must be like others within the human race. He is born, sleeps, works, excretes, and reproduces. This is the basis of the life in which he lives in slavery to the human needs of his body. But he rises above this in the Atma Sarup and becomes a greater being in the eyes of the SUGMAD, because he no longer needs the social lie. This social lie makes him have the artificial needs of life to which he becomes attracted, and he cannot leave in spirit when death comes to him. The less that he has in life, the greater is his liberation.

The loneliness of liberation comes of not being able to take sides on issues of the day in the humanistic world, or to find security in the crowds; of no longer believing that the rules of the game are the laws of nature. It is the transcending of the ego into the security of the greater individuality. This greater individuality is always lonely, because all those who have not entered into it will attack it in ignorance.

Liberation thus begins at the point that anxiety or guilt becomes unbearable, where the chela feels that he can no longer tolerate his situation as an ego in opposition to an alien society, to a universe in which pain and death deny him, or negative emotions overwhelm him. Ordinarily, he is not aware that his distress arises from a contradiction in the rules of the social game. He blames people, himself, and God for his distress, but none of these are responsible.

He begins to wonder about the major issues of life and wants to escape the wheel of birth and death. Thus he begins the search for the MAHANTA, the Living ECK Master, although he may not even be aware that such a person exists. He will find the pseudogurus scattered throughout the world; some in India, others in various parts of the world. He will find the false prophets and the so-called teachers, but none will give him anything worthy of what he seeks. He will not find satisfaction in anything in life until he comes to the MAHANTA, the Living ECK Master in humility.

The Living ECK Master will introduce him to the path of Eckankar. It is a disciplined and rugged path to follow. There is nothing to teach but life itself, and the chela must learn to obey in order to find himself in the true realization. If he doubts, there is no place for him; but if he believes in the ECK, all will be given to him.

The MAHANTA, the Living ECK Master is so frank about everything in life that no one believes him. For his part he seems to take the world and its suffering as if it were just a dream. Usually the chela thinks he, too, can reach this same level if only he finds the right method for transforming his consciousness. Yet it is not possible to be accepted for ECK training without considerable persistence. All sorts of barriers are put in the way of the applicant during his first year, yet in many cases the more barriers, the more eager becomes the aspirant. But some feel that there is nothing to be gained and drop out of ECK, feeling a sense of injustice.

Those who stay think that the barriers are only obstacles; that the MAHANTA, the Living ECK Master is guarding some deeply spiritual secret and testing them for admission to become an elite in the works of ECK. All the chela's problems and karma are put squarely back upon his shoulders to work out himself instead of the Living ECK Master taking them upon himself.

The point being made here is that once the ECK chela commits himself to accepting the MAHANTA, the Living ECK Master as the guide for his spiritual journey, he becomes engaged in an intense struggle in which all his energy which has been used in exercising his ego will be withdrawn. He soon learns in this struggle between the ego and his true self, Soul, that nothing he can do is right, spontaneous, or genuine; he cannot act independently of himself. On all sides is nothing but defeat. But in this moment of defeat, he, the agent of all his actions, cannot act, does not act, and does not see any future, past, or present in his life which is worthy of anything.

When he has come to this point, the realization bursts

upon him that he has nothing to prove and nothing to lose; but he has only to be himself and live independent of all other things.

Once the chela enters into this state, he is not aware that often such insights have a habit of wearing off. Knowing this, the Living ECK Master tells the chela that he has gained very little because he has only entered the gate. To get the greater understanding, then, he must practice more diligently, which is of course a test to see if he will continue or have an idea that there is still something more in ECK to learn and grasp. On the other hand he may go away with the idea that there is nothing more to be had in Eckankar.

This occurs because the MAHANTA, the Living ECK Master has purposely planted a doubt in his mind. As long as any doubt remains in the chela's mind, he has not finished the task of grasping the true insight on ECK. If he, the chela, returns, the game continues day by day in some subtle way, ploy by ploy, until at last the chela has gained a deeper insight into ECK. As for the MAHANTA, it's known all along that he cannot lose the game, because he doesn't care in the least whether he wins or loses. He has nothing to prove and nothing to defend.

The whole relationship of the Living ECK Master is the same, not only with unfolding the chela to greater spiritual heights, but he actually doesn't care whether he lives or dies. This is true in the sense that he has no ambition to be great, have fame, or leave a name behind him, nor any ambition to be courageous and create anxiety. He clearly sees the idea of the ECK behind all acts, behind all thoughts and feelings, and that all else is illusion. Therefore, he knows that the Kal force controls all life here, so he doesn't fight with it, and will try to get all chelas under him to be detached, if at all possible, from the Kal and its effects.

When one blocks his mental action, there is doubt or hesitation. It is the lack of the ego in going directly ahead; it is a sign that one is not thinking out his problem, that he has stopped thinking. He has a kind of anxiety, going blank, through which flows the emotions of eagerness to win or fear to lose. It is a double bind on the part of the individual who puts himself in this position. Not until he turns the problem over to the MAHANTA, the Living ECK Master will it begin to unravel itself.

The paradox is that pure consciousness is simultaneously both the positive and negative, something and nothing, a fullness and an emptiness. Therefore, the assertion of the greater consciousness is completely paradoxical. The positive side is that it is an actual and positive consciousness. When the chela reaches into it, it is found to be that peace which passes all understanding. Therefore, it is quite correct to say that when one empties all objects and contents of the mind, there is nothing left. This is the negative side of the paradox. What is left is sheer emptiness, and this is the fearful side of consciousness. It leaves its participant filled with terror and wondering where he went astray. It is often called the "awful works of Kal."

The common thought for the positive is that it is sound and light and for the negative, darkness. This is the darkness of God that so many experience while on the path to God. It is darkness because all distinctions disappear in it just as all distinctions disappear in physical darkness.

The paradox is therefore that the light is darkness and darkness is light and sound. Most of those who have experienced both have come to this conclusion. They can tell little difference between the positive and the negative, because they have both the qualities, and both are the qualities of ECK.

Most persons seem to take for granted that the spiritual experience is a religious experience and spirituality is necessarily a religious phenomenon. They seem to believe that spirituality and religious mysticism are one and the same thing. It is true there is an important connection between the two, but it is not nearly so direct and immediate as most persons seem to think and simply cannot be taken for granted as an obvious fact.

When the spiritual experience is stripped of all intellectual interpretation, such as that which identifies it with God or with the Absolute or with the world of Spirit, the only thing left is the undifferentiated unity. This brings out the fact that when the chela has reached this state, there isn't anything left at all. Some interpret this as the "union with God"; however, this is only an interpretation and is not the experience at all. This is only the speech of those who have analytical minds. But most persons do not have such minds, and therefore what is, is that "all" which enters into their experience. This and nothing more!

The experience is personal, yet it is not such, because it grows into the impersonal. During contemplation upon such an experience, after going through it, the individual often finds it to take on a religious form of some sort. This is only an afterthought and not that which actually happened at the moment of experience. It can be said to be reality and hardly anything more.

The individual who experiences this sort of introvertive reality has several different ways of describing it. He may feel the movement of himself through areas beyond space and beyond time, and may see and know what is happening. There is another reference which is used: a melting away, a passing into something greater than the individuality of the human self. It appears to be a loss of personality, but this is only the first phase, the movement through the Mental world where the mystics experience cosmic consciousness and believe that it's the ultimate. He has not learned to move beyond the worlds of time and space, since the mental region is still within the boundaries of spirito-material planes.

This is the experience which leads mainly to selfish motives. When one has the mystical and religious experiences, he usually does not want to serve his fellow man. Too many monks and religionists reach this stage through meditation and drugs and become more interested in living in such states than being active and wanting to give to the worlds. Soul Travel has nothing of this kind. The experiences which one has in this give him the purpose and motivation to serve, to get to the heart of God and become a Coworker. He has the true ideal in mind and will accept nothing but it, whereas those who attempt to get cosmic consciousness and do have the experience of it want only to give up life, to live it selfishly because it gives them a certain dreamy, peaceful, and happy state that demands nothing of them but a voidness of energy and lack of service. All this will eventually lead to death, decay, and unhappiness. It is one of the tricks of the Kal power.

In other words, mysticism is an escape from life and its duties and responsibilities. The mystic retreats into a private ecstasy of cosmic consciousness, turns his back on the world, and forgets not only his own sorrows but the needs and sorrows of others.

If a chela is in the act of Soul Travel and sees that someone on one of the lower planes is in need of his help, he should leave his journey and go serve that person. The very act of entering into the heavenly worlds, via Soul Travel, brings with it an intense and burning love of the SUGMAD which must meet the need of the overflow into the world for all fellow men and creatures, and this must show itself in deeds of charity, mercy, and self-sacrifice, and not merely in words.

The MAHANTA, the Living ECK Master is not one who merely gives predictions of the future, but he is the ECK prophet. There is a vast difference in the two. Those who give predictions are merely the readers of the psychic files from the lower planes, generally those of the Astral world. But the MAHANTA, the Living ECK Master gives divine utterance from the SUGMAD. He is the channel for the Voice of the SUGMAD, and in this case nothing comes from the mind, but directly from the heart of the Almighty.

He is that Voice which speaks from the impersonal. Nothing is from him personally. He gives what there is to give, not of himself, but from the divine source, and not of a religious nature, but of truth itself. He often does this from what may appear to be the normal function of his life; but then again it can be from a deep ecstasy in which he might be in a trance state.

This is part of the works of Eckankar known as the ECK-Vidya, and the MAHANTA, the Living ECK Master is often the only one who can give this type of telling forth. Again there is a difference between telling forth and foretelling. Telling forth comes from the central spiritual region above the Anami Lok, in which the SUGMAD dwells. Foretelling is merely prediction which is of a psychic nature. The ECK chela will soon come to know the difference between the two and will give up anything of any psychic nature which might be a detriment to himself and his spiritual unfoldment into the heavenly worlds.

Prophecy is of a highly specialized nature, and few, if any, can become one who can read the ECK-Vidya records for others. It is usually the MAHANTA, the Living ECK Master who is the prophet of the followers of Eckankar.

This is of central importance because it purports to show that no one can establish himself as a prophet without proper background, the certification of the

SUGMAD. Anyone who proposes to act as a prophet without the highest initiation in Eckankar is apt to believe that he might be one. But this is self-deception on his part, and because of this he will make many statements from out of the mind which are considered to be truth. He is only one who can predict with a reasonable amount of accuracy, which is only from the psychic worlds. So many times his prediction will not hold true, nor will it show any accuracy after a certain period of time.

Predictions do not hold true under many circumstances because they are subject to the temporal power of Kal, who rules the negative worlds. These world-mind planes are what man knows as the psychic regions and therefore are unreliable. They are also subject to change, because in dealing with people and circumstances, the changes come with the movement of time through space when connected with personalities and events. A prediction about a person on a psychic level can be true at one time but not at another time. Therefore, timing is the greatest problem for the one who is giving the predictions. He cannot set the prediction exactly right in time because he normally cannot see it in the psychic world. The event may come about now or in the far future. If he puts a definite time upon the occurrence, this all comes out of the mental region and is not at all reliable.

Therefore, it's best to stay away from the psychic foretellers, for none can give the future. They only guess at it. Only the prophet knows and hears the Voice of the SUGMAD. The prophet is the MAHANTA, the Living ECK Master; he alone can give the truth. He awakens the faith and Spirit in every individual with whom he comes in contact, whether it is in the flesh or the Atma Sarup. He speaks with the pure essence of the ECK. This is the ultimate purity and unity, the all-embracing wholeness, the quintessence of truth.

The essence of the ECK belongs to neither death nor rebirth; It is uncreated and eternal. The concepts of the conscious self are individualized and discriminated by false imaginations. If it could be free from discriminative thinking, there would be no arbitrary thoughts to give rise to appearances of form, existence, and conditions.

Soul has two aspects. The metaphor of the two doors of Soul means that It can look outward into the space-time of the Pinda world, the world of becoming, or It can look inward into the worlds of Sat Desha, the pure spiritual worlds of God, the world of being. Entering into the true Soul consciousness, the chela empties himself of all multiplicity, the things of the physical and psychic worlds. This is the apex of Soul consciousness, for then It may behold with clarity what the SUGMAD wishes for It to know, see, and do in this dazzling world.

There is the appearing and disappearing aspect of Soul, that which is thought of as entering into a body and withdrawing from a body whenever that body is born or dies. Because the human eye and senses cannot see or know about the aspects of Soul, there are questions which arise constantly with the chela about the existence of Soul, should he never have had experience outside the human consciousness.

The essence of Eckankar consists in acquiring a new viewpoint on life and things generally. If one wants to get into the inmost life of ECK, he must forgo all his ordinary habits of thinking which control his everyday life. He must try to see if there is any other way of judging things; or rather, if his ordinary way is always sufficient to give him the ultimate satisfaction of his spiritual needs. If he feels dissatisfied somehow with this life, if there is something in his ordinary way of living that deprives him of freedom in its most sanctified sense, he must endeavor to find a way somewhere which gives him a sense of finality and contentment. ECK will do this for all concerned, and It assures one of the acquirement of a new point of view in which life assumes a fresher, deeper, and more satisfying aspect. This is natural, but it's the greatest mental cataclysm one can go through in life. It is no easy task; it is a kind of fiery baptism, and one has to go through the storm, the earthquake, the overthrowing of the mountains, and the breaking in pieces of the rocks.

The acquiring of a new point of view in the chela's dealings with life and the world is called the ECKshar by those who are followers of the ECK. This ECKshar can be said to be similar to the enlightenment known to religions, except that it contains both the Light and Sound. Without It ECK would be like the sun devoid of its light and heat.

The ECKshar is not a conclusion reached by reasoning, and it defies all intellectual definitions. Anyone who has experienced it is always at a loss to explain it coherently or logically. Yet when it is explained either in words or gestures, its contents more or less undergo mutilation. The uninitiated are unable to grasp it by what is outwardly invisible, while those who have had the experience understand and discriminate what is genuine and what is not. The ECKshar experience is always characterized by irrationality, inexplicability, and incommunicability.

Rebazar Tarzs says that it is like a great fire which scorches the body so much that one cannot speak of the pain. He only experiences it, and thereafter everything in the experiencer's life has been changed.

It is noticeable that the divine wisdom contained in the ECKshar is concerned with the universal life and at the same time with the experiencer's aspect of survival in eternity. However, this knowledge is not final, for it will come again and again when the chela is in the throes of the ECKshar, stronger each time, with greater capacity for knowledge and wisdom of the SUGMAD. The best description of what the ECKshar might be is that it is a form of perception, an inner perception, which takes place in the innermost part of the consciousness. When one receives it, there comes about a sense of authoritativeness which the uninitiated do not understand and will resent. This sense of authority is final, for it casts out all negativeness, that is, the Kal forces, from the mental realm and replaces it with the affirmative.

Although one has the experience of the ECKshar in that part of the spiritual universe beyond time and space, he feels it to be rooted elsewhere. He feels that the roots of the ECKshar are in something permanent which makes it ready for acceptance in authoritativeness. This permanency is that which we know as the SUGMAD, where all roots are attached and dependency placed. The experience is impersonal, yet there is the knowingness that the roots are in the heart of God. All this appears to be in the impersonal, yet every experience is personal to the experiencer. There is this feeling which inevitably accompanies the ECKshar which consists of the breaking up of those former restrictions imposed on one as an individual being in this material world. This breaking up of these restrictions is not negative but is significant because it means the infinite expansion of the consciousness of the individual.

The general feeling, though the chela is not conscious of it, which characterizes all his functions of consciousness is that of restriction and dependence. This is because consciousness, itself, is the outcome of two forces conditioning or restricting each other. The ECKshar, on the contrary, essentially consists in doing away with the opposition of the two, and goes beyond it into the heavenly worlds where there is only freedom and joy of being.

To be released from this restriction the chela must become a Soul Traveler who moves into that arena where all things are intensely exalted. When one has experienced the ECKshar, a hut may become a splendid palace because of the sharp increase of awareness in the spiritual sense. While on the other hand, without the ECKshar, the splendid palace may be that which looks dull and uninspiring, like the hut to the outer senses.

The ECKshar comes upon the chela in many ways. It may come abruptly and in a momentary experience, yet on the other hand it may come gradually, and the experiencer may stay in it for hours, maybe days. At the same time he is able to continue with his daily duties without others noticing. He may have a specific time daily for entering into this experience, if he has trained himself, and stay in it for a definite time and then withdraw into the world of matter again.

Therefore, the study of the mind and its aspects is imperfect. The chela soon learns that the illumination of the intellect is that of the lesser way to God. If he wants true knowledge or divine wisdom, he must seek the ECKshar through the MAHANTA, the Living ECK Master. Even so, if he takes up the path of ECK, seeking the ECKshar, he could become a wandering outcast, for society often rejects the ECKist.

He is the outcast because the way of the ECK is that he makes himself alienated from all orthodox life, because now he is the possessor of wealth and power which is not attainable in this world by mortal beings. However, this does not give him a high feeling of self-glorification, for the inflow of the ECK into him to use him as a channel gives a feeling of humility. He has come to realize that the ECK has chosen him instead of the reverse, mainly for the very reason that he has disciplined himself to receive Its riches and wealth of power.

He can do nothing else now except serve It in this world. Should he believe that by becoming a channel for the ECK there will be nothing in his life but glory, happiness, and joys of this material world, he has made a terrible mistake. The SUGMAD does give the heavenly glories to all who have been chosen to attain them; however, it is only after one has disciplined himself to the ways of the ECK.

The sensory-intellectual consciousness, which is the highest aspect of the Kal forces, is dropped when one enters into the ECKshar and stays in its own place, only to be used when necessary by the chela in this world of matter. The use of the sensory-intellectual consciousness to reach the solution of a problem is the difficult way. It is thinking in a circle, the looking at two sides of the question. He is never satisfied with any answer and seeks further, like a man thirsting for a drink while walking the vast stretches of the waterless desert.

He is like a man trying to remember something, a person who has forgotten something upon which his very life depends. This is the state of spiritual tension which may be resolved, should the chela meet with the MAHANTA, the Living ECK Master. Although he may communicate in vocal sounds, it is usually in that inner communication that lies between the Living ECK Master and chela.

Upon meeting the MAHANTA, either inwardly or in the flesh, he generally trembles, sweats, and feels the excitement of something which may be anticipated or dreaded. Then the answers come to him in a flash, and he can see everything clearly. The moment of understanding is often brief, but to him it may be that of an hour, a year, or more. Yet the message is profound, impressive, and glorious, and often he is able to see, know, and understand, but it takes time to grasp it in its entirety.

This is the ECK, the everlasting gospel.

3
The Four Zoas of Eckankar

The man who cannot live by faith alone, who must satisfy reason and intellect, must learn that contemplation on the ECK is the way. The contemplation is a tremendous force. It has been said that Lai Tsi, the great ECK Master, kept asking the SUGMAD to send him spiritually inclined people, and soon after that, those who later became his disciples or devotees began to appear.

This spiritual contemplation of the ECK is the greatest resource of strength that the chela may have for himself. It is the ultimate lift for him and will help him where intellect and all other things have failed him.

If the chela came to the MAHANTA, the Living ECK Master and said that the spiritual contemplation of ECK did not appeal to his temperament, he would be given counsel to frequently associate with those who have gained the stature of the Mahdis, the initiates of the Fifth Circle. These are the ones who have had real spiritual experiences. Constant contact with them will assist him to bring out his latent spirituality. The Mahdis are the higher ones who turn the minds and wills of the chelas toward divine objects. Above all, they stimulate an intense longing for the spiritual life. Therefore, the society of such men and women is important as the first step, and often the last.

Man finds no peace except in the eternal worlds. If he seeks elsewhere, it is eventually learned that he is on the path of Kal and will spin around on the Wheel of Awagawan—the coming and going, the agelong cycle of births and deaths, transmigration, and reincarnation.

Therefore, metaphysical speculation is discouraged, for it keeps man on this Wheel of Awagawan. Within this worldly life everything is relativity. Within the worlds of God it is found that nothing is in relation with another except through the ECK. The ECKist knows that he must steer himself on the path to God, and that not even the MAHANTA, the Living ECK Master can give him help unless he works in accordance with the laws of Eckankar. What he requires is restraint, compassion, self-awareness, and wisdom. Restraint does not involve self-mortification, but avoidance of excess and mastery over the senses and emotions. Compassion involves the negative virtue of avoiding harm to others and the positive virtues of helpfulness, generosity, and sympathy when needed.

Self-awareness includes scrutinizing one's own actions and motives, sitting back, as it were, to watch his passions and desires in action, observing the thoughts which slip through his mind, and making a careful study of his bodily functions such as muscular movements, the pulsing of the blood, the process of breathing, and other functions. This awareness helps one to come to realize the illusory nature of the ego. Wisdom means the intuitive wisdom that dawns when the mind is stilled. It is started by simple drills like breath control given in many of the Spiritual Exercises of ECK, and this leads to the achievement of one-pointedness of mind.

It is found that compassion and wisdom interact upon

each other. Compassion, besides making man good to his fellow man, is beneficial to himself. Gifts of thought, time, energy, goods, or wealth are all expended at the cost of the ego, which diminishes accordingly. With the diminution of the ego, wisdom arises, and with wisdom's dawning, compassion increases; for the clearer it becomes that the distinction between the "I" and the other is unreal, the more natural it is to be compassionate. The radiant wisdom that gradually manifests itself within the peacefulness of the mind and heart is that which comes into the full enlightenment of the ECKshar.

The aim of man's life on this earth is to set a limit to his reincarnations, for reincarnation is a lesson somewhat in the form of punishment which Soul is compelled to inflict upon Itself; for as long as It does not feel that It has reached purification, It cannot return to the SUGMAD. To attain the last phase—that is, never to be reborn again upon this earth or within this planetary system—is the ideal. To be assured of eternal happiness, assured that the earth shall no longer behold Soul returning to cloak Itself once again in Its gross substance, is the goal of all who must live in this Pinda world.

This purification, this progressive dematerialization, this renunciation of all egoism, begins when Soul begins Its life here and is continued through all phases of existence. But one must first of all accomplish all the duties of this active existence. For all must know that none shall achieve absorption into the heart of the SUGMAD by prayer alone, nor by good deeds, nor the motives of charity and love for one another. Not alone will any of these take Soul into the heart of the SUGMAD. Yet if anything can give help, it is detachment from materialism, the act itself, where one single deed or action is worth more than a thousand good thoughts and can bring about that which takes Soul into the heavenly world. But as long as man is attached to something, and as long as he is looking for good deeds alone to give him the way into heaven, he is lost. It is only when he has gained detachment from worldly goods and actions that he will make spiritual progress.

The world is sustained by every action whose sole object is sacrifice; that is, the voluntary gift of self. It is in the making of this voluntary gift that man has performed the action without respect of materiality. The sole object of action should be to serve others. He who sees inaction in action and action in inaction is wise among men. He is attuned to the true principles in whatever action he may perform. Such a man, who has renounced all interest in the result of his action and is always content, depends on no one but the MAHANTA, the Living ECK Master. All his ideas are filled with wisdom, and all his actions consist of sacrifice, and his deeds are indeed noble.

All men have the death wish ingrained within themselves. This is part of the Kal consciousness which wishes for self-destruction of the individual and others. It is that which creates wars and brings about violence and destruction of property. It is that which causes man to inflict torture upon himself and death to either himself or his neighbor. The mass suicide in certain species of animals and in some primitive tribes is noted to be a part of this Kal force to get rid of the body, and the idea of doing so brings about the death wish.

The social taboo on the subject of suicide is wrong. Some prefer to deny suicide rather than to discuss it. Families will deny that certain members died from a form of self-destruction, claiming instead that it was an accident. The drug habit in itself is an expression of some partial suicidal wish. The sickness and malaise of man cannot be healed until at last he attains a pure consciousness which contains no contamination of the Kal forces within itself.

Suicide is an aspect of life in this material world. It is brought about by man's continued hold on his material life, with everything attached to his mind and heart. This attachment is the basic reason for suicide in man as he develops the Kalistic traits, including hostility, as he withdraws from life. Anyone who withdraws from his family or community feels like an outsider, yet guilty about his own betrayal of biological ties. The ambiguity of loneliness and individuality and man's conflict about the will to live in isolation and dignity is a keynote to the problem of suicide. There are people who cannot live independently of others; they must have their social ties or die. This is a part of the attachment to the material life.

Between life and death is always that empty time which is called the future. The creative self in man is that through which the ECK forces work, and the destructive self in man is that through which the Kal forces work. These two do not fight many open conflicts. The inner battle between life and physical death usually lies deeply hidden in man, and the struggle frequently shows itself, usually in the most paradoxical way.

Some of these paradoxical ways are the fear of failure in many things, or perhaps of physical danger, such as walking across a bridge over a high canyon. Another is social failure, in which one loses all his material goods or has a great social downfall. In the Orient this is called the loss of face. Either one is a threat, only a step away from potential death. In his fears many a man finds himself unwittingly facing self-destructive tendencies that he is not aware of within himself.

He is afraid of stepping or falling into nothingness. This is because he stands always before the abyss, the great vacuum, and should he fall into it, would return to his unborn state. The state of nothingness would mean suicide, the returning to that awful gulf of nothingness.

Yet the suicide believes that it means the freedom of getting away from the protective dependency of the aggressive world and accepting the challenge of self-consciousness, of being an eccentric observer standing outside the world. Man has always sought distance from the world and at the same time hated being that far from it.

Every disgruntled person in this world has played with the idea of suicide, self-destruction, at some time or other. He has put it this way: Either my will and wishes be gratified, or I choose death. Yet, most men do not know what they want or how to search for death, and as a substitute man may build himself a delusional world of having extreme power and expect the final end to occur in hazardous and heroic exaltation.

In the world of this earth planet, within the physical universe, where primitive drives are exalted into heroic ideals, man has to murder either himself or others. He kills something in himself by throwing himself into the turmoil of his instinctive drives. It may be called killing his ego or murdering his inner self. When life becomes too bothersome, man regresses easily to the state of a primitive being. In his primitive rage he reverts to ideas of primitive magic and expects somehow in death to be reunited with mother earth. For him death means the magical union with what created his physical body, or in killing others he expects to enlarge the powers of his inner self. But through all this regression to primitive imagery, he kills something of the pure self within; and the wisdom, self-awareness, and everything that the ECK has been giving him now leaves him.

These primitive fears can kill him. Knowing that he has broken the laws of the spiritual worlds can cause such an inner panic that man's vital organs are paralyzed and starvation and death overcome him. Yet even in a less primitive civilization, wild, rampant emotions can kill an individual, just as sudden fright and bodily shock can cause a man to die. The illusion of lost hope makes many a disease incurable, and the man who worries may kill himself with faulty thinking. He doesn't use any weapon to do so but destroys himself nevertheless with paralyzing morbid anticipations.

Self-destruction can be a reaction to outer stress or an inner burden—a protest that is chosen when no other form of escape seems to be possible. It can be a substitute for an attack, or an alternative to somatic disease, or a replacement for mental disintegration.

Therefore, committing suicide is a human phenomenon, for conscious interference with one's own fate is possible. There are animals who surrender passively to destruction, but in their state it can often be said they are only reacting to panic. Only man has the conception of life and death within himself. It is sometimes found in primitive tribes that it is a requirement for the old and feeble to freely commit suicide in order not to be a burden to those who are younger and must support the families.

Suicide in the human race can be cited as a negative measurement of happiness. Most people are no longer alive after they enter the age of maturity. They commit a token self-destruction by stopping their growth and expansion in the spiritual experiences. They bury themselves in old, accepted habits and customs, drowning their sense of curiosity regarding new spiritual experiences. They become contented in apathy.

The law of the SUGMAD does not allow self-destruction in any form. It is said that when a person destroys himself to escape the problems of life, he must return to life almost at once in a new bodily incarnation in order to work out the karma which he refused to confront during the life he just left.

It is known that the suicide trait is in the human consciousness; therefore it will provoke a multitude of protests. Anxious escapists and breeders of dogmatic rules become angry over trifles. They want to deny the disguised self-destructiveness hidden in some of their rigid and repetitious habits. The automation of actions and self-destruction denies all vitality, spontaneity, and creativity in man. These types of people have become automatized and will raise their psychosis to the position of some true, human ideal in the field of sociology to deny the despair and hidden suicidal wish in themselves. This is part of their compulsion to repeat and their resistance against change.

Suicidal tendency in a family or community is infectious because it arouses the suppressed self-destructive inclinations in everyone. When one threatens suicide, it is usually not carried out but used as a threat to get one's own way. The social stigma in a family in which there has been a suicide can be part of a revenge. Children often wish to punish their family or parents with this sort of suicide revenge.

Many depressed people like to exhibit their sorrows in an effort to arouse pity and empathy in others. It affords a paradoxical gap of communications between them and their listeners. They try to acquire love and affection from others, which they believe is their inherent right. Punishment, rejection, or a prejudiced attitude on the part of the family or public can drive one to suicide. Hatred and insult are curious weapons, but they can be toxic and dangerous.

No ECK Master will acknowledge his appearance to another person. This is neither modesty nor is it a hiding of something; in a sense he is letting the individual or individuals decide for themselves whether it was really him. He wants them to decide if it was reality. In this way he is not telling, nor confirming his presence with them in the Atma Sarup, but allowing them the independence of knowing and understanding whether it was actually him.

If a person makes up his mind that the Living ECK Master really appeared to him, then he knows it, and this cannot be taken away from him, regardless. However, if he has to be told that it was the ECK Master, then he is always in doubt, for it was an outside source which gave him this information and not himself. It is superficial knowledge and not from his own inner sources.

He must always remember that the MAHANTA, the Living ECK Master is not the one to tell him of his inner experiences, nor whether the ECK Master has appeared to him. But he must know this with a faith that is beyond anything that he has ever experienced, and, therefore, it will stay with him. Otherwise it may fade in time, and the experiencer soon forgets whether it was really the ECK Master.

One of the most interesting points in connection with the last statement is that so often the individual is rather doubtful about his experiences with the ECK Master if he doesn't gain that inner conviction at the same time. So often he calls upon the Living ECK Master for something, a healing or a divine gift. It is given to him because this is the right moment to receive, but later he forgets and leaves the ECK Master because someone else who claims mystical powers appears to give him anything he desires when he makes the request.

The four Zoas (laws) of Eckankar for the Mahdis, the initiate of the Fifth Circle, are (1) The Mahdis shall not use alcohol, tobacco, or drugs; gamble; or be gluttonous in any way. No Mahdis shall be existent on the animal level. He is a leader, and he must fix his attention above the psychology of the brute. (2) The Mahdis shall not speak with tongue of vanity or deceit or unhappiness, criticize the actions of others, blame others for wrong-doings, quarrel, fight, or inflict injury. He shall at all times be respectful and courteous to his fellow man and show great compassion and happiness. (3) The Mahdis shall have humility, love, and freedom from all bonds of creeds. He shall be free from the laws of karma which snare him with boastfulness and vanity. He shall have love for all people and all creatures of the SUGMAD. (4) The Mahdis must preach the message of ECK at all times, and prove to the world that he is an example of purity and happiness. He must show that the disciple in the human body must have a Master in the human body. This is a fixed law of the SUGMAD. At the time of his passing, every Living ECK Master turns over his work to the next Living ECK Master who is in the body, and he carries on until his time to translate from the human body into the other worlds. Those who translate shall continue with the ECK chelas they have initiated on earth, when those chelas have passed across the borders of death into the upper worlds. Their ECK Master meets them, and they begin their further studies under him in the heavenly worlds.

These are the four laws for the Mahdis, the initiate of the Fifth Circle. They shall be abided by and shall have the respect given to the MAHANTA, for each law within itself has great authority and power. The works of Eckankar depend mainly upon the Mahdis.

To practice ECK out of curiosity, in search of new sensations, or in order to gain psychic power is a mistake which is punished with futility, neurosis, or worse. None should seek initiation into the mysteries of ECK from unworthy motives, for disaster will certainly result.

Also to try praying for someone else or to use any type of healing, such as putting him in the white light, is to bring a lower power into being. This means that if anyone should try to pray for the MAHANTA or any of the ECK Masters, either for them or to them for anything, those who are in receipt of the prayers will have to come down to the psychic level to comply. Prayer and healing in any other way than through the ECK of Itself is to deal in the psychic worlds. There is no permanency about this type of request and healing.

No ECK Master has ever taught that every gift offered by the chela without any thought of compensation is already returned to him. The purpose of the Living ECK Master is therefore to give all he possesses in return to the chela for giving all that he has.

Mental acrobatics or tortuous, complicated philosophical gymnastics are not required in ECK. Nor is there any necessity for a chela to pore for hours over a page or an extract from some book or writings in order to grasp what the author means. The ECKist needs none of this. The truth of God is too simple for the seeker after complexity, looking for things he cannot understand. The intellect creates its own problems and then makes itself miserable trying to solve them. Truth always expresses itself with the greatest simplicity.

There are also four principles, or precepts, which the ECK chela must have imprinted upon his heart and mind. These are: (1) There is but one God, and Its reality is the SUGMAD. (2) The MAHANTA, the Living ECK Master is the messenger of the SUGMAD in all worlds, be they material, psychic, or spiritual. (3) The faithful, those who follow the works of ECK, shall have all the blessings and riches of the heavenly kingdom given unto them. (4) The Shariyat-Ki-Sugmad is the holy book of those who follow Eckankar, and there shall be none above it. Spirituality, therefore, cannot be taught, but it must be caught. Once one has learned the secrets of ECK at the feet of the MAHANTA and is enlivened with the life impulses received from him, it is no longer essential to be in constant physical association with him. The chela will have inner association with him anywhere and everywhere. He may even make frequent visits or write whenever possible and report on his spiritual growth.

Thus it's found that by attending the ECK Satsang classes one is able to make contact with the MAHANTA, the Living ECK Master. *Sat* means true or unchangeable, and *sang* means union. Therefore, union with that which is pure and imperishable is Satsang, the ECK Satsang gathering. On the material plane Satsang will mean the coming in contact of man with the Living ECK Master. In the absence of the Living ECK Master, the study of the works of ECK may also be called the ECK Satsang, for that also gives inducement to go within oneself to explore the higher planes. The study of the works of ECK is Satsang; the company of the Living ECK Master, or one of the higher devotees, is Satsang; hearing or reading his discourses is Satsang; going in and making contact with the ECK Sound Current is Satsang. The union of one with the Living ECK Master is Satsang.

The trinity of Eckankar is the following: (1) The Sat Guru, the MAHANTA, the Living ECK Master; (2) the ECK Satsang, or his company of followers; and (3) the ECK, or the true name which is the Bani, or the Sound Current. Whenever there is a desire to develop spiritual awakening in order to attain the goal of God, one should yield to it.

The most important fact which differentiates the spiritual discipline this teaching gives is the realization of the SUGMAD. The steps are first, Self-Realization; second, God-Realization; and third, entering into the kingdom of heaven, either in this life or in the next.

All this being said, it's noted that no chela is referred to any teaching other than Eckankar, the way of entering and realizing the kingdom of heaven while still living here in the human body. This is the goal of every chela who takes up the path of Eckankar during his lifetime. Not merely to be freed of his karma, nor to receive the higher initiations, but to realize the kingdom of heaven while still living in his body. This is the sum and substance of all the teachings of ECK.

The concept of a Supreme Deity which is different from that of orthodox religions is certainly extraordinary to most people. But it's truth, and many are too steeped in their own religious traditions to ever break away from such concepts of their individual and collective ideas about a God who rules over them. Eckankar never expects to break the image of these people, because it would deprive them of a certain amount of spiritual security, despite the fact their own belief is in a deity which does them little good in prayer or daily inner life.

Most religions have always believed in a space god of some nature. This space god was one whom they could not put into a geographical position; therefore, they made it one who was everywhere, in all things. This led the clergy into thinking that the space god was within as well as without. This is merely a mental concept which fails when man is faced with some deep crisis that calls for materialistic resolve. That is, if the problem lies in the mental and physical worlds, he soon finds that whatever he is calling upon as a space god will not respond to his request to dissolve his problems.

This is because he is putting his god into a dualistic image. No man can serve his god in this manner, as the ECKist has learned. He must become a nondualistic believer, for the SUGMAD doesn't perform Its deeds in the same sense as the orthodox believer has his faith. Its actions and works are of the ultimate reality which is entirely impersonal.

Within the lower worlds It allows the Kal to take its course and manage the affairs of all Souls within this realm. Therefore, It does not interfere in matters of personal importance when man calls upon It for comfort and relief from pain or disease, and freedom from worldly matters. If man is answered in these categories, it's because the Kal power gives him temporary relief for its own reasons.

When man begins to think that he can manipulate the mental powers for his own use in this world, he is wasting his time and energies. All the promises of the metaphysicians that he can take charge of his mind and have control over it are either ignorance or falsehoods.

Such deeds and doctrines often lead the individual into personality disorders, which makes him a ready victim for psychic attacks. The methods of any metaphysical teachings without discipline and careful organization are met more or less with defeat for the individual. In many of the metaphysical and psychic teachings, the religious aspect or the worship of the Supreme Deity is lost, and they become merely a method of mental manipulation for purely personal gains, though not necessarily and deliberately evil.

Hypnotism is the worst of the psychic arts, for it is used in so many different ways by the practitioners who charm and fascinate men and women, influence their thoughts, control their desires, and make the practitioner master of every situation in which they are involved. Life is full of alluring possibilities for those who master the secrets of hypnotic influence, and for those who develop their magnetic powers.

It is said that through hypnotism one can be put to sleep at any time or banish pain and suffering. But little is said of what can be done by those who practice evil upon their fellow man. They can create robbery and murder through a victim if he should be nursing a sense of injury and desires to be revenged, or loves power for its own sake.

The case of a patient being regressed into past lives through hypnotism is often without foundation. Many an entity loves to participate in the luring of a hypnotist and friends into false beliefs. It will take over and proclaim almost impossible incarnations without any evidence. This is when the ECK chela must distinguish very carefully between psychic experience and subjective hallucination. One must be sure the person who states such experiences is not hearing the reverberations of his own dissociated complexes taken over by some astral entity. The difference between hysteria, insanity, and psychic attacks is an exceedingly delicate and difficult division; frequently a case is not clear-cut, with more than one element being present. A severe psychic attack can cause a mental breakdown, and this lays its victim open to invasion from the astral entities.

Fear is the motivation of any attack of this nature on a person. Usually such fear is based upon a bitter experience. The labyrinthine windings of the left-hand path are as extensive as they are devious; but while exposing them in something of their horror, it's maintained that the right-hand path of initiation and spiritual knowledge is the lofty way to God. It is a means of lifting the burdens of human suffering.

The trouble with the left-hand path is that its aspects have an unfortunate knack of waking up spontaneously. So much of the psychic knowledge is abroad in the world today, and so much is going on of this nature unknown and unsuspected in our midst, that it's very desirable that the ECK chela should always be aware of the forces which men of evil will pervert to their own ends.

If man looks at the universe around himself, he cannot fail to realize that there must be some overruling plan coordinating its infinite complexity. If he takes into his hands and examines minutely any living thing, however simple, he must equally realize that the ordered diversity of its parts is built upon a determining framework. Science has sought in vain for its organizing principle, but it will never be found on the physical plane, for it is not physical. It is not the inherent nature of atoms which causes them to arrange themselves in the complex patterns of living tissues.

The driving forces of the universe, the framework upon which it is built up in all its parts, belong to another phase of manifestation other than the physical plane, having other dimensions than those to which man is habituated and perceived by other modes of consciousness than those to which man is accustomed.

He lives in the midst of invisible forces whose effects alone are perceived. He moves among invisible forms whose actions he seldom perceives at all, though he may be profoundly affected by them. In this mind side of nature, invisible to man's senses, intangible to his instruments of seeing and knowing, many things can happen that are without their echo on the physical plane. There are beings that live in this invisible world as fish live in the sea. There are those who, with trained minds or special spiritual aptitudes, can enter into this invisible world as divers descend to the ocean floor. There are also times when, as happens to land when the sea dikes break, these invisible forces flow in upon men and swamp their lives.

Such things normally do not happen, for man is protected by his very incapacity to perceive these invisible psychic forces. There are four conditions, however, in which the veil may be rent and he meets the unseen. First, man can find himself in a place where the forces are concentrated; second, he may meet with those who are handling these forces; third, he may himself go out to meet the unseen psychic force, led by his interest in it, and get out of his depth before he knows where he is; and last, he may fall victim to certain pathological conditions which rend the veil.

The most common form of psychic attack is that which proceeds from the ignorant and malignant minds of others. Not all attacks are deliberately motivated. The persecutor may well be a victim himself without knowledge of this. Therefore, one should never bring himself down to the moral level of the attacker, but rely upon the more humane methods of ECK, which are in reality more effective and less dangerous to handle.

Some come into touch with the psychic forces through the influence of places. A man who is not actually psychic, but who is sufficiently sensitive to perceive the invisible forces subconsciously, may go to a place where such forces are concentrated. Where they are concentrated, unless the individual is very dense-minded, he begins to be dimly conscious of something which is affecting him and stirring him within.

It can be that the barrier between the human consciousness and the psychic is dense in some people, and they are never able to grasp what is going on about them. They merely have the sense of oppression and general feeling of restriction which leaves when they are in another place. Consequently the condition may never be discovered, and it could lead to years of misery and poor health.

This is why anyone who gets into such psychic phenomena as aura reading, aura adjustment, and psychic studies is without foundation. The teacher or reader and those who make such adjustments could be psychic thieves and be stealing energies as well as taking control of the person. A sense of fear and oppression is very characteristic of an occult attack which can come through these three aspects. It is an extremely rare thing for an attack to manifest without reason. One must first put himself in a position to be attacked, for man is not in his normal state of mind, body, and circumstances when he finds himself suddenly in the midst of an invisible battle. An approaching psychic attack or influence makes its shadow on the consciousness of its victim before it becomes apparent to those who are not at all psychic.

Nervous exhaustion and mental breakdown are the most common results of these astral attacks among people. Odors and bruises are found on the body after a psychic attack during sleep. However, these are for those who are uninitiated. They are the things which hardly any ECK chela will experience. He is immune to these things because he finds, sooner or later, that the fundamental idea is that man, as known to most in the state of human consciousness, is not a complete being; that nature develops him up to a certain point and then leaves him to develop further by his own efforts and devices, or to live and die such as he was born, or to degenerate and lose capacity for development.

The evolution of man in this case means the development of certain inner qualities and features which usually remain undeveloped and cannot develop by themselves. Experiences and observation show that this development is possible only in certain definite conditions, with the efforts of a certain kind on the part of man himself, and with sufficient help from those who have begun similar work before and have already attained a certain degree of development, or at least a certain knowledge of methods.

Without effort, spiritual development is impossible. Without the help of the MAHANTA, the Living ECK Master, it is also impossible. After this the chela must understand that, in the way of development, man becomes a different being and must learn and understand in what sense and in which direction he must become a different being: that is, what a different being is and means to the spiritual senses.

All men cannot develop and become different spiritually, because most of them do not want it. Only a few seek God-Realization, but many seek psychic development, which is all wrong. This is because they do not know about God-Realization and will not understand without a long preparation what it means, even if they are told.

The chief idea is that in order to become different in the spiritual sense man must want it very much and for a very long time. A passing desire or a vague wish based on dissatisfaction with external conditions will not create much of a desire to become numbered among the God-Realized.

The spiritual evolution of man depends on his understanding of what he may get and what he must give for it. If he does not want it, or if he does not want it strongly enough and does not make the necessary efforts, he will not unfold. If he is forced to become anything that he doesn't want to be, this would be an injustice.

The truth lies in the fact that before unfolding any faculty or powers which man has within himself and doesn't know about, he must acquire and learn about faculties and powers which he has and never uses. This is the missing link and the most important point in the spiritual evolution of man. It is that point which has always been made—that man does not know himself.

This is the crux of the nature of man.

4

The Shab, the Lover of Life

The love of life begins with the descent of Soul into this physical universe. It is the great survival factor which all Souls have, some greater than others; but it is always there, instilled in each so deeply that often it must be uncovered by the MAHANTA, the Living ECK Master to give the seeker something creative in his life. Unless the seeker has a creative goal in his life, there is little survival factor left for him.

Soul, as the inner guide of man, seeks out that which is imperishable, apart from which there is only suffering. Man may contemplate on the infinity of space, the infinity of reason, and the nonexistence of nothing; he may seize the moment of illumination which brings with it the deliverance which no one can teach, and which each must find for himself, and which is ineffable. This purifies Soul in order to spare It, that it be possible for It never to return to this world after death of the physical body.

The Shab is also known as the Bhakti, which is the initiate of the Seventh Circle. Unless one is the lover of all things, he is never eligible to enter into the heavenly initiations. He abandons all pious practices and acts of austere devotion, and applies his intellect solely to the contemplation of the great SUGMAD, the First Cause; and, exempt from all evil desires, Soul is then already on the threshold of love, while the mortal self flickers like the last glimmer of a dying lamp.

Those who enter into this state of loving life are always self-sustaining and never supported by another or by public charity. None who is a Shab ever boasts of his mastership nor of his spiritual attainment and powers. If any man claims to have attained the highest in spiritual development, that claim of itself may be taken as conclusive proof that he has not done as stated. The Shab always shows the utmost humility, but he never makes his humility obtrusive. He never does anything to advertise this humility or exhibit it in public.

The Shab never complains of treatment at the hands of others; even if he is abused, he will not reply angrily, nor will he speak of it afterward. He never speaks of ingratitude nor of being down on his luck. He never finds fault or blames others, either to their face or behind their back, no matter what the provocation may be. He does not speak ill, and he never lectures others concerning their shortcomings. He always exalts their positive virtues, keeping silent about the evilness of Kal, except to answer questions.

The Shab is never given to ascetic practices or unreasonable austerities. This is the quality which differentiates him from certain types of teachings from the Orient. He is always the giver, never sits around in idleness or wants anything from his fellow man but love. He practices the ECK, which is the Audible Life Current, and teaches It whenever anyone will listen.

The Shab tries to show all around him that the Brahm, the lord of the Mental world, is not the supreme

God. He carefully points out that the way to the SUGMAD is through the MAHANTA, the Living ECK Master. Anyone who is teaching differently is too full of himself to see and recognize the true path to the heavenly kingdom.

The Shab is to help the seeker prepare to meet the MAHANTA, the Living ECK Master. No one can discover the Living ECK Master until certain inner preparations have been made. This is the whole secret of the mystery in finding the MAHANTA. Few will catch the glimpse of the whole, but these few will be the enlightened ones who take the message to the masses of humanity. All the virtues of the ethical system which man must live by are not forgotten in these books of the Shariyat-Ki-Sugmad: charity, kindness, self-control in speech and action, chastity, protection of the weak, benevolence toward the lowly, deference toward superiors, and respect for the property of others, even to the smallest details, will be found expressed in admirable language.

The ECK is merely the most perfect degree of the human being in the spiritual sense. It goes without saying that the MAHANTA, the Living ECK Master, who reigns as the Avatar over the external order of the universe, is himself but a perfect man. Between the human state and the divine state there is but a difference of degree. Man is in the process of development; at the end, of course, he becomes the ECK. According to this concept, the ECK is an eternal becoming, not God complete in Itself.

Such being the universal order, it is evident that he alone may enter into the life of the ECK who has already become this Itself before knocking at the gate of the SUGMAD. Therefore, the highest life of man consists of transforming himself into the ECK. Man becomes perfect when he lives as the ECK, when he makes the journey that all ECK Initiates make to arrive at the goal of God-Realization, which is becoming the ECK of Itself.

Starting from the same point of departure in the unknowable, this journey is the worship of and the search for the ECK within man himself, and the return of man to the SUGMAD, the Godhead. The upright man, that is the man who has all his life striven to find the ECK and to give ear to Its voice, when liberated from the body, does not merely become the ECK, but he becomes the eternal vehicle who acts as the channel for the Voice of God.

The SUGMAD is not born, for It could not be born save of Its own like or of Its contrary; two hypotheses of which the first is futile and the second absurd. One cannot call It infinite nor finite, for if infinite, having neither middle nor beginning nor end, It would be nothing at all; and if finite, It would be encompassed by limitations and would cease to be One. For like reasons, It is neither at rest nor in movement. In short, one cannot attribute to It any characteristics.

This acceptance of the SUGMAD is more clearly formulated by the ECK Master Fubbi Quantz in a statement to an audience interested in his words: "No one understands, no one ever will understand the truth concerning the SUGMAD and the things which I teach. If anyone did happen to come upon the absolute truth, he would never be aware of the encounter. Nowhere do we find anything more than probability."

He went on to say, "On the periphery of the circle, the beginning and the end are one. Divinity is itself the origin and the end of the individual life. Unity is divided into plurality, and plurality is resolved into unity; but unity and plurality are contemporaneous, and the vibrations from the bosom of the Divine are accomplished by the incessant return to divinity."

If all is God and necessarily immortal, it is nonetheless certain that men and things and worlds would disappear. From this moment one bids good-bye to the logical consequences of the great confession of ignorance to enter into the labyrinth of theories which are no longer unassailable and which, for that matter, are not at the outset put before us as revelations but merely as metaphysical hypotheses, as speculations of great antiquity, born of the necessity of reconciling the facts with what is too abstract and too rigid for deductions of human reason.

The SUGMAD is the first cause of all things and is unknowable to all but those who set out to find the answer to all life. None, however, are capable of doing so unless they have taken up the path of ECK. In the finality, the true Deity would not be the SUGMAD unless It understood Itself, unless It were all things. Its infinity inevitably gives rise to pantheism, for if It is everything, everything partakes in It, and it is not possible to imagine anything that can set bounds to It. The cause of life itself, or part of the cause, proceeds from the SUGMAD. From this pantheism proceeds, in its turn, the belief in immortality and the ultimate hope, for the SUGMAD being infinite in space and time, nothing that is a part of It or in It can be destroyed without destroying the SUGMAD.

Since this is impossible, the SUGMAD takes control of all life through Its counterparts such as the ECK; the lords, rulers, and governors of each plane; the ECK Masters of the Vairagi; and those beings who are the Coworkers of Itself. All these work through and with the MAHANTA, the Living ECK Master, whose spiritual body is stationed on every plane within the universe.

Therefore, one is concerned with the worlds and the universes of the SUGMAD. None of these perish, but disappear and reappear alternately throughout eternity, especially the lower worlds through maya, the illusion of ignorance. When they no longer exist for man or for anyone, they still exist virtually where man cannot see them. Similarly, when the SUGMAD sets bounds to Itself in order to manifest Itself through the MAHANTA and to become conscious of a portion of Itself, It does not cease to be infinite and knowable to Itself.

Unable to know the SUGMAD, man contents himself with seeking and questioning It in all Its creatures, and above all in mankind. He thought to find It there, and the religions were born, with their gods and service to a secondary cause, with their cults, their sacrifices, their beliefs, their moralities, hells, and heavens. The relationship which binds them all to the SUGMAD is more and more forgotten, reappearing here and there in some religion, but then again disappearing in some metaphysical meanings and trappings.

The great secret of the ECK, which has been hidden with such care beneath mysterious and sacred formulas, beneath rites which were sometimes terrifying, beneath formidable reticences and silences, comes alive again and again through the ECK Masters to give to the few who accept them. This is the way that it has been and will be for a few centuries, because the idea of the truth about God and Its aspects is too much for the smallness of man's brain.

The greater secret, therefore, is that the only secret is that all things are secret. When one takes up the path of Eckankar, it is learned that those who have preceded him had little more knowledge than he and that they learned little more than he during their respective lifetimes upon their planet. This great secret that all is secret remains a mystery throughout the ages, and since few, if any, can resolve it, the unknowable stays in the hands of the ECKist.

Man does not think, move, or speak of his own accord. He is a marionette pulled here and there by the invisible strings of the Astral worlds. If he understands this, he can learn more about himself and then, possibly, things may begin to change for him. But if he cannot realize and understand his utter mechanicalness, or if he does not wish to accept it as a fact, he can learn nothing of the great secret of ECK, and things cannot change for him.

Man is a machine, but a very peculiar machine. He is a machine which, in the right circumstances and with the right treatment, can know he is a machine; and having fully realized this, he may find ways to cease to be a machine. An individual traveling the path of ECK soon learns that he is more than this, that he is a spiritual being with full control over his emotions and desires. But before he can acquire any new powers and capabilities, he must develop in himself those qualities which he knows are within himself. This he does through guidance under the MAHANTA, the Living ECK Master.

His spiritual unfoldment does not begin on the basis of self-deception. He must learn who he is and what he is not, through Self-Realization, within this Kal world. This means that he must realize that he does not yet possess the qualities already described but must educate his consciousness and will in the spiritual manner.

The most important and the most misleading of these qualities is consciousness. The change in him begins with the change in his understanding of the meaning of consciousness, and after that with his gradually acquiring command over it.

The definition of consciousness lies in the reality of a particular kind of awareness in man, which is independent from the mind's activity. It is, first of all, an awareness of himself, then an awareness of who he is and where he is, and further, an awareness of what he knows and of what he does not know. Therefore, the individual is himself able to know whether he is conscious at a given moment or not. Only man himself can know if his consciousness exists at the moment or not. This means that the presence or absence of consciousness in man cannot be proved by observation of his external activities. The importance of consciousness has never been fully understood, because it has always been connected with the understanding of consciousness as spiritual activity.

When one speaks of the various states of consciousness in connection with thoughts, feelings, moving impulses and sensations, he is basing everything upon the fundamental mistake of mixing consciousness with psychic function. But when he speaks of the states of consciousness in regard to the various planes, then he is working in the spiritual consciousness.

In reality there is no degree of consciousness; but one must take the position that this must be so, for the very reason that the mind cannot grasp the whole. It must think in terms of parts, because this is the way it has been doing in the lower worlds. Since it cannot reach into the higher realms of God, the mind must then begin to think about the consciousness of self on the psychic planes.

The problem here is that man is not always conscious of himself, if at all. The illusion of his being conscious of himself is created by memory and thought processes, while at the same time he realizes only four states of consciousness on this physical plane. They are sleep, waking state, self-consciousness, and objective consciousness.

In ordinary life, man knows very little about objective consciousness, but he does believe that he possesses self-consciousness, although this comes in rare flashes, and even then he probably does not recognize it. That is because he does not know what it would imply if he possessed it. These glimpses of consciousness come in exceptional moments, in highly emotional states, in moments of danger, and in very new and unexpected circumstances and situations.

With the Spiritual Exercises of ECK and the right effort, the chela can acquire control of consciousness and can become conscious of himself, with all that it implies. The human machine has seven different functions: first, the intellect; second, emotions; third, instinctive functions, which are all the inner work of the organism; fourth, moving functions, all the outer works of the body movement in space and time; fifth, sex; sixth, self-consciousness; and seventh, objective consciousness.

The first five functions of the human machine can be studied and become a part of that which is known as self-knowledge. This is what is sometimes known as self-realization, in a manner of speaking. But self-study must begin with the study of the four functions: thinking, feeling, instinctive function, and moving function.

The first, or the lowest, state of consciousness is sleep. This is purely a subjective state, for man is surrounded by dreams, and all his psychic functions work without any direction. This is why the psychic field is so strangely without strength, for few, if any, psychics know what is happening, and when they do cannot control the direction of this force.

The only way that sleep and dreams are handled is through the direction and guidance of the Living ECK Master. No ECK chela is given freedom in the sleep state, for he must be led by the Living ECK Master through the levels of dreams until reaching the higher worlds. If he allows himself to be guided by the Living ECK Master, there is, of course, the opportunity to study the Shariyat-Ki-Sugmad directly in certain Temples of Golden Wisdom in the other worlds.

The second state of consciousness is the awakened consciousness. That is when man is not asleep, but in this state he has feelings of contradiction or impossibility which are absent during sleep. So many times what has taken place during sleep and dreams will influence man in his awakened state of consciousness.

These two states, sleep and waking, are the two main states of consciousness in which man lives. It is hard for him to become adjusted to any other state of consciousness. But he can win any higher states by and after a prolonged struggle with himself, should he have the desire and willingness to do this.

The third state of consciousness is that in which man becomes conscious of himself. Man generally thinks that he possesses self-consciousness, that is, that he is conscious of himself at any moment he wishes; but in truth self-consciousness is a state which can be ascribed to one's self without any right. It is a state in which man becomes objective toward himself and, for the first time, begins to have possible cognition of truth about himself and his actions.

In the fourth state of consciousness it's found that one becomes objective toward all life. In other words, he becomes detached and can look at life with a viewpoint that makes him separate from the emotional state of feelings. He can look and study things in themselves or as they really are in life.

Morals have little to do with any of these states of consciousness, as one has been taught in this physical world. This is one of the acquired things in man's life, which goes along with the artificial likes and dislikes which are acquired by imitation and imagination. These artificial likes and dislikes play a very important and very disastrous part in man's life. He will get along all right in life until personality begins to dominate his life, which brings many wrong results of many kinds.

Man must have a certain amount of personality, which is ego, in order to live in this world. But at the same time, he cannot allow it to dominate him. When it is prominent, he finds himself partial about things. Some things may please him, others will annoy him, irritate him, and even horrify him. He cannot stand aside and view life in all its aspects as he would a distant star, but must live within life and be a part of it. He will discover signs by which he will know harmful manifestations in himself. Then he will further discover that the more he can control these manifestations within himself, the less harmful they can be; and the less he can control them, that is, the more mechanical they are, the more harmful they can become. For example, lying is a mechanical manifestation which, in some, cannot be controlled but takes over and controls them, as well as controlling other functions within them.

The next feature about man which must be closely watched is his imagination. Very soon after starting his observation of himself, he comes to the conclusion that the chief obstacle to self-observation is imagination. He wishes to observe something, but instead imagination takes over on the same subject, and he quickly forgets about observation. Soon he realizes that imagination, as others see it, is artificial and has little meaning in the sense of a creative or selective faculty.

He soon comes to the conclusion that imagination is a negative, or Kal, faculty which he cannot control, and it always carries him away from his more conscious decisions in a direction he had no intention of going. Imagination, in this sense, is almost as bad as lying, for he starts to imagine something in order to please himself and, very soon, he begins to believe what he imagines, or at least some of it.

Another negative effect is in the expression of negative emotions, meaning all the emotions of violence, depression, self-pity, anger, suspicion, fear, annoyance, boredom, mistrust, jealousy, and many others. Ordinarily, one accepts such expressions of negative emotions as quite natural and even necessary. Very often this is called sincerity, but it has little to do with sincerity. It is simply a sign of the Kal in man, a sign of negative emotions and of his incapacity to keep his grievances to himself. These are mechanical manifestations which come to light when the chela reaches the Fifth Plane and experiences Self-Realization.

After the expression of negative emotions, the chela will notice in himself another curious mechanical feature. This is talking; and while there is no harm in talking, by itself, with some people it becomes a vice. They talk all the time, everywhere they happen to be—while working, traveling, and some even while they are sleeping. They never stop talking to someone if there is someone to talk with; and if there is no one, they talk to themselves.

Man will have difficulty in seeing these four mechanical manifestations in himself—lying, imagination, the expression of negative emotions, and unnecessary talking. He will always have to struggle against them, life after life, without the spiritual help of the MAHANTA, the Living ECK Master; that is, without new knowledge and without actual assistance. For even if man has received certain materials, he forgets to use them, forgets to observe himself. He falls asleep again and must be awakened to observe them. With the guidance of the MAHANTA, he will not have this problem of sleeping.

Identification is a curious state in which man passes more than half his life. He will identify with everything—with what he says, what he feels, what he believes, what he does not believe, what he wishes, what he does not wish, what attracts him, what repels him. Everything in life absorbs him while he is in this sleep state, and he cannot separate himself from the idea, feeling, or object that absorbed him. That is, man in the state of identification is incapable of looking impartially on the object of his identification. He will even identify with the smallest object, thus making himself vulnerable to the mechanical reactions which plague him, such as the manifestations of lying, imagination, the expression of negative emotions, and constant talking.

He will find that none of these will exist without identification; and if he could get rid of the identification, he could get rid of many useless and foolish manifestations. Yet, he doesn't know that identification means death to the physical and mental organism. He moves more in this direction by considering himself in a state in which he constantly worries about the social opinions of others; whether he is important in the lives of other people; what others think about him; whether they admire him; and the doubts, fears, and suspicions about his relationships with people. This considering plays a very important part in the life of man, but with some people it becomes an obsession. Their lives are filled with considering doubt, worry, and suspicion, and there is no place for anything else left in the consciousness.

This is just what the Kal desires, for then it has control of the individual. Its greatest trap is to keep the individual from seeing faults in himself, but easily seeing his very own in others. The separation of one man from another is simply in the language barrier; that is, not the actual language of itself, but the communication and understanding of what the other is saying and wants to get across. This is the greatest problem which the MAHANTA, the Living ECK Master has with his chelas.

The chelas, having been raised in different environments and having varied attitudes, fixed opinions, and ideas about religions, do not understand and cannot open themselves to the words and teachings of the Living ECK Master. Mainly, they do not understand that he is speaking to each on the Soul level, that he knows and understands that each is immortal within the limits of the universes of God and, therefore, he speaks to each in this manner.

This can be said to be the new language, but so few understand it. It is a different set of ideas, united in a reality that is not universal in thought. This expression as a universal language must not be taken in a metaphysical sense. The language is universal in the same sense as mathematical symbols are universal. This is the language of ECK, and it includes in itself all that people can think about. Even a few words of this language can give the chela the possibility of thinking and speaking with more precision than is possible in ordinary language.

Reincarnation and social reconstruction go together in this physical world; in other words, there is a vast interest in society in the fields of reincarnation and karma. Both offer society a sound basis upon which to proceed in dealing with all sorts of human irregularities. Therefore, it's found that the basis for reincarnation and karma is that of character in the individual. When the individual is undergoing disciplinary training in the spiritual works of ECK, it's noted that he is running off his karma and will reach that point in which he will never have to return again in this physical life.

The knowledge of reincarnation makes a great deal of difference in the treatment of both men and animals. It teaches man that he is bound up in one karmic bond. It shows that civilization and governments have changed from age to age, in each age taking shape to correspond with the spiritual development of its citizens. It is a fact, since man has descended from a golden age, that sooner or later it must be acknowledged that kings, rulers, courts, priests, lawyers, and legal punishment are all marks of racial degeneration and not indices of a high degree of civilization, as so many believe. It would do well to ponder this point. As evil tendencies become more and more manifest in society, some regulations are necessary to adopt to protect the members of society. It is an old trick of priests and kings to teach the masses that whatever they give out is the will of God.

The righteous law is called danda. It treats the divine rights of the people as well as that of kings. When it works both ways, it means that neither can trespass upon the other's rights. To have to write law upon the books and use this as a guide to keep society within the moral standards of life is to bring about disorder in a society. As the human race enters upon its decline in civilized standards, there is, and was, a transfer of the center of government from within man to enacted statutes; in other words, from moral standards deeply embedded in the inner consciousness of people to laws written in books. When the time came that the fundamental danda, the Law of Righteousness, was no longer in the hearts of people but in books, then the decline of civilization set in for society.

It is only the ECK Masters who have witnessed such changes and have tried to lift the human race above the decline of every civilization in the history of mankind. The task is hard, but since the Golden Age, long since passed, every ECK Master who has spent time upon this earth has gone through the Silver Age, the Copper Age, and others to witness the degenerative changes. Slowly has come the Iron Age, which marks the lowest ebb in individual and social degeneration. It is during this period that modern laws, governments, and social regulations began to appear. Men, supposedly wise in nature, hailed these changes as progress. But it's not true that man has progressed in nature, but has decreased due to the workings of the Kal forces. He usually does not recognize such a negative force and, if he does at all, he scorns it as being nothing in his life.

Karma, of course, is bound up with reincarnation. It is separated into two parts: cause and righteousness, which are the basic factors that create karma. It is the disobedience of the Law of Dharma, which is rightness or righteousness—the Law of Life or what ought to be done—that brings about karma for the individual or groups. But nowhere does anyone tell exactly what cause or righteousness might be, which causes the karmic forces to enter into the life of man. This is because all people go by a book of laws. No one, except the ECKist, can live by the laws of God. Nearly all commandments say, Do right, but few know what is being said here except the Living ECK Master, who gets to the heart of the problem. Most religions, instead, write down their laws in a book and assign penalties for their violations. Nearly all of them sum up the matter by saying, Do the will of God.

When this statement is investigated, it's found that the commands of the lawgiver are assumed to be the will of God. Those who are and have been responsible for the will-of-God statements have been the priests, prophets, kings, and, of course, the dictators. Once their credentials are challenged, they are upset and quote their authority from some religious writings. They have no understanding of what constitutes good or bad conduct and other problems of a moral nature.

The MAHANTA, the Living ECK Master says that whatever bears the quality or character of any of the five mental passions, or in any way hinders or delays Soul in Its progress and unfoldment toward spiritual freedom, is wrong and brings karma. Therefore, whatever creates good karma is right, and whatever creates bad karma is wrong. If a certain act has the effect to delay anyone else on the path of spiritual liberation, then that course of action must be considered wrong.

No one is to be impeded on his way to God-Realization. But if any given act has the effect of helping another party in his spiritual progress, then that is to be considered good, whether the individual most concerned likes it or not. The ultimate effect upon the higher interests of all concerned must be the prime consideration.

The old slogan "the greatest good to the greatest number" is unfortunate, for it is utterly misleading. Sometimes it is used to justify murder in the name of society, but nothing can be morally good if a single individual has to be sacrificed to gain it. Therefore, the cure for evil is the unobstructed Sound and Light. When this occurs, as in the case of the Living ECK Master, then all darkness and evil vanishes, as the night disappears when the sun rises.

One of the most provocative of all things in the works of the ECK is the gathering of the lowly and the ignorant at the feet of the MAHANTA, the Living ECK Master. It's puzzling to realize that they find him, when millions of the best people of the world have failed to find him. Whatever moves them to seek spiritual liberation when they scarcely know any more than to eat, sleep, breed, and work? But it is doubtful that many know what they are seeking, or what urge has brought them to this strange quest.

The key to the divine mystery is the great mercy of the Supreme SUGMAD and the great love of these people. The best of things in this world is not superior intelligence, but love. No one ever comes to the MAHANTA, the Living ECK Master until his good karma brings him. Therefore, these Souls must have a lot of good karma even though their appearance and position in this worldly life do not indicate it. Their good karma is not utilized to purchase worldly position and wealth, but applied to secure something vastly more important; that is, the Darshan, the meeting with the Living ECK Master. They come to him with a love, a capacity to love, an inheritance which has brought them directly to the feet of the Living ECK Master. They have but one idea; that is, the Living ECK Master will take them up out of the miseries of this world. This is all that is needed, for no one needs anything else, for finding the way to the Living ECK Master is far better than all the riches and comforts of this world.

The paradox of life is that mercy and love bring one closer to the Living ECK Master than any other qualities in the individual. That is the mercy of the SUGMAD giving life through the Living ECK Master, and the love of the lowly, humble people. These followers have nothing but the richness of their love, and this they give freely to the Living ECK Master. The capability to love is the most noble of all qualities of Soul, for to love is a greater ability than to rule over one's fellow man.

These humble people trudge the dusty highways, bearing their rolls of bedding and only a handful of food, some walking for days in order to reach the Living ECK Master. These are more greatly blessed than the ones who need expensive transportation and rich foods in order to see the MAHANTA, the Living ECK Master. Therefore, it's found that love is the passkey to the kingdom of heaven and, once again, none can take it from him who has gained it.

Thus it means that love, faith, and humility are the virtues which must first be established in the seeker before he can come unto the MAHANTA, the Living ECK Master. These are the virtues that are gained by the poor and lowly ones, the simple and childlike virtues which all must have in order to enter into the kingdom of heaven via love. It is love and love only which will admit the seeker to all the heavenly worlds, for it is the golden coin which must be presented when entering the high regions of Spirit. Nothing else will do, because the doors of these worlds will not open for any other reason.

If the karma of man has brought him nothing more than a capacity to love, then he has not lived in vain for a thousand past lives. It is this love which makes the most humble of Souls so great that it lifts him beyond all human life into the worlds of God.

Every person who loves, even a little, in purity and unselfishness, contributes that much toward the elevation of the whole of the human race. Therefore, when the mists have been cleared, when one of these poor and lowly shall stand side by side with the man of great intellectual learning on the bright shores of the Sach Khand world, what will be the difference between them? What advantage will the intellectual man have over the other? The answer is none, for his intellect has never taken him this far, to the shores of the Sach Khand region. Intellect alone will never do this, for it is love and love only, with the help of the MAHANTA, the Living ECK Master, which can take him there.

The mind goes only to the region to which it belongs: that which is called the First Grand Division of the universes of God. There it is discarded, for it is of no further use to the Soul which desires to enter into the heavenly worlds of true Spirit. When a Soul such as that of a beggar, stripped of its poor mental equipment, shall stand by the side of a mental giant, there will be no difference between them. Both are drops from the same infinite ocean, and the entire ocean is that of love and mercy. Nothing exists in the ocean except that of pure Soul and a boundless love.

The pure act of love lies mainly in the personal mantra of the ECK Initiate. It can be described mainly as a sacred prayer-song which, when repeatedly chanted over a long period of time, gradually converts the devotee into a living center of spiritual vibration which is attuned to some other center of vibration vastly more powerful than his own. The user of this mantra is able to appropriate this energy and redirect it to the aid of himself and others.

Mantras are ubiquitous in the life of the ECK chela and are used at every significant step in his unfoldment to God. This is the love power which builds for him that great aura of everlasting mercy and compassion. For example, when a chela enters into the ECK Master discipline, the Living ECK Master will sometimes assign him a special mantra for life. This generally occurs at the Second Initiation, and the Living ECK Master is also under an obligation to see that the disciple keeps up this chant of his special mantra, because it constitutes a spiritual link between them. This is one of the reasons why the Living ECK Master always asks for a monthly report, for he can tell if the chela is keeping up his chant through the report as well as other means of spiritual insight.

The MAHANTA, the Living ECK Master may select the mantra on the basis of his insight into the spiritual condition of the individual chela or, alternatively, he may instruct the chela to bring the mantra out of his own inner self by observing his spiritual experiences and dream states.

The actual recitation of the mantra may be either verbal, whispered, or silent. Since the chanting of the mantra at times goes on for several hours, these various intonations of it can be alternated in order to maintain concentration. All the usual means of interpretive expression can be used in the chanting, such as variations in tempo, volume, voice, and other things. However, in order to preserve the essential power of the mantra intact, the original melody, word, and rhythm must be strictly adhered to and used with some constraints, because there is room for an enormous range of emotional expression.

Mantra chanting produces a whole series of spiritual effects, mainly that of love. When one concentrates the mind on the mantra, a deep sense of peace and love arises. Mantra chanting focuses the mind to a sharp point that is capable of penetrating through the ordinary thoughts to the deeper layers of Soul which lie beneath.

To the ordinary man, the mantra would appear to be nonsensical, a sound which is only the response of the brain to a certain range of vibration transmitted by the air that surrounds him. Nevertheless, it is a powerful instrument of love and detachment for that ECK chela who practices it regularly. He reaches out to people whom he will never know and changes the course of their lives from the Kal forces which might be gripping them to the ECK, which will lead them to God. Few, if any, will ever learn what has happened, but the mantra built up by the ECKists, either individually or collectively, will bring about a change in the worlds: first the world of man, and then that of the spiritual heavens where necessary.

It is the Living ECK Master who brings the opportunity of love via the mantra to the chela. He gives the secret mantra to those who deserve it, and thereafter the responsibility lies in the hands of the chela, who can make the best of it if he is at all spiritually observant and energetic.

5
Gakko, the World of Being

It is claimed by some occult following that there is in existence on this earth a perfect race of beings who are as far removed from the present state of man and his human consciousness as man is from the animal and vegetable kingdoms. Although there is a great deal of truth in what is said, it must be pointed out that those who believe this outside of Eckankar have been looking and listening to the wrong teachings and teachers.

Within the world of being these entities, or Masters, live, but it is a state of consciousness that few know and understand. These beings are the Adepts of the Vairagi, known in the works of Eckankar as the ECK Masters. These are the true spiritual Masters, and none other exist. The use of the word *perfect* is relative, for it is like the horizon, forever receding; but the state known as Gakko, which is within the Atma Lok, the world of Soul, is that state of relative perfection where all or most of the ECK Masters live who are not doing duty in the other planes and worlds.

It is known that having attained the stature of an ECK Master that there yet lies beyond this higher and even higher stages of spiritual evolution. One of the three truths of ECK is that Soul is immortal, and Its future is the future of a thing whose growth and splendor has no limits. Therefore, when the Gakko, Soul, a fragment of the Absolute SUGMAD, begins Its long pilgrimage into matter, It first enters into the elemental kingdom, and from there It passes into the mineral kingdom.

In this state, the mineral kingdom, Its consciousness sleeps imprisoned in Its rocklike substance. Although to the naked eye It appears inanimate, yet the eternal life dwells within. For consciousness ensouls all forms from a grain of sand to a mighty cosmos. From this It passes into the vegetable kingdom, where consciousness dreams in an almost half-awakened state, responding to external stimuli as nature cares for It with the warmth of the sun and the rain. Next, in the animal kingdom, consciousness awakens and becomes directly aware of Its surroundings. Unlike the other previous kingdoms where the forms remain static, the animal moves about and becomes aware of different environments.

When Soul in the animal consciousness makes Its transition into the human element, not only is Its consciousness enormously enhanced, but It becomes individualized. There is the old saying that a man knows that he knows, but an animal merely knows. Even within the species of *Homo sapiens* the range of consciousness varies from the primitive bushman to that of the scientist, artist, or philosopher. The previous kingdoms are guided in their evolution by certain high spiritual beings, but man, with the birth of the "I" consciousness, begins consciously to determine his future evolution through the Living ECK Master.

Therefore, man is unfolded until he gains an insight into the spiritual kingdom again. He now begins to realize that there are those superbeings like the ECK Masters; but where do they live and what do they look like?

Since many possess physical bodies, they appear to man as individuals with distinct personalities. Fubbi Quantz, Rebazar Tarzs, and other ECK Masters, all having attained a high degree of consciousness well beyond the level of man, appear differently to man.

The ECK Masters, along with yet higher entities, form an inner, esoteric ring. In Eckankar they are known as the Adepts of the Vairagi. Their existence has been known to mystics and occultists in every age, and they are the "just men" in the sacred scriptures of the West made perfect. The religious orders of the Orient have long known about the ECK Masters and their strange adeptship; their existence has been accepted as authentic.

The state of the ECK Master is that he must be as perfect as the ECK or that which is known as the SUGMAD. This perfection does not mean perfection of the physical body, but that which is known as the Atma body, or Soul. His human body, through which he operates, is in a state of health and is retained as long as his position is necessary within this physical world, several hundred years if necessary. Spiritually, the Living ECK Master lives in a state of God Consciousness for twenty-four hours a day. Also he has developed, but doesn't seek, what is known as the various siddhis powers, due to his high state of evolution.

To the average man they appear to be miraculous, but to him they are only powers to be used whenever necessary. However, he never uses them because so many of his followers would never understand. All the Masters of Eckankar generally live in a retreat or inaccessible places, or, if in Western countries, every effort is made to conceal their identity. Their presence is universal: in India, Tibet, Egypt, China, Lebanon, Cyprus, Hungary, and other nations of the world. However, there is only one MAHANTA, the Living ECK Master, who has charge over all until he is relieved of his spiritual title. The next one who steps into his place takes the reins and assumes the responsibility.

These ECK Masters are also on every plane and planet in the universes of God. Their work is to help forward the evolution of humanity, to find and train disciples. They see that these disciples come to the Living ECK Master so that he can take them under his charge to bring about qualities of love and wisdom in this world. None can force man to follow these aspects of God, but can only guide and inspire. Each man must tread the path of ECK himself. He is foolish indeed if he does not listen and gain the knowledge of the divine from the MAHANTA, the Living ECK Master.

Many times the Living ECK Master will mock up illness, pain, anger, and other emotions in order to bring about certain reactions with one or more of his chelas. He may even lay discipline on a chela to bring him into the realization of humility, modesty, or understanding of courtesy toward all his fellow men. If the chela has shown a lack of discipline, he may be in for some very rough treatment from the Living ECK Master, while on the other hand, the ECK Master is extremely gentle and kind to another chela. He treats all chelas individually and never as a collective group of persons.

The path of ECK is not a selfish one, for every time one individual attains perfection, the whole of the human race is lifted up a little higher, just as the yeast leavens the bread. No one shall be without spiritual help as long as he desires it, but once he enters into ECK there is no turning back, for the chela must go on until he reaches the region of Gakko, that world of being where all the Adepts of the Vairagi have established their home.

There has probably never been a greater gift from Eckankar to the world than the present book, *The Shariyat-*

Ki-Sugmad. It contains the quintessence of the most profound doctrine of all spiritual works. These are not obsolete or forgotten doctrines recovered from out of the past, which blossomed and died long ago, but that very essence which is life itself. The doctrine of ECK has been handed down to the present age through an unbroken line of ECK Masters who have kept it alive despite whatever suppression has been made against Eckankar.

The suppressions have been many, for all orthodox religions have fought to keep it underground or tried to destroy it because of the great power which it has gained as a force on this planet in the past. Those who took part in the suppression of ECK, causing it to go underground, suffered from the Laws of Retribution. In ancient times long before the Western nations became civilized and were no longer tribes, the teachings of Eckankar were being expounded to a chosen few among the learned of Tibet and India.

In the beginning, the original teachings stated that, having practiced the ECK contemplation and spiritual exercises, a communion was established between the human mind and the ECK spiritual forces, or between the normal human consciousness and the supernormal cosmic consciousness, and by this means, man attained a true knowledge of himself.

He realizes intuitively that the Knower, which is the SUGMAD, and all objects of knowledge, or all knowing, are inseparably linked together; and simultaneously, with this realization is born what is known as the great symbol which signifies his spiritual illumination. This symbol is known to every ECKist as the ECK, the "E . . . C . . . K," either sung or placed in the mind as a symbol. It purges from the mind the dross of ignorance, and the human is transmuted into the divine by the spiritual alchemy of Eckankar.

The Shariyat-Ki-Sugmad is a guide, for it directs the ECKist on the path of ECK, leading to complete God-Realization, enlightenment, and emancipation. Not until the lower self has been absorbed into the Higher Self can the illusion of personality be broken, and not until then can the continuity of the SUGMAD be realized as having no beginning and no ending, as being eternally in at-one-ness with Itself and the all-knowledge of the ECK. It is thus that the human is raised to the divine Self and set to confront the pure wisdom of the ECK.

The temporal instructions are only to serve as a guide for the laymen who are traveling the path of ECK to the higher way of life. Once the decision is reached by the seeker to take the first step on the path of ECK, the disciple is no longer in need of the temporal, or the outer, instructions only, for he begins to acquire those which are spiritual, in contrast to the unenlightened multitude who are mentally unable to understand them esoterically.

The refuge of the chela, once he has taken this step, is in the ECK, but he must think of the ECK being in the form of the MAHANTA, the Living ECK Master. This means that the chela must believe that it is through the intercession of the MAHANTA that all beings go for refuge in the SUGMAD. The resolution, then, is that the chela resolves to become an ECKist so that he might be able to aid all sentient beings to reach the ECKshar, the enlightenment, or supreme consciousness.

The ECK chela will pass through the three lower stages, which are the Astral, Causal, and Mental bodies, to reach the first stage of the ECKshar which is experienced on the Atma, or Soul, Plane. He will have to contend with the psychic powers which come in certain waves, sometimes called gift-waves. These are waves of psychic energy which stimulate spiritual development and greatly assist the aspirant seeking the ECKshar, the enlightenment. These waves are sent forth telepathically from the MAHANTA. The Living ECK Master will assist in the granting of these waves, otherwise known as the conferring of power, which constitutes the true spiritual initiation.

The chela must reach at-one-ment, both with the MAHANTA, the Living ECK Master and, through him, the ECK power, in order to reach the God Worlds. It makes little difference if he ever meets the MAHANTA during his lifetime; but as long as he seeks his refuge in the Living ECK Master, he will have his opportunity to enter into the heavenly worlds.

Prolonged contemplation may cause tiredness of body and mind, leading to drowsiness and sluggishness. By way of diversion and to overcome these hindrances, the chela is directed to go to a place like an isolated room or an outdoor place where he might not be disturbed, such as a garden, an orchard, or a hilltop, in which no human sounds can be heard. Here one attunes the body with the mind, which becomes rhythmic with Soul. It is to be remembered that the life-giving part of the air inhaled is not chiefly the oxygen, which is absorbed into the bloodstream through the functioning of the lungs, but the ECK, which is essential to all the psychophysical activities of the body and mind, as well as the Soul, in the lower worlds.

Unruly thoughts are the enemy of the chela practicing the Spiritual Exercises of ECK. He must learn to cut off any thought at the root the very moment that it arises. In contemplation, one finds that because of the mind responding to stimuli, thoughts crop up continuously. Knowing the birth of even a single idea should be prevented, the chela must try to inhibit this continuous cropping up of thoughts by exercising mental alertness. As soon as a thought sprouts, try to eliminate it, root and all, and continue the spiritual exercises in which one is engaged.

By prolonging the period of contemplation in which the effort is made to prevent the arising of thoughts, the chela finally comes to be aware of thoughts following closely on one another, so numerous they seem to be interminable. This is the recognizing of thoughts, which equals the knowing of the enemy; the enemy being unruly thoughts, or what is normally called the Kal force. This stage is called the first resting-place, which is that level of mental quiescence attained; and thereupon, the ECK chela looks on unperturbed at the interminable flow of thoughts as though he were sitting on the riverbank watching the water flow past.

If the ECKist is successful up to this point, he will have attained freedom from the mental tyranny of thoughts and will be ready for the still greater tasks ahead of him on the path of Eckankar. But once the mind has attained the tranquil state for even the briefest moment through the act of Soul Travel, rising above the mental state, he begins to understand the rising and cessation of thoughts. This understanding makes one feel as though thoughts are always rising, but there is neither an increase nor a decrease of them. Thoughts are born instantly; and that which is apart from and capable of arresting the birth of thought is the ECK, the divine reality.

Rising above the Time Track in which the thought process has its modus operandi is the manner in which the ECKist operates. He does not try to stop any thought process, but rises above it. He leaves unshaped whatever concept or idea appears and is somewhat indifferent to thought, neither attempting to impede it nor to fall under its influence. In other words he is working from the Atma Plane, the fifth region, and is not concerned with whatever the mind has to say or how it acts.

He is interested only in whatever the actions of Soul might be and, therefore, follows any instinct which might be given to It by the ECK. The practice of keeping the mind in its place is his greatest discipline and nothing else. He then is concerned only with Soul Travel in the upper regions of God. Yet thoughts should be kept under control with the consciousness, like a shepherd watching over his sheep. The effort to stop thoughts from arising, of controlling them or not controlling them, has inevitably created other thoughts. The aim is to reach the highest level of tranquillity. Each strand of the rope represents a thought. The rope represents the continuity of the thought process which, like the rope itself, is to be broken.

One must keep the mind like that of a small child looking with interest at a toy. It is the ECKist's attitude that the mind is hardly anything more than a machine, or like a child which sometimes becomes unruly and wants attention at once or it will create a disturbance. All one must learn to do is to handle the mind as he would a small child. Less trouble is had with the mind when under such supervision.

The individual mind is a part of the Universal Mind, or Kal power, which is that force that rules the lower universes. It is the psychic power and is not to be considered anything more than an inferior force. However, many religions worship this force as the true spirit, and their followers are always in trouble whether they pray for material things or to God for the many things which are needed to make up living on earth. It gives only temporary relief and must be avoided at all cost by the ECKist who wants the true reality of the SUGMAD.

The ECKist is independent of book learning in making his analysis of himself or of the spiritual forces of God. He seeks knowledge only in those worlds beyond which he lives, and is usually successful in doing so. The intellectual measures experiences in terms of the external world, because he has never learned the true spiritual life.

In this connection Rebazar Tarzs has said, "I have never valued word-knowledge which is set down in books. This leads only to mental confusion and not to such practices as the Spiritual Exercises of ECK, which bring actual realization of truth."

Therefore, all things which serve as obstacles in life must be considered as aids on the path of ECK. The underlying principle is that all trials and tribulations must be regarded as aids to spiritual living. For example, the traveler, who is walking at night along a road, finds what he considers a snake and leaps in terror to smash it with his staff. Regaining his confidence, he strikes a light and sees that it's only a coil of rope. So he ties the rope around his waist to help keep his robe from drooping about his legs. He has found a way to use the obstacle which otherwise might have impeded his journey. Ignorance of the divine knowledge will bring terror and fright of many things which have no power to harm man. But in the face of it all and by using the ECK power, man can dispense with such things which are considered evil in his life and hold back his progress toward the spiritual goals.

He can bring about the ECK indifference of non-attachment to all phenomena, his body and mind relaxed in the state of quiescence of the highest realization. Once he gets into this state, his mind and heart assume a rhythmic vibration in touch with the vibrations of the ECK power, of which the cosmic creation is the phenomenal fruit.

Up to this point the chela has been contemplating on the created substance of the lower worlds. Now he enters into the Atma worlds, which are the uncreated universes of God, and all is vastly different from the worlds below. It is here that the laws change, for all creation here is that which the individual Soul does of Itself and must hold if the chela is to be at all successful in the world of true spirituality.

The realization that birth, death, and time have no existence in themselves is of vast importance within Soul. The present thought that any of those aspects of the material life have but a momentary existence is true, for no sooner than such is born, it passes away. It cannot be fixed or identified as being present. It is, in fact, inseparable from both the past and the future, whence it arose in the present and in the past had vanished. The purpose of this type of contemplation is to cause the ECKist to realize that the past, present, and future are an inseparable unity, and that the materialistic view of time is erroneous; for time, itself, being like all other material things or concepts, is illusory.

All things perceived by the unenlightened mind are seen only in their materialistic aspect. They are real to one who has no concept of the great divine nature of the SUGMAD. They are of the stuff that dreams and illusions are made, in accordance with the true reality.

Transmutation into the true worlds of God is a spiritual process dependent upon the Spiritual Exercises of Eckankar. Its purpose is to aid the ECKist, both mentally and spiritually, to realize the complete selflessness of the ECKshar state of the heavenly worlds to which he has always aspired. Within this state he can hear the heavenly Voice and witness the heavenly Light of the SUGMAD. These are the twin aspects of the SUGMAD which every seeker on the path of ECK can witness, provided he puts forth an effort into the practice of the Spiritual Exercises of ECK.

It is in this state that he reaches the bliss of the perfect enlightenment, the true state beyond all sorrow, pain, and grief, beyond all emotions of the Kal power. The man immersed in the materialistic is wise only in sensations, in knowledge derived from experiences in a sensuous universe. All his worldly learning is, in fact, unreal and, by its egotistical character, obscures the true wisdom. It is for this reason that the ECKist calls it *avidya,* ignorance of truth, or a lack of enlightenment. This is the state in which the unenlightened multitude exists as in a feverish nightmare, knowing nothing of the path of ECK which leads to the supreme awakening into freedom.

Each aspirant for the ECKshar enlightenment must be a law unto himself. He himself, not the Living ECK Master, must tread the path of ECK. One must eat the food for oneself and, as it's taught by the MAHANTA, the Living ECK Master, each upon the path must be his own Light and Sound, his own refuge. The realization of God is not to realize by the proxy of an ECK Master, but by the ECKist himself.

The passing beyond sorrow is the goal of every ECKist. The path through the material worlds, the spirito-materialistic regions, ends when one realizes that which is called Self-Realization, that which Soul realizes as Itself upon reaching the Atma, Soul, Plane. But this state known as the ECKshar must be considered as a spiritual rest house on the highway through eternity. Although one finds his true spiritual companions known here as the Gakko, the world of being, Soul, or the fully enlightened one, he finds no line of demarcation exists between the spirito-materialistic worlds and the Atma Plane. He lives in both states, and for him neither state is an abiding or fixed state. Were the Gakko an abiding state, that is to say a state of finality like the heaven of the orthodox religions, no further evolutionary progress would be possible beyond it.

There are three errors which can arise in doing the Spiritual Exercises of ECK. These are the overfondness for analyzing thought and thought processes, an overfondness for reflecting upon the analysis, and an overfondness for the quiescent state of mind. When the ECKist grows too fond of, and becomes habituated to, any of these three errors or all of them and attached to any or all, he is prevented from further progress on the path of ECK.

There are some ECKists who have grown too fond of the quiescent state of mind; and unless safeguarded by the MAHANTA, the Living ECK Master, they make no effort to advance beyond it and not infrequently develop the illusion that they have attained the goal of God-Realization. So, for these reasons, it becomes the duty of the Living ECK Master not only to expound the teachings of Eckankar, but to impress upon the chela that the path of ECK has many pitfalls and that many misleading will-o'-the-wisps of the senses are certain to be seen while practicing the spiritual exercises before the goal of God-Realization may be attained.

Another great error which the ECKists find in reaching certain spiritual levels, especially that of the mental realm, is from such egotistical thoughts as *I shall never come back to human birth again; I am living on earth for the last time; I shall quit all material experiences forever; I have reached the goal; I have realized the ECKshar.* Not until all self-consciousness be eradicated, be transmuted into selflessness, into all-embracing altruism so overwhelmingly selfless that no thought of self be left, can there be attunement with the ECKshar, which is the goal of all those who follow the path of ECK.

This is the state of Self-Realization. It is that state of consciousness which brings about the knowledge of the Self and the overwhelming experience of Soul realizing who It is and the mission that It must accomplish. This mission will be that of God-Realization and the assignment that It receives to serve within the universes of God. The conviction is there for Soul. It will not have to be told what Its goal may be and what the assignment for Its duty and responsibilities might be throughout all eternity.

The worlds of ECK are always mysterious to those who know naught of It. Yet they are simple when one finds them through the MAHANTA, the Living ECK Master when traveling via the Atma Sarup, the Soul body, throughout the various worlds. They are as follows:

1. The Physical Plane is the First Plane, when counting toward the Ocean of Love and Mercy where dwells the SUGMAD. This is the plane where Soul is trapped by the five passions: vanity, greed, anger, attachment, and lust. It is a plane of illusion, time, space, and matter. It is the region of the illusion of reality (maya), science, and day-to-day events in life. The sound one hears on this plane is that of thunder. The word, or chant, is *Alayi.* The ruler is Elam. In the Sanskrit language this world is known as the Pinda.

2. The Second Plane is the Astral, or the emotional, world. It is the highest plane reached by astral projection and is the source of most occult sciences, ghosts, flying saucers, spirits, etc. The sound is that of the roaring sea. Its word, or chant, is *Kala.* The ruler is Jot Niranjan. The classical name is Sat Kanwal-Anda, also described as the Turiya Pad.

3. Next is the Causal, or Third, Plane. The word is *Mana.* The ruler here is Ramkar, or the Maha Kal Brahm, who rules over negative reality and affects all below. It is that plane where memories, karmic patterns, and Akashic records are stored. Here is where those who can do Akashic readings look for the source of trouble in past lives and embodiments. On this plane one can hear the tinkling of the bells.

4. The Fourth, or Mental, Plane has the word *Aum* for chanting, and the sound of running water is heard. This plane is that of the Universal Mind Power, and this is where the ruler of the three worlds of Vedanta, Buddhism, and Hinduism dwells. He is Omkar, the Brahm,

the great Brahman, spoken of in the Hindu sacred writings, and is the source of all moral teachings, ethics, philosophy, aesthetics, and conventional Gods and religions.

The top of the Mental Plane, the Etheric Plane, is known as the unconscious, because it is a clearer channel for those seeking to become the instrument of God. Psychologists call it the subconscious. It is the source of the primitive thought and is a very thin line between the Mental body and the Soul body, the Atma Sarup. It has the word *Baju* for chanting, and the sound is that of the buzzing of bees. The ruler here is Sohang, or the Saguna Brahm.

5. We now come to the Fifth, or Soul, Plane which is the dividing line between the lower and upper worlds, separating the psychic regions from the spiritual planes. It is the first step of Soul into the worlds of God, the kingdom of heaven. Within the upper regions we gain freedom and individuality which is self-recognized and allows Soul to reenter into that state called God Consciousness, or God-Realization. The word here is *SUGMAD,* spelled out in each individual letter for chanting. The ruler is Sat Nam. The sound is the single note of a flute.

6. The Sixth Plane, or Alakh Lok (*lok* means plane in the Hindi language), is the second of the true worlds of God, or the invisible plane. The word for chanting is *Shanti,* and the sound is that of a heavy wind. It represents the Alakh Purusha, the supreme creative energy and ruler of this plane. Those who reach this plane must have great determination to go beyond it, for they experience peace and happiness here.

7. The Seventh Plane is the Alaya Lok, the endless world, for it seems to have no end and is the third of the true worlds of God. It is sometimes called Sach Khand, where eternity begins and ends. The word here is *Hum,*

like humming with the lips closed, and the sound is much like a swarm of bees or a high electrical sound.

8. The Eighth Plane is the Hukikat Lok and is the highest state that Soul can usually reach. The word here is *Aluk.* The sound is that of a thousand violins.

9. Agam Lok is known as the Inaccessible Plane, for few, if any, ever enter into this world. The word here is *Huk,* with a short barking sound made deep in the throat.

10. The Tenth Plane is the Anami Lok, the nameless world. There isn't anything to say about it. It is beyond any vocabulary in the human language. The word is *HU,* the universal name of God, which is in the language of every living thing. It is everywhere, in everything.

11. The Eleventh Plane is the SUGMAD world. Here is the beginning of the abode of the SUGMAD. Only those who have become ECK Masters reach this world. Out of this world flows the Word of God, the magnificent music of the universes. Anyone who has ever heard It will never want to live in the material worlds again.

12. SUGMAD. This is the SUGMAD, the Living Reality. It is the Ocean of Love and Mercy. Beyond this plane is the Akshar Realization which covers all worlds. This plane can only be experienced—never put into words or even thought. Here the sound is the Music of God.

Eckankar does not say there are only twelve planes, for above the Anami Lok there are numerous ones not yet accounted for in the explorations of the ECK Masters. But in order not to confuse ECK chelas we give only the number listed here. Also, one must remember that there are many planes listed within these twelve regions.

All those who follow ECK must have faith in the words of the MAHANTA, the Living ECK Master because he is the Godman, the representative of the SUGMAD in each and all of the great spheres within the living universe of the divine reality.

Rebazar Tarzs once said, "Let your faith, your inner trust and confidence stream forth; remove your inner obstacles, and open yourself to truth." It is this kind of faith, or inner awareness and open-mindedness, which finds its spontaneous expression—its liberation from an overwhelming psychic pressure—in the sacred sound of the HU. In this mantric sound all the positive and forward-pressing forces of the human—which are trying to blow up its limitations and burst the fetters of ignorance—are united and concentrated on the ECK, like an arrow point.

However, if the genuine expression of profound spiritual experience comes too soon, one often falls victim to speculation. He knows not what this experience is and its value in his life on the path to God. But it's mainly because he has no one nor any part in the overall experience himself to analyze its results. He usually wants to discuss the quality of the Light and Sound of God before he has even started penetrating the darkness; and while mentally going over such experiences, he usually builds up an elaborate theology into which the Voice of God is woven so artfully that it becomes impossible to extricate It.

Therefore, instead of relying on his own forces, he expects the help of the MAHANTA or some supernatural agency. While speculating about the goal and the direction, he forgets the effects which result from his efforts in the Spiritual Exercises of ECK. He forgets that there is really a way out of his personal misery of every kind; out of the meaninglessness of life; out of boredom, discouragement, failure, obsessive anxiety, or depression; and out of fear. He learns that there is a way out of these Kal effects into the freedom of life. That way is the ECK way.

The ECK is the root and background of all life, all religions and daily living. It is the principle by which all life, the entire universes of God go forward. It is truth, and it is beauty. No matter what language one speaks, he does not have to go to any special place to get in touch with the ECK, nor wait for a special time or a special person; he can make contact with the ECK now. It matters not what religion he is brought up in, he can connect with the ECK here and now. The ECK is beauty. The ECK is the essence of the SUGMAD.

Man does not want to be involved in invidious religious distinctions. Many of the arguments which develop into war between men have arisen out of arguments over the definitions and incarnations of God. Most of this arguing goes on among people who have not observed the vastly more important principles of the ECK. They have not listened seriously to their own or other great teachers.

The ECK is the living power which embraces all the universes of God; It sustains and governs the primal creative powers of all living things. It is the power which governs all, including man, and will show him how to live if he will permit it. But he has refused to permit it. In departing from the ECK and ignoring the ECK does man come to the state of the Kal, which furnishes him with the weakness and misery of the human consciousness. This brings the war that splits him, raging within him, and makes him the battlefield between the ECK and Kal forces within the consciousness of the individual. Man is the prodigal son of the ECK.

It is the first and most important task of Eckankar to bend and restring the bow of Soul by proper training and discipline. After the self-confidence of man has been restored, the new doctrine of ECK has been firmly established, and the ornaments and cobwebs of theology and metaphysical speculation have withered and fallen before the sacred word of HU, it can again be attached to the Spiritual Exercises of ECK.

It has already been mentioned how closely the HU is connected with the development of the individual in ECK, which, as a kind of integration of thought upon every mental and spiritual system in existence, gives some sort of experience, whether it be psychic or spiritual. Therefore, it is not surprising that the works of the ECK have been handed down from the ECK Master to the chela by word of mouth instead of through public announcements or by the written word.

It is now, in the age of liberation from traditions and thought, that the ECK can become known to all persons. It is only now that It can be put into the written word because there is less opportunity of being persecuted. It is only now that man, as a mass, has collectively been lifted high enough to have a grasp and understanding of the ECK. Man has reached that level for the awakening of faith, for the liberation from inner hindrances, and for the concentration upon the supreme goal of Samadhi, Self-Realization, and eventually the Nirvikalpa, God-Realization.

The true ECKist does not expect the MAHANTA, the Living ECK Master nor any of his disciples to accept prayers or to act on behalf of any person in a miraculous way. Anyone asking for healing or any specific spiritual work for another person will generally be ignored. The person who needs spiritual aid must request it himself, for it is the universal law that anyone who desires such must appeal to the MAHANTA, the Living ECK Master on his own initiative. An appeal for another will not be considered unless that individual has given specific permission. If an individual makes a request for spiritual aid for anyone else, without permission or upon assumption, or without the knowledge of the other, he is subject to punishment by the great law.

Each new experience, each new situation of life, widens the outlook of the chela and brings about a subtle transformation within himself. Thus the nature of every chela who is earnest and serious about the works of ECK is changing constantly, not only on account of the conditions of life, but by the constant addition of new impressions, the structure of the mind becomes ever more diverse and complex. Whether it is called progress or degeneration depends upon how one looks at it. But it has to be admitted that this is the law of life, in which the spiritual and the psychic coordinate and balance one another in the world of the spirito-materialistic, where Soul must serve out Its time for perfection.

Religious and deeply rooted philosophical attitudes are not individual creations, though they are given their first impetus by the individual alone. They grow from the germs of creative ideas, experiences, and visions. They grow through many generations, right or wrong in what they are, according to their own inherent law, just like a tree or any other living organism. They are what might be called the natural events of life, because they are being watered and fed by the Kal force. But their growth, their unfoldment and maturity need time, for Kal does not work in a hurry. Though the whole tree is potentially contained in the seed, it requires time to transform itself into visible shape. This is the way the Kal works to bring religions and philosophies into this world so that man will be blinded by them instead of seeing truth.

What the MAHANTA, the Living ECK Master teaches in words is only a fraction of what he teaches by his mere presence, his personality, and his living example. The MAHANTA is always conscious of his own worldly shortcomings and limitations of words and speech, which cause him to hesitate to teach the works of ECK by putting into words something that is too profound and subtle to be grasped by mere logic and ordinary reasoning.

Despite this, the MAHANTA does disclose the truth, out

of compassion, to the few whose eyes have hardly been covered by the illusion. However, he strictly avoids speaking about the ultimate things and refuses to answer any question concerning the supramundane state of realization or similar problems which go beyond the capacity of the human intellect. He confines himself to showing the practical way which leads to the solution of the problems of man in his spiritual capacity. He always explains the essential teachings of ECK in a form which corresponds to the capacity of his listeners.

The advanced teachings of ECK have been described as esoteric, or secret, doctrines. However, their purpose is not to exclude anyone from the attainment of higher realization or knowledge, but to avoid the empty talk and speculation of those who try to anticipate, intellectually, these exalted states of consciousness, without trying to attain theirs through the Spiritual Exercises of ECK.

The teaching of the works of ECK means that each individual, race, and creed, including nations and various nationalities, must find their own form of expression, individually, and the best methods of teaching, in order to keep the idea of ECK alive. This is not a philosophical thesis nor a metaphysical dogma but an impetus toward a new attitude of spiritual endeavor which must be taken from the Soul viewpoint, or that which might be called the "non-I."

By the reversal of the viewpoint from the physical to the high level of Soul, all things suddenly appear in a new perspective insofar as the inner and outer world become equal and mutually dependent on the state of the higher consciousness. This consciousness, according to the degree of its development, experiences a different kind of reality, a different world, that of the Gakko, the world of being, in which all true ECK Initiates dwell.

6
The Records of the Kros

The Records of the Kros are most important in the life of this world. They are the ancient transcripts of the past history of this earth planet and what will become of it. History and prophecy are within these records, and those who are able to read them will know the past and future of what will take place in the physical plane.

These records are history and prophecy. So in the beginning it is known that the Records of the Kros are hidden in the Katsupari Monastery, under the guardianship of the great ECK Master Fubbi Quantz. This monastery is found in the remote Buika Magna mountain range.

These records tell us that the legendary paradise of man, thought of as the Garden of Eden, was laid on the lost continent of Lemuria, which was sunk by earthquakes and tidal waves fifty thousand years ago. This continent was in the midst of what is now the Pacific Ocean, and many of the islands which dot its vast surface were once part of Lemuria's vast mountain ranges.

It was a strange land of some one hundred thousand inhabitants who developed one of the greatest civilizations on earth. These records describe the creation of man in this mysterious country. Centuries later, writers of religious literature used fragments of these records to write their own version of creation. One of the greater records which came out of the Kros was that of the ancient Naacal writings of the primitive tribes and civilizations on this earth planet. But the Kros goes back even into the early days of the formation of the whole planetary system in this universe.

Only the great spiritual giants walked the earth and the planetary worlds in the ancient days. The world was a paradise, for every living creature could maintain and preserve its survival through the fruitfulness of the earth. The world was filled with inhabitants who were innocent of any known evil, and happiness reigned.

The first era was called the Satya Yuga, the Golden Age. It was the era in which truth and righteousness reigned. There was not any social law nor courts to punish or threaten the individual, because everybody acted right and believed in truth. The forests were still intact because no one cut timber for ships or houses, and no fortifications were built around cities and towns. The earth brought forth all things necessary without the labor of plowing and sowing. There was a perpetual spring that lay over the land, flowers grew without planting, and yellow honey was distilled from the great trees.

The Golden Age was succeeded by the Tretya Yuga, the Silver Age. Inferior to the Golden Age, it's found that the spring was shortened and the year became divided into seasons. Then, for the first time, man found that he had to endure the extremes of cold and heat. Houses and homes became necessary for every man. Caves were the first dwellings that man found for himself. Crops would no longer grow without planting, and the farmers were forced into sowing seeds and using oxen and horses to draw the plow as they toiled in the fields.

The next to follow was the Dwapara Yuga, or that known as the Copper, or Brass, Age. Men found themselves growing more savage of temper and ready to manufacture swords, spears, and helmets to fight neighbors at the least provocation. When they found their neighbors gaining wealth which they did not have, they attacked them to seize anything of temporary benefit. These were the beginning of the destructive eras. The Kal power came into strength during this period to make man subject to him so that he could hold back Soul on Its road to perfection.

The Iron Age, or that which is known as the Kali Yuga, is the one that we are dwelling in today. It is the worst and most violent of all ages, for crime has flooded the world, and all that is and was known in the past as truth and modesty has vanished. Fraud and the cunningness of man have taken their place. Violence has become rampant. This is why it's said that man shall never find peace on earth again, at least not in this lifetime, for the Kal has become the leader of this world and will continue to be king until the SUGMAD has destroyed the lower kingdom.

These are the mahayugas, or the manvantaras, which are the cycles of cosmic history. The current yuga embraces the Kali Yuga, which is one-tenth of the duration of the whole cycle. The Satya Yuga, the Golden Age, embraces the first four-tenths of the cycle, or 1,728,000 years. The Tretya Yuga, or Silver Age, embraces three-tenths of the cycle, or 1,296,000 years. The Dwapara Yuga, or Copper Age, embraces two-tenths of the cycle, or 864,000 years. The Kali Yuga, or the Iron Age, which is the dark era of the cycle, embraces one-tenth of the duration of the cosmic cycle, or 432,000 years. These descending numbers represent the physical and moral deterioration of man in each age. The four yugas represent an aggregate of

4,320,000 years of man and constitute a great yuga, or mahayuga.

A great yuga is the period of time in cosmic history which consists of approximately five million years. Soul lives and struggles in the physical and psychic worlds during these cycles. But at the end of each, the SUGMAD lifts those Souls which have not reached perfection into the Atma Lok, the Fifth Plane, where they sleep while It readjusts the lower worlds. After several million years, the SUGMAD ends the cosmic cycle and places each of these sleeping Souls back into the lower worlds so they can once again start their long journey to perfection. The cycle begins once more in the Satya Yuga, the Golden Age, where all is peaceful and man lives in harmony with all nature and creatures.

It is the longing for peace and love which has always been developed in the highest form during the Golden Age. Man remembers this through Soul forces and always seeks peace and love on this planet.

This will never come because of the Kali age which is that of darkness and unhappiness, where illusion reigns. Yet man has not realized this and must follow the MAHANTA, the Living ECK Master, who will lead him through all the maze and destruction of the Kal forces into the heavenly worlds. Either this, or he shall suffer through all the ages and sleep for five million years in the heavenly world, while his world is being readjusted so that he may enjoy life again.

Several orthodox religions are built upon the memories of the Golden Age. These religions do not know that life in the lower worlds is temporary and that Soul unfolds and progresses upward through the planes into the heavenly kingdom. They only look to the material promise of life and cannot grasp that the Golden Age comes only once every five million years or so. That, too, it is temporary and will give way in time to other ages as man goes down in moral and physical degeneration.

All the things that man does here upon this earth plane are a game under the guidance of the Kal Niranjan, the king of the negative worlds. The sooner man learns this, the quicker will he find himself on the path of ECK, and then his karma begins to work off.

By the command of the SUGMAD, the primitive spiritual force which is known as the ECK was formed, which gave law and order to the spiritual and material universes. Following this, It gave four commandments which are (1) that all heaven and the planets be formed out of the gases and waters that floated over the surfaces of the many worlds; (2) that man be formed and established upon the earth planet, and other beings be put on the other planets; (3) that the female be formed out of the rib of man and established to be his mate on the earth planet, and the same was done with the beings of other planets; and (4) that man and the beings of the other worlds live in peace with one another; that each love the SUGMAD, and love his brother and sister likewise.

This was done in all the lands of the Satya Yuga. It was the era of peace and happiness for man upon earth. He followed out the commandment to live in peace and love the SUGMAD and love his brother and sister likewise. It was a land in which everything was beautiful, tropical country with vast plains, surrounded by a peaceful ocean. The valleys and plains were covered with grasses and fields, while the low rolling hills were shaded by luxuriant tropical vegetation and fruit trees.

It was a gay and happy world, this land of Lemuria. Its people were highly civilized and enlightened, and there was no savagery on the face of the earth, nor had there ever been. This particular land was the ruling kingdom for all mankind on earth, and all lived under a code established by the rulers and their governing powers. The destruction of the kingdom of Lemuria and all its colonial empire came about by gas pockets under the crust of the earth that formed some hundreds of thousands of years ago.

Language, mind, and reality were uppermost in the thoughts of the people of this age. The idea, entirely unfamiliar to the modern world, that nature and language were inwardly akin was the mainstay of this age. The mantra of the HU was the sacred chant of all the people in the Satya Yuga. It was a manifold of conscious patterns contrived to assist the consciousness into the noumenal-patterned world. Because the ECK was the greatest force of these times, the Satya Yuga was maintained for 1,728,000 years before the Tretya Yuga, or the Silver Age, took over.

The idea of sex was, of course, much different in these times than in the modern world. Sex is divine, and its origin in the Satya Yuga, the Golden Age, was only for the procreation of children in the state of a union between the male and female under the sponsorship of the ECK Master. It has degenerated through the various ages to the present age, the Kali Yuga, in which it has become the phallic system practiced by so many who do not understand the five deadly passions of the mind: kama, or lust; krodha, or anger; lobha, or greed; moha, or undue attachment to material things; and ahankara, or vanity and egoism.

Kama, or lust, is the passion whose chief function is to pull men and women down to the common animal level and keep them there. It makes them keep their attention fixed upon that which is common to both man and brute.

If sex is used for its legitimate purpose, it becomes the highest expression of love; otherwise, it falls into the trap of degradation, which is one of those set up by the Kal Niranjan to keep Soul in this world. When one falls into the trap of self-indulgence, he begins to descend toward the animal plane. Nature has furnished man and woman with the proper means of perpetuating life upon this planet. It is within the human species to decide what is best for themselves on the sex level; however, if they do follow out the divine law that sex is not to become an instrument for self-indulgence, then all will be well. However, if sex is used for lust, man simply wastes energy and clouds his mind, ending at last in blank stupidity like an ordinary animal. When sex controls the individual instead of him controlling it, the degeneration of that individual is already an established fact. He has fallen from the state of *Homo sapiens* to that of a biped.

Therefore, sex in the form of lust is the chief phase of kama, whose central core is self-indulgence. Kama, or self-indulgence, is the principle of sickness and evil in the Kali Yuga. Every single act in self-indulgence lowers one's moral status and binds him to the world of senses. It pulls one down to the creature plane, when Soul should be rising toward the Atma Lok, the Fifth Plane.

The Tretya Yuga, or Silver Age, came after the breakup of the previous age, when Lemuria, by earthquakes and tidal waves, went down under the seas. Atlantis became the great capital empire of the world. It was located in the mid-Atlantic Ocean between northwest Africa and South America. The climate was mild, and everything grew without too much labor, to feed the population of the Atlantic empire. Its boundaries as an empire extended to Egypt, Greece, the Middle East, and parts of the area around the Black Sea.

Atlantis was first known about twenty-five to thirty thousand years ago. Its inhabitants were chiefly tall, white-skinned, fair-haired people with blue eyes who spoke a mixture of Lemurian and what was earlier considered a Scandinavian dialect. They were great sailors and traded abroad with the remnants of the old empire of Lemuria, around the areas of the China Sea and the Far East.

In the beginning Atlantis was governed by kings, but these were gradually taken over by the sage kings (wise men), who were later driven out by the tyrants and dictators. The latter posed as sage kings and leaned upon the corrupted priestcraft to manage the masses. It wasn't long before this super civilization went down under a tide of water, created by terrible earthquakes and upheaval of land masses, because of its morals, corruption, and degeneration of sex. Nothing was left for anyone to know that a great civilization was once a part of this world where the waters of the Atlantic now roll in turmoil under the winds and storms.

The next age opened with what is known as the Dwapara Yuga, or the Copper Age. This was the ancient world, of which there is some historical data preserved in the records of mankind through archeology and burial grounds. The Hittites were the first to be recorded in this era; and they were the ones who found that copper was good for the making of weapons, and possibly the first known sword, although swords had been used a little in the Silver Age. They were among the first known conquerors in the annals of mankind. Their history shows that the civilizations of the Middle East were the first of the races of mankind, for all had been forgotten of the Golden and Silver ages.

This was the beginning of man according to the sacred scriptures, and the biblical Garden of Eden lay somewhere along the Tigris River near what later became Babylonia. Man depended upon oxen for plowing and planted grain for his survival. He hunted, rode the horse, and found lands beyond his own horizon. Egypt began its long history during this period, and Greece began to stir into awakening when stories of the Trojan War brought the talents of the blind poet Homer into existence.

This was the age when man began to divide up the ECK power into many powers, which hence became gods and goddesses. This was the era of the ancient gods of Greece and the other lands: Egypt, India, Italy. The SUGMAD had been blanked out of the minds of the masses, and the priestcraft became strong, to control all people including the rulers.

The Kal power came into greater strength as the years passed and eventually was the ultimate power. Man and his consciousness were ruled by it. Sex was the strongest power of any because of its urge to reproduce new species upon the planet and within the other physical worlds. It became a strength in its own right and at once was the strongest emotion of all within man and the worldly creatures.

The Copper Age came to an end—about three thousand years before the change in the world calendars—during the time of Narmer, one of the earlier pharaohs, through a series of earthquakes which shook the Mediterranean and changed the land masses. The next age that came into existence was that of the Kali Yuga, the present age, which is to last approximately 432,000 man years. The concept of one God has come back into the consciousness of man, but it's only a god on the lower planes. Man generally worships the Sat Nam, the first manifestation of God, who rules the Fifth, or Soul, Plane.

The Kal is in complete charge of the lower worlds during this period of time. Man worships materiality and sex. He believes that nothing lies beyond the grave and it is useless for him to struggle to save himself. He has forgotten all which preceded him; a veil has been pulled over his spiritual eyes, blinding him to his birthright and his past lives. He lives like the animal, suffering and believing in whatever god or gods have been given him by an outside source. He is concerned here with the power of maya, which produces the illusory forms of appearance of man's mundane reality. Maya itself, however, is not illusion in a manner of speaking, but the way that man looks at reality. The illusion is within himself. So he who masters this power gets the tool of liberation in his hand, the magic power of ECK: the power of creation, transformation, and reincarnation.

The power of man's inner vision in ECK produces forms and worlds which, when he becomes aware of them, can fill him with such a feeling of incredible reality that, compared with it, the reality-content of his mental, everyday world fades. It is here that he experiences something that means nothing to his emotions and thoughts, and yet it is reality. This is the way the divine SUGMAD outwardly and inwardly moves toward the fullness of Its reality into inner awareness; and Soul is that part of man's being which has the power to ascend and descend the steps toward the heavenly worlds.

Maya, then, is something that has become, that is frozen and rigid in form and concept, and which is illusion because it has been torn from reality and is limited in time and space. The individuality of the unenlightened person is that which tries to maintain and preserve its illusory self in maya in the negative sense.

Therefore, it's also found that the body of the enlightened one such as the MAHANTA, the Living ECK Master is maya, but not in the negative sense. This is because it is the conscious creation of a mind that is free from illusion, unlimited, and no more bound to an ego.

Thus it is that maya is a part of the creative principle within the limitations of the human consciousness, and that which is used mainly by the metaphysicians, religions, those engaged in witchcraft, and by black magicians. Compared with the highest, or absolute, reality, in all forms in which this lesser reality appears, there is the deception that all things appear illusory. This is because they are only partial aspects and, as such, incomplete—torn out of their connections and deprived of their universal relationship with the true reality. The only reality which is called absolute is the ECK Itself, that of the all-embracing whole. Each partial aspect must, therefore, constitute a lesser degree of reality; the less universal, the more illusory and impermanent.

Within this world it is called a one-dimensional consciousness, in contrast with the nondimensional, point-like consciousness. Therefore, beginning with the Physical Plane, one finds he must begin with the one-dimensional consciousness; the Astral will be the two-dimensional consciousness; the Causal will be the three-dimensional consciousness; the Mental will be the four-dimensional consciousness; and the Soul Plane will be the five-dimensional consciousness. Beyond the Soul Plane the traveler comes into the nondimensional consciousness.

When one reaches the position of the fifth-dimensional consciousness, he arrives at the perception and understanding of the law of action and reaction, the Law of Karma. If he observes the various phases of a karmic chain reaction in his relationship to other sequences of karmic action and reaction, he becomes conscious of the individual interrelationship of himself with all life and the spiritual worlds. He also becomes aware of his interrelationship with nations, races, civilizations, humanity, planets, solar systems, and finally the whole universe. He arrives at the perception of a cosmic world chain which begins with himself and ends in the Ocean of Love and Mercy of the SUGMAD. Within this enlightenment he realizes the universality of consciousness in the world of worlds and no longer seeks the psychic things and power of the lower worlds.

Seen from the consciousness of the ECK, all separate forms of appearance are maya. But maya, in its deeper sense of being, is reality in its creative aspect, or the creative aspect of reality for the lower worlds. This is why the religionists and metaphysicians believe that maya, or whatever it represents, is God Itself. Therefore, maya can become the cause of illusion, but when it's seen as a whole with the ECK, in its continuity, in its creative function, or as an infinite power of transformation and universal relationship working with or against the ECK as a counterforce, it becomes a part of man.

As long as man is living in the human consciousness, maya is to be a part of him, the creative side which brings forth all the aspects of civilization as the culture of a nation. It can be found as a part of the creation of man and his relationship with the outer world. When man stops at any of its creations and tries to limit it to a state of being, or self-confined existence, he falls prey to illusion. He does this by taking the effect for cause, the shadow for substance, the partial aspect for the ultimate reality, that which is momentary for something that exists within itself.

One begins to understand and know where maya is a part of himself and why he acts upon certain impulses which he believes are from God. Thus he comes to learn that such an impulse is only part of the psychic forces which make up his material bodies, such as the Physical, Astral, Causal, and Mental. In fact he soon learns to distinguish which is from the beyond, that which could be cause and not effect. He learns to separate his physical and mental problems from the psychic disturbances which are buried deeply within him.

He must always be constantly on the alert for the psychic disturbances. Most persons who are victims of psychic disturbance are invariably highly sensitive and suggestible. The study of psychism is not a normal way for unfoldment in any individual, for it leads to instability, liability to violent emotional reactions, and, in general, aberrations of conduct which are associated with cranks and fools.

Unless a psychic is trained, disciplined, protected, and watched over by the MAHANTA, the Living ECK Master during his training to reach the higher worlds of spirituality, he is found not to be reliable, for he is blown about by every wind or influence. The psychic and the neurotic are closely associated in their reactions to life; but the neurotic differs from the psychic because he has not yet been exposed to the public mirror as has the psychic, who can be quite exaggerated in his public conduct.

The result is the same, however, between the force and the form, with the consequent inability to maintain a central, reasonable control of himself and his conduct. He becomes the result of the effects of the psychic power and cannot get away from this in either case, whether psychic or neurotic. The way of handling one's discipline in either matter is largely directed toward maintaining control of the disparate forces, which compensates for the sensitiveness of the psychic and protects him from the evil forces which may greatly influence him.

Progress is necessarily slow and laborious in the usual case of a person who has taken up the path of ECK for the first time. But a Soul which has taken any type of initiation in occult and psychic groups may reopen the latent faculties so rapidly that the problem of keeping him coordinated in his personality may become a serious one indeed.

It is common, in the case of anyone who has never before contacted the psychic world, to experience psychic disturbance. Often this is referred to as evil influences or evil entities, which is not always true. It is mainly that the consciousness of the individual is disturbed by a force to which it is not accustomed. These unaccustomed vibrations are upsetting and are usually the results of psychic indigestion. The best cure for this is that the Living ECK Master will take him off the path for a short time, or restrict his activities in his study of ECK.

Another cause of psychic upset may lie in the partial recovery of the memories of past incarnations, if these include any painful episodes, especially such as those connected with his spiritual studies. The entry of any psychic concepts into the conscious mind tends to awaken the subconscious memory of similar experiences in the individual's past lives.

The emotion which surrounds a memory is part of the test about a past life. It is the most accurate of memories for anyone's past lives. This type of shadowy emotion can hang about for a long time on the threshold of consciousness before the images clarify sufficiently to become tangible to the chela. If the emotion which appears is of a painful nature, it may cause considerable disturbance, and if there is no spiritual adviser, or if one does not have the Living ECK Master, it may be attributed to an evil influence or entity which bothers the chela.

It is difficult to determine whether the chela has reasonable grounds for his complaint, if this is his feeling, or if it is his own imagination which is creating the problem. Therefore, it is wise to look into the records of the chela, for few persons, even though filled with lofty ideas, are able to keep a level head with clear and somewhat unbiased judgment. They often do make mistakes in their work with persons who have psychic disturbances.

The vagaries of the sex instinct in the individual whose life urges have been repressed, who is no longer young, nor in circumstances that permit him to follow a normal life, could run him into serious problems if the path of ECK, or any other spiritual path, is started. This is true for anyone who receives the initiation when first joining any group, whether it be psychic, occult, or spiritual. The inexperienced, love-starved chela is overwhelmed by what is taking place and often steps into the mire of psychism. The ritual of initiation is a very stimulating thing with each individual, as religious groups have found, sometimes to their sorrow. Any individual taking an initiation, especially if he is ignorant of the facts of life, will find himself strangely stirred. Often the head of the group becomes a father figure, with magnetism only placed in him by the chela. If it is a woman, there is always the reaction of the female in the presence of any leader with strong individuality.

Many women, ignorant of the facts of life, may fall under that which is known as self-hypnosis without realizing that nature, or the Kal, is the hypnotist. Such persons may feel that such disturbances within themselves are deliberate, and they could bring about charges which are completely without foundation, based mainly upon what they felt happened. Substitute love is often the downfall of a chela who, instead of being normal about his love for family, friends, and dear ones, will give up this type of affection and fasten it upon the MAHANTA, the Living ECK Master.

Such disturbances have come about because most of the chelas fasten their own image on the MAHANTA, the Living ECK Master, thinking that this is what he should be like, instead of allowing their thinking and imagination to be free. This is known mainly as making a father, lover, or friendship image of another instead of letting it be its own. Those who are used to high-tension psychic forces will experience some of these disturbances on first entering the path of ECK.

The person who is ripe for development will unfold into the higher spiritual consciousness rapidly, whereas he who is not may find these influences profoundly disturbing. No ECK Master will allow unsuitable persons, or those who are not stable, to enter into his magnetic field. Anyone claiming to be a spiritual teacher who does so is not worthy, because of his lack of discrimination and discretion. Generally, he has not had experience with the psychic forces, nor has he been unfolded enough to be able to handle the forces which he emanates involuntarily in his magnetic field and, therefore, he cannot help himself.

This is one reason why the higher ECK Masters live mainly in seclusion, for not only do they need solitude for their work, but their influence upon the unprepared Soul produces too violent a reaction, and it ends in violence such as many saviors have suffered, ending in their physical death by mobs and other forces.

The layman is usually unprepared to handle any psychic attacks or to manage the ways of the chela who might be upset by psychic influences. But one must always remember that the Kal force will never let up. It always wants its way with those living steadily in the human consciousness. No chela in Eckankar is ever alone, that is, isolated. The life of the chela is lived within and nourished by the life of the whole of the ECK, so that one really makes up for what another lacks.

It is useless to try to explain that health, wealth, and happiness are not to be expected in a life based on the desire to do God's will. For many, the religious or spiritual life is the last refuge, should they be crossed in love or have disgraced themselves in some dramatic way and must live out the rest of their lives safely hidden away from the public eye. There is the assumption that the only people who could be expected to enter into the spiritual life are those who are naturally pious, or who, at least by their own efforts, have attained a certain standard of sanctity; who, as it were, have got at least a general unfoldment and head start on others. This idea has, perhaps, been reinforced by some of the language about "states of perfection" to which some make the assumption, but they have never really thought out the relationship between vocation and avocation.

Accordingly, a housewife can be further advanced than many who think of themselves as saints, or those who put tremendous effort into becoming perfected. Entering into the spiritual life is very much a question of finding out if it is suitable to the individual, his own way of thinking, and his own outlook on life. It depends on a number of things, mainly, if one is going to depend on some private revelation before making up his mind about accepting God or entering into the path of Eckankar.

The belief that one is called to the spiritual life, like any knowledge of the will of the SUGMAD, comes in various ways. Sometimes it comes quite clearly, as an answer to a petition, realized either while in contemplation or at some other time. Sometimes it comes through other people, directly through the Living ECK Master or through some other chela, or indirectly while listening to the MAHANTA talk, reading a book, and even from drama on the stage or life events. Often it comes through circumstances; through recognized needs, temperaments, or the character of others; sometimes through inclination, where this is not obscured by a rigid conviction that God's will must be the opposite of one's own thoughts. There is little need of mixing motives; human motives are always mixed, and what matters is what God makes of what the individual does, rather than the motives which lead one to do it.

There are some who doubt the spiritual life on the grounds that it represents a desire for false security and flight to a refuge from the necessary tensions of living in the human consciousness. It is certainly true that the desire for security may sometimes be the factor in the awakening of the consciousness for needing God; there is nothing wrong with this of itself, for in fact the ECKist believes that the only security is in God, and that the desire for it is one of the desires that can only be satisfied by and in It. What is certain is that anyone going into the path of ECK only out of desire for security would not last very long, and anyone seeing it as a flight from tensions would be sadly disillusioned.

Often it is family difficulties or other psychological pressures which have led a person to the MAHANTA, the Living ECK Master. This might be obvious to others but not to the chela. But this does not in any way invalidate the seeker's motive and may indeed be an example of the way in which the SUGMAD leads a person to the form of life which is necessary for his spiritual perfection.

The SUGMAD supplies what is necessary for each Soul as well as for every other aspect of the person. The SUGMAD knows whom It has called, and Its call is based on that knowledge of the individual, of his needs as well as his gifts. But in the case of the person who has reached up to God, if he is honest and sincere with himself, it is his recognition of weakness and inadequacy which makes it possible for him to act in the strength of God. Anyone who counts his gifts and volunteers from a position of strength to do service in the name of the Living ECK Master would not know what obedience or holiness is about. He must, as said before, work from the position of his weakness and inadequacy.

Sometimes the spiritual life helps to overcome a defect or weakness. Thus the strength of the common life may bring out unsuspected depths in a diffident or apparently weak person; or the enforced, continual contact with others may be the means whereby a life rooted in the ECK and the guidance of the MAHANTA, the Living ECK Master begins to point in the same direction. Then it is a sure indication that the time has come for one to prepare for the next step into the higher planes. It is easy to say that God has made man's mind to function in such a manner, and that It works through man and his mental apparatus; but one begins to see the truth of what is spiritually taking place in his life when he begins to see and study the small coincidences which come about, and to compare them with what he knows of God's will.

The Records of the Kros also tell man that in the life of the ECKist God's saving acts have taken place once and for all, at the turning point of history; that creation is already finished within the lower worlds. It is known, then, that all possible psychic and human situations are already-made states of consciousness. Every aspect of life has already been worked out as mere possibilities as long as the individual is not in them, but each is an overpowering reality when he is in them. Soul is, therefore, not the state, but these states of consciousness must be distinguished from the individual Soul in those states. These states of consciousness change, but the individual Soul never changes, nor does It cease.

When Soul is within this lower state, It is within the human state, or existence itself. Therefore, love or affection becomes a state when divided from imagination. This is important to remember, for the moment a chela realizes this for the first time in his life, it becomes a most momentous occasion, in fact a changing point in his consciousness.

The moment that any chela of Eckankar realizes this great truth—that all things in his world are a manifestation of the mental activity which goes on within him, and therefore a building and destroying of his karma; and that the conditions and circumstances of his life only reflect the state of consciousness with which he is fused—life changes for him. This truth is common to all, but the consciousness of it, and even more the self-consciousness of it, is another matter.

This experience changes him from the ordinary individual into the highly experienced person who recognizes the difference between the human, psychic, and spiritual lives which are within. First, it reveals to him that he is supreme within his own circle of consciousness and that the state with which he is identified is that which determines what he experiences in life. Therefore, it should be shared with all, for to know this is to become free of the Kal Niranjan, the greatest tyrant of the lower worlds. Secondly, it frees him from belief in the second cause, which is always the Kal itself.

The world of creation is finished for the lower worlds. Its original is within each Soul. Each Soul saw it in the Golden Age and has since been trying to remember it and to activate any part of it. There are infinite views of it, and man's task is to get the right view through Soul's eyes. Then one learns the course of time as jumps of attention are made between the moments of eternity; for an infinite abyss separates any two moments of time within this world.

One must think of the worlds as containing an infinite number of states of consciousness from which they may be viewed. These states are like rooms or mansions in the house of God; and like rooms in any house, they are fixed relative to one another. But Soul is the living, moving occupant of such a great mansion of God. Each room contains the events and circumstances of life, with infinite situations already worked out but not activated. They are activated as soon as Soul enters in and magnetizes them with action. Each represents certain emotional activities.

To enter a state, man must consent to the ideas and feelings which it represents. If he enters into the Astral world, he must let himself enter into the ideas and feelings of this astral state of consciousness. These states represent an infinite number of possible transformations which man can experience.

To move to another state, or room—consciousness as it is generally known—necessitates a change in faith and beliefs. All that one has ever desired is already present and only waits to be matched by his faith. This is certainly true of the ECK, for Soul must go in and possess the land which is without ownership until he takes over and tills the fields. It becomes the individual's home from which he views the world.

7
The Renunciation of Life

The renunciation of life is usually repulsive to those who have no knowledge of the eternal. Yet many who do are not naturally docile people who find obedience easy, but those who see things clearly and are sure of their own judgment, whose strong wills need to be disciplined if they are not to become self-willed.

Often, they are not people who find detachment natural and easy, but men and women who enjoy life so much that they risk being completely immersed in it, those who humanly not only love but are in love with life, those like Rebazar Tarzs and Gopal Das. A good ECKist is not a person who is naturally unaffectionate, to whom people mean little and human love and affection are unknown. One has only to think of Fubbi Quantz, Lai Tsi, and many other ECK Masters, including Kata Daki, one of the ECK Masters in the Ancient Order of the Vairagi who is a woman, to understand the great love, the intensity of which would be a danger to themselves and others if they used it selfishly.

The danger lies mainly in the fact that each has the power to arouse love in others to serve God; otherwise, if they had aroused personal love in chelas, it would have defeated their purpose in life. It is unworthy to impede another, whose call has been to serve God, with personal love and other emotional charges. The call of God to the individual to serve is not always for the same purpose in life, such as serving directly through work in a monastery or other sacred place, but often in the ways of a career or motherhood. Yet it is the means of perfecting that person called and is, therefore, the sphere within which he can be of most use to others.

Those who follow the ECK believe it is when they are completely what the SUGMAD wants them to be that they can contribute most to the total life of the body of the MAHANTA, the Living ECK Master, of which they are a member, and to the life of the whole human race to which they belong; a belief based on their whole understanding of the spiritual works of ECK as the body of the MAHANTA, and of the whole world as created by the SUGMAD. Therefore, it functions properly only when every part of it is in complete obedience to God. Thus in Eckankar, selfishness, as understood by the ECKist, and service are not antitheses, for obedience to the SUGMAD is both the way to self-fulfillment and the only valid form of service.

The basic principle is that all Souls can become perfect, and the path of the ECK is the way in which God calls and enables Soul to fulfill Its command. The life in ECK is often considered a school in the Lord's service, for the chela must learn obedience which will give him discipline for reaching the heavenly worlds.

Eckankar never makes a claim that it is built on a historical foundation. Yet to deny it would be making false claims, for it has been a part of every age in the history of the lower universes as well as that of the heavenly worlds. There never was a time when man did not have the opportunity to accept ECK, for it has always been before him, although so many times he could never see his opportunity to grasp it. It has always been a life of worship, and the life of heaven can only be expressed in terms of sheer worship and adoration. The vows of ECK which the chela takes at his initiation always represent a freedom from limitations, which is a foretaste of the life of heaven—a freedom from care for material needs; a freedom from limitation upon love; a freedom from temptation to self-will, through a life lived in willing obedience. And finally the life of the ECK within itself is in anticipation of the joys of heaven and of the stability of a life lived entirely in God.

Those who follow the ECK have to live this life in and for the world. So rather it is an entry into an inheritance which one already possesses and has begun to enjoy. What is confidently expected in the future is worked out and anticipated in the present, and it is the experience of God in the present which leads to confidence in It in the future.

The very form of the chela's life is a foreshadowing of the life of heaven and those high worlds. It is primarily a life of worship and adoration, for all ECKists must live a life in the Spiritual Exercises of ECK, which brings about the simplicity of living in joy and happiness. At the heart of the ECK life lies the conviction that the ECK is the way as well as the goal. Therefore, whether the way is long or short, and whatever blind corners it has, every moment is as important as the goal. It is only because to live in the MAHANTA that to die is to gain.

In practical terms this means that every moment is known to be of infinite value, not because of what precedes or follows it, but because it is the moment of communication with God, in which eternity is a present reality as one holds and possesses the whole fullness of life in one moment, here and now, the past, present, and future.

The past is always put behind without regret, and the future, when plans have been made, left in God's hands. Life is lived in the present moment, which is the particular realization of the nowness of the eternal.

The life of an ECKist cannot in any manner be understood with the tension between this world and the other worlds, between what the ECKist already is and what he is becoming, between the present lived as in the eternal nowness of God and the present as in anticipation of the final goal. If the ECKist's life cannot be understood without these dualities, it's not likely that his whole purpose in seeking God will be understood. This is why, in a way, it is impossible to make any sense of the life in ECK in the terms of this world.

The primary task of the chela is service to God through the MAHANTA. If the Spiritual Exercises of ECK have any place in his life, then he cannot live in isolation from this world, for they are offered for and in his behalf to be spiritually perfected and to give service to all concerned. Even in the joy and release of the ECK within oneself, the agony of the world's pain must not be forgotten, for the agony of the world's pain is also the pain of the chelas as well as the MAHANTA himself.

If the doctrine of the body of the MAHANTA as the spirit in and of the ECK is taken seriously, and due significance given to the variety of tasks within the body of the MAHANTA, then the ECKist's life can be seen as one of those tasks, complementing others and complemented by them. For every chela there are spiritual exercises and other activities, but the relationship of these two sides of life in ECK will vary from individual to individual. There will be many within the body, who, if they are doing the tasks to which they are spiritually called, will have little time for the conscious offering of the spiritual contemplation and worship of the SUGMAD. Because this is so, such active lives are not second best but just as valid as any other vocation within the whole body of the MAHANTA.

The ECKist has a visible place in the life of the world as well as of the Satsangs. The history of the world would be totally different without the influence of the ECK Masters and those who have followed ECK over the centuries, from the beginning of time in the physical universe. It was the ECK Masters who civilized the human race, who kept not only learning and even literacy alive, but taught the primitives farming and, during the latter ages after the golden era, the raising of cattle. Those who have done the most for the human race in its intellectual and spiritual aspects, as well as its material life, have been the ECK Masters of the Ancient Order of the Vairagi. But nothing other than giving the human race an uplift of spiritual value has ever been the aim of the ECK Masters. Rather all else, other than the spiritual aim, has been the consequence, almost the by-product, of their search for helping man reach perfection through the Spiritual Exercises of ECK.

The desire to be useful to God and one's fellow man may be one of the motives leading a person to the path of Eckankar, but it is not the aim of that life. One of the arguments constantly advanced by well-meaning relatives and friends against aspirants to the path of ECK is that it brings about a neglect of their lives in some orthodox religion. In actual fact, the aspirant usually finds his talents and conduct of life used for more than he could imagine possible on the path of ECK, more than in any other way of life. But the value of a particular life or work cannot be calculated to some form of counting, and, basically, the ECKist does not have to ask where his talents can be most useful. Instead it should be, What is God asking me to do?

Temperament and talents may be one factor in answering that question and, for the aspirant to the spiritual life of ECK, may sometimes be relevant in discovering the path of ECK. But fundamentally the question is, Could one do more good in ECK than elsewhere? It is hardly possible for anyone to return to his old position in the new spirit of ECK. The only thing that really matters is obedience to the command that comes to all those who hear the MAHANTA, the Living ECK Master.

It is the search for perfection through withdrawal from the world which brings about many of the mistakes of the chela, for not all can retire into a monastery or live by himself in some cave and achieve perfection, as the popular thought has led many to believe. The life in Eckankar is made for the active Souls and is purely an individual search for God. It is not a battle with the Kal, which those who believe in the worldly affairs are confronted with daily. As long as the individual looks at his daily battles with the Kal, his attention will always be upon this and not upon the ECK. He must constantly look to the ECK for his salvation, his way to freedom, and never to any limitations.

The living membership of ECK is most important to all those who are ECKists. This does not mean that they are banded together in some community to serve in a communal way, but as individuals linked together in an invisible but secret way, and who can communicate with one another regardless of the distance between them. This should be remembered, because it is one of the great secret principles of Eckankar.

The purifier is not a cave in some remote mountain area, nor is it a retreat in some hidden desert oasis; but it is the individual who is able to discipline himself to the extent that he can commune first in the secret recesses of his heart with the Living ECK Master, and then with others through this same modus operandi. The results are amazing, for he finds that to withdraw from society is unnecessary, and that he can live and talk with his fellow ECKists without the means of outer communication. He can receive instructions from the Living ECK Master without having seen him in the flesh for years, and knowing that he might be thousands of miles away.

The emphasis is not to resist what the chela must do in order to gain the heavenly joys of life. Those who start with Eckankar must not wander from place to place to seek knowledge from others outside of ECK. If they do, it will harm anyone who seeks such knowledge, and they will not have long to live in this world. If a hen stops sitting on her eggs, she will hatch no chickens, grow old and fat, and soon meet death without being productive. The ECKist who moves from place to place and teacher to teacher grows cold and dead in faith.

He who struggles with the problems of understanding the kingdom of heaven needs no other than the MAHANTA, the Living ECK Master. His greatest problem is trying to identify the heavenly realm with his own ideals of the material life. The two cannot meet without conflict. The ways of the old religions always gave man hope that his gods would feed him through the grain in the fields and the flesh of animals in the forest, and secure him a home in some cave. This ideal has never been forgotten by man, for today he is told by the metaphysicians and priests that God will take care of him if only he prays for his requests. It doesn't particularly mean that he must live in goodness, for God forgives and gives to any who worship It in prayer.

These statements are lies based upon the clergy desiring to cater to a congregation. No person can have the goodness of God in his life unless he is obedient to the spiritual laws; and often, when asked, he could not even name one. Therefore, it appears that man has forgotten his own image in God and will not return to ECK where he belongs. His work consists of physical survival, and he does not give any thought to survival beyond this world until old age is upon him. By then he is so established in traditional thinking that he cannot be freed from this in order to have any new ideas enter into his consciousness. He is hidebound in his ways and will not, even if he could, change to enter into another path. He makes claim that this is possible, but once any new ideas conflict with his religious background, he is ready to fight before dropping anything learned during childhood and that which he acquired during his whole lifetime.

In the realm of the heavenly kingdom there is neither time nor space. This is not to be argued philosophically, but stated as a fact which anyone who is accustomed to operating on the inner planes will have shared. If the chela thinks of a person, he is in touch with that person; if he clearly pictures that person in his mind, he is more closely in touch with that person. Being in the mental vicinity of that person, he can create a thought atmosphere by dwelling upon certain ideas in connection with the other person. This is how spiritual healing is done, and how control is sometimes taken over by the other person; something which no ECK chela can handle.

If the healer uses his contemplation periods to get his mind in certain emotional states, then his condition will effectually influence the emotional body of the individual from whom he has had a request and will put him in rapport with that individual. This is the use of the ECK power, and one only uses It wisely so that the sharp edge of the sword will not harm himself. As long as the world is ignorant of the use of the ECK power, it is better that nothing be said by those who know, because knowledge, if spread abroad indiscriminately, might do more harm than good, giving information to those who ought not to have it.

Any message to another person must be couched in very simple terms, because the mind thought is a primitive form of mentalism developed before spoken language was known to mankind. The primary aim of this is to create an atmosphere about the individual, whether that person is to be uplifted or healed of some physical ailment, until a sympathetic response or reaction is elicited within Soul Itself. Once this reaction is achieved, the battle is almost over, for the gates of Soul have opened from within, and there is free entry for the MAHANTA, the Living ECK Master to enter into the heart of the individual and give succor or unfoldment in spiritual affairs.

There is the modus operandi of giving help to those who are unable to help themselves. If the individual has been attacked by a discarnate entity, a being of another order of evolution or from another plane, in all cases the gambit is the same. Until the aura is pierced, there can be no entrance to Soul, and the aura is always pierced from within by the response of fear or desire going out toward the attacking entity. If one can inhibit that instinctive emotional reaction, the edge of the aura will remain impenetrable and will be sure defense against psychic invasion. This is the reason that those who do aura readings, healings, or adjustments can be considered either devious persons or ones who do not know anything about what they are doing. They can, unwittingly or purposely, open the aura for those entities who can do harm.

The Astral Plane and its subplanes are ones of violence. The true Astral Plane has more pure essence, but it's seldom that anyone who is not properly developed can reach this plane. It takes those who have had the discipline and training under the MAHANTA, the Living ECK Master to be able to reach the pure regions of the Astral world.

Within this material universe the Law of Polarity, or the Law of Opposites, operates. Nothing exists except in relation to its opposite. This is also true within the psychic worlds: Astral, Causal, and Mental. However, within the heavenly worlds this is not true; for here there are no opposites, although the sacred scriptures of the worlds say so.

These scriptures claim that the good go into some heavenly paradise, while the evil will be punished forever in some fiery region. This is the Law of the Opposites, or Polarity. Those who are good attract the good, and those who are evil attract the evil. But in the heavenly states, it's found that polarity or chemistry within two objects no longer exists, and that Soul is free to do whatever It desires as long as it falls within a general pattern of the heavenly law. This law is: Love is all, and do as thou wilt.

This means that all Souls who enter into the heavenly state must abide by the law which they establish for themselves. The self-abiding law is for the individual Soul to recognize that It is Its own law. First of all, It must love or give out goodwill to all beings within the heavenly worlds. Secondly, It must make Its own law to abide by, and this must be in harmony with the great law: Love all things.

Within the psychic and material worlds nothing can exist except in relation to its opposite. Without the mountains there can be no valleys. Without the shadows there can be no perception of light. There is no such thing as evil unless it's compared with good. Without wisdom there can be no ignorance, and without age there can be no youth.

When Soul enters into the regions of immortality, the worlds of true Spirit above the psychic worlds, It finds no opposites. Light is light, and there is no opposite to it and the sounds of ECK, only the polarity of the highest qualities. Therefore, the ECKist is a realist, for he knows how to use the Law of Polarity. When he has to use his consciousness in the psychic world, he is able to take advantage of the Law of Opposites. But when he is in the world of the true Kingdom of God, then he is able to use the Law of Polarity for his own benefit through this conscious state.

There can be no total consciousness within the psychic and materialistic worlds because of the two principles, the male and female. The male is positive, active, and progressive, while the female is passive, reactive, or responsive, as it may seem to the observer, and retrogresive. Until the ECKist can recognize these principles within himself, it is possible that he will always be at their mercy.

There is no such thing as a total male type in this world, nor could there be a total female type either. Since man and woman are living in a negative, or passive, world of matter, all concerned have a certain amount of the negative within them, merely to keep those living in the physical body alive, to adapt to the needs of existence. This is where the metaphysician makes his mistake, for he doesn't take into consideration that in order to live in this world man, right from birth, is trained in the ways of the negative—to be at least materialistic enough to learn to support himself in this world of matter. Therefore, all his prayers are to a negative god, regardless of what man calls him or believes he may be.

Thus we find that the human consciousness is trained to react to manifestations of any sort. Man is schooled in becoming the slave of phenomena. Since the human consciousness, or the negative state, is decay and death, he is trained less in the art of living than in the art of dying. Therefore, it's found that the passive and negative contains the qualities of reacting and needing, and is dominated. This means that anyone who is strongly negative is the slave of his materialistic world. Reacting to the things of this world simply puts one in need of something, and by one subjecting himself to this quality of the Kal force, he puts himself deeper into the power of the negative, and thus becomes more so. He subjects himself to the liability of more grief.

This is why the MAHANTA, the Living ECK Master has always advised the chela against reading literature on sacred religions, the occult, and psychic matters. That is, until the chela is strongly entrenched in Eckankar; otherwise he is liable to find himself reacting to what is said in some of these works and eventually depend upon them in some manner or other, via certain modus operandi like prayer and requesting the space gods for help.

It is a law of the Kal that like attracts like. Those who seek materialistic solutions of life attract one another, while those who seek the spiritual life attract one another also. No one can explain the spiritual works to another who is interested only in the material things of life. One reaps great spiritual benefits by placing himself where the gains are to be made. Thus, if he reads the lives of the spiritual giants and lives quietly in a place where the life of ECK is greater, he gains in his unfoldment. However, he does not gain unless he practices the Spiritual Exercises of ECK regularly. This places him in those regions where the ECK is greater, and thus enables him to make spiritual gains.

Since the human consciousness is trained to be negative or dominated by the Kal force, there are few who can bring themselves to believe there is anything holy, other than what is found in their own religions, including any ECK Master. They have their own vices, and they are certain that the ECK Masters will have their own vices also. Perhaps they conceal them, but they feel that the Masters still have them. If anyone should tempt the Masters with so-called good food, housing, and all the vices of the Kal, it will be quite a surprise to find these materialistic things are rejected.

Those who wish to hurt others are being driven by a motive. They are being dominated by the Kal force, the slave of the negative, and sooner or later will have to pay tribute to it. To master anything or anybody, the chela should never allow himself to become dominated by it, to become its slave.

To react or to respond to anything is to be in sympathy with it and therefore become a part of it, itself. There is the law of Kal that if anyone responds to worry, he establishes fresh cause for worry. All men have a tendency to let themselves become slaves to the Kal power. This is the herd instinct, and a crutch, for all in the human consciousness have the tendency to want to follow a leader; this is the rule of Kal. Out of pure laziness they let someone do their work, do their thinking, and take over their responsibilities, but the leader simply loads them down with more of the same.

Most of those dwelling in the human state of consciousness want more material things, because the habit has been acquired, and many are without the will to help break such habits. The law of ECK is that desire is the source of all pain. This means that whosoever sets a price on himself finds that nobody wants him. But whosoever refuses to set a price on himself and his talents will find that others will swarm on their knees to him because they feel that he can be trusted.

Passive resistance succeeds because it is a positive force. It is the same principle as the boycott; once anyone demonstrates he can do without anything, it will be thrust upon him, especially if he is abased or smirched by it. Once this is done, it is assured that he will be overwhelmed by it, for he will be a challenge to the whole materialistic world.

There is an old ECK proverb which states, There is always the lover on one hand and the beloved on the other. Therefore, when anyone needs another person in the human state of love, there is bound to be rejection. This is why the human race has taken up the pursuit of God. Since God does not need mankind, and mankind does need It, there has always been a race between the priestcraft and the clergy to vie for honors as to who would be the intermediary, for the position of serving the human race as the voice of God.

There are none who can serve the human race or Soul except the Living ECK Master. He is the only one who is in a position to stand as the intermediary between Soul and God. All others are dealing with the Astral or psychic planes, and this leaves everything in doubt as to what they say. Those who seek God are doing so at the risk of losing It. When man ceases to seek God and settles down to let life *be,* to accept the MAHANTA as the Living ECK Master, and looks only to being the individual who is himself alone, and nobody else, there will be peace and happiness.

Those who believe in the SUGMAD consider themselves superior, and those who believe in the Kal consider themselves inferior. This is the very reason that man thinks of God, or his own version of the Supreme Deity, as being the greater, and the Kal is, of course, subject to It. But in his pursuit of the Supreme Deity he forgets that he is acting in the manner in which the Kal desires him to do. It is the masculine way of trying to receive the Light and Sound of God. Yet, on the other hand, it is the feminine way to be too passive. So what does the chela do if he is to enter into the heavenly worlds and receive the Light and Sound of the SUGMAD? The way is the neuter path, the way which is neither masculine nor feminine in his approach to the ECK, to God.

At first he accepts the MAHANTA, the Living ECK Master as the only way to enter into the heavenly worlds. Until he has reached this particular point, he is always seeking, always struggling to enter into the path which will bring him to the Atma Lok, the Fifth world, which is the beginning of the spiritual worlds. He must begin by putting himself in the state of not needing anything. When one adopts this attitude, he is not chained to facts by response. He accepts the Living ECK Master not because he needs the Master, but because he loves and cherishes him and accepts the love which the Master pours upon him.

The chela should never accept the fact that a certain housing, building, or structure is his home, but that the universe, with all its worlds, is home to him and all Souls. Admiration or envy of others brings about pain, but trust and love of the MAHANTA, the Living ECK Master bring about love and peace. The MAHANTA is of no danger to anyone, for he does not covet anything that others may have, nor does he withhold his love from those whom he knows dislike or hate him.

By traveling the middle path does the chela reach the gates of heaven. By allowing the MAHANTA, the Living ECK Master to take him out of his body consciousness into the higher worlds, by trusting him, and by putting his life into the Master's hands, will he reach that particular world in which he should be as the perfected Soul.

Man must learn the extremes of life the difficult way. Otherwise he has no experience by which to judge himself and his position within the worlds of matter and Spirit. He must always seek control and balance because he needs them as self-discipline, and by doing this he will have little need to simulate passion. His first experience in divine knowledge is that knowledge is not what a man has been told, shown, or taught; it is what he has found out for himself by long and rigorous search.

There is a sharp distinction between knowledge and opinion. Only the permanent, not the transient, can be the material of knowledge; only what is not the objects of the senses which are always becoming something else. The ECK Masters have a saying which is truth within itself: The knowledge of the divine reality is the beginning of wisdom. But when man reaches this position, he does it by a very difficult road. The knowledge of what is comes only through a life given up to intellectual striving, the introduction to which is the study of the holy works of ECK, for this leads the mind away from gross objects of the senses to the contemplation of things more real.

The unchanging realities can be apprehended only by Soul; the senses can show man only the transient and imperfect copies of reality. Of the realities, or the ideas, the highest is the good, and although there are times when none can formally identify the good with the SUGMAD, a few know about its divine nature in such a way that formal identification will make but little difference.

Such is having the knowledge that Soul can do no wrong; it is virtually the knowledge of being, of the good, of the SUGMAD. It is much richer and wider than man's intellectual knowledge, and a moral as well as an intellectual passion in its driving force. Its object is the truth that embraces everything; it belongs, in fact, to the same order of things, however different it may be in kind, as the state of grace that some seek. It is the culmination of the search made by the worldly thinkers for the inner reality, the Logos, the Word of God.

Therefore, man must have complete freedom from any form of religious mysticism. Freedom such as one might expect from the ECK through Soul Travel. Freedom of this nature allows the individual to use his faculties to gain the divine knowledge directly. But this comes through self-discipline, and never should any chela try to gain anything of the divine nature without such discipline. If he does, then there is the terrible and thorny path which he must follow. Never should he indulge in idle jest with the name of the SUGMAD or the MAHANTA. If this is done, he will have to pay the penalty which comes with such idleness of mind.

Within this sort of life no one seeks anything but the unfoldment of his faculty to see things as a whole. No ECKist can be called a fanatic because of his loyalty and devotion to Eckankar. Nowhere in the works of ECK does anyone find that the chela seeks the religious excesses of Eastern cults, nor of ancient and medieval times, nor the excesses of commercialism. The ECKist knows the strange and beautiful ecstasy which comes of the union with the ECK, by reaching the heavenly worlds through Soul Travel; but this is one part of the definite scheme of things.

The sharp distinction between ECK and the religious worlds of the lower planes has normally been drawn between Soul and body, and the spiritual and physical. Naturally, this is foreign to the religionist, for being one who is directed by the Kal, he associates most everything with the spirito-materialistic. But to the ECKist there is nothing more than the whole man. To him the physical body is the tomb of Soul, which is indeed an idea that is met almost everywhere on the path of ECK.

The ECKist must learn to live with extremely few physical needs or apparatus. He can live on a smaller amount of food than most men; he can have less leisure time than most men, since the majority of his time is spent in contemplation and the Spiritual Exercises of ECK. But most of all, he is mainly concerned with being himself and living, which means that he has learned to live with himself through self-discipline. He is responsible to himself and works toward a happiness which becomes a part of the whole of himself. In other words, he is integrated and is now a part of the universe instead of being only a part of his community, nation, and race.

The ECKist, in a sense, does not have to seek the Supreme Deity, for he knows instinctively that he is already with It. His seeking will be of little concern, while those who are not certain of themselves will become frantic in the seeking of God. There is an old ECK saying which goes like this: No one who has little faith can be convinced in God, and one who has faith needs little convincing.

The mind of a people is expressed more immediately in the structure of its faith and happiness than in anything else, but in all the works of ECK is found this firm grasp of the idea of the SUGMAD, and Its expression in clear and brilliant form. This is the secret of what has been called the ECK miracle; and the explanation, or the important part of it, lies in the fusion of cultures, if not of the ECKists too.

The strength of any religion or cult depends upon the power that it generates. It never depends upon the number of those who belong to it, but on the faith and hope by which they live in their particular religion, and the love of their master. This is why the ECKists have the strength and power, because of the love of the MAHANTA, the Living ECK Master. Since all religions and faith spring from the ECK, there is none to compare with the greatness of It.

In all religions there is a form of dualism, but in ECK there is only the totality of the SUGMAD for every chela. No ECKist should be happy to stay in the psychic worlds where dualism is part of the natural way of life. Every chela knows that life is a totality and should never be satisfied with anything less than this. All ECKists are free

Souls, and all others are slaves to their illusions and psychic phenomena. There is little obeisance in the ECK works, for this is an affront to Soul. The ECKist is polarized to the SUGMAD, and the Kalist is polarized to the Kal Niranjan.

The sense of the wholeness of things is perhaps the most typical feature of the ECKist mind. The mind of man in the psychic worlds divides, specializes, and thinks in terms of categories; the ECKist instinct is the opposite, to take the widest view, to see things as an organic whole. This is the strength of the ECKist who is able to face every problem in life and bring about his own solution to it without having to depend on another.

It is the person with a mediocre mind who attacks a personality. No one who has any sense of the relative world would care about an assault against another. But this goes on constantly, for it is the work of Kal that brings such into action, deceiving the individual who makes such mental, verbal, and physical assaults against his fellow man. But the fact that this goes on reminds all that this is only the Kal at work with everyone who persists in the human consciousness.

The emotional cliché, which all mediocre clergy and persons use, that "God blesses you" when one pulls out of a crisis is, of course, not true. So many in the state of human consciousness feel that God has taken a personal interest in their lives and saved them from dangers or loss of life. Naturally, the ignorant man wants to feel, through his egotism, that God took an interest in him and saved his life. But for what reason? Apparently thereafter, such individuals may lead a better moral life, but this is really a matter of egotism. The whole case lies before man as to why some were saved and others lost their lives.

In this lies the crux of the answer to this baffling question. The fact is that God never takes an interest in anything, creatures or man, in these lower worlds. It cares nothing about the human or the physical elements and never interferes with the way and the karma of life within these lower worlds. It administrates the worlds through the MAHANTA, the Living ECK Master. The Master is like all men, for living here in the physical body, he, of himself, can do nothing. He must depend upon the power of the ECK, that essence flowing out of the Godhead, to use him as Its channel to reach all that will respond to his efforts to get them to become one with the ECK.

It is said: "He who hates you hates me, and he who loves you loves me."

This is the SUGMAD speaking to the MAHANTA, the Living ECK Master and telling him that all is well; that whosoever shall try to interfere with the works of ECK shall be subject to the Law of Retribution. But those who love the Living ECK Master and are willing to give all their love to him will win everything in life. It is as though when one gives up life, he shall gain life.

The taste of the principle of giving up one's life to gain life is the letting go of everything mortal, and by being absent from the body consciousness with the MAHANTA, the principle. This great sea of consciousness is the home of Soul.

The only means to salvation is the letting go of the idea of a separate existence and in becoming conscious of that which *is.*

8

ECK, the Sacred Teachings

No problem greater or more moving confronts man than that of possible awareness of his own consciousness, the deep significance of the place he occupies in the world as a whole, and the purpose he should first discover and then pursue.

The consciousness of Soul is the primal Eckankar experience, which, while causing one to penetrate into one's own innermost being, at the same time causes one to penetrate into the universe. Therefore, man cannot behold this universe as he could some spectacle before his own eyes, for he, himself, is a part of it. He aids in its formation; he is, as it were, a fellow actor in a kind of drama, the variation of which depends upon his subjecive life which expresses its manifold incidents.

His affective states are not to be considered as mere accidents, of interest to no others but himself, to which the universe remains impassive, for thereby he penetrates into its intimacy and participates in the innermost workings of its life to gain the revelations of its mystery.

Nor does he halt here. He continues in his penetration into the mystery of himself. This is done through the science of Soul, whose modus operandi is Soul Travel. The surface is skimmed when man looks into the mysteries of the outer universe, regardless of whether he studies and discovers the answers to many other things in life. The true understanding comes from the inner study of the many planes of the spiritual worlds. This is what he is seeking but never finds until that moment arrives when he learns of the ultimate reality.

Man wanders from the cradle to the grave, yet never knows his true destination, which is not the tomb, but rather the discovery of himself as Soul which must eventually make Its way back into the heavenly world again.

For centuries man has accepted the tradition of the existence of two worlds—one the world of appearance, the other the world of existence; and having assumed that, as the knowledge of things always means his linking them to his beingness, he knows the appearances alone are accessible to mankind.

Therefore, the chela starts with and from the ECK to build or construct life, never from the Kal, for from it he goes down with the negative flow. ECK is upward and constructive, while the Kal is downward and destructive. This is the laying of the foundation for divine knowledge via the senses, and all in ECK know this as the operative principle working toward the heavenly works of the SUGMAD. He who works from the Kal principle is not building life, but is either paralyzed or destroying the world around himself.

Therefore, it is found that those who practice the meditation techniques have no freedom in the spiritual worlds. ECK, unlike the orthodox religions which make up the social orders of mankind, is an indivisible part of all social orders because It is life; and man is always acting or living out of It and never forming or molding It, for It is doing this to him through the inner self. This is why the meditation techniques are of little use to him. He would be trying to use life to gain for himself; while the Spiritual Exercises of ECK are letting the flow of life work through him without opposition.

He who loves the ECK greater than himself will find food for Soul. Meaning, of course, that anyone who loves the ECK and performs all deeds only in Its name, shall have the patience to wait for understanding and entrance into the kingdom of heaven.

If anyone suffers at the hands of his fellow man, be not discouraged, for the MAHANTA is always with him as long as he keeps his attention upon the MAHANTA, the Living ECK Master. The chela will always suffer at the hands of others, but he should never allow this to bother him, for he is on the path to heaven, and knowing this should give him happiness and gladness.

Do not surrender to the Kal Niranjan, the negative power, although the way is hard and the suffering greater, for the MAHANTA, the Living ECK Master is always watching and guiding every chela under his wing over the shoals of life. He will protect ten thousand on his right hand and all others under his left. No ECK chela shall be without the protection and guidance of the Living ECK Master.

Every chela who wants to reach the ECKshar state must become a fanatic on the path. He must have that inspired faith, that zealot's drive to serve the cause of ECK without any question. He should, by all means, be able to find new energies that will overcome the psychic powers and those physical energies that seem to smother him on the lower planes. This builds the proper attitude in him so that he can have victory in the end by entering into the ECKshar.

Every chela in Eckankar should know upon entering the path of ECK that overt acts against the MAHANTA, the Living ECK Master will bring about repercussions via the ECK. It is that which most chelas must learn the difficult way. Metaphysics is the lower path and the way of suffering. The ECK chela cannot indulge in it, nor in phenomena. Orthodox religion is also a way of suffering.

All religions have had a beginning and an ending. Even the modern religions of the day will have an ending, whether or not anyone believes it. But with ECK it is vastly different. No one can establish any beginning of It with a founder or such, for ECK cannot be placed within the framework of matter, energy, time, and space, for It is the creation of all these elements. It is life itself. It just *is,* and there is nothing else that man nor even Soul can say about It.

Of course, all men, creatures, and life are living in ECK. Man is living in the human senses, in the body, and the mind must have stable data upon which to anchor itself as a matter of survival. If it didn't, man would wander about like a comet in the sky and likely be somewhat of a menace to his fellow man. Therefore, he must think of ECK as life. It is that essence, that fluid, or Holy Spirit which flows out of God to be used as the creative force for the feeding and maintenance of all things in every universe of the SUGMAD, whether it be a piece of mineral, a particle of soil, an animal, or a man.

All the same, It is the basic reality, the chain of invisible atoms that man breathes for survival in the flesh, that he uses to create thought, that is the basic but necessary element by which life is created and maintained. It cannot be anything else but this, and when It is viewed from the eyes of Soul, or what is often called the esoteric viewpoint or the viewpoint of the Atma Sarup, It appears to be simply a great, radiant sheet of blazing light, too great for the human sight, stretching from infinity to infinity, without a beginning, without an ending. It sometimes appears like a great, calm, brooding sea, reflecting a thousand times the light of a brilliant sun. This is the consciousness of the MAHANTA, the Living ECK Master.

Therefore, how can the common mind grasp this; how can those with a narrow perception of the human self know and understand when an ECKist says we cannot fix dates like BC and AD, for ECK is life. This enlarges but staggers the ordinary mind; but the ECKist is not astounded, for he realizes eventually that ECK is greater than all other things which have come into his life, that It is the spiritual phenomenon of all worlds of God.

The only physical element of human consciousness that most men can fasten their minds upon, to keep from wandering about and gaining a totally unreal historical measurement of life, is the MAHANTA, the Living ECK Master, whom all know as the Ancient One, reimbodied life after life, in every generation, for the opportunity of Soul to find Its Master. He is the divine one with whom Soul can make Its first contact in order to take up Its path again to God.

Therefore, each chela can honestly say to himself that life begins with his first meeting with the Living ECK Master, be it in the inner worlds in the dream state or when the Master first gazed upon his countenance at some meeting, whether by chance or deliberately. This is the historical moment in the chela's life. This is, in a sense, the fixed date when he can say BE, before the ECK Master, or when living in his own ancient or primitive times; or AD, after death, which means after the death of the old consciousness, which represents his ignorance or forgetfulness of his divine origin, or the many times before this life when the chela met the MAHANTA, listened to and examined his words, but did not take him seriously.

Reality can only be attained by traveling the path of

ECK. The divine strain of God's music hums around man constantly, yet he is of such gross nature that he cannot hear It. Only by entering into the divine silence of the Spiritual Exercises of ECK, and closing his ears to the world of illusions, can he catch the celestial melody. Otherwise, he is yielding to the illusions of his imagination and reaping bitter misery.

The discovery of Soul within man is first of all an act of inner retirement; it is what is termed *the going within.* Man penetrates the invisible world, but unless he has direction from the Living ECK Master, he will have occasion to cry in anguish and never have the ability to conquer this inner world.

Whosoever goes upon a pilgrimage needs a guide to show the way, for few can travel the path without a guide. The outer universe withdraws and fades away as does the most beautiful dramatic scenery when the play ends. But soon enough the chela can experience the joy of revelation, and the universe is now no longer an object outside himself, an enigma to be solved. He no longer contemplates it from without, but from within. To each it reveals its own secrets, and this discovery brings each confidence and light. Having long lived in the world as a stranger, the chela now takes refuge in solitude; his perception is of a new world which welcomes him, and eventually he obtains the direct knowledge and sight of newer and superior planes.

Truth does not demand violence. It needs only an inward reverence and a willing ear to hear the divine music of God. Truth reveals itself only to those who seek and love it.

The inner illumination is the holy fire and is united with an infinite love for the divine reality. This inner flame, this simultaneous love and knowledge, when born, rises and grows until finally, through an impersonal ecstasy, the whole being of man is kindled with a supreme desire for the SUGMAD. This impersonal state is that of intuition in which thought is no longer divided into an internal thinking process and an external world, but rather the separateness of the outer world is abolished by its integration into the personal consciousness.

Man cannot hope to possess true riches greater than those he already bears within himself. He should use them and not neglect them, but they are so familiar that at times they do not appear to be of any value to him. Therefore, he pursues tawdry chattels whose possession is denied him, because man is so weak that the world is sometimes obliged to rebuff him to cause him to detach himself from the world.

The kingdom of heaven is here with man constantly, in the very heart of those who realize God, and the whole purpose of life is to make God a reality. Therefore, it's simpler to find a way into heaven than to find one's way here on earth.

Disappointment and all the negative qualities of man are his, provided he expects such in his life. The simple way of defeating all these qualities of the Kal force is to trust the MAHANTA, the Living ECK Master. ECK is Spirit, the divine essence, infinite love, the immortal life, and the sole power within all the worlds of God. Therefore, all reality is spiritual and perfect, because the SUGMAD has desired all to be this way. It forever blesses Its creation with limitless joy and well-being. Under the control of God, man is not subject to chance, mistakes, misunderstandings, or to the vagaries and frustrations of the material senses.

The negative aspects of life are really an argument of the Kal power which claims it has power to build up expectations and then dash those expectations by withholding the desired results. But the Kal powers, or the mortal self, have no power to cause or do anything, for love is omnipotent. Spiritual understanding includes the right expectation and fulfillment, and excludes failure and disappointment in the Living ECK Master.

If man had wisdom, he would not be carried away by human desires but would trust that the MAHANTA, the Living ECK Master would open him as a channel to serve God, for further progress and happiness. The MAHANTA knows what things every individual who is under his protection has need of, before he asks of him.

The negative aspects of man, including disappointment, can be salutary, for often they force man to review his thinking and to see more clearly that God is to be trusted. To replace with Its works the uncertainty of human expectations, man needs the sharp experiences of belief in the supposititious life of matter, as well as disappointments and ceaseless woes, to turn him like a tired child into the arms of divine love.

As the chela begins to trust the MAHANTA, the Living ECK Master and recognize that the negative aspects of life are only that of the human state of consciousness with which he must live in the flesh, then regardless of the situation, he will unfold spiritually.

The ECK, therefore, brings to pass that which is best for all; any sense of frustration or discouragement can be replaced with the inspiring realization that divine love is all.

This world is perishable, and all things worldly are ephemeral. The wise man is he who realizes the transitory and illusory nature of the affairs of this world and makes the best use of his body and mind in service to the SUGMAD. He thus derives benefit from all that the SUGMAD, through Its grace, has placed in the body. Then that priceless jewel, the essence of all, the Atma, or Soul, is taken to Its real abode.

Soul is sometimes called the Tuza, Surat, or the Jivatma. It has come into the body from the higher planes, the Soul Plane, and from the heart of the SUGMAD. It is detained here by the sense organs, and the mind. It has become difficult for It to free Itself from the bondage of the body and things related to it. Freedom from the body ties is called salvation. The internal bonds are formed by worldly pleasures, the family, and other relationships. The Jivatma, or Soul, is so limited by these bonds that It has no recollection of Its real home. It has been so far removed from that home that It finds it is practically impossible to return to it without the grace of the MAHANTA, the Living ECK Master, who is the Vi-Guru. The supreme thing to be done is to take Soul back to Its divine source. So long as this is not done, one is not free from the pains and pleasures of this world.

The aim and purpose of Eckankar has always been to take Soul by Its own path back to Its divine source. The successful devotee is he who, by practice and use of the Spiritual Exercises of ECK, lifts himself as Soul to Its real abode with the help of the Living ECK Master. This frees Soul from all bonds, both internal and external, gross, subtle, and causal. It separates the mind from the physical worlds and gives Soul freedom to move in any direction, either upward into the heavenly worlds or downward into the psychic worlds. The perfect devotees, the true lovers of the SUGMAD, are only those who reach the final stage of the journey to the heavenly source of all things. Those who only talk of the MAHANTA, the perfect Guru, or read his teachings to others without practicing them, are only intellectually educated people.

If the divine reality did not exist, there would be a void where It should prove Itself as a living thing. Free from thought, reality abides in the heart, the source of all thought. It is, therefore, called the heart by orthodox religionists and thinkers. To contemplate upon It one thinks of It as living in the heart of all things.

Those who have the intense fear of physical death seek refuge at the feet of the MAHANTA, who knows neither death nor birth. Dead to themselves and their possessions, the thought of death occurs to them time and again. In their own thinking they are victims of life, but it never occurs to them that they are deathless.

The ECK devotees of different historical periods, started by the force of the spiritual works of ECK toward the heart of the SUGMAD, have not all reached the final stage. Some of them have stopped at the First Plane, the Physical world, and others at the Astral Plane. A few have reached the Causal Plane, and some the Fourth. Only those who have been faithful over the incarnations of centuries and devoted in their faith to the MAHANTA, the Living ECK Master, and who have gone through the initiation, will never return to this world again in the flesh unless it is to serve the SUGMAD as a Coworker. Those fortunate to have reached the highest stage, the heart of God, are few indeed. This is the place of the original departure of Soul toward the lower region. During Its downward journey, Soul descends from the intermediate stages, such as the Sat Lok and the psychic planes, until It reaches the world of matter. Those who have not yet reached the highest stage and finished their upward journey in the lower planes feel that Soul originally descended from the planes of the psychic world. Not being instructed by the MAHANTA, the Living ECK Master, they naturally look upon the lower worlds as the source of life.

Likewise, they regard the Kal Niranjan, lord of the lower worlds, as the creator of all creation. They have then taught their disciples to worship the lord of each plane as the true lord and to believe in him as the Supreme Being. But it should be known that the region of the SUGMAD is the highest of all. This is also the name of the true Lord God.

The world of the SUGMAD is sometimes called the Akaha, the unspoken, or the Ocean of Love and Mercy. This is the region of the endless, the original, or the eternal. It is from this that all other regions are created or manifested. This is the Lamakan, the beyond-all, which cannot even be termed as a plane or a region.

The holy personages of this world have never reached the Akaha, and all rank much below the ECK Masters. In their upward journey they have stopped at different planes and founded religions corresponding to their spiritual attainments. Any stage that was reached by any one of them was regarded by each as the final region, and the presiding deity of that region was looked upon as the supreme deity, and its worship began.

This mistake is due to the fact that all of the different regions are so created by the Supreme SUGMAD as if each were a reflection of the Ocean of Love and Mercy. Thus there is some resemblance between the higher and lower regions. But there is a lot of difference in regard to permanence and other conditions. Each region has its own distinct creation, marked by different grades of subtleness and purity. Only he who has seen all of the planes of God can appreciate the difference. The effulgence of the lord of each plane reached is regarded as limitless, boundless; and that deity is considered the supreme one. The ecstasy of the moment of realization causes the devotee to lose himself in what he considers an indescribable state of eagerness and blissful intoxication.

Soul acquires special knowledge of every stage that It reaches. At every stage It feels as if It controls and predominates over all below that plane. For instance, on reaching the next higher plane, the lord of that world appears to be the creator and governs all the worlds below it, as if he were their manifestor and creator. Since these individual Souls have no knowledge of any higher region, they have taught their disciples to regard the lord of that plane as the supreme deity. Only the MAHANTA, the Living ECK Master, the Vi-Guru, knows of the higher worlds. If any of these teachers are instructed and guided by an ECK Master, those higher regions are revealed to them, and they become channels for the Living ECK Master.

Anyone who has crossed the First, Second, or Third Plane in his heavenly journey is looked upon as perfect. A devotee acquires all the power over the lower regions when he reaches the Ocean of Love and Mercy.

In the beginning, Soul descended from the region of the Sach Khand, and all the regions below it only mark the stages in the descent of Soul. The Light of the SUGMAD spreads into Soul, and thus descends into the various bodies—the Physical, Astral, Causal, and Mental, which It wants to use as a clear channel for Its own Light and Sound.

By the power of contemplation and the upward journey, the force of desire is lessened. Temporary suppression might lead one to think that it has been annihilated. But as long as Soul does not reach the Sat Lok region, desire cannot be fully eradicated. It is not surprising, therefore, that a devotee who has only reached the first and second regions may not be able to withstand the influence of the Kal forces and its aspects, the maya, and strong impulses of sensual pleasures. One may falter, though soon recover strength and regain lost ground by the practice of the Spiritual Exercises of ECK and the help of the MAHANTA, the Living ECK Master.

It is, therefore, better for a devotee of ECK to take

himself to the higher planes where no such temptation can assail him, beyond the influence of all sensual appeal, where he may enjoy the bliss of living in the presence of the Sat Nam, lord of the Fifth world. After this, one escapes all temptations and has no downward pull, because he is out of the influence of maya. He is then entitled to be called a Mahdis. Because they had not reached this high plane, many great rishis, munis, mystics, and prophets have been tempted by maya and ensnared, thus forgetting their exalted states.

Yet those sages mentioned did not incur such deep spiritual losses, for it is always possible to move further into the higher worlds once the individual understands the devices that the maya uses in order to deceive him. Although they have reached high stages in their development, they have not attained that region which is out of the scope of maya. That region is the world of Soul, the Fifth Plane and above.

The first and foremost region, which is the highest and largest, the name and location of which cannot be described in mortal language, is that of the SUGMAD, or Akaha, the end of all worlds, the Ocean of Love and Mercy. This is the beginning and the end of all; it circumscribes all worlds. It is the love and power of this world which is vibrating in every place, by the force of its first principle. In the beginning, the divine current emanates from this world and comes down in the form of the Word, best known as the ECK. This is the region of the Supreme ECK Masters. Only the ECK Masters and their followers ever have the opportunity to reach this plane.

The last world of the true spiritual universes is that of Sat Nam, or the Fifth world, better known as the Soul Plane. It is highly effulgent and pure, a region of pure Spirit (ECK) and consciousness. It is the beginning and end of all creation below it in the psychic and material worlds. The ruler of this region is the first manifestation of the SUGMAD. The primal Word, the Adi-ECK, manifests and moves into the lower worlds. It is that which gives the life substance to all things. It is not subject to destruction and change; It is always the same. The ECK Masters are the true embodiments or incarnations of the Sat Nam, the lord of this region. The MAHANTA, the Living ECK Master is the manifestation of the SUGMAD, the only true representation of the divine reality.

Those who live in the heavenly worlds enjoy the presence of the MAHANTA, the Living ECK Master, for he dwells on all planes in the bodies furnished him by the SUGMAD. They drink the nectar of immortality; and death, karma, and all pain are entirely absent in these worlds.

It is only after freeing Itself from the subtle bodies (the Astral, Causal, and Mental), that Soul reaches the plane of the Fifth world and is fit to worship the Supreme Deity. The devotee who reaches the Sat Lok regions with the aim of reaching the SUGMAD, having full faith in what he is doing, can also reach the heart of the SUGMAD.

When Souls descend from the Ocean of Love and Mercy, they stay in the Soul Plane before entering into the psychic worlds. Each is given special training before entering the lower planes so that It can have a greater opportunity to escape the snares and traps of the Kal Niranjan, who will certainly try to keep It within the lower worlds as long as possible.

Below this is the mind world, or the Par Brahm region, where the Universal Mind and its aspects manifest themselves under the Kal Niranjan. The Universal Mind Power is the male creative energy which the religionists call the Father, or the God of the universe. We also find that the Universal Mind has another energy, which is matter, sometimes called the prakriti. The trinity of energies arises here, which is called the Father, Son, and Holy Ghost by the Western religions; the Orientals know them as the Hindu trinity of Brahma, Vishnu, and Shiva. These are the sons of Kal Niranjan, the king of the lower worlds. The female counterpart of the Brahm is Shakti, who represents a minor creative current. Out of the union of these two great currents at the top of the Mental world, the three subordinate currents flow into the lower worlds, and to these are attributed the creation of all the lower worlds. These three became creators, lords, and governors of the lower worlds under their father, Brahm, and mother, Shakti. They are more directly under the supervision of Shakti, their mother. They represent the creative powers of the Kal, for they carry the creative powers from the greater powers above. These negative, creative powers become personal, take individual form, and assume individual duties. These three have been accepted since ancient times as the Hindu trinity of gods.

These gods have invaded other religions, both East and West, creating the belief that each religion has the original truth it has been able to give out to its followers. These negative powers, however, are only servants to man, although millions worship them in spite of their subordinate position. They each perform a certain function in carrying on the work of the world, in producing human bodies and in keeping these bodies going. They are only the agents of the SUGMAD, and not gods to be worshipped. They are almost menials in the grand spiritual hierarchy, but each has certain powers and prerogatives, and within his own sphere he is all-powerful. Each must carry on according to the definite laws and rules which are laid down for his government. These are laws of nature; and the trinity—no matter in what religion it may be represented—as Brahma, Vishnu, and Shiva, may be regarded as servants of the Kal Niranjan, the negative power.

Lower than these three, there is another current of power, or god, who is the working force helping to carry on the administration of the physical universe. His Hindu name is Ganesh, but other religions give him different names. He stands almost at the foot of the ladder of subordinates whose business is to serve mankind and help carry on the work of the world. Therefore, as it is seen, man worships the wrong gods; for all religions, whether or not they deny it, are pantheistic, which means many gods.

Metaphysics, occultism, orthodox religion, and witchcraft deal with the minor gods of the hierarchy. This also includes the elementals and angelic forces in the lower scales of the hierarchy, who dwell in the subtle regions close to the earth. These great hosts of beings are called devas, devtas, bhuts, prets, and other names. They are beings somewhat above the ordinary man, and they help to serve man in many ways. They have great power and are quite willing to help those individuals who are in harmony with them.

Man is the in-between being, between the spiritual hierarchy and the lowest of the beings: the beasts of the fields, fowls of the air, creatures of the seas, the elements of the soil. But if he works in harmony with all of those powers above him, he will surely receive their help and will eventually rise to the position where he will meet with the MAHANTA, the Living ECK Master and then succeed in returning to the heavenly world, his true home.

The teachings of the works of ECK are at once, therefore, both the oldest and the newest known. It is the oldest and the purest of the known works of God since its revelation; no one can say when this happened, for eternity has no beginning and no ending. The ECK Masters have instructed the devotees of this spiritual work so long ago that historians of the human race cannot attempt to trace it on this planet. It was ages old before the Vedas of the Hindus were ever heard of, and it was only when the pure teachings of the ECK Masters began to be obscured and corrupted that the Vedas arrived here in this world. ECK was taught to those who were receptive long before the Chinese sages started to speculate upon the abstruse and the unknown God. It was old long before the great cataclysm changed the face of the continents and raised the Himalaya Mountains to their present magnificent heights. It was old, of course, when the first known empire stretched back into the Satya Yuga, the Golden Age. Naturally it was old when the Sanskrit language came into existence in the central empire of the great, prehistoric civilization known as Uighur that built its civilization on the great plateau which is now Tibet and the Gobi Desert.

The Vairagi, the ancient order of Adepts of ECK Masters, which has extended itself from the Ocean of Love and Mercy to the lowest plane in this universe, have watched the decline of all known civilizations. The MAHANTA, the Living ECK Master is therefore not a product of modern civilization, as many believe. He has been, as well as the Order of the Vairagi, the chief factor in producing all civilizations, including the present modern civilization. The MAHANTA, the Living ECK Master has existed in this world for millions of years, and the works of ECK have been given to the selected chelas for millions of years. As always, during the prehistoric periods when the human race was on the decline, in descent toward savagery, the ECK Masters held up the spiritual truths as a torch lighting the way for all those who had eyes to see.

The works of ECK must never be confused with the various systems of philosophy and orthodox religion, for the ECK is neither a philosophy nor a religion. Many of the world religions and philosophies have features which are similar to Eckankar, but the most essential point to make here is that the reason for this is that all religions and philosophies are the offspring of ECK. It is the fountainhead of all life; therefore, all other things are the children of the ECK.

It is for this very reason that so many, preoccupied with their own systems of religion and philosophy, seem to find something in ECK which appears to be like their own. It is because their founders have taken from Eckankar, for each individual religion and each philosophy has sprung out of the Godhead of Eckankar. There is no way to analyze ECK, nor is there any way to explain It. It is just what It is, and attempts to make It anything else bring about confusion and failure.

The existence of Eckankar is a fact, and sooner or later all men will ardently yearn for it. Some advanced individuals claim a knowledge of it, but those who approach this discovery realize that it is the appanage of an extremely limited number of persons. Up to the modern times, few have been granted the privilege of having the revelations of the ECK Masters in common language. Before this, the philosophical and spiritual teachings have been veiled, and this is why such teachings were classified as esoteric, knowable to only a limited few of the initiated. Initiation was gained through secret revelations, allegorical and symbolic writings, possible of interpretation only by those possessing the key and direct teachings of the MAHANTA, the Living ECK Master to his disciples. The uninitiated were unable to penetrate the teachings, and only the spiritually advanced Souls could grasp the imagery of the language, the divulgement of which was prohibited and the meaning of which, without the key, was impossible to interpret.

To practice ECK out of curiosity, in search of new

sensations or to gain psychic powers, is a mistake which is punished with futility, neurosis, or even worse. None should seek initiation into the mysteries for unworthy motives, for disaster will surely follow. But there must be a way to believe without proof in the beginning. There must be a faith for all who are able to establish themselves on the path, with hardly anything more than their willingness to accept the MAHANTA, the Living ECK Master as the truth and the way. The answer is ECK, for once the individual accepts this as his way to God, he surrenders completely, giving up all in this material world to find happiness, joy, and love in the arms of the MAHANTA, the Living ECK Master.

This is the sacred teaching of Eckankar!

9
The Visions of Lai Tsi

The ancient Chinese ECK Master Lai Tsi had contemplated for fifteen years in various caves and retreats high above the Yellow River in north-central China. Nobody knew him; nobody had heard of him. He was one of the many thousands of unknown monks who had received his higher education in one of the great monastic universities in Tibet, and though he acquired a title of Geshe, or Doctor of Divinity, he had come to the conclusion that realization could be found only in the stillness and solitude of nature.

He had come from a family whose wealth was great, and his father had been a physician to the court of the ancient kingdom. But they had forgotten him, and he had forgotten them, as well as the world. This was not the result of indifference on his part; rather he had ceased to make a distinction between himself and the world. Instead, he had forgotten himself, the ego which existed because the world existed.

He became friends with wild animals that visited his cave, and his compassion went out to all people, all living things. He never felt lonely in his solitude, but enjoyed the liberation which was born from the visits of his Master, who came daily in his Atma Sarup (Soul body) to teach him the wisdom of God, to take him into the far worlds of the spiritual planes where he found the tremendous love of the SUGMAD.

One day a sheepherder in search of a lost ewe came into the inaccessible wilderness of the Yellow River caves. He heard the strange rhythmic plucking of a lute, as used by hermit monks. He did not believe his ears, because it seemed impossible for anyone to live in this forbidding place. At first he feared the sound, thinking it might be some demon luring him into its claws. But torn between curiosity and fear, he followed the sound as if it were a magnet drawing him on. Soon he saw the great ECK Master seated before a cave, absorbed in contemplation, his face lit with inspiration and devotion. The sheepherder lost all fear and approached Lai Tsi, and when the Master touched him, there was a stream of bliss that flowed through his body. Immediately he forgot all the questions to ask and, instead, requested the Master's blessings.

Soon, rumors of the blessed Lai Tsi spread throughout the river valley, and people rushed to see him. They wondered how he had lived in the cave during the icy winters. But in gazing upon his face, they saw the peace and happiness there and knew that here, at last, was the great ECK Master that had been promised them so many years ago.

In reply to a question raised about his life there, he answered, "I have indeed been blessed, for the good ECK Master Yaubl Sacabi has come often to give his great words of wisdom. I have left my humble body here and traveled with him through the spheres of the SUGMAD's universe to find the joys and happiness which are unknown in this miserable world.

"I am only the vehicle for the works of the ECK, and can only give you what It must give through my own self.

"You call me the perfect one, but this is not true, for in the eyes of God no one nor any thing is perfect until we are in Its arms for our final resting-place. Neither you nor I am able to hold truth and perfection in the human vessel, which encases the Atma of all while dwelling in this earth world. You must learn to be good and do good to all your fellow men, be kind to animals and love all things, man and creatures. I am most fortunate to have the works of ECK, even at an early age in my life. Too many wait until they are older before entering into the life of ECK. Each feels that he must exhaust everything else before he comes to the works of ECK, although knowing that It might be the way into heaven, that is, the true and perfect way.

"I was lifted up into the worlds of the true ECK, into the Anami Lok, where the music of the SUGMAD was, without doubt, the most beautiful, and the sound of the whirlpool became a part of myself. The Light and Sound was of a wondrous whiteness, like falling snow and sucking noises of water and air in a gigantic whirlpool. I beheld the benign features of the SUGMAD, and yet today I cannot describe one thing I saw of It. It was more like being in a world of compassion, love and mercy. I now know why It is called the Ocean of Love and Mercy.

"I never knew how long I lay on the cold floor of the cave, nor how long the animals, the beasts and the birds, came to see if my body was still alive. The lion cooled my brow with its rough tongue, and the wild deer lay down beside me to keep the cold air from freezing my limbs. The birds and butterflies brought nectar and other edibles. Everything in nature seemed to want to see that I survived. Later, however, I knew that it was the SUGMAD that urged them to give me sustenance, warmth, and companionship.

"It was learned after I came back from that marvelous world of beauty that I had been out for three days and nights. Beside a merry, blazing fire sat an ancient-looking old man whom I recognized as Tomo Geshig, the wondrous ECK Master who had visited with me for seven years in the Atma body and taught me the wonders of the SUGMAD before I found him in the flesh. He wandered about in the heights of the Himalaya Mountains alone and with hardly a shred of clothing except tattered robes. Under normal circumstances, any man would have died from exposure and starvation, but Tomo Geshig is not a normal person; in fact he must be as old as Yaubl Sacabi. It seems that in the ancient days they were both trained under one of the earlier Masters of Eckankar, Gopal Das, in Egypt. That must have been at least five thousand years ago.

"Gopal Das is now the guardian of the fourth book of the Shariyat-Ki-Sugmad, on the Astral Plane, while his two chelas are now ranked high in the Ancient Order of the Vairagi Adepts. Yaubl Sacabi is now the guardian of the second book of the Shariyat-Ki-Sugmad and the head of the spiritual city of Agam Des. Tomo Geshig is in the sixth world, the Alakh Lok, where he has charge of the Shariyat-Ki-Sugmad there.

"'All things are passing; only the SUGMAD is changeless. We are journeying in the same direction, only we travel by different paths.' Thus said Tomo Geshig to me before I journeyed into the heavenly worlds with him. I found now that the only thing that counts is the SUGMAD; not God as this world knows, but that wondrous, changeless being that few except the ECK Master and the devotees know.

"Here is a short contemplation seed which I found in myself upon returning from the heavenly worlds:

"'Show me Thy ways, O SUGMAD;
Teach me Thy path.

Lead me in Thy truth, and teach me;
On Thee do I wait all day.
I remember, O Beloved, Thy guiding light
And Thy loving care.
For it has been ever Thy will,
To lead the least of Thy servants to Thee!'

"Should anyone be in distress or need to reach the great SUGMAD, use this contemplation; repeat it slowly, and it certainly brings results.

"If you work, if you study, if you love, if you contemplate, and if you do any of these things for the love of truth or the love of the SUGMAD, then, whether you know it or not, you are already practicing the works of ECK.

"All those who gaze upon the countenance of the MAHANTA, the Living ECK Master shall be lifted up spiritually and be healed of all their afflictions. This is the right act which strikes a cord that extends throughout the whole universe, touches all spiritual intelligence, visits every world, vibrates along its whole extent, and conveys its vibrations to the very bosom of the SUGMAD.

"Therefore, anyone who has been healed of all their afflictions by gazing upon the countenance of the MAHANTA, the Living ECK Master shall find that not only does it assist them in every way, but it shall, as stated above, vibrate to the extent of the whole world and help those nearest him with astonishing results.

"The SUGMAD never appears in the flesh except as the MAHANTA, the Living ECK Master, and only in the consciousness of men as the ECK. Therefore, man must become conscious of good and the good works. Without the good works, there will be more sickness and less than good works in store for man in his consciousness of thoughts. His consciousness of thoughts and ideas dominates all his being. His powers, his life, and his flesh and bones, for better or worse, are subjected to what the ECK gives unto him, or what the Kal furnishes him. It depends upon what his consciousness is open to, as a channel. He is what he thinketh, in a sense, for man never changes until he changes his attitude. Spiritually, man's health, life, or conditions are no better or worse than his thoughts, or mind's consciousness of them. Man has five senses: seeing, smelling, tasting, hearing, and touching. Above all these, which seemingly appears to be unknown although used daily, is the sixth sense: the laughter and the greater of the indwelling powers and presence of the ECK, the ever-present help for every need. This is only known and active when man's consciousness is open and not hardened.

"To the enlightened man whose consciousness embraces the universe—to him the universe becomes his body, while his physical body becomes the manifestation of the ECK, his inner vision an expression of the higher truth, the highest reality, and his speech an expression of eternal truth.

"Here the mystery of body, speech, and mind finds its ultimate consummation and reveals itself in its true nature on the six planes of action in which the psychic and spiritual events take place.

"In a man who lives in his ideals or in the ECK, which goes beyond the realm of individual interests and experiences, the conscious body extends into the universally valid truths, into the realm of the beautiful, of the creative power, of aesthetic enjoyment and intuitive insight.

"The ego personality of a spiritually undeveloped human being is confined to its material form of appearance, the physical body. The personality of a spiritually advanced man comprises not only the material part of his form of appearance, but also his psychic and spiritual functions, his consciousness body which reaches far beyond the limitations of his physical body.

"The duality is the discrepancy between Soul and the physical body of man. This duality is annihilated when Soul has reached the heavenly planes and entered into the heart of the SUGMAD.

"None of the ways observed or described by man, in which things happen or events occur, is the master way by which nature works. No word or name can disclose the way of ECK in its deepest secret. Creation begins in an event which is not identified and, therefore, has no name. All creatures, nevertheless, can be traced to a common matrix which exists only in the ECK.

"The secrets of ECK, the constant, formative way from which no event is exempt, is disclosed only to those who can be rid of their personal wishes or prejudices about the ECK. One comes to grips with It, as It lies hidden beneath appearances, by disregarding his own point of view. Prejudiced ears have no place on the path of ECK.

"The secret and its containers are separated only by abstraction and persistence. In the nature of the ECK, either of these are invariably paired. This pairing, or principle, of life with matter, is the most profound feature of the world. It is the clue to the understanding of all existence.

"It is always said that the palace rises in beauty only against the ugliness of the dwellings of the poor, that man's goodness is attended by his wickedness.

"So generally, positive and negative, being and nonbeing, pleasant and unpleasant, good and bad—such qualities and values come in pairs. They are relative to human feelings; they arise from the individual point of view. They do not appear in the way of ECK, nor in Its virtue.

"The ECKist knows nothing and does nothing of himself; he is quiet and lets the ECK act through him in Its power. He takes no pay in any form—neither fame, nor service, nor property, nor personal power—and since he does not, they all come to him. This is the way that It works in man, which is the natural vehicle for Its power.

"Looking down into the unfathomable depths of the ECK, I wonder at Its hugeness, vastness, and timeless way. The power pours out of It; you can never exhaust It. No one except the MAHANTA, the Living ECK Master knows from where the power of ECK comes and that It is never exhausted. It is always flowing from the Godhead into the worlds of worlds—sustaining life, uplifting Souls, and giving all the path to the heavenly worlds.

"Too much talk means too much exhaustion, so it is far better to keep your thoughts to yourself. Silence is golden, for it brings to the seeker more than gold. It brings him the heavenly treasures which cannot be measured in gold and silver. But man seeks too much the gold and silver of the world when he should be seeking the Window of Heaven through which, when opened, all the treasures that he believed were possible will now come pouring to him.

"The treasures of heaven are not merely gold and silver, but the treasures of Soul—the peace, contentment, and happiness which come with the opening of the Window of Heaven. None will know this until each has a glimpse of the broad skies and the beautiful gardens, the running waters and the wonderful colors of the world beyond, by the opening of the window.

"The man of wisdom chooses to be last, and by so doing he becomes the first of all. He knows that by denying himself in life, he is saved from the worldly attachments of this earth and the lower planes. In so doing, he fulfills the duties of the unselfish man. By serving the ECK first, he finds life more abundant to help serve all others.

"The object of the ECKist, therefore, is peace and wisdom which come from seeking the highest through selflessness. He who is sharp and scheming can never open the Window of Heaven, nor can he find it.

"Resignation, the action of returning good for evil, temperance, purity, the subjugation of the senses, a knowledge of the Shariyat-Ki-Sugmad, that of Soul, the worship of truth, and abstinence from anger—such are the principles which should be the conduct of a true ECKist.

"Contemplation upon the delights of the SUGMAD, needing nothing, living beyond the reach of any sensual desire, with no society save himself and the thought of the Supreme Deity, man should live in the constant expectation of everlasting happiness.

"Whosoever has been initiated, no matter what may be the degree to which he may belong, and shall reveal the sacred formula, he shall be punished by the Lords of Karma.

"Whosoever has been initiated into the third degree and shall reveal the superior truths he has been taught to the candidates for initiation into the second degree before the proper time, he shall suffer death many times over.

"Whosoever has been initiated into the second degree and shall act likewise with those who have been initiated into the first degree, he is declared impure for the period of seven years, and when that time has elapsed he shall be turned into the lower degree—the first degree.

"Whosoever has been initiated into any degree of Eckankar, and shall divulge the secrets of his initiation to others who are barred from knowing them, as though they were contained in a sealed book, he shall be deprived of his sight and tongue in order to never again be able to say anything about the degrees of initiation in Eckankar.

"Anyone who thinks that what has been said here about the initiations is not in accord with the ECK Masters of the Ancient Order of the Vairagi is foolish. Since all wisdom, and wisdom only—not knowledge or opinion—comes directly from the Source of all sources, the SUGMAD, one cannot think otherwise, for it is the SUGMAD who really gives the initiation through the MAHANTA, the Living ECK Master, who, in turn, appoints the Mahdis to give initiations in his place.

"The wisdom of God, the SUGMAD, is channeled to the nine unknown ECK Masters who dwell on the plane of the Anami Lok. Unless you are at this level of life, you cannot have the true wisdom. The passions of the worldly life are like heavy clouds which shut out the wisdom, like they shut out the sun entirely or obscure the brilliancy of its light. They may be compared to a violent wind which agitates the surface of the water so that it cannot reflect the splendor of the skies above; to the cocoon of the butterfly, which deprives it of liberty; and to the shell of certain fruits, which prevents their fragrance from diffusing itself abroad.

"Yet we know the butterfly breaks its way out of its cocoon, makes itself a passage, and wings its way into space—thus conquering air, light, and liberty.

"So it is with Soul. Its prison in the body, in which earthly troubles and tumultuous passions keep It confined, is not eternal. After a long series of successive births—the spark of wisdom which is in It being rekindled—It will finally succeed, by the long continued practice of penitence and contemplation, in breaking all the ties that bind It to the earth; and It will increase in virtue until It has reached so high a degree of wisdom and spirituality that It becomes identity. Then, leaving the body which holds It captive, It soars freely aloft where It dwells forever with the SUGMAD.

"Having reached the fifth degree of initiation, it is the duty of the initiate to improve, to spiritualize himself by contemplation. He is supposed to pass through the four following states: First is Salokiam, which signifies the only tie with the lower worlds. In this state Soul seeks to lift Itself, with the assistance of the MAHANTA, the Living ECK Master, to the true spiritual worlds and to take Its place in the presence of Divinity Itself; It holds communication with those Souls who have gone before into the regions of eternity and makes use of the body left on earth as an instrument to transcribe, under the permanent form of writing, the sublime teachings It receives in these worlds of true spirituality.

"Second is Samipiam, which signifies proximity. By the exercises of contemplation and the disregard of all earthly objects, the knowledge and idea of the SUGMAD becomes familiar to It. It becomes farseeing and begins to witness marvels which are not of this world.

"Third is Souaroupiam, which signifies resemblance. In this state Soul gradually acquires a perfect resemblance to the ECK and participates in all Its attributes. It reads the future and the universe has no secrets for It.

"Fourth is Sayodiyam, identity. Soul finally becomes closely united to the MAHANTA, the Living ECK Master. This last transformation takes place only through the death of the physical body, that is to say, the entire disruption of all material ties by translation.

"The passage of Soul through these four states may be explained by the following comparison: When we wish to extract gold from a compound mass, we shall never succeed if we subject it to the process of fusion only once. It is only by melting the alloy in the crucible several times that we are finally able to separate the heterogeneous particles of which it is composed and release the gold in all its purity.

"The two modes of contemplation most in use are called the Shabda-SUGMAD and the Shabda-MAHANTA, or intercourse with the SUGMAD and the MAHANTA Consciousness.

"It is by persistence and making use of the Spiritual Exercises of ECK, anywhere—in the home, in the desert, in the jungle and forest—that the Mahdis, the contemplatives, prepare themselves for the lofty heights of heaven.

"The spirits of the first grand division, the Pinda (Physical worlds), the Anda (Astral), and the Brahmanda (Causal and Mental), should be ignored. They are not to be worshipped nor listened to, for they are only the shades of those ancestors who have passed on or are waiting in between incarnations. They are not wise, nor are they usually happy, because they can see no future and are only too concerned with becoming possessed with anyone on the Physical Plane. The former drunkard whose shade now is in the Turiya Pad (Astral world), deprived of the satisfaction of his thirst for alcohol, will try to take up with anyone on the Pinda (Physical) Plane to have his joy of drinking vicariously through a living physical being. The same will go for those shades who were living in passions of their vices on earth.

"The true Master of Eckankar is he who is familiar with the practice of daily virtues; who, with the sword of wisdom, has lopped off all the branches and cut through all the roots of the tree of evil and, with the light of reason, has dispelled the thick darkness by which he is enveloped; who, though surrounded by mountains of passion, meets all their assaults with a heart as firm as a diamond; who conducts himself with dignity and independence; who has the love of a father for all his chelas; who makes no distinction between his friends and enemies, whom he treats with equal kindness and consideration; who looks upon gold and jewels with as much indifference as if they were bits of iron and potsherds, without caring more for one than the other; and who tries with the greatest care to remove the dense darkness of ignorance in which mankind is plunged.

"The sacred scriptures of the Shariyat-Ki-Sugmad should not be taken in their apparent meaning, as in the case of the orthodox scriptures. Of what use would it be to forbid their revelation to the profane if their secret meaning were contained in the literal sense of the language usually employed? We must look upon the Shariyat-Ki-Sugmad in the following way:

"As Soul is contained in the body in the beginning,
As the almond is hidden by its hull,
As the sun is veiled by the clouds,
As the garments hide the body from view,
As the egg is contained in its shell,
As the germ rests within the interior of the seed.

"So the sacred ECK has Its body, Its hull, Its cloud, Its garment, Its shell, which hides It from the knowledge of the world and the eyes and ears of the profane.

"All that has been, all that is, everything that will be, everything that ever has been said—is to be found in the Shariyat-Ki-Sugmad. But the works within these sacred books do not explain themselves, and they can only be understood when the MAHANTA, the Living ECK Master has removed the garments with which they are clothed and scattered the clouds that veil their celestial light.

"The ECK is like the precious pearl that is buried at the bottom of the ocean. It is not enough merely to have the oyster in which it is enclosed, but it is also necessary to open the oyster and get the pearl.

"You, in your pride, who would read the sacred works of the Shariyat-Ki-Sugmad without the assistance of the MAHANTA, the Living ECK Master, do you even know by what letter of a word you ought to begin to read them? Do you know the secret of combinations of the threes and the nines? Do you know when the final letter becomes an initial and the initial becomes final?

"Woe to him who looks upon the ECK as a simple knowledge of life expressed in ordinary language, for if that is really all It contains, we can frame an image of the ECK much more worthy of admiration. If we are to regard the ordinary meaning of the words, we need only turn to that which is the human consciousness and serve its laws and limitations. We have only to imitate these rules and frame laws after their model and example. But it is not so, for every aspect of the ECK contains a deep and sublime mystery and meaning.

"Nothing is begun, and nothing is ended. Everything is changed or transformed; life and death are only the modes of transformation which rule the vital molecule, from the planet up to the ruler of the highest plane of the SUGMAD, and including the SUGMAD Itself.

"It is the ECK which envelops all bodies of man within Itself. These bodies are composed of the five selves, which are under the control of Soul, and the words spoken by man. The words are seals of the mind—results or, more correctly, stations—of an infinite series of experiences which reach from an unimaginably distant past into the present, and which feel their way into an equally unimaginably distant future. They are the audible that clings to the inaudible, the forms and potentialities of Soul, that which grows and unfolds into perfection.

"The essential nature of words is, therefore, neither exhausted by their present meaning, nor is their importance confined to their usefulness as transmitters of thoughts and ideas; but they express, at the time, qualities which are not translatable into concepts. This is like a melody which, though it may be associated with a deep meaning, cannot be described by words or by any other medium of expression. It is that irrational quality which stirs up our deepest feelings, elevates our innermost being, and makes It vibrate with those with whom we are closely related in love and work.

"The birth of language was the birth of humanity. Each word was the sound-equivalent of an experience connected with an internal or external action. A tremendous creative effort was involved in this process, which extended over a vast period of time, and due to this effort man was able to rise above animals and other forms of life.

"All that is visible clings to the invisible, the audible to the inaudible, the tangible to the intangible, and, of course, the thinkable to the unthinkable.

"The seer, the poet and singer, the spiritually creative, the psychically receptive and sensitive, and the saint—all know about the essentiality of form in word and sound, in the visible and the tangible. They do not dislike what appears small or insignificant, because they can see the great in the small. Through them the Word becomes flesh, and the sounds and signs of which It is formed become the vehicle of mysterious forces. Through them the visible takes on the nature of symbols, the tangible becomes a creative tool of the ECK, and life becomes a deep stream flowing from eternity to eternity.

"The highest goodness in man, like water, is characterized by humility. A good man or a good king is self-effacing, like the ECK. Consequently, his object is peace; and the picture of peace consists of families secure on their land and the people thoughtful, kind, and sincere.

"All must be able to control their animal nature enough to be pure in heart, never distracted from the way of ECK. Each person must be capable of personal discipline that will enable him to love unselfishly, wield virtue, and, at last, understand all, while denying himself. He must put life into others without trying to own them. He must never depend upon anyone. He can be the king, but never the tyrant. This is what the ECK requires of all people.

"Can anyone isolate the ECK and say, 'This is It!'? It

is as real as the spokes in a wheel, as real as the hub of the wheel where the axle rests. The hole is a void in the hub, but it exists as a window exists when part of the wall of the house is torn down. This is like the ECK, which exists like the emptiness of a bowl on the table. So it is with the ECK; but It is functional and cannot be isolated, and none can do without It.

"The MAHANTA, the Living ECK Master has other titles. He is the Godman, the Vi-Guru, the Light Giver, protector of the poor, the king of heaven, savior of mankind, the scourge of evil, and the defender of the faithful. He is the real and only power in all the universes of God. No one can harm him without his consent, for all that is done to him is given permission by the ECK, with his consent.

"He never seeks power, for he already has power. He never seeks love, for he already has love. He remains as much as possible in the background and doesn't come forward in the affairs of the world unless he is asked. He has the basic control over all life and never needs the social things of man, nor the necessities of life that people want, and over which they often quarrel and kill one another.

"The ECK is invisible, inaudible, and intangible to the common man, and It must be accepted as such for him. Its presence can never be put to a definite test; so that being present, It gives no light; being absent, It leaves no darkness. It meets no specifications of human standards.

"Deep in all, there is a stillness where the Self of life is; and the Self is God, from whom destiny proceeds; and without knowledge of that Self, the eternal Self, man is constantly blind to It, and instead of finding good in all, will, therefore, work evil. When the chela comes to know the Self, he will find himself taking on the stature of a great king whose goodness will endow him with the best of life and make him at last divine, because the ECK is at work within him. He may die, but he will never perish, for he has learned that survival lies beyond the grave.

"The ECK, Itself, is impalpable, immaterial, and yet out of It issues all life.

"The ECK has existed throughout all eternity, yet from ancient times until now, from the beginning, the ECK has been presented under an endless number of names. How may I know you know It? By what can you tell It? It is known only through your insights, your intuitions, your experiences with what is eternal, and what you know as truth.

"If the chela is to put faith in the MAHANTA, the Living ECK Master, his faith in the ECK must be great. His hope for success lies in the ECK and Its power; if he were to abandon It, he, himself, would be abandoned indeed.

"Everything in the universes of the SUGMAD takes its greatness from the ECK, and of this, the MAHANTA, the Living ECK Master is the human symbol. He is the Godman who, through the earth and heavens, connects all of us with the ECK.

"The man of faith in the ECK reflects the world around him, for the principles of both worlds are the same. Certainty is to be found in the heart; confusion is bred in the outer worlds. So look at yourself and know where life might be for you.

"Everything depends on your relationship with the ECK, especially the form of virtue which is appropriate to each field of interest and endeavor. This leads to the consideration of the chela in his home, city, nation, or world. The man in the street, through which the ideal is contemplated, is the channel for the ECK to reach all within his environment. Once you set your feet firmly on the path of ECK, you become the ideal and the standard by which all men are judged.

"If there is to be peace in this world, if this world is

to be won by the ECK, it must be let alone; then only will the ECK take over. This is shown in the fact that the more men act, the more they have to act. With all the ruling and doing that men do, the world goes badly; it would be better if we were to let it alone altogether. If we did that, people would be free and, naturally, they would return to the simplicity and honesty of their original nature. This is what the ECK desires of the human race.

"The history of Eckankar, the Ancient Science of Soul Travel, has been written in the blood of all men—men tortured in ignorance, those suppressed and discredited by orthodox religions, men seeking power, the mundane masses, the priests trying to gain control over their subjects, and the tyrants who live by terror and death.

"No man shall be called father who is not the parent of his children. Therefore, no orthodox religion is able to appoint its priest to be called father. Only the Godman, the MAHANTA, the Living ECK Master has attained this position to be called the Baba, or Babpu, of his people. But even he does not go by this title, because he realizes that all men are equal and should not look upon one another as superior, and because he is the ECK in the human form and, therefore, subject to the laws of the world.

"Evil cannot harm the ECK chela. He is above all of this, for the protection of the MAHANTA, the Living ECK Master has taken over his human and spiritual affairs, like the mother hen who has spread her wings for her chicks to take cover when the hawk is hovering over them.

"The ECK has always been attacked by the orthodox believers, because none understand It. This failure to understand is moral rather than intellectual. Compassion, frugality, and humility are absent from the worldly man. Their absence could be fatal to the human race. It is chiefly compassion that connects the chela to the MAHANTA, the Living ECK Master.

"He who can yield can survive both here in life and in the invisible worlds. This is what makes marriages last throughout the years, what makes friendships everlasting, what makes nations friendly in relation to one another, and what allows Soul to live in eternity.

"Never being able to bend will bring about death. The soldier who doesn't know when to strike or when to yield will never find victory. The strong and mighty topple from their place because they are not able to yield, while the yielding, the soft one, rises above them all.

"I have seen and told you what was to be given. Only those in the higher worlds know what truths and divine wisdom can be given to your ears. I am only the humble vessel through which they flow to you."

10

The Arch of the Heavenly World

"The immortality of Soul lies in the sacrifice and hardships of life within this physical realm and its counterparts." So said Tindor Saki, the marvelous ECK Master who dwells on the Atma Lok and is guardian of the Shariyat-Ki-Sugmad in the Temple of Golden Wisdom there.

He also said, "When a man is willing to sacrifice all that he has for the ECK, to give up the clothes on his back for his fellow man, or to give his life for all—that is the MAHANTA, the Living ECK Master. When he goes to his death with love for his very enemies, although they have burned his flesh and caused him suffering, he reaches the immortality of the Atma Lok."

It is written within the golden books of the Shariyat-Ki-Sugmad that Soul is the arch of the heavenly world. It is purified by Its suffering for the sake of the MAHANTA, the Living ECK Master, who has always given his life, and his various bodies throughout the planes of the psychic worlds and within the heavenly realms, for the sake of man.

The Living ECK Master has always been in this world; therefore, there has never been a time when man could not receive salvation. He has always had the opportunity to be with the ECK Master, and never at any time has he been denied, despite his actions and his deeds in any particular life. The past experiences of man's life always rise up in him, perfectly mastered, mild and beyond measure, but he never recognizes this. He hardly realizes the intangible and his particular link with the MAHANTA, the Living ECK Master.

The Living ECK Master gives him everything in life, gives him all that he has, suffering so many times for man's own karmic misconceptions and the manner in which he has conducted himself during the many lives in which he has lived. The MAHANTA will sacrifice of himself to give spiritual assistance to the whole race of men upon this earth, those who dwell on other planets, and all beings and entities within the lower worlds of the SUGMAD. He sacrifices in blood, pain, and agony for all the karmic debts which man owes to the Kal. He brings about perfection through his giving up of all material things of life, through his giving of himself to mankind, all beings, and all things of the human nature.

If one who has nothing wishes for food in the MAHANTA's presence, he will break bread with him. If one who has no cloak for his back shall wish for a cloak in the MAHANTA's presence, he shall be given the Master's cloak. If he wishes for the MAHANTA's blessings, even though he is an evil man in this world, then the Living ECK Master shall give him his blessings.

The MAHANTA's very presence in the human body shows that the principles of cause and harmony lead to human reason, to the absolute notion of a superior and universal cause of the SUGMAD Itself. "He who denies this cause for the whole has no right to assign any cause to any particular fact. If you say that the MAHANTA exists because the SUGMAD wishes it, it is unnecessary to go any further;

man lives by facts, and he has no assurance otherwise of the invariability of the laws of the ECK," says Tindor Saki.

The MAHANTA knows all things that go on around him—in the affairs of his chelas, the minds of all men, and the past, future, and destiny of the human race. He understands the Kal Niranjan, whose very duty is to destroy him if at all possible. Cunningly, the Kal sets about establishing the minds of men against the MAHANTA, in hope of destroying the sacred vessel which is created upon this earth to raise up all mankind. So, very often the Kal succeeds, but more often fails. When the agents of Kal offer up something to the MAHANTA, in false worship and subtle attacks, the MAHANTA realizes that it is for another reason, which is to get rid of his physical body. But this is only an illusion, for he will reappear in another place, in another time, as solid as ever in the body form. Those acting as the agents of the Kal are always defeated, for the MAHANTA does reappear to prove that he can overcome death, to show that his life is eternal and not merely subject to the laws of this world. Always, when his body is destroyed, he rises again from the tomb to show his closest followers that it is possible to defeat death, even in the destruction of his own body.

"The MAHANTA is he who exists by himself and who is in all because all is in him. It is he who exists by himself, because Soul alone can perceive him who cannot be apprehended by the physical senses. It is he who is without visible parts, except the human body, but is eternal—the Soul of all beings. None can comprehend him except those who live in the high worlds of ECK in the Atma Sarup. He is one, immutable in the MAHANTA Consciousness, devoid of parts or form, infinite, omniscient, omnipresent, and omnipotent. It is he who has created the life and energies of the worlds, as the instrument of the SUGMAD. None other is before him." So said Tindor Saki.

The immortality of Soul is also the law of eternal love. Soul is one, but man is two; he is also three. Man contains the two principles, masculine and feminine, and the union of these two principles produces the third, which is the neuter, or that which is above the masculine and the feminine, the balance of the two in one.

Man is one, and he is that which is called the allness of this world. This contains the husband and the wife, and the love of the husband for the wife and of the wife for the husband, which produces the third, which is the child. And the child becomes the balance of the two principles: masculine and feminine.

It's found that in the immortal life everything is contained and preserved in the one fluid known as the ECK. Everything is changed and transformed by the ECK. All creation must be kept in secret, or the heart of the secret will leave the indulger. This is the foundation of the immortal life, the heart of eternity for Soul. If the chela reveals any secrets given him by the MAHANTA, the Living ECK Master, his way into the heavenly worlds may be blocked by insurmountable obstacles. All secrets are contained in whatever the MAHANTA tells the chela in any personal sense, whether it be in the commonplace or that which is the greatest of all secrets. His word shall never be given to the public or private ear unless the MAHANTA gives his permission.

The indulgence of any secret given by the MAHANTA, or whatever prophecies that he might make about them, will at any time be that which is of the most minute value to those who wish to indulge the secrets of their own life or lives with one another. Since ECK is the path of universality, it is, then, the holder of the secrets. Such idle talk only reestablishes karma within those who wish to talk about themselves or their experiences and give life to their own egos.

Truth, goodness, love, and beauty are commonly regarded as poetic ideas, but they are, in essence, spiritual facts. These are the ideas which one should include in his speech and thoughts. They are the language of Soul and must bring about an awakening of that pervading, persuasive urge in man to realize himself in his totality, as a being essentially spiritual and eternal. Truth, as given by the ECK, is neither esoteric, strange, nor fanciful. It is at once sublime, universal, and profoundly practical.

If truth is to be of actual value, it must be experienced and manifested in the chela's life. The ECKist is the truly spiritual man, is the most giving of all men. His universal vision naturally compels him to see the presence of the MAHANTA in all beings, and he unceasingly speaks to the essential nature of all beings. His very existence inspires others to manifest their own higher nature. It is as Tindor Saki says: "What a man receives in contemplation, he must pour out in love." Therefore, this spontaneous giving of one's own self is an inevitable outcome of his contemplation and spiritual exercises. The state of selflessness attained through these spiritual efforts will penetrate his character entirely. The great world movers of the ECK Masters in the Ancient Order of the Vairagi have been those whose characters have been penetrated by the SUGMAD's state of selflessness.

Those who have reached this state of selflessness learn that death is stingless. Death is only a translation from one body to another, and man transfers his awareness to the Soul state. As a disciple of the ECK, he knows that no obstacle can stand in his way as long as he is following the MAHANTA, the Living ECK Master. His very glimpse of heaven, through the MAHANTA, will erase the fear of death. He will gladly pass through the portals of death for the sake of ECK, to dwell in the heavenly worlds.

For a mere glimpse of heaven, men have sacrificed

themselves and died. In the pursuit of some religious goal, men have sacrificed themselves for no worthy purpose; but within the ECK, should man give up his life and die for It, he is worthy of the MAHANTA's attention and shall have salvation within the aura of his sacrifice.

In the pursuit of the ECK, shining as a beacon to men struggling in an unequal battle with nature and their fellow creatures, too many have died, stifled by their own attempts to perpetuate, codify, and evangelize the vision of heaven. But not until each has come to the conclusion that this vision, this reality, is the very freedom which he seeks, is there any evidence of success.

The MAHANTA, the Living ECK Master is the only one who can know the future of this world and change it, should he decide to do this. He realizes that all followers, all disciples, and chelas of ECK should and must participate in bringing about peace when the times become too chaotic. He is willing to teach each to be a channel for the ECK, and through every channel or instrument the ECK causes all environments to change from that of turbulence to peace. This modus operandi can and does exist through the lower worlds, for the MAHANTA is unfolding Souls everywhere so they can reach spiritual perfection. In doing so they become his channels for the peace of the SUGMAD.

If a chela of ECK can have no peace within himself, it is written that he cannot bring peace to others. The mystery of peace is found only within one, and he has to distribute his state of selflessness to others to bring degrees of peace; that is, if they are ready and willing to accept this quality of God within themselves. Each environment is unique within itself and must be treated differently by the chela who is desirous of bringing peace within its boundaries.

The mystery of speech is more than that of mere words or concepts; and it, too, belongs in the element of peace. It is the principle of all mental representation and communication. Yet there are times when speech alone contains the elements of peace. Those living in the state of selflessness will speak gently and carefully, selecting their words to give life to others.

The mysteries of speech, sight, and hearing in the physical world are indeed strange. The dark things of Kal will mislead the chela, for when you hear strange sounds in another's voice it isn't unusual. These are utterances much unlike the nature of that person, and one will have the feeling that something was said which really wasn't. This is always the work of the entities under the leadership of the Kal Niranjan who are trying to fight the chela and get him under the Kal's control.

He can see visions and objects and get a glimpse of these entities through the side-vision of his sight, at the edge of the normal eyesight. They flip into the boundary of the range of his eyesight, but never into the full vision, only to let him know that they are there and dangerous to his well-being, should he slip from his loyalty and obedience to the MAHANTA, the Living ECK Master.

He can also hear them speak at times through his left ear, calling to him, telling him that he is to follow particular instructions of the MAHANTA. But this is false, for the MAHANTA speaks only through the inner channels and never in the outward to his chelas, except in the physical flesh or by letters. If he instructs, it is often via the inner channels or by the written word. Sometimes these entities will even attempt to change the written words in those letters and personal instructions which the MAHANTA might send to his chelas. It is not often done, but these entities of the Kal Niranjan are always seeking opportunities to do harm to the chelas to get them away from the ECK, which is to their own discredit. They are always promising something greater to the chelas in order to lure them away from the path of ECK.

They speak in the voices of the false prophets and the pseudomasters. They bring about obstacles and troubles to the minds and the flesh of the chelas. They interfere with plans and raise their voices to drown out any of those who are speaking truth in the works of ECK. They will falsely represent themselves as the teachers and Masters of Eckankar and will use those who are the simple, the guileless, and the naive to listen to the voices of the false teachers and masters who claim they are teaching Eckankar.

These entities, these false prophets and pseudomasters who make claim to being the ECK Masters, or who teach in other faiths with the title of spiritual masters, are simply the coworkers of the Kal Niranjan. They live and exist in the psychic worlds only and cannot give true spiritual liberation to Soul, yet they make claims that their works are worthy of this greatest of tasks. The ECK works are the most powerful in this world; and the MAHANTA, the Living ECK Master, who is the vehicle and channel for the ECK, is the most powerful being within the physical world, as well as the planets and all the planes within the worlds of God.

ECK is the thread—so fine as to be invisible, yet so strong as to be unbreakable—which binds together all beings in all the worlds of God, in all universes, throughout all time, and beyond time into eternity. In prehistoric times, man took an enormous leap upward from the animal life with the development of consciousness. ECK is always giving the human race the opportunity to take another equally great step upward into the higher consciousness by making Its appearance again in this world. The effect of this reappearance will be that man will make greater spiritual progress by this second step than he has made, materially, through the first.

Therefore, those who claim to be masters have not had the experience to render or to back their claims. Those who follow these pseudomasters will find themselves, at death, standing before Yama, the King of the Dead, through whose court all uninitiated Souls must pass. If those false prophets and masters make claim to giving initiations, they will reap the works of the Kal and degenerate in their spiritual and physical growth.

Those who have reached the higher initiations, such as that of the Mahdis, become members of the inner circle of the MAHANTA. The Mahdis must show initiative, resourcefulness, and a fanatic loyalty to the ECK; otherwise they are not worthy of this station of life. Each, if he is found to be true to the ECK, is taught the deepest secrets of the magnificent works, the modus operandi of leaving his state of consciousness, and the ways of ECK in some specialized way or other. But once the chela has become a member of the inner circle, he cannot resign. Woe be unto him if he does, for the result is known among those who have reached these lofty heights and witnessed the consequences of the few who have. Those few have found that spiritual decay sets in immediately, affecting the health, material life, and spiritual life, and brings death more swiftly.

These inner-circle members shall give complete obedience to the MAHANTA. Each must be willing to stand by the ECK through bloodletting, violence, torment, poverty, unhappiness, and destruction. If he does succeed, there will be happiness, light, and greatness of character, and he shall be rewarded. He shall be the greatest in the spiritual kingdom, the most successful in the eyes of the MAHANTA, and shall sit on the right side of the Living ECK Master in the heavenly worlds.

Each new spiritual experience, as well as each new situation in life, widens the perception of each chela and brings about a subtle transformation within all concerned. Thus the spiritual nature of the disciples of the MAHANTA changes continually, not only the conditions of life, because it is the law of all life to either progress or degenerate. If there is strict obedience to the will of the ECK, there shall be no problem for any initiate who is desirous of reaching the Akshar, the imperishable consciousness.

Men are so busy putting faith into some orthodox religion, or using science to discover what is believed to be the effect of nature, that they have not learned that ECK is the most powerful of any force in all the universes of God. It is the mover of all things, the force which can create or destroy any universe, any creature, any form of life, and anything which is desired by the SUGMAD and Its vehicle, the MAHANTA, the Living ECK Master. Therefore, the MAHANTA is the most powerful being within the universes of the SUGMAD. With a flick of his finger he can create or destroy nations and any form of life. But in his compassion for all life, he desires to create and build instead of destroy. It is the will of the SUGMAD that the Kal exists; therefore, the MAHANTA does nothing about the evil ways of this lord of the lower worlds. It is written in the heavens that the Kal is only the servant of the MAHANTA and the Supreme Being, and whatever it does is only planned in the destiny of the Books of Life.

Whatever suffering takes place at the instigation of the Kal Niranjan upon the personage of the MAHANTA is allowed by the Living ECK Master, for it's the will of the SUGMAD to give man an example of what he must do in order to reach spiritual perfection.

The MAHANTA always gives himself to the Supreme Being and allows his own physical body to suffer, giving up his blood and making a sacrifice of his physical body in the end, to prove unto man that there is survival beyond the grave. He proves that ECK is the highest of all powers within the universes, and that the SUGMAD is the Supreme Being. The teachings that he gives by word, whether spoken or written, are a mere shadow of what he gives to the world by his presence, personality, and living example. He discloses the works of ECK to his chelas without speaking or writing, in so many of his gestures and physical actions. A touch, a smile, an embrace, a handshake, or a kiss on the cheek brings about an uplifting of man's spiritual unfoldment. It quickens his awareness and gives him added energies and life, new visions, and the whole of all things.

The whole history of Western civilization, including that of nations which have accepted orthodox religions, was established upon the principle of the religious idea of sin. No pagan religion and culture could withstand the force of the idea that man was born in sin and never had any release from it to gain salvation until he accepted the respective savior.

This is all built upon a false premise, and today man is learning that this is not true. Therefore, he is finding himself in a quandary of trouble arising from a multitude of new ideas and forces, mainly from the new concepts of what is going on around him with the welter of words from orators and written means. But the idea of man being born in sin is one of the oldest traps that the Kal Niranjan could establish and use to hold Soul in ignorance of Its original plan, that is, to spend a certain amount of time in this world and then become purified in order to leave it and enter into the heavenly kingdom to become a Coworker with God.

It has proven out that the idea of the religious concept of man's iniquity in sin is archaic. Soul, not man, is dependent upon Its own state of affairs, mainly that of recognizing that Its true liberation lies in the initiation by the MAHANTA, the Living ECK Master. Until this time arrives in the affairs of Soul, It goes on without any true concept of Its own life on earth, with a guilt pattern generally established by Its belief in the religious path which It might be following during Its worldly existence.

The body's rate of vibrations is most important. Often the problem of the individual's health is that the vibrations are too slow or too fast. The Living ECK Master can raise or lower them according to whatever proper adjustment is needed. This is the reason so many persons suffer and cannot get help; it is because their leader does not know anything about adjusting the vibrations of the one who seeks him out for healing.

The healing of the individual depends mainly upon his response to the manner in which the Living ECK Master adjusts the vibratory rates of whoever is making the request. His faith must be strong or the healing will not occur. There is a saying that if one believes a thing is impossible, his despondency shall make it so. But if he perseveres in his thoughts and heart for faith in the ECK Master, he shall overcome all difficulties.

Discrimination is, therefore, practiced by the MAHANTA, the Living ECK Master in order to be an example for those who follow him. He tries to show each individual, personally, what is best for him. The enlightenment is never forced upon those who do not care for it or who are not ripe for it. It is given only to those who thirst for higher knowledge, and it is given at the proper time and the proper place.

Spiritual unfoldment can be found in the little things of life. The drama and fixed things which are getting the attention of man are generally those of the Kal. It is the nature of the Kal to force man's attention to the dramatic things of life, such as war and politics. But it is in the small events, such as goodness in the daily things of life, being kind to a child, speaking softly to those who can be hurt easily, noninjury to a fellow creature, and the giving of one's self to others who are without the essentials of life, that spiritual unfoldment can be found.

Truth cannot be taken as one's own discovery, but it has to be continually rediscovered. It has to be reformed and transformed if its meaning, its living value, and spiritual nourishment are to be preserved. This is known as the Law of Spiritual Growth, which results in the necessity to experience the same truth in ever-new forms, and to cultivate and propagate not so much the results, but the methods through which Soul obtains knowledge, experience, and reality.

If the individual man will keep up the Spiritual Exercises of ECK, it's found that this process of spiritual growth is repeated and experienced in him. It does not only mean that the individual will become the connecting link between the past, the present, and the future, but that his past will become revitalized and the present rejuvenated in his experiences. It also transforms itself into the creative process of the future. In this way history is reshaped for the individual into his present life and becomes a part of his own being. It is not merely an object of learning or veneration from some past mistake which creates guilt patterns and heavy karma, but with the help of the MAHANTA, the Living ECK Master the original causes are easily transformed into a pattern of Light and Sound and become essential to that individual.

The individual merely grows out of his past into the present, without having to get into the past problems which are part of his karmic debt to life. He finds that, with the help of the MAHANTA, it becomes somewhat easier now to become aware of his present conditions and viewpoints on life, and he can reestablish his future. Man cannot understand his past, nor that of the nature of historical peoples who populated the earth for many years, because he cannot understand the language barrier, the attitudes and customs, as well as the habits of those in former lives. This is why he fails to grasp the significance of his karmic debt. He may be able to see and understand what his past lives have been, but he cannot make any progress because of a lack of knowledge of how the people of certain particular lives spoke, acted, and performed their duties toward their own social conditions.

However, it's found that the essential nature of Eckankar cannot be found in the spaceless realm of abstract thought, nor in the dogma hallowed by antiquity, nor in the speech, customs, and habits of the ancient peoples. It is only in the unfoldment of Soul in time, space, and the heavenly worlds, in the immensity of Soul's movement and development, in Its all-encompassing influence upon life in all its aspects, in Its universality.

It might be said that ECK is a work of life which appeals equally to those who wish to gain their own liberation and to those who wish to work both for their personal liberation and for the liberation of others. ECK does not make suffering a vanity, although suffering is a well-known essential which one must go through in order to become purified and reach the heavenly worlds. No sacrifice that one makes for another is in vain, even if it is not recognized or is misused by those for whose benefit it was intended. Each sacrifice is an act of renunciation, a victory over ourselves, and an act of liberation.

The more man loses his ego and breaks down the walls of his self-created prison, the greater becomes the clarity and radiance of his being and the convincing power of his life. This is through deeds of charity and not merely pious words and religious talk. Those who keep aloof from the works of life miss the opportunities of sacrifice, of self-abnegation, of relinquishing one's possessions by giving up what was dear or what seemed desirable to give service to others. To help others while helping oneself go hand in hand, for one cannot do one without the other.

None should force his good deeds upon others from a sense of spiritual superiority, but act from spontaneity, from that natural kind of selflessness which flows from the heart.

The MAHANTA, the Living ECK Master is always testing his initiates and chelas. A touch, a glance, a request, and a command are often in the testing. He is always looking and seeking to see who will be loyal, who is developing vanity and egotism, and who is only with him seeking favors. He is seeking to learn who will be silent about the communications between him and the individual whom he has tested. Those who complain about their relationship with the Living ECK Master, or talk about what went on between them behind closed doors, will not be worthy of the trust and faith which he puts in them. If he speaks and acts in secret to a chela, that one who has so been trusted to keep the secrets which have been given him should never reveal such to others. If anyone gives away such secrets or betrays the trust the Living ECK Master has put in him, there shall be a delay in his spiritual growth.

A true seeker should learn who is the MAHANTA, the Living ECK Master and then go to this perfect guru, whoever he might be. He should understand that the worship of the MAHANTA implies the worship of the ECK, the worship of the SUGMAD. He must show love and complete devotion to the MAHANTA, and he will gain his object of enlightenment, the ECK Master's blessings and the opportunity to enter into the heavenly worlds.

Tindor Saki said, "Within the MAHANTA is the true temple of the SUGMAD, and he who seeks to bow to the divine reality should bow before him. The SUGMAD has said to the humble one that It does not live in a particular place, either on earth or in the heavenly worlds, but It lives in the hearts of Its devotees, and if you wish to have me, go and beg for me."

Therefore, it is proper that every true seeker should search for the true Living ECK Master of his own times, get instructions from him, and show love and regard for him in all respects. It is written in the heavenly books that any chela of the ECK who wishes to see the SUGMAD, and wishes to serve and love It, should serve and love his fellow devotees who are ECKists. This will be his service; he will be pleased to be with them and serve and love them. The SUGMAD says It lives neither in heaven above nor on earth below, nor in any paradise, but It lives in the hearts of Its devotees who love It.

The human form of the MAHANTA, the Living ECK Master is only the outward manifestation. His real form is one with that of the SUGMAD, as he always enjoys the bliss of the divine reality. A true seeker, so long as he cannot realize the form of the Supreme Being within himself, should contemplate the human form of the MAHANTA as that of the SUGMAD Itself, and should believe in and love the true self in this manner. Some believe that the scriptures are the highest one can receive from the MAHANTA, the Living ECK Master. But this is not true. The secrets of spiritual practices, which can be known only by the MAHANTA, cannot be reduced to writing, nor are they clearly mentioned in any scriptures. There are only vague references to them here and there. They serve only as a testimony in those writings. The complete secret can only be imparted by the MAHANTA. The study of books can impart only intellectual knowledge, but books cannot show the way to see the SUGMAD. Books only assist the understanding of the student, for they show only what is morally right and wrong. The chela who is sincere will follow what is right and attain the ECKshar. The roots of passion, anger, greed, attachment, and vanity are within the very core of the mind. They can be destroyed only by such devotion to the MAHANTA, the Living ECK Master, as to how much love is fostered for him. When sufficient love for him is engendered within, the chela's purpose will be accomplished.

Those who waste the whole of their lives in the attachments to this world go alone when they die. They are followed to the graveside by their families, but beyond death they go alone. People are usually troubled when alone, even in this world. At the time of death this loneliness is intensified. One's family may keep company with him so long as he is in this world, but only the MAHANTA can go with him at the time of death. Even the purpose of living in the body can be fulfilled only if one has the company and help of the MAHANTA, the Living ECK Master. If he has the company of the Living ECK Master, there is no pain at the time of death. If one cannot have the ECK Master's outward form with him, he should always keep the Master in his thoughts and heart at all times.

A person may be well-versed in all sorts of religious knowledge, but if he has no love for the ECK, it profits him nothing. The same is true of the chela who may worship the MAHANTA but has no real love for him. So long as there is no love for the ECK, there can be no spiritual unfoldment. Those who never think of the ECK except in times of necessity never make any spiritual progress. But in the case of the one who has deep love for the MAHANTA, the love and spiritual unfoldment becomes great within himself.

The disciple should be unaware of this world in the spiritual sense and should act only as ordered by the ECK. He should not impress his own logic and reasoning upon his spiritual life. As long as he maintains the attitude that he is right about this world and regards himself only a man of the world, he will be just that. His spiritual progress will be slowed to a trickle like that of a stream in the desert during midsummer. If he believes wholly in the MAHANTA, the Living ECK Master, continuing his spiritual exercises and increasing his faith daily in the ECK, he will become a real disciple.

The maya, which holds the whole world in its grip, is itself under the control of the MAHANTA, the Living ECK Master. If anyone is anxious to separate himself from the illusions of the maya, he must seek the help of the MAHANTA. He must do this regardless of praise, slander, or rejection by the world. Only then can he become a true follower of ECK. If he is a disciple of ECK only under pleasant circumstances, ready to drop ECK as soon as he would be slandered or rejected by the world—things which are meant for his spiritual progress—he can never become an initiate of ECK. He can only be a true initiate when he is willing to endure all things in this life.

The root of all bondage in this world is in egotism. When man grasps the principles of ECK, all the principles are grasped; but if he misses one or two, then all have not been grasped. In much the same way, one who enjoys the grace of the MAHANTA gets the thread of his vanity removed and obtains freedom from all bondage of this world. Those who are without the MAHANTA, the Living ECK Master are pagans, little better than those life-forms just below that of man. This statement is meant for the true followers of the ECK, and not for the men of the world who, instead of believing, hold the works of ECK in antagonism.

It is through the Word only that Soul has descended into bondage, and as long as the MAHANTA, the Living ECK Master will withhold the Word from the chela, that Soul is unable to return to Its true heavenly home again. It can only reach those divine planes by traveling the path of ECK via the secret name of God which is imparted to him by the Living ECK Master. There is no other way to escape from the captivity of the lower-world bondage.

It is important to do the things first which are calculated to induce humility. The society of the Mahdis is the best place to develop it, other than the company of the MAHANTA, the Living ECK Master. Those of the clergy who are anxious for wealth and fame are not apt to develop humility; instead, they will gain greed, unhappiness, and vanity. If anyone is anxious to acquire humility, he must first seek the MAHANTA, the Living ECK Master. He should not accept anyone else.

The MAHANTA, the Living ECK Master does not perform miracles. He always acts according to the will of the SUGMAD and keeps the possession of such powers a secret. He may exhibit his powers in miracles if the SUGMAD wills that he should in any particular instance, but not before the world at large. When he performs miracles, it means that he is to leave the world soon, much to the grief of the true followers of ECK. The insincere people gather around him in crowds. Those who are anxious to see miracles are not true seekers.

Soul is surrounded by enemies who are the friends of the Kal. No one is Its friend, not even the mind, which watches Soul just as a cat watches the mouse. Even those Souls who are the followers of Kal and obey its orders suffer pain. All are subject to pain as long as they are in the realm of mind and matter. Those who follow the MAHANTA, the Living ECK Master enjoy his blessings, and even the Kal is afraid of them. It is, therefore, the part of wisdom for one to submit himself to the MAHANTA, for he is able to save him, both in this world and the next.

The followers of the MAHANTA do not feel any pain at the time of death. Rather, they enjoy great peace at this time. They are perfectly conscious of the approaching crisis and attend to all of their affairs in calm detachment.

Their connection with the world is cut off. The fruits of the spiritual exercises, which are hidden to the human eyes but not to those who are the disciples of the MAHANTA, result in the grace of his help when it comes to death in the human body. Faith is a prerequisite to spiritual advancement, for without it spiritual progress is impossible, and nothing can develop; with it those followers can be taken across the borders of death by the MAHANTA, the Living ECK Master, bypass Yama, the King of the Dead, and be placed in that plane which they have earned in their past life.

11

The Culture of Eckankar

Those who follow the teachings of the MAHANTA, the Living ECK Master generally form an inner community which is noticeable on those planes beyond this world. However, there are groups who live together either in communes or within their respective societies as small groups. Yet it can be said that the ECK society is that which is within the whole of the mainstream of any society, in any nation, or on any plane beyond this realm.

This is called a culture within a culture, for the ECK, working as a force, uses Its own, individually or collectively, to bring about changes in various environments. Outwardly, a true follower of ECK is not concerned with reform. He is seeking what is true, and that very search has transforming effects on society. Therefore, the MAHANTA, the Living ECK Master is not seeking followers, nor does he care too much about revolutionary changes, and he certainly is not interested in political reform. Yet wherever he goes there are revolutionary changes which occur and political reform which comes about.

This is done principally through the inner channels, for not once does he preach that changes must be made; but in allowing the ECK to flow through himself, It will bring about many human and spiritual upheavals. If the chela is endowed with the wisdom of the ECK, such changes are always apparent to him, and he can see them where others cannot. He is without doubt, for the MAHANTA always brings truth in a way that even the most simple person can understand.

The culture is the way and the teaching of the ECK. Such is always unique within Itself; and once the ECK has made Its impression on the followers of Its ways, they seem to come together without being urged, because they speak a common language and have the same cause at heart. One of the basic ingredients which brings them together is that of nonviolence. Few, if any, followers of ECK ever believe in force or violence to gain their objectives in the spiritual works of Eckankar. They realize there is no need to do this, because the acts of violence, anger, and complaint really belong to the Kal. These are among the five passions of the mind, and they are the children of the Kal Niranjan; none belong to the chelas of Eckankar.

The community of ECK is international, interplanetary, interpsychic, and interspiritual. This means that the community does exist, but the followers of ECK have intercommunication with one another which isn't found on the visible planes. The community is scattered throughout the worlds of God. Some may be living in communes and others living alone, but between each and all there runs an inner telephone which keeps them together. It is a two-way communication which allows the inner conversations to keep them together.

Those who have reached the Fifth Initiation, that which is called the Mahdis, are banded together in deep spiritual ties, which act as one for all, and all for one. They live within a deep spiritual bond that is all their own. These are known as the Brothers of the Leaf, which has a deeper significance than what is known and seen on the surface. They are few in number, but once anyone becomes a member of this precious little band, he never turns back—he never leaves it, and his goal is always forward, to give help to the rest of the world. He must always be ready to serve those less fortunate than himself.

The community of ECKists, that is those who are initiates, can and do talk, hold conversations, and communicate with one another via the inner channels. This inner communication is hardly known to any of those who practice the methods laid down by the parapsychologists and the psychic practitioners, as well as those who call themselves occultists. It is a method known only to those who have been initiated and found that it is a part of their spiritual exercises.

The reason for failure among so many who take the discourses of Eckankar and cannot practice Soul Travel, or the inner communication with another in the community of heaven, as this is called, is simply that they have no discipline. This discipline is important to everyone who belongs to the ECK culture. Those who practice their spiritual exercises, as laid down in the various discourses and written materials of ECK, will find results in some manner or form.

Those who have gained the true essence between the Second and Fifth Initiations know that it cannot be obtained by recitations, austerities, and vows of silence. No one has ever obtained the secret of the ECK by such exercises, even though he may exhaust himself by the exercises. Only those who have entered into the ECK and have gained the higher degrees of enlightenment through the MAHANTA, the Living ECK Master have been able to enter into the community of heaven. The secret of entrance into this holy community is through submission to the MAHANTA, the Living ECK Master. To give up, to surrender oneself to him, will bring about an opening of the door to the heavenly worlds where dwell those who are the beloved of the MAHANTA, the Living ECK Master.

Therefore, the secret is in self-surrender and devotion to the ECK. It is therefore necessary for all who wish to approach the MAHANTA, the Living ECK Master to do so in the spirit of surrendering. It is not easy for anyone to escape temptation, and many are led astray and are unable to ever enter into the community of the ECKists in the heavenly worlds. But, if they find the MAHANTA, the Living ECK Master, they may easily pass their lives in virtue, living among their own. But, if anyone accepts only an educated person as the Guru, and is led into the worship of him and other idolatrous things, he only wastes his time and cannot escape the bondage of birth and death. It is necessary that he should find the perfect Vi-Guru, the MAHANTA—even if he dies in the search. So long as his quest is in earnest, he need not worry, for the desire to find the MAHANTA, the Living ECK Master is itself worship of the SUGMAD, and It will certainly manifest Itself to all of Its disciples in due time, in the form of the MAHANTA, the Living ECK Master.

It is unfortunate in these times that people, instead of believing in the works of ECK, run after the teachings of the orthodox and the false, even without any visible evidence in their favor. The Kal has so cleverly designed this world that people easily believe what suits their purpose. They will not believe the MAHANTA, the Living ECK Master, who tries to present truth to all in the best possible manner, but demand miracles of him. This shows they are the victims of the Kal, because they believe what his followers say without evidence, while they demand miracles of the MAHANTA.

Ignorance is so prevalent in the human race that many

persons wish to join so-called holy orders and waste their lives listening to the educated who have had no experience in life. Instead of joining such orders, they should seek the perfect Master, the MAHANTA, the Living ECK Master, and spend their time in his service. They would be taught to perform the inner spiritual exercises and would become ascetics in the true sense of the word. Instead of wasting their time, they would eventually reach their true home, the spiritual community of Honardi, in the world of the Atma Lok, the fifth region of Soul.

No one can escape the round of birth and death by following the pseudoteachers and masters, or even Brahm, the lord of the Mental realm, who is the founder of the orthodox religions in the lower worlds. Yet he, himself, cannot go beyond the cycle of transmigration. This is true, especially in present times when the majority of pseudoteachers are merely educated men, not true teachers or masters; for one never finds the real Master until he meets the MAHANTA, the Living ECK Master. All are in the cycle of transmigration because the Living ECK Master is the only one who can save people from remaining in this cycle and lead them back to their real home.

The spiritual community of ECKists is that place in which the hearts of all those following ECK dwell. It is here that they can communicate with one another over vast distances and bring about love, wisdom, and happiness with each other. No other followers of any master, teacher, cult, occult or religious group can do this. It is the privilege of the ECKists to be able to communicate with the MAHANTA, the Living ECK Master in his subtle form, and with one another in their own subtle bodies. This is the defeat of the Kal and that which brings about the tremendous love and understanding that each ECKist has for the MAHANTA, the Living ECK Master and for one another.

The Kal Niranjan has spread his net in this world. Those who are engaged in all manner of worship and devotion imagine they are worshipping the Supreme Deity, receiving praise from their fellow man for their holiness, but are found, upon examination, to be far removed from the real teachings of Eckankar. They busy themselves with sacred places, fasts, and idols, spending their time in recitations, ceremonies, and ritualistic observances. This sort of worship only induces vanity. The SUGMAD is not pleased with such forms, nor can they ever liberate anyone from death. The masses are ever driven on, in the cycle of births and deaths. If anyone is to escape this cycle, he must devote himself to the MAHANTA, the Living ECK Master and serve through him. There is no other way of escape.

Many persons regard certain scriptures as their guide and teacher, but there is no benefit to be derived from such belief, and no commandment for it. No scripture or sacred writing can help anyone spiritually. It is not possible to serve any written scripture, for it is inanimate and without help of any nature. True devotion lies in carrying out the only real commandment that most written scriptures give; that is, seeking out the Living ECK Master, submitting to him, and carrying out his instructions. Those who believe in substituting any written works for the MAHANTA, the Living ECK Master are like image worshippers. This is certainly true of those who follow the path of orthodox religions.

Those who fall into this trap have created their mistake because they have not found an honest teacher who will point the way to the MAHANTA, the Living ECK Master. Therefore they are being led in ignorance and superstition. Those who teach them have never surrendered themselves to the Living ECK Master, hence they know nothing about the true nature of the SUGMAD and mislead their followers. Those of the so-called holy orders and orthodox religions, occult followings, and others know nothing about the MAHANTA, the Living ECK Master, nor do they understand what he is. They are the ritualistic slaves of books, scriptures, customs, and rites, and likewise enslave their own followers. This never happens in the spiritual community of ECK, where those who can communicate between one another via the inner channels have pure freedom.

However, it is only the MAHANTA, the Living ECK Master who is capable of teaching the works of ECK, that path which leads to liberation of Souls. Fortunate are those who believe the truth of the SUGMAD and seek out the MAHANTA. The masses always look for miracles and want a show of supernatural powers; because of this, they are not fit for the spiritual company of the MAHANTA, the Living ECK Master. Such demands cause strain on the body and mind of those who make them. Blessed indeed are those who believe that the MAHANTA and the Holy Name are supreme.

Worldly people do not believe that there is a spiritual community of the ECKists. They think in terms of the outer things, like good clothes and dainty dishes. The food which is dearest to the chela is that of the words and discourses of the MAHANTA, the Living ECK Master. Faith in the MAHANTA is the armor of the chela and the attitude of the true and pure seekers of truth. Each loves the things which the world utterly rejects as being impractical and much too dreamlike.

The clergy and the pseudoteachers consider their sacred scriptures superior to the ECK. They are making the supreme mistake in their spiritual quest. They regard some of their own members as saints, even though they have made but little spiritual progress. They do not know, in reality, what truth is and seem to care little about it, but only care to dress themselves in splendid robes and strut among the followers. These persons are not equal to the humblest disciple of the MAHANTA, the Living ECK Master.

Those who believe that a good education will give them greater spiritual progress are working in an illusion. It will help them find employment, of course, which is good, but as far as helping them to unfold spiritually, it is not worth much. Naturally, employment is needed, for every chela must stand on his own feet and accept his responsibility here in this world and those worlds beyond.

The MAHANTA, the Living ECK Master has come into this world during the age of the Kali Yuga for the salvation of Souls, and to make known the mistakes and defects of all religions, while at the same time to point to the straight path of liberation for all Souls. The masses will not believe the MAHANTA, but will believe the varied sacred scriptures by hearing or reading them. No spiritual exercises are required for such reading or hearing the scriptures read. The people do not believe the word of the MAHANTA, the Living ECK Master; otherwise they would have learned the system of spiritual exercises long ago and would now be performing them. Such exercises cannot be learned by mere study of discourses and books, which usually produce more vanity, further rendering the mind impure and unfit for the purpose of spiritual exercises. One often comes across those who talk much about the Spiritual Exercises of ECK but who perform none of them.

All true seekers of the SUGMAD must find the Living ECK Master and surrender themselves to him, because this is the only way of purifying the mind in this Kali Yuga age. As long as the mind is not purified, there can be no liberation of Soul. Only the MAHANTA, the Living ECK Master is familiar with the Ocean of Love and Mercy and can take his disciples to this final region. No one else knows the supreme secrets of the path of ECK. Only by his grace is liberation attained. There is no other way into the worlds of God.

The MAHANTA, the Living ECK Master is the only being who is eligible to make known the true path to God. All others mislead their followers, because they themselves are misled. The blind who themselves have lost the way are misleading others instead of serving them, as they pretend to do. How can the blind lead the blind? This is why it is so important that the MAHANTA, the Living ECK Master shall be sought out. So long as he is not found, the inner secret of the path of ECK cannot be known. The MAHANTA is the one who is devoted to the Word of God. He reveals the inner secret of the Word and shows the way for Soul's return to the heavenly worlds, where It is truly liberated.

The MAHANTA, the Living ECK Master cannot be judged by his external appearance. The blind of the world cannot judge the MAHANTA, but he can manifest to them in any way he chooses. It is best to know and understand, in the beginning, that he gives to the chela the secret of the body, that he teaches the works of Eckankar, and that he himself is engrossed in the true Word of God. If the chela finds him, it can be assured that he may be accepted by the MAHANTA, the Living ECK Master.

The inner secret of the body can be made known only by the MAHANTA, and he is the only one empowered by the SUGMAD to reveal it. The MAHANTA, the Living ECK Master does not depend upon any book or scripture for his teachings. He is the true representative of the SUGMAD and in possession of the Word. As long as one does not practice the Spiritual Exercises of ECK as taught by the MAHANTA, depending upon his grace, he will never reach the region of the Ocean of Love and Mercy. Out of the MAHANTA's mere will and grace, the MAHANTA can redeem a being in any way he likes. Therefore the belief in and devotion to him are essential. It is entirely within his prerogative to decide the course a chela should take; that is, he knows the inner workings and the thoughts of his chela so well that he can direct him in the way he knows is necessary for the spiritual welfare of that individual.

If any lover of God believes that he can eventually become that which enters into the heavenly kingdom without the MAHANTA, the Living ECK Master, he is mistaken, because it is utterly impossible to find one's way into the upper heavens, or to become a member of the spiritual community of ECKists, without the Living ECK Master. Even this longing for God may vanish in the presence of an imperfect preceptor, and the desire to find the Living ECK Master may disappear. He who seeks God will not have any success until he submits himself to the perfect Master, the MAHANTA, the Living ECK Master. On the other hand, the company of an imperfect or pseudo teacher will develop only vanity in the chela and lead to failure. When one has the Living ECK Master, there can be no failure.

Resignation to the will of the MAHANTA, the Living ECK Master is difficult but of vast importance to the chela. Many may say they have submitted to him, but, as a matter of fact, anyone who has truly submitted to the Living ECK Master holds no other being as dear to himself as the MAHANTA. Only these chelas are entitled to claim that they have completely submitted to the MAHANTA, the Living ECK Master. Those who know the secret of the Living Word and are in the holy service of the ECK are extremely fortunate, for the company and the society of the ECKists in their community, as well as that of the MAHANTA, the Living ECK Master, is precious in this age of the Kali Yuga.

That Soul which is not in the works of ECK is in the clutches of the Kal Niranjan, the god and creator of the lower worlds. He brings life, creates, nourishes, and destroys the universe. He has separated Soul from Its real form, subjected It to the cycles of births and rebirths, and associated It with all sorts of enemies, within and without. This has entangled Soul in a net of passion, anger, greed, attachment, and vanity; while externally It is attached to mother, father, son, wife, friends, wealth, honor, and all the sensual pleasures of the world. What profit, then, is there to worship a god who has made so much trouble in this world for Soul? It is, then, the best of wisdom to turn to the MAHANTA, the Living ECK Master, by whose grace alone can Soul escape the net spread by the Kal Niranjan and attain the regions of heavenly peace.

The secret name of God, which the MAHANTA, the Living ECK Master may reveal to the initiates through the Mahdis, is not to be found in any scriptures. Only he who possesses this name is entitled to be called the MAHANTA. Many persons belonging to different holy orders call themselves saints and masters, but they are not. Only he can attain the MAHANTAship by being chosen during his early youth by the great ECK Masters and trained through childhood, youth, and maturity. Even so, he may fall by the wayside before he is able to accept the Rod of ECK Power. He is constantly under the watchful eyes of the ECK Masters who have him in training during those years. If he falters or fails, it is possible that he may be taken out of this position; and if he falters in his responsibility while serving as the MAHANTA, the Living ECK Master, it is possible that he must step down for another to take his place.

Vanity is the greatest Kal passion which those in training for the ECK Mastership must watch. It is subtle and can reach out, putting its claws into the mind and heart of the trainee, and without his knowing it, he practices vanity. Those in training serve their Master with care and happiness. The eyes of the trainee are blessed by looking at the MAHANTA, the Living ECK Master.

Within the works of Eckankar there is no worship of those who are the leaders in the teachings. If anyone feels that he must hold a strict worship of the MAHANTA, the Living ECK Master or any of the Mahdis, those who are the Higher Initiates, they are mistaken. The SUGMAD, in Its own Self, never asks any of those who are following the path of ECK to worship It. This is different from all the orthodox religions, occult groups, and sects of the lower worlds. The Kal Niranjan demands worship of himself, because he is an inferior being to all in ECK and is never sure of himself.

The Kal requests that all love him. That all persons, whoever they might be, love him and worship him, because his claims are that he is the Almighty and must be revered. Any religious group making claims of this nature is false and should never be considered by the chela as being a true source of reaching God. This is the illusion that the Kal has established, the worship of himself in an illusionary manner, making everyone believe that he is the greatest of all beings and must be worshipped. The human race must have a standard by which each individual is able to find love for something outside itself; therefore the Kal establishes a worship of himself. The ECK does not demand such materialistic belief, nor does It, in a sense, ask for a faith, which often turns out to be a blinding belief in, and never a return of, anything for the chela. The ECK gives and receives. Those who have faith in It will also receive the faith of the ECK within themselves. If anyone admires, adores, and has faith in the ECK, It will return these a hundredfold; and if any chela loves and respects the MAHANTA, he will receive these qualities back in the same amount of love and respect, only a thousand times more. The same is true of the love for the SUGMAD, only it will be returned in multitudinous quantities for the chela. There is never a one-way love between the higher ones and the individual, except in the case of the MAHANTA, the Living ECK Master, who loves all creatures, persons, and beings equally. He never loves them simply because they love him, but because they are part of that which *is*. He, himself, loves all, whether or not they love him. Whatever is good for each individual is equally good for the MAHANTA, the Living ECK Master. Therefore, he never deprives anyone of anything, nor gives to anyone something which is greater than he gives another. All things are given in proportion to how much the chela can receive.

If it appears that he takes away something in the material world, then he must replace it in another way for that individual with whom he is working to reach perfection. Some persons imagine they have renounced everything for the MAHANTA, yet they continue to read the orthodox religious scriptures. This is a mistake, for they have not yet tested their minds and senses; so when they come face-to-face with the allurements of sensual pleasures or are flattered by riches, the wealthy, or the powerful, they see how the mind yields to such seductions. They will also see how the mind reacts to censure, dishonor, and the denial of the objects of desire. They will find that worldly desires are more powerful than spiritual ones. It is a great error to look upon outward renunciation, detachment, or the reading of books as true spiritual attainments. By such means the mind is never defeated. The only way the mind can be conquered is by surrender to the MAHANTA, the Living ECK Master and the Spiritual Exercises of ECK, as laid down by him.

When one has no idea of such things, he cannot expect

to control the mind and make spiritual progress. The masses of people are even more ignorant because they follow the ignorant and so drown themselves in ignorance while depending on the drowning to save them.

Most of those who are among the educated and sophisticated will make claims that it is a natural habit for the mind and senses to indulge in anger and other sensual pleasures; that Soul is separated by a spiritual gulf between the senses and Itself. Even many of the clergy will speak of righteousness or hold anger. But this is a mistake, for it is only the Kal which brings about the problem, as he alone will encourage the building of the mind, through education, while neglecting the spiritual self.

There is no difference between the priest and the layman who secretly entertains the desires for education and sensual pleasures at the expense of Soul. Both are subject to birth and death, rebirths and more deaths. They are simply reaping the rewards for their actions. They are forgetting the higher teachings and giving way to their own sensual indulgences. It can be seen that such persons become angry and impatient when they are dishonored or criticized, or when they see others honored and praised. They are filled with pain, and they devise all sorts of schemes for the fulfillment of their desires and even ask for help to accomplish their purposes. For their own benefit, they should give up their pseudoteachers, who are merely the results of their own education, and the sharpening of their senses on words and books, and seek out the MAHANTA, the Living ECK Master and submit themselves to him.

No other path will lead to emancipation, for no priest nor clergyman can redeem any individual on earth. They claim that their founder and savior can, but this is not true, for he is not a living Master, and the saviors who are worshipped today in this world are gone. They have entered into other planes, and their individual help for the masses has passed. Only a Living ECK Master can help, for he is here and now present in this world, ready to give of himself, here and beyond. Only he can spiritually feed the hungry and poor, whereas no priest is able to save one Soul nor feed the spiritual hunger. It is essential that the chela shall sacrifice both his mind and body via the MAHANTA, the Living ECK Master for everything in ECK.

Many educated and clever persons are not fit for the society of the MAHANTA, because they are filled with vanity and do not believe in him. He tells all people who will listen that he sees and knows, but the educated depend on what they hear or read, and wish to set up their own way because of their own superior intelligence. But their minds are filled with vanity, wavering thoughts, and sensual desires. They desire miracles, but the MAHANTA, the Living ECK Master does not exhibit miracles, for love is not based upon miracles. Miracles are shown only to true seekers who believe in and love the MAHANTA. These disciples are shown miracles at the proper time, but those who are not in earnest, being desirous only of pleasure and fame, are not worthy to see miracles or even to stand before the MAHANTA. Those who are the true followers of the MAHANTA should be wary of such persons.

Worldly people are afraid of death because they are engrossed in the world and its attached pleasures. But an ECKist is not afraid of death, knowing that this world is full of pain and it is not his home. He lives in this world simply as a traveler and is anxious for the joy of seeing the radiant form of the MAHANTA, the Living ECK Master. Therefore, he feels no pain at the approach of death. During life he becomes accustomed to passing through the changes of death and remains immersed in the joy of often viewing the Atma Sarup, the radiant form, of the MAHANTA.

There are no special rules in ECK for people to abide by, for the MAHANTA does not wish to compel people to believe in him or the ECK. He wishes to correct false beliefs only by teaching about Eckankar. The superior type of person, one who has listened to ECK over the centuries in other bodies and has gained much spiritual unfoldment, believes in him and the ECK. But the majority of people take a longer time to deliberate and come to the conclusion that ECK is the only way into the heavenly worlds. At the same time there are still others who do not accept nor understand the MAHANTA and will not stay with ECK. They become floaters and weave in and out of the various religions.

However, the ECK chelas should not be impatient with any of these people; nor should they be anxious that all should be compelled to believe in the MAHANTA, the Living ECK Master, or for those that get away from the society of ECKists. There is no gain for the chela if such persons go away, but they themselves suffer loss. If these nonbelievers would stay in the groups, they would, in time, evolve by constant association and begin to conduct themselves as true followers of the ECK. It only takes time, and nothing is gained for either side by asking them to believe or to leave.

When the individual chela cannot understand the physical form of the MAHANTA, the Living ECK Master, it is for certain that he cannot accept or understand the subtle Atma Sarup, the Soul body, of the MAHANTA. It is necessary to devote oneself to the Living ECK Master in order to become an ECKist. If anyone should turn away from the Living ECK Master and try to make claims that they are on the same level as he in spiritual unfoldment, or that they themselves are above him, in order to gain a certain following, then they are adding to their karma by telling falsehoods, and they are doomed on the path to the spiritual worlds. No man is the equal of the MAHANTA, the Living ECK Master, and no man becomes a Master until he has been so designated by the MAHANTA, the Living ECK Master. For any chela who leaves the MAHANTA and establishes himself as a master to gather up a following does so at his own spiritual risk. His followers do not know that he is acting out of ego and vanity, and his spiritual growth and unfoldment has halted and will not be resumed until he returns to the MAHANTA, surrenders himself fully, asks for forgiveness, and allows himself to be taken in hand once again. Otherwise he will struggle through life after life, building up his karma, until the day comes when he realizes that he has been led astray by the Kal Niranjan and rushes to find the MAHANTA, the Living ECK Master in order to get back on the path of ECK once more.

Priests and the clergy are honored in this world, but such persons are revered only by those who are not anxious for spiritual perfection. They do not possess the secret which, if known, would lead each Soul to Its true place in the spiritual heavens. Those priests and clergy have acquired only knowledge, or joined religious orders for the sake of their livelihood. A true seeker of the ECK cannot have much regard for such persons. Outwardly he might entertain them and even donate to them of his means, but he will not give his mind and heart to them. Such persons do not belong on the same spiritual level as the chelas of Eckankar, but if they are sincere, they may gain some enlightenment. Otherwise they will only disgrace themselves.

For anyone to go to a place where the MAHANTA, the Living ECK Master might be, in order to enter into a false and insincere discussion, is only to belittle himself. The MAHANTA will show great forbearance, but usually his chelas are not always so generous. The true ECKists are always selected from the masses, while the hypocritical and the insincere will not remain very long.

The Mahdis, who are the initiates of the Fifth Plane, are the gatekeepers of the high spiritual worlds. They must protect all who are eligible in entering into these worlds. No preacher nor priest can or does have the same spiritual rank as the Mahdis, and they are the only ones other than the MAHANTA who are able to expound the teachings of the ECK. They surround and protect the MAHANTA as needed, although this is hardly ever necessary. But they are always there to serve as his spiritual bodyguard, should the need arise.

If there were power in the name of the SUGMAD, or his secret name, alone, surely those who know it would have great influence. But this proves that power does not lie in the Word alone; it is in the MAHANTA, the Living ECK Master. Fortunate are those who are devoted to the MAHANTA, the Living ECK Master, for even those who have committed foul deeds and created the worst of karma are forgiven when they have submitted to the Living ECK Master. But those who have been supposedly cleansed but refuse to submit to the Living ECK Master will stand in the same class as those who have committed trespasses against the MAHANTA.

Those who are believers in name only of the ECK (expecting It to take care of them), and are vain, haughty, and do not take the word of the Living ECK Master seriously, will always have to bear the burden of their troubles. The commandments of the Shariyat-Ki-Sugmad are for everyone to seek out the MAHANTA, the Living ECK Master for liberation. That none should accept the scriptures as a substitute for the MAHANTA, the Living ECK Master. Scriptures are usually words without life and cannot give the help which is necessary. Only the Living ECK Master is able to give spiritual assistance to anyone who is able to accept him and the living words which he may give to them. No person who is versed only in religious literature can secure the Jivan Mukti, spiritual salvation or liberation of Soul, during this lifetime.

During this age of the Kali Yuga, the MAHANTA, the Living ECK Master is the real salvation. All who follow his commandment, that is perform the sort of devotion he outlines for his chelas in this age, will be emancipated. But those who reject this commandment, engaging in any other ways of devotion if there are such, will increase their vanity, and they will never get off the wheel of life which keeps spinning around like a squirrel's cage. They may forsake their devotion but never their vanity and their ego, for often their leaders will never let them go, because their efforts on such paths often form a religion, which is a source of income for the priestcraft.

The human body is impermanent, and it is foolish to be proud of its beauty. Just as the leaves of the tree will fall in the autumn of the year, so will the beauty of the human body fade in its brief time here on earth. Only Soul is beautiful, and nothing can bring about beauty of the human form in comparison with the beauty of Soul. Relationships with people outside the ECK bring pain more than happiness, and this is why the ECKists all band together in a spiritual community. They are looking for the best in life and will give up everything to be with their own under the MAHANTA, the Living ECK Master.

Man is subjected to three illnesses which are manifest and three which are hidden. He is anxious to treat the manifest ills but is ignorant of those which are hidden. Only the Living ECK Master can make known to the chela the ills which are within. If one is fortunate to find the ECK Master, he will become aware of all his ills and consider the means for their removal. The first of the outer ills is that of constant birth and rebirth. Second is that of the struggle with the mind, which is the universal power of the lower worlds. Third is that of absolute ignorance. It is evident that none of these ills can be resolved by merely reading books or by following a pseudomaster.

The three inner ills are vanity, anger, and lust. It is also evident that none of these can be cured by book reading or trying to follow the adjuncts of any sacred scriptures of religious nature. It is only the MAHANTA, the Living ECK Master who is able to bring about a healing for any of these ills that man may have, both outwardly and inwardly.

Only those who are seeking the sublime in the SUGMAD are able to find the communication between themselves, as vehicles or instruments, in the spiritual community of the higher worlds. If they seek the ECK through the MAHANTA, the Living ECK Master, It shall be found, and they shall gain life everlasting.

12
The Circles of ECK Initiations

The initiation for the seeker of God on the path of Eckankar is the gateway into the mysteries of the SUGMAD. It is through the rites of initiation that the uninitiated gains deliverance from the lower self and enters into the worlds of freedom and immortality.

The initiation into Eckankar is the true way, and the radiant form of the MAHANTA, the Vi-Guru, the Light Giver, lights up every Soul who enters into it, with the sacred word for each, which is personal and secret to each one who is looking for enlightenment in God.

There are many initiations in Eckankar, thereby giving each Soul an opportunity to advance to a higher degree of spiritual unfoldment. Twelve initiations include the whole of those for the ones who are traveling the path of ECK. However, it's found that the very advanced, those in training for the MAHANTAship, can go further, for their greater spiritual advancement, in initiations above these twelve so mentioned here.

The initiations as given at the present time in the world of matter are (first) the Acolyte, the initiate of the First

Circle; (second) the Arahata, the initiate of the Second Circle; (third) the Ahrat, the initiate of the Third Circle; (fourth) the Chiad, the initiate of the Fourth Circle; (fifth) the Mahdis, the initiate of the Fifth Circle; (sixth) the Shraddha, the initiate of the Sixth Circle; (seventh) the Bhakti, the initiate of the Seventh Circle; (eighth) the Gyanee, the initiate of the Eighth Circle; (ninth) the Maulani, the initiate of the Ninth Circle; (tenth) the Adepiseka, the initiate of the Tenth Circle; (eleventh) the Kevalshar, the initiate of the Eleventh Circle; and (twelfth) the Maharaji, the initiate of the SUGMAD Realization. This is the Allness in the Allness.

The initiate is given a secret, but sacred, word in each initiation, which is all his own, and it supersedes all other words which he uses in the Spiritual Exercises of Eckankar. It must never be divulged to another person, even within one's own family, unless the initiation is given together.

When the family takes the Second Initiation together, and its members consist of children who are unable to understand the meaning of any word which has been given to them, these young ones will need an explanation when of age to grasp truth mentally. This means that the child does not have to be initiated again, but made to understand that he has been initiated into Eckankar and may practice the word given at the time of initiation. The child need not be present at the ceremony and may even be born after the parents receive their Second Initiation. The age that the child can be told about his initiation depends upon his mental development. It also depends upon the parent's judgment about him and his ability to grasp the explanation of what has taken place.

There is also the thought of what is going to happen to the child when he comes to that stage in his life, perhaps as a youth or during his early adult years, when he might feel that ECK may not be his way of life. There is not much to do about the decision which he will make, because if he wishes to step away from his own native teachings, it is entirely up to him. However, since he has been initiated into ECK, there is the knowledge that he cannot leave Eckankar, although it may appear to be that he does so. He who enters into Eckankar must be aware of his responsibility toward himself and others, and above all the ECK. If he has no pure motivation for becoming a part of the ECK, there is a possibility that everything will reverse itself and cause him problems.

The *Acolyte,* who is a member of the First Circle of ECK, receives his initiation during the dream state. When he begins the ECK discourses, even though they might be the most elementary ones, he is eligible for initiation after six months. His initiation comes in the dream state, which is often vivid to him and can be recalled after awakening from the dream state. Others may not be this fortunate and may find themselves unable to remember anything, although they are aware that something happened; they may write or talk with the MAHANTA, the Living ECK Master or one of his representatives about it.

Sometimes the Acolyte looks upon this initiation as merely a gesture toward the spiritual life and takes it in a light vein—that all he is doing is entering into the ECK out of curiosity or because of some benefit which may come from belonging to the ECK. If he does not remember anything about the First Initiation, which was received in the dream state, he has missed a great deal, because there is a deep responsibility which goes with his spiritual development during the time he spends in the First Circle of ECK initiation.

The chela may not realize that he has entered into the heart of life when he has received the First Initiation. This means that he is not able to leave Eckankar, should he desire to ever do so. Nobody can leave ECK if he has become an initiate, for this is impossible. It is like saying that one wants to drop out of life. Nobody can leave ECK, because ECK is life, and life is ECK. However, few ever realize this, for they cannot seem to find what they are seeking, and this something—or what we think of as the unknown—is missing. They cannot grasp or understand just what it is that happened to themselves, but usually feel that it is nothing, because they can neither describe it nor find any description of what took place. This causes unhappiness, and they are liable to dismiss the whole affair as if nothing happened to them. This is a great mistake, for sooner or later they will recall what really happened.

The whole Eckankar movement is rather that of a secret society; the world knows that it exists, but they do not understand what it is and many times do not even try to find out. The veil of mystery which surrounds it still holds, and most people do not know today what ECK is and consists of in Itself. The mind is incapable of grasping reality; therefore, it is necessary to undertake a course of discipline that enables one to take the path of ECK that will allow the lower emotional and intellectual centers to come into contact with the higher ones. This is what the First Initiation is all about, but few persons, if any, know about this.

Man is a machine ruled entirely by his subconscious machinery; in other words he becomes a creature of habit. The First Initiation teaches him how to withdraw from everything in this world, and from himself. This is the state of self-remembering. It is to realize that he is perceiving, or otherwise sensing, the object of his sensations as the Higher Self and, at the same time, is aware of himself as the observer of what is going on within himself. Thus he has a twofold duty: to be in the center of the activity, whether it is Soul Travel or not, and at the same time to be the observer of this inner activity.

Man, in his ordinary mind, is a machine, and the First Initiation awakens him to his potential. His first Self-Realized state comes when he begins to perceive the world objectively, as it really is, and not as the veil of subjective illusions under the rule of the Kal Niranjan.

It is what one acquires in the initiation of the Second Circle that starts him on the path to Self-Realization, which he will acquire on the Fifth Plane, the Soul Plane. It isn't knowledge that he will get through the senses that will be of any use to him. Man is capable of writing learned books and undertaking all sorts of pseudoscholarly activities, and still be sunk in deep sleep with no possibility of awakening and with no understanding. Among such learned ignoramuses are men of authority in this world.

The initiation of the Second Circle is where the limited consciousness in man comes into the state of decision. This decision is what road shall the chela take: the left-hand path, which is that of black magic; the right-hand path, which is that of white magic; or the center path, which is the road of the purified Soul.

If the chela decides to take the middle path, he is safe from all evil. If he takes either of the other paths, he is not sure of himself and will come to naught on all his endeavors to achieve life as it is in ECK. He becomes subject to karma and accident. He becomes the mechanical man subject to the statistical law, which is that of accidents, which applies to all circumstances in his life.

He falls under the principle of conscious evolution, which is entirely opposite to that of mechanical evolution. All conscious evolution is carried out through opposing mechanical evolution by substituting conscious action and deeds. It is only by destroying mechanicalness that the initiate is able to achieve perfection in consciousness.

This transformation brings about the first stage of Self-Realization, and those who enter into the Second Initiation of Eckankar must learn that here discipline starts. Any of the five vices of the mind that he has with him will start to be given up. Unless he does this, there are no other initiations available for him. Also it is here that he receives his first personal word, which will go with him through the period between the Second and Third Initiations. He is the *Arahata,* the teacher, who gives the knowledge of ECK to the Acolyte and those outside the works.

The *Ahrat* is the initiate of the Third Circle. This is the Causal world in which the initiate must learn to look at his past lives in order to live in the present. He receives another personal, but secret word which is not for sharing with anyone. This initiation word will be kept and used for his spiritual exercises during the period in which he serves as an initiate of the Third Circle.

Those who have taken this initiation come under the cycle of the threes in which, accordingly, every phenomenon, every action, every event, every physical and psychological change is the result of an instant action of the three forces which come under the Kal Niranjan. These forces are the positive, the negative, and the neutralizing force. They appear in the second field of initiation; that is, the initiation of the Second Circle, whereby one must make the choice of which way he wants to go to find himself. Within the Second Initiation they are recognized as three roads, or paths, which branch off simultaneously and give the initiate a choice of which way he wants to go.

Perpetual change is the very essence of manifestation, and in that transmutation, the medium for the action of the neutralizing force, by this very change, now becomes the medium through which the active force of ECK acts and enters into that Soul which has selected the middle path for perfection.

The aspect of the number of threes is that it is directly connected with the evolution of consciousness. This means that the conscious evolution in any sphere is guided only by the inner knowledge as to how to fill in those areas created by aberrations and actions of men, especially in the case of fear. Man's behavior has always been triggered by fear. This knowledge alone about him has been used throughout history to degrade him. But the mechanical man has never been able to recognize the insidious mental degradation of superstitions and the social, pseudoscientific, and pseudoreligious actions which have crippled his mind and left Soul untouched. Thus the Third Initiation will begin the true unfoldment of the consciousness into true spirituality.

The initiation of the Fourth Circle is that of the intellectual realm. It is the evolution, or development, of the mind in the results of the power of sensing time, matter, energy, and space. This is a remarkable development in man when he begins to have an insight on all these phenomena of nature. But when he begins to realize that these are all illusions, as he will when entering into the Fifth Plane of initiation, he has started arriving at perfection.

The initiate of the Fourth Circle is the *Chiad.* It is here that he realizes that the five passions of the mind are the enemy that must be overcome. The function of this realm is thought, and the evolution of intelligence is his greatest gain. But it must always be remembered that this is not the final answer to life, as so many believe. If man depends upon thought alone, he will be most unhappy, because thought and intelligence only lead to unhappiness. Mind, consciousness, and intelligence are the ruling factors upon this plane. The outward manifestation of these three is thought, which so often becomes confused when trying to analyze the works of ECK, or what could be called the chewing of the mental processes on some parts of the ECK works.

The evolution of the intelligence that is in the Fourth Circle, the Mental Plane, is the gradual rising out of the world of psychic reality. This illusionary world is typified in the Indian philosophy by the word *maya,* which means illusion. In the Buddhist philosophy it is known as *mara,* and in Christianity as Satan, or the devil. It is known in the works of ECK as the Kal Niranjan, king of the lower worlds.

The gradual emergence of the higher states of consciousness begins in the Mental worlds. Man's perceptions on any concept which is beyond him develops into trust and faith that all will be well provided. He will leave the ECK alone and let It work in him to grow into the mighty stream, which It assuredly will, in time. This is the development of the progressive knowledge of the SUGMAD; it will create the illusions of problems, because man will not want to turn from his acquired knowledge, gained from books and discourses, to enter into the full trust of his inner senses. He wants to let himself argue and chew mentally over the aspects of the illusions, creating damage to his faith, his health, and his thinking process. Thus he becomes like a cork on the waves of a great ocean, tossed about in the storms, and has little control over his destiny.

This is the highest of the psychic worlds, and man still suffers under the illusions of space and time. He still sees all time as motion and thinks in terms of traveling inwardly through time and space. Those who believe in Soul Travel as motion in time and space are suffering under the illusions of the Kal. They are thinking, then, in terms of the movement of Soul through space and time. This is the belief of those who are outside of the works of ECK and have little knowledge of It.

Neither reason nor logic offer any way to find truth. Both deal merely with the world of appearances. Only the ECK can give the initiate an opportunity to rise above the Mental Plane and enter into the heavenly worlds. But it's found that the growth of consciousness is frequently accomplished by certain mental distresses, and also by physical illnesses. The latter indicates that, with mental changes, deep-seated and lingering remains of old illnesses will come to the surface and be passed off. The body slowly adapts itself to the new mental state.

The *Mahdis* is the initiate of the Fifth Circle. He finds himself above the psychic worlds, in the first of the true worlds of Spirit, which is a new and different world. Man, in an ordinary state of mind, has a balance, although it is a false balance, but when he reaches this world, all this is swept away, and a new and truer one must be found. It is during the first few weeks or months that the initiate is on trial, for he has left the beaten track of the ordinary seeker of truth, and attacks upon himself must be expected before he settles into the true ways of the Mahdis.

This is the period in which the Mahdis learns that foxes have holes and birds have nests, but he who dwells in the realm of the Atma Lok has no place to call his home. This is why none but an ECKist can recognize the nature of the individuality of his fellow ECKist and understand the problems which arise; all of which become a part of each initiate in the Fifth Circle, for it is here that he first faces what is known as truth, or the Reality of God. If he fails the tests which must be confronted constantly during his daily life, then he could slip back into the world of the mind, where the mind itself chews upon all ideas and thoughts before releasing them, thus giving rise to the phrase "dwellers on the threshold"; for this is actually the entrance into the first plane of enlightenment, that which is called the Atma Lok.

The initiation of the Fifth Circle is sometimes known as the transfiguration. This transfiguration takes place when the mind has finally come under control and is balanced with the rest of the personality so that the fire of Soul and the Light of the plane, along with the ECK Sound Current, affects it, reflects upon it, and can permanently illuminate the personality. From this time forth the Mahdis is an illuminated person. He knows and sees the spiritual realities and understands those around him, and his and their standards of achievements.

He begins to use and control all the psychic faculties within himself for a greater cause. These are interjected into his own spiritual senses, to be used to work practically and systematically for the progress of the whole human race and those beings in every plane within the universes of God. When the mind, and all its aspects within the human self, has come under control of the individual Soul, there is a new type of person. He is now ruled by Soul and can view all life from this lofty position. By this time his consciousness is focused in the spiritual planes of the Fifth Circle, and he begins to organize his life from this position.

This is the new consciousness for the old. It has no connections with institutions, rituals, ceremonies, and rites, but is concerned entirely with one's evolution to states of the higher worlds. The spiritual exercise with its individual, special word given in this initiation develops new ways for breaking up conceptual thought patterns, or thoughts based on evidence of the senses. This is the first of those worlds in which there is no meaning to time and space. This will bring about a new means of understanding for the initiate and, at the same time, lift him into the higher worlds.

The *Shraddha* is the initiate of the Sixth Circle, which is the Alakh Lok. It is found that with this initiation comes complete sacrifice and uttermost suffering. The period preceding is, therefore, called the way of pain and unhappiness. It is during this initiation that the initiate must lose everything in life that means anything to him and sacrifice himself even unto death. If the Acolyte, the initiate of the First Circle, knew what lay ahead for him, he might leave the path of ECK at that point. But by the time he has come to the Sixth Circle he has been tested time and again by the MAHANTA, the Living ECK Master. He has become so strong as Soul, and his character so expanded, his inner knowledge so great and his sense of values so different, that if he could look forward to what is in store for him through the ECK, he would consider what he must do and pay the price; it would mean nothing.

After the Sixth Initiation, the initiate can work consciously with the ECK Masters and beings of the various planes with intelligence and consciousness of what is taking place. His knowledge of the universes of God is ever-expanding, and now he sees it extending far beyond the material universe into the worlds of the true heavens. He has become more wholly the spiritual man, which he has struggled all these many lifetimes to become, and never succeeded until the moment he was chosen by the MAHANTA, the Living ECK Master to take the initiation of the Shraddha, the initiation of the Sixth Circle.

No longer does he need anything in the psychic and materialistic worlds, for he has now fully surrendered himself to the MAHANTA, the Living ECK Master. All he is concerned with now is the service which he gives gladly, without complaint and without hesitation on his part.

The initiate of the Seventh Circle is known as the *Bhakti*. He enters into the path of pure love, for it is here that he surrenders everything and keeps nothing for himself. This is the world of silence, for the forces which have brought him this far are now broken apart and gone. He has become entirely ECK in principle and spirit. He speaks and acts mainly in the name and service of the MAHANTA, the Living ECK Master, for he has nothing else to live and have action for during his existence here in this world.

He now has the right to choose whether he will pursue the rest of the way on the path of Eckankar. There are five more initiations for him to take before entering into the true circle of the Adepts who are the brotherhood of the ancient Order of the Vairagi. He has long passed the stage of mysticism, which has its basic principle in unknowingness; that is, God is best known by negation; that we can know more about what God is not than about what It is. This is true of all the works of orthodox religions. But here it is learned that no initiation is of any value unless it is an ECK initiation, because the MAHANTA, the Living ECK Master is the only living being within this world who has true contact with God.

It is here that the initiate begins to attain direct, conscious experience. This is something which the intellectual senses cannot give him. This type of experience is concerned not with words and concepts, but with the unexplainable spiritual senses. The initiate has learned that by self-surrender he does not resist life, but goes along with it in an active manner. He is like the willow bough which is weighed down by the winter snow and does not resist but bends spontaneously under the weight so the snow falls off. In his relationship with the MAHANTA, the Living ECK Master he accepts all the burdens of life because they will be destroyed by their own weight.

The initiate of the Eighth Circle is the *Gyanee.* He is now at the crossroads of eternity, for now he has the right to choose whether he will sacrifice himself to remain upon the earth to help with the progress of humanity, or whether he will pass onward to the realm of spiritual development outside this planet, and even beyond the psychic worlds into the spiritual regions. If he retires into the invisible worlds to contemplate and put himself into the realms of the true spiritual planes, then he will eventually have to return to the worlds, because upon reaching the final goal of spiritual purification, the SUGMAD will send him back to serve humanity or those beings upon some plane within the universes of It.

Now he has directed his footsteps toward the Mastership, and he can never turn back, because life forces him on to the complete perfection of God. He finds that there is not only one great Deity, but many deities who start at the bottom rung of the spiritual ladder and end with the SUGMAD, the greatest of all. As the Gyanee, he cannot do anything but obey the wishes of the MAHANTA, the Living ECK Master. This means, then, that he is the pure disciple who has come this far on the path of the ECK because he has voluntarily given up all within his life with love and passion to serve the MAHANTA, the Living ECK Master. The great change comes over him, for he has become one among the chosen few who will come to the true knowledge of the SUGMAD. He often, in the beginning, has a great sadness, because his world has changed, and he feels indeed that there is no place for him here. It presents the experience that everyone is either asleep or dead.

The initiate of the Ninth Circle is the *Maulani*. The Maulani is that one who is given the power to wield the law, or work with the vibrations governing all the phases of planetary life. Of course, he cannot understand what this means at the stage of development in entering into the Ninth Circle, but it isn't long before his intellectual senses grasp the full significance of it.

It is then that he is given the insight of the spiritual unfoldment which, as it is taught, lies inevitably ahead of the teeming masses of humanity. The history of the human race, for the past, present, and future of the human race, is taken into consideration, with its karmic pattern, as he views it from this lofty position. The Maulani, the planetary spirits, the devas and deities, the Adepts and initiates, all are striving upon the path to reach the glorious heights of the Ocean of Love and Mercy.

The Maulani is now the vanguard of the race who is graduated to his higher position because he has suffered, sacrificed, and surrendered himself to the ways of the ECK, under the MAHANTA, the Living ECK Master. He is the vanguard for the human race and acts out the parts which those advanced Souls must play in the unfoldment of the masses of the human race. From the time the initiate left the circle of the Fourth Initiation, he has been watched carefully by the Adepts of the Vairagi, for he is one of the selected few whom they know will eventually enter into the glorious heights of the Ninth Lok (plane), where his responsibility is exceedingly greater and cannot be shirked.

The Maulani is the one who sacrifices everything for his fellow ECKists, for if it is necessary for him to put himself in debt for them, or share their cell in prison, it must be done. The initiate of the Ninth Circle can do no less than this, for it is now his duty to perform as such through his existence as the initiate of the Ninth Circle.

The initiate of the Tenth Circle is the *Adepiseka.* This is the initiation which enters into the divine wisdom pool, which is far different from anything that comes out of the planes and worlds below the Tenth Circle. This is the true wisdom, not that which is read in books in the lower worlds, or in those writings called sacred and holy by the priestcraft. It is a wisdom beyond human capacity, and only when one enters into the Tenth Circle does he have any concept of what is taking place.

No initiate takes his teachings on trust, especially in the Tenth Circle, for it is here that the spiritual fire growing within him finds truth and belief that the ECK is the only part of life worth living. What is being given out as the wisdom of God in the material worlds is false and without truth, unless it is the message of Eckankar. He is the accepted disciple who enters into the Tenth Circle, for this is the Anami Lok, in which the word is HU, that which is the goodness of all goodness. The music heard here is the sound of the whirlpool. There is nothing but the Sound and the Light which instill wisdom into the initiate. If he is so fortunate to find life as it is here, then he has really entered into the worlds of the true nature of the SUGMAD.

Life is given only by the SUGMAD, and it is found that when one goes into this plane he must have true direction. It is the way to the Godhead, yet it is not the way, and it is this paradox that brings about true wisdom for all those concerned in the Tenth Circle, or the Anami Lok plane. By now he begins to see the wisdom of the three basic principles of ECK. First, Soul is eternal. It has no beginning nor ending. Second, whosoever travels the high path of ECK always dwells in the spiritual planes. Third, Soul always lives in the present. It has no past and no future, but always lives in the present moment.

The initiate of the Eleventh Circle is the *Kevalshar.* This is the initiate's entrance into the SUGMAD world, which is the high world of God which few, if any, may enter. It is the world of the unspoken Word, the Voice of the SUGMAD, which comes out of the whirlpool of life. The Sound here is the Music of the universe, and life itself swirls round and around one, so that anything which enters into it will return purified and happy.

Rebirth is gained in this world which is the land of the SUGMAD. This rebirth is that which is known as God-Realization, and those who are fortunate to have gone this far are able to know the twin aspects of God: love and wisdom. This rebirth is the apotheosis of the deification of Soul; for the way to this rebirth in the SUGMAD, a guide must be found. It is only the MAHANTA, the Living ECK Master who can serve as the spiritual guide to lead the initiate into this world. The initiate shall enter into these high worlds in true humbleness, for insolence or arrogance, which are the result of ignorance, can keep the seeker away from any true spiritual unfoldment.

When the initiate reaches such heights as the world of the Eleventh Circle, or the SUGMAD world, it becomes known to him that hardly anything can be said about ECK, for It is the beginning and ending of all life. It is the whole of It, and that translator of messages by the SUGMAD. All the works of ECK spring out of the three principles which the initiate found in the Tenth Circle. But here he finds the great overlying principle upon which all life is anchored: Soul exists because of God's love for It. He now begins to see the wisdom and love embraced in this final principle in Eckankar and works steadily for every being on every plane throughout the universes of God.

The initiate of the Twelfth Circle is the *Maharaji.* Here it is learned that the ECK is not energy of Itself, but It controls and directs energy in all the worlds of God. That the end product of spiritual evolution by man on earth is by instruction and discipline, and that he must see to it that he is free at all times to follow the MAHANTA, the Living ECK Master. So many times he may be hypnotized by someone who will keep him under their own influence for several lifetimes. Both being reincarnated at the same time and in the same environment will keep that individual under the influence of the other. But if that one who has been hypnotized should come under the MAHANTA, the Living ECK Master as a chela, a disciple of the path of ECK, then he will no longer be under the spell of anyone. Those initiates of this higher circle, the Twelfth Plane, can break any so-called spell put upon anyone, provided it comes to their attention, either by the individual involved or his relatives.

Those who reach these heights begin to learn that they are now, in essence, the leaders within the spiritual community of ECK. They are ready for Mastership and will be approached by those ECK Masters who are the body of the brotherhood of the ancient Order of the Vairagi, for membership with this august body.

The Living ECK Master, as a *Maharaji,* is not the MAHANTA as of yet. This is summed up as the Master who is of the body but not yet ready to wear the crown. This is the form, the body which all persons who are within their earthly bodies can see, and can hear his voice giving the message, and can correspond with him by written language, or read the discourses which he supplies to all who are concerned with the reading of the works of ECK.

There are two more initiations within the ECK works, but these are secret and cannot be revealed. First is the *MAHANTA Maharai,* who is an initiate of the Thirteenth Circle and the second is the *MAHANTA, the Living ECK Master,* who is the initiate of the Fourteenth Circle. Neither of them reveals their secrets to the world, and it is needless to try to understand and grasp, through the intellect, what they are doing in all the worlds of God.

The MAHANTA, the Living ECK Master is the Vi-Guru, the Light Giver who lights up the worlds of God when he inherits the spiritual mantle of the title. There is only one who appears in this world every five to a thousand years. He is a product of the spiritual evolution of the ECK refined in the worlds to save it from all the destruction of the Kal Niranjan. He is usually persecuted, tormented, and troubled during his time because of the lack of understanding by his own chelas and the race of men in general. Nobody will grasp the full significance of his presence or have the least concept of his true existence as a savior not only of the human race, but of all life, no matter where it exists, anywhere in the universes of God.

There is a difference between the Maharaji, who is the Living ECK Master but not the MAHANTA, and the MAHANTA, who is the spiritual consciousness, the true representative of the SUGMAD manifested within the worlds of God as Itself. The Maharaji lives only in the body and does not have the spiritual power which the MAHANTA does, for the latter inherits the ECK Rod of Power, and the Maharaji is only appointed to his position.

These spiritual Masters are within their own line of spiritual descendents and do not concern themselves with those of religious or philosophical groups. The ECK Masters are of a true, clean-line spiritual family that does not include those commonly known in the orthodox religions.

The collective body of initiates work for a common cause, to assist the MAHANTA, the Living ECK Master to spread the message of Eckankar to all worlds including the physical universe. Each is a channel within himself, not a spiritual medium, but that through which the ECK power reaches the world. The initiate channels the power to uplift and enlighten all those within the worlds who have not been touched by the divine message of ECK.

There are four orders within the body of ECK Initiates which each initiate may become a part of to give service to the MAHANTA, the Living ECK Master and ECK Itself in specific paths. These orders are, first, the Arahata Marg, the teaching order. Within this path the initiate is able to give spiritual assistance by being a teacher of the message of ECK. He definitely works for the higher cause of ECK by giving out the message to those who want to know and understand more about it.

Second, the Bhakti Marg, the order of love. One gives service by volunteering in the works of ECK because of his great love for the MAHANTA, the Living ECK Master and the ECK Itself.

Third, the Giani Marg, the order of wisdom. The initiate gives his services by writing, painting, and other forms of creative arts for and about Eckankar. He gains himself while at the same time giving of himself to others through the creative forms.

Fourth, the Vahana Marg, the order of the missionary. The initiate gives of himself to the ECK as a carrier of the message of ECK into the world and among the masses of mankind. These are the preachers and true messengers of the spiritual truths of Eckankar.

These four paths are generally the way to serve the MAHANTA, the Living ECK Master, although an initiate does not have to look for hard lines drawn between these paths. In fact, he can be a little of each if he doesn't particularly want to become one or the other. However, it is good to be within the confines of one path and say this is the way for himself, as it means the initiate can concentrate his strength, energy, and mind in one direction. Such as in the Bhakti Marg he can give and serve by working among the poor, in the hospitals, and with the elderly. He can take up spreading the truth of ECK through service to the blind and the needy, bringing love and happiness to those who are handicapped.

Every initiate in ECK is linked up with the ECK, the Audible Life Stream, and is an added force for the whole movement of Eckankar. Therefore, he becomes a channel of his own under the Living ECK Master, and his responsibilities should never be lightly taken, for each initiate is a potential light of the world.

Index